Advancements in Business for Integrating Diversity, and Sustainability: How to Create a More Equitable and Resilient Business World in the Developing World

About the Conference

This book is the collection of selected articles that appeared at the First International Analytics Conference 2023 held in Hyderabad in virtual mode on February 2nd the 3rd 2023. In the fast-paced, ever-changing world of business, the pursuit of diversity and sustainability has emerged as a dynamic catalyst for progress. This illuminating volume takes you on a journey through the evolving realm of business, where innovative approaches are redefining corporate strategies and values.

Discover the groundbreaking advancements in integrating diversity, which encompasses not only gender, race, and culture but also a diversity of ideas, perspectives, and experiences. Delve into how these inclusive business practices are driving innovation, fostering collaboration, and enhancing the resilience of organizations in an increasingly interconnected world. Simultaneously, explore the vital thread of sustainability that runs through modern business practices. From eco-friendly supply chains to ethical corporate governance, businesses are embracing sustainability as a cornerstone for long-term success. Learn how sustainability initiatives are not just responsible but also profitable, leading to the growth and development of businesses worldwide.

'Advancements in Business for Integrating Diversity and Sustainability' is your compass in navigating the evolving world of commerce. Join us on a thought-provoking journey, as we showcase the pioneering efforts and transformative potential of businesses that are embracing diversity and sustainability as essential pillars of their future success.

Advancements in Business for Integrating Diversity, and Sustainability: How to Create a More Equitable and Resilient Business World in the Developing World

Edited by

Dimitrios A. Karras

Srinesh Thakur

Sai Kiran Oruganti

Routledge
Taylor & Francis Group
New York London

First published 2024
by Routledge
4 Park Square, Milton Park, Abingdon, Oxon OX14 4RN

and by Routledge
605 Third Avenue, New York, NY 10158

Routledge is an imprint of the Taylor & Francis Group, an informa business

© 2024 selection and editorial matter, Dimitrios A. Karras, Srinesh Singh Thakur, Sai Kiran Oruganti; individual chapters, the contributors

British Library Cataloguing-in-Publication Data
A catalogue record for this book is available from the British Library

Library of Congress Cataloging-in-Publication Data
A catalog record has been requested for this book

ISBN: 978-1-032-70828-7 (pbk)
ISBN: 978-1-032-70829-4 (ebk)

DOI: 10.4324/9781032708294

Typeset in Times LT Std
by Aditiinfosystems
Printed and bound in India

Contents

*Advancements in Business for Integrating Diversity, and
Sustainability – Dimitrios A. Karras et al. (eds)
© 2024 Taylor & Francis Group, London, ISBN 978-1-032-70828-7*

List of Figures

Advancements in Business for Integrating Diversity, and Sustainability – Dimitrios A. Karras et al. (eds)
© 2024 Taylor & Francis Group, London, ISBN 978-1-032-70828-7

List of Tables

Advancements in Business for Integrating Diversity, and
Sustainability – Dimitrios A. Karras et al. (eds)
© 2024 Taylor & Francis Group, London, ISBN 978-1-032-70828-7

Editor's Biography

Proceedings of the International Analytics Conference (IAC 2023)

Edited by

Dimitrios A. Karras received his Diploma and M.Sc. Degree in Electrical and Electronic Engineering from the National Technical University of Athens (NTUA), Greece in 1985 and the Ph. Degree in Electrical Engineering, from the NTUA, Greece in 1995, with honours. From 1990 and up to 2004 he collaborated as visiting professor and researcher with several universities and research institutes in Greece. Since 2004 he has been with the Sterea Hellas Institute of Technology, Automation Dept., Greece as associate professor in Digital Systems and Signal Processing, till 12/2018, as well as with the Hellenic Open University, Dept. Informatics as a visiting professor in Communication Systems (the latter since 2002 and up to 2010). Since 1/2019 is Associate Prof. in Digital Systems and Intelligent Systems, Signal Processing , in National & Kapodistrian University of Athens, Greece, School of Science, Dept. General. He is, also, adjunct professor with GLA University. Mathura, India and BIHER, BHARATH univ. India as well as with EPOKA and CIT universities Tirana. Moreover, he is with AICO EDV-Beratung GmbH as senior researcher as well as Director of Research and Documentation at ADIafrica N. G. O. He has published more than 80 research refereed journal papers in various areas of pattern recognition, image/signal processing and neural networks as well as in bioinformatics and more than 185 research papers in International refereed scientific Conferences. His research interests span the fields of pattern recognition and neural networks, image and signal processing, image and signal systems, biomedical systems, communications, networking and security. He has served as program committee member in many international conferences, as well as program chair and general chair in several international workshops and conferences in the fields of signal, image, communication and automation systems. He is, also, former editor in chief (2008-2016) of the International Journal in Signal and Imaging Systems Engineering (IJSISE), academic editor in the TWSJ, ISRN Communications and the Applied Mathematics Hindawi journals as well as associate editor in various scientific journals. He has been cited in more than 2560 research papers, his H/G-indices are 20/52 (Google Scholar) and his Erdos number is 5. His RG score is 32.78.

Srinesh Singh Thakur is a distinguished hardware engineer with a profound expertise in FPGA and embedded systems. With a notable tenure at the Laser Research Institute of the esteemed IIS Fraunhofer in Germany, Srinesh contributed significantly to cutting-edge research in the field. Holding a Masters in Electrical Engineering from Darmstadt University of Applied Sciences, Germany, he honed his skills in the heart of technological innovation.

Currently, Srinesh wears multiple hats, demonstrating his entrepreneurial prowess. He stands as the founder of Anvita Electronics Pvt. Ltd., a company at the forefront of technological advancements. Likewise, as the founder of Atya Technologies Pvt. Ltd., he continues to push boundaries in the ever-evolving tech landscape. Additionally, Srinesh serves as a co-founder of the SPAST Foundation in Hyderabad, India, demonstrating his commitment to social causes and community development. With a rich tapestry of experience and a visionary approach, Srinesh Singh Thakur is a driving force in the realms of technology and philanthropy, leaving an indelible mark on both the industry and society at large.

Sai Kiran Oruganti, a seasoned academic and researcher, held the position of Assistant Professor at the Indian Institute of Technology Tirupati from 2016 to 2017. His Ph.D. work made significant strides in the domain of Zenneck Wave Power transmission across shielded metal zones, resulting in the filing of 16 patents. Following his tenure in India, Dr. Oruganti played a key role in establishing ZN Ocean Technologies in South Korea. Between 2019 and 2022, he continued his academic journey as a Full Professor at Jiangxi University of Science and Technology in China, under the Foreign Talents Program, where he continued to specialize in Zenneck Wave type Wireless Power Transfer. He also co-founded the SPAST Foundation and currently holds the position of CEO at the Technology Innovation Hub of the Indian Institute of Technology Patna.

Advancements in Business for Integrating Diversity, and
Sustainability – Dimitrios A. Karras et al. (eds)
© 2024 Taylor & Francis Group, London, ISBN 978-1-032-70828-7

Foreword

Within the expansive and ever-evolving landscape of the International Analytics Conference (IAC) 2023, we embark on a journey that not only reflects the conference's dynamic themes but also the transformative forces shaping contemporary business. "Advancements in Business for Integrating Diversity and Sustainability" stands as a distinguished part of the Proceedings of the International Analytics Conference (IAC) 2023, held virtually on February 2 & 3, 2023, uniting participants from around the globe in Hyderabad, India.

This volume serves not only as a compendium of insights but as a beacon illuminating the path forward in the world of commerce. It delves into the intersection of diversity and sustainability, which are rapidly becoming the cornerstones guiding business practices toward a more inclusive, responsible, and equitable future. In these pages, we encounter a wealth of ideas, experiences, and perspectives that extend far beyond demographics, propelling innovation, fostering collaboration, and enhancing the adaptability of organizations. As we dive into the remarkable advancements in integrating diversity, we see that it is not merely a choice but a fundamental catalyst for progress.

Simultaneously, we embark on an exploration of sustainability initiatives within contemporary business practices. These encompass eco-friendly supply chains, ethical corporate governance, and responsible business models. Here, sustainability is not just an ethical imperative but a pragmatic framework for long-term success, guiding businesses towards growth and development on a global scale. The narratives contained within these pages are more than mere accounts of corporate achievements; they are chronicles of adaptability, visionary foresight, and active engagement with the challenges of our time. They represent the unwavering belief that businesses, participants in IAC, and professionals worldwide are not passive spectators but active contributors to a world where diversity and sustainability are integral components of business success.

As you delve into this volume, we invite you to contemplate the transformative potential of businesses in integrating diversity and embracing sustainability, recognizing that this is not only a reflection of the conference's themes but also an integral part of a brighter, more inclusive, and sustainable future. This book is dedicated to those who envision a world where business is not solely about profit but also about purpose, where diversity is a celebrated asset, and sustainability is a fundamental principle guiding business endeavors.

Welcome to a world where business, diversity, and sustainability converge to create a more equitable and environmentally responsible future. We invite you to partake in this intellectual journey, where commerce is a dynamic force for positive change, diversity is embraced, and sustainability is woven into the very fabric of business success.

Dilrabo Bakhronova
Uzbek State University of World Languages, Tashkent, Uzbekistan

Nita Sukdeo
University of Johannesburg, South Africa

Preface

The Proceedings of the International Analytics Conference (IAC) 2023, conducted virtually on February 2 & 3, 2023, in Hyderabad, India, represent a collective endeavor to explore, share, and foster collaboration among a diverse global community of researchers, experts, and forward-thinkers. Within this repository of knowledge, we proudly present "Advancements in Business for Integrating Diversity and Sustainability" as an integral part of this intellectual journey. IAC 2023 provided a unique platform where intellects from across the globe convened to examine essential themes in the field of analytics. This conference was not merely a platform for the exchange of ideas; it was a testament to the collective commitment to progress. The volumes contained within these Proceedings serve as a tribute to this commitment.

"Advancements in Business for Integrating Diversity and Sustainability" is far more than a compilation of scholarly contributions; it represents a comprehensive exploration of the transformative influences shaping contemporary business practices. It delves deep into the dynamic interplay between diversity and sustainability—two core pillars driving innovation, inclusivity, and corporate responsibility in the modern business landscape. As we venture through these pages, we encounter the profound advancements in integrating diversity. Here, our understanding extends beyond traditional demographics to encompass a richness of ideas, experiences, and perspectives. This approach is presented as not only a means of enhancing the work environment but as a potent force for progress and success in the global marketplace.

Simultaneously, the exploration of sustainability initiatives within the business sphere unveils a paradigm where corporate responsibility and environmental stewardship are integral to profitability. Sustainability is not just an abstract ideal; it is a practical framework that fosters responsible business practices, nurtures eco-friendly supply chains, and upholds ethical governance. The narratives and insights contained within these Proceedings are a testament to the transformative power of human innovation and collaboration. They exemplify the belief that in a rapidly evolving world, businesses are not passive observers of change but active agents in shaping it. Diversity and sustainability are not mere buzzwords but are fundamental drivers of success and purpose.

As you immerse yourself in this volume, we invite you to explore the transformative potential of business and its pivotal role in integrating diversity and embracing sustainability. We hope that these Proceedings serve as a wellspring of inspiration, not only in the context of IAC 2023 but also as a clarion call for those who are passionate about seeing business as a force for positive change. These Proceedings are dedicated to all those who envision a world where commerce is propelled not solely by profit but also by purpose, where diversity is celebrated, and sustainability is the guiding principle for businesses worldwide.

Welcome to a world where business, diversity, and sustainability converge to create a brighter, more inclusive, and environmentally responsible future. We invite you to embark on this intellectual journey with us, where knowledge is shared, innovation is celebrated, and progress is the cornerstone of our collective efforts.

Dimitrios A Karras

Acknowledgements

Chairs

Nita Sukdeo
University of Johannesburg, South Africa

Dilrabo Bakhronova
Uzbek State University of World Languages, Tashkent, Uzbekistan

Organizing & Publishing Commitee

Dimitrios A Karras, PhD
University of Athens (NKUA), Greece

Sudenshna Ray,PhD
RNTU, AISECT University Bhopal, India

Advancements in Business for Integrating Diversity, and Sustainability – Dimitrios A. Karras et al. (eds)
© 2024 Taylor & Francis Group, London, ISBN 978-1-032-70828-7

1

Transforming Insurance Industry through InsurTech

Umasankar M*, Kavitha Desai
Christ University, Bangalore, India

Padmavathy S[b]
Kongu Engineering College, Erode, India

Abstract: The modern customer accesses his insurance needs through his smart devices. Based on our examination of the literature, we find that there are no particular studies on Insurtech entry into the Indian market. As a result, our major goal was to evaluate the level of penetration that insurtech provides to the Indian market. Our research looks at how insurtech will change the insurance sector and its impact. According to the primary goal of this research is to comprehend the power of insurtech and how it has aided in the improvement of customer service in the insurance business. Primary data was gathered using questionnaires, and secondary data was gathered from official websites. According to the data gathered, Insurtech provides more product availability and security while reducing processing time and providing better customer assistance than traditional approaches.

Keywords: Insurance, Insurtech, FinTech, Digital economy

1. Introduction

This research is based on How insurtech has revolutionized the insurance industry and to study the impact of the same. Today's consumers use smart gadgets to access their insurance needs. The tracking tools for insurtech, which enable consumers to obtain insurance in a matter of minutes, include wearable technology, auto-monitoring devices, and phone apps. When a vacation itinerary is last-minute, insurance is a must, and customers don't want to waste time poring over policy paperwork when they could be packing. Customers want readily available mobile solutions that condense information on coverage, liabilities, and premiums. Like this, new businesses might need insurance protection for a day or perhaps only a few hours. Insurtech can assist with that. Additionally, insurtech has improved the efficiency of underwriting, claims processing, and asset management for insurance businesses. The fundamental components of insurtech are Big Data, AI, and the IOT.

*Corresponding author: umasankar.m@christuniversity.in

DOI: 10.4324/9781032708294-1

2. Purpose of the Research

Study's main purpose is to investigate the impact of insurtech on insurance penetration in India. It also coupled with other two objectives, that are to identify the building blocks of insurance penetration and to understand the consumer perception variance towards insurtech.

3. Literature Review

Especially in regions where the FinTech environment has expanded extensively, the insurance industry is seeing a rise in technological advancements to its operations and products globally. India is unique in terms of InsurTech due to its sizable uninsured population. Insurance industry pioneers will surely pay attention to the insurtech sector in the next years. Through this, we were able to comprehend the essence and significance of insurtech in the current market. (Suryavanshi, 2022) Information asymmetry and moral hazard are features of the Indian insurance industry. As a result, using insurtech has become essential. While telematics, a type of InsurTech, is rapidly gaining momentum on a global scale, it is still in its infancy in India. In light of this, the current paper examines how Telematics might help the Indian motor insurance industry by decreasing information asymmetries, enhancing the risk assessment process, and guaranteeing that the insurance premium reflects the risk assumed by the policyholder. The study is unique since it is one of the few that has looked into the use of telematics in the Indian environment. (McFall & Moor, 2018)

Due to its outstanding performance and promising future, the Indian insurtech sector has experienced substantial growth over the previous five years. The growth has so far been evenly distributed throughout all of the major sub-segments. The current paper's purpose is to explore the growth narrative and identify the causes driving it. The report makes an effort to evaluate significant trends in the Indian insurtech market that have the power to alter the course of events. It evaluates the difficulties the sector will have in maintaining its momentum. (Sarkar, 2021)

This study tries to offer a definition of fintech by outlining its key characteristics in light of the academic community's theoretical advancements in the area. Based on criteria like impact factors and citation counts, these papers were selected. A definition of the FinTech ecosystem is provided after a review of the literature, explaining the roles that different stakeholders—including regulators, investors—play in the sector. This concept takes the Au and Kauffman framework into account (2008). The writers also describe the primary business models used by fintech, such as blockchain, crowdfunding, payments, insurance, and wealth, and they label fintech as a disruptive innovation. (Siddiqui & Rivera, 2022). FinTech and InsurTech offer technology that can improve the efficiency of financial services but also have the potential to upend the sector. InsurTech investment and research have increased considerably since the beginning of 2015, giving them a higher visibility than they have had in the previous five years. Prior to considering potential insurer responses and strategies, I quickly scan the FinTech and InsurTech scene. The study discuss each step of the customer journey, from the first interaction to the settlement of claims. (Mai, 2017). The insurance industry has been quickly growing as a result of the FinTech phenomena, and a number of companies have appeared to offer services that are referred to as "InsurTech." These services apply ideas from the sharing economy, artificial intelligence, blockchain, and digitalization to several facets of the insurance sector. This abundance of technology promises a number of advantages in terms of improving efficiency and cutting costs for businesses or individuals who use insurance as their primary source of protection as well as insurers and intermediaries. But as InsurTech develops, there are associated dangers and regulatory issues that aren't yet taken into account by the conventional regulatory approach. This essay will look at potential hazards posed by the use of insurtech and consider how existing rules might get in the way in the development of InsurTech. (Lin & Chen, 2020)

The newest buzzword reshaping the insurance industry worldwide is surtech. Insurtech is essentially the combination of insurance and technology. In India, where insurtech is still in its infancy, start-ups are fundamentally changing the market's dynamics. In this study, the financial health of insurtech businesses in India will be investigated and the financial soundness of these two enterprises will be compared. Go digit and Acko, two prominent insurtech businesses, are used as the study's sample. For the analysis, three years of financial data from 2017–18 to 2019–20 were used for these two businesses. The CARAMELS model's financial indicators were utilised. The models' parameters include management soundness, earnings and profitability, asset quality, reinsurance and actuarial difficulties, and capital adequacy. (P. & Pathak, 2020)

When insurance 5.0 arrives, insurance 4.0 will become obsolete. Insurance 4.0 has a bright future. As soon as the insurance 4.0 strategy is implemented, all aspects of the company's business model should alter permanently. In the coming years, new businesses known as insurtech might transform the insurance landscape. It should be even more successful if established corporations and insurtech work together. The perspectives of insurtech organisations are presented in this chapter along with a model. Sustainable insurance is highlighted in Insurance 4.0. With its units, services, and distribution, the organisation becomes specifically engaged in insurance 4.0 and significantly contributes to the welfare of the company, the community, and the regions in which it operates. (Nicoletti, 2021)

Finding the answers to the following three questions will make it easier to define insurtech. then how? The first set of inquiries to be answered is, "Who or what is driving the industry-wide shift in insurance and insurance technology? Does the term "InsurTech" refer to a particular kind of startup or to the entire ecosystem of businesses engaged in the development of insurance technology?" The second group of inquiries is as follows: "What activities do those startups have in the InsurTech ecosystem? What is their main objective?" How are InsurTechs redefining the insurance industry is the third and final query. The key components for providing a precise and thorough explanation are the solutions to these three sets of mysteries. (Ricciardi, 2018)

The chapter looks at the current growth plans of the new technological start-ups in the insurance industry. It makes the case that these developments shouldn't pose a threat to established businesses because other aspects of the digital world, such as home automation systems and Big Data analysis, don't directly compete with traditional business. The chapter emphasises how crucial it is to keep in mind that the entire financial and insurance ecosystem will be profoundly altered by digitalization. Traditional insurers will eventually respond by developing new digital capabilities and/or forming agreements with IT companies. (Cappiello, 2018)

4. Research Methodology

The study's primary goal is to comprehend the impact and degree of penetration of insurtech in the Indian insurance sector.

This research study is descriptive in nature. The target population for the study were people who have a proper level of income and might have insurance policies. The Primary data was collected using a random sampling technique. The questionnaire was sent to the target population with the help of LinkedIn and have received over 250 responses. Part A of the questionnaire is used to collect the demographic details and Part B of the questionnaire contains questions on Insurtech. Part B of the questionnaire asked items on a scale of 1-5. SPSS software was used to analyse the gathered data.

Analysis

Table 1.1   Regression analysis

	Unstandardised		Standardized	t	P	Alternate Hypothesis Result
	Beta	SE	Beta			
(Intercept)	.514	.172		2.994	.003	Yes
Product Offering	.167	.043	.194	3.893	.000	Yes
Customer Service	.122	.052	.123	2.348	.020	Yes
Security	.112	.064	.090	1.750	.081	No
Process Sequence	.051	.064	.045	.801	.424	No
Payment Options	.537	.061	.503	8.786	.000	Yes
a. Dependent Variable: Satisfaction						

Source: Primary Data

The above Table 1.1 we can see that the satisfaction is the dependent variable and the study constructs are the independent variables. R value for the analysis is 0.819. The R^2 is calculated as 0.670 and the adjusted R square value is 0.663. From the above table we can see that Product offering, Customer service, and Payment options have a significant level of impact on the level of satisfaction while Security and process sequence don't have a significant level of impact on the satisfaction of customers while using the insurtech software.

Findings

From the above study using the annova analysis and regression analysis we can see that most of the respondents are from a age category of 21-30. While the Martial status of majority of the respondents being

Married. Almost all the respondents have a insurance policy and have heard about One or more Insurtech support apps. It is also visible from the collected data that most of the people tend to allocate at least 21-30% of their income towards the Insurance purposes. We have used 6 study constructs in the study and they are Product offerings, Customer services, securities, Process sequence, Payment options and satisfaction. From the above ANOVA analysis and regression analysis we can clearly see that there is always a high level of significance on product offerings no matter what the independent variable is and there is always a low level of significance in security and payment options no matter what the independent variable is. Thus we can see that there must be a significant improvement has to be made on those specific sides. From the above regression analysis we can see that Customers' happiness with utilising insurtech software is significantly impacted by the availability of products, customer service, and payment alternatives, but not significantly by security and the order of business processes.

5. Conclusion

Insurtech is one among the most growing technology and as India is moving fast in the digital economy with the implementation of UPI and other Online payment platforms. It is one among the key player in Improving the efficiency of the Insurance firms and helps them gain more customers. In a fast-paced world, Insurtech also helps the end consumers to speed up the process of getting a insurance on their finger tip which was first considered a hectic and Lengthy task. In the modern digital world where everything is accessible through the internet, Insurtech pushes insurance on the same platform and makes it have a higher reach and make it more attractive and customizable for the end users. From our study and literature review we came to a conclusion that Insurtech has indeed increased the penetration of insurance in India. The people who are mostly in favour of Insurtech are people between the Age group of 18-40. The key factors that distinguish Insurtech are the capability to customize the scheme, the variety of options to pick from, easy access and the security reasons.

REFERENCES

1. Cappiello, A. (2018). Digital Disruption and InsurTech Start-ups: Risks and Challenges. *Technology and the Insurance Industry*, 29–50. https://doi.org/10.1007/978-3-319-74712-5_3

2. Lin, L., & Chen, C. (2020). The promise and perils of insurtech. *Singapore Journal of Legal Studies, 2020*, 115–142. https://doi.org/10.2139/SSRN.3463533

3. Mai, H. (2017). Preface: Fin- & insuretech. *Digital Marketplaces Unleashed*, 329–341. https://doi.org/10.1007/978-3-662-49275-8_32

4. McFall, L., & Moor, L. (2018). Who, or what, is insurtech personalizing?: persons, prices and the historical classifications of risk. *Distinktion: Journal of Social Theory, 19*(2), 193–213. https://doi.org/10.1080/1600910X.2018.1503609

5. Nicoletti, B. (2021). *Future of Insurance 4.0 and Insurtech*. 389–431. https://doi.org/10.1007/978-3-030-58426-9_15

6. P., K., & Pathak, D. (2020). Financial Soundness of Insurtech Companies in India – An Analysis. *International Journal of Case Studies in Business, IT, and Education*, 203–211. https://doi.org/

10.47992/IJCSBE.2581.6942.0090

7. Ricciardi, V. (2018). InsurTech Definition as Its Own Manifesto. *The InsurTech Book*, 6–8. https://doi.org/10.1002/9781119444565.CH1

8. Sarkar, S. (2021). The Evolving Role of Insurtech in India: Trends, Challenges and The Road Ahead. *The Management Accountant Journal, 56*(12), 30. https://doi.org/10.33516/MAJ.V56I12.30-37P

9. Siddiqui, Z., & Rivera, C. A. (2022). FinTech and FinTech ecosystem: A review of literature. *Risk Governance and Control: Financial Markets and Institutions, 12*(1), 63–73. https://doi.org/10.22495/RGCV12I1P5

10. Suryavanshi, U. (2022). The Insurtech Revolution in Insurance Industry: Emerging Trends, Challenges and Opportunities. *International Journal of Management and Development Studies, 11*(08), 12–19. https://doi.org/10.53983/IJMDS.V11N08.002

Advancements in Business for Integrating Diversity, and
Sustainability – Dimitrios A. Karras et al. (eds)

Impact of e-Service Quality on Perceived Value, Brand Experience and Loyalty in D2C Channel

2

Priyansha Shami*, Leena Fukey

Christ (deemed to be university), Bengaluru, India

Abstract: Marketing academic is undergoing change due to shifts in today's marketing environment and one of the important reason being is digital transformation. The study aims to shed light on the current trends of modern retailing. This paper intends to uncover the impact of digital platforms on branding activities of businesses and firms with reference to D2C channel. Therefore, this study will highlight the importance and rise of new ecommerce channels and its impact on consumer shopping behavior, Direct to Consumer (D2C model). This study proposes a conceptual framework based on previous literature with regard to online shopping behaviour of consumers and emphasize on the factors relevant in building loyalty toward brands in online shopping. The framework proposed will provide a basis for enhanced understanding of impact of e-service quality on customer satisfaction, perceived value, brand experience and loyalty in virtual D2C channel. The framework proposed lacks empirical verification and can be a ground for future studies.

Keywords: D2C channels, Customer satisfaction, Brand experience, e-commerce, Loyalty

1. Introduction

Shopping experience has been revolutionized through the availability of various digital platforms. Digital markets have reduced market prices of products and increased the wellbeing of both consumers and producers. Direct to consumer channels are those where manufacturers and brands sell their products directly to consumers eliminating any intermediaries. Technically the term direct-to-consumer describes a sales channel rather than a type of company. D2C is a brand selling their goods under their own brand name, rather than the name of a retailer, like a department store when sold through department stores, they have the relationships with customers not the brands. So once brands were able to set up their own e-commerce sites and acquire

*Corresponding author: priyansha@res.christuniversity.in

DOI: 10.4324/9781032708294-2

their own customers they eliminated the "middlemen." D2C channel emphasizes on facilitating premium customer experiences including quick-to-respond customer support, personalized emails and customized offerings. Direct-to-Consumer (D2C) channel allows brands to directly engage with their customers using social, mobile, and other digital platforms. Firms are increasingly choosing direct online channels to communicate with their customers. D2C channel is beneficial for consumers as well as for firms as it offers various advantages like lower prices, convenience, wide assortment of products and exclusive online collection.

2. Problem Statement

E-marketplaces and e-retailers have emerged into new competitors to brand manufacturers. One of the reasons being is that they have access to huge consumer data base like recommendations, reviews and feedback. These shopping digital platforms have facilitated e-retailers customize their product and prices according to consumer expectations and turn their private labels into brand competitors. This changing role of retailers has negatively impacted the well-established brands. Brand manufacturers are unable to deliver personalized experience to their customers due to lack of direct touch with their customers which is also the major reason behind setting up of web stores by brand manufacturers. Manufacturers want to directly communicate with their consumers as they want to know their consumers with the aim of delivering customized products and services.

Therefore, this study will focus on framing a conceptual model on how D2C channel impact brand relationship with customers through online purchases. Also, this study

will closely focus on the influence of variables generated by the customer during the service experience offered by the firms and how it impacts consumer brand experience, satisfaction and loyalty. Therefore, the study frames following research questions:

RQ1. What factors impact the consumer brand experience and brand loyalty in D2C virtual interactions?

RQ2. How online buying experience from firm's own website impacts consumer satisfaction and brand loyalty?

3. Theoretical Background

The environmental cues have been increasingly explored as a means to create loyal customers. Firms own website is a major tool for establishing relationship with customers. It performs following four major functions: Firstly, establishing the brand identity; secondly, informing and educating consumer about their products; Thirdly, shaping consumer brand experiences. Therefore, two main approaches have been used to explore the impact of environmental cues on consumer behavior, the (S-O-R) Stimulus organism response model given by (Mehrabian and Russell, 1974) and later (Bitner, 1992) coined the term service scape. Bitner further extended this theory and adapted S-O-R model which he applied to service organizations which is also known by the term servicescape. Servicescape is defined as physical surroundings that have an impact on consumer behavior (Bitner, 1992). This framework identifies three main environmental dimensions that have an impact on consumer behavior: spatial layout, ambient conditions and symbols and artifacts. Therefore, the model proposed is based on Stimulus organism Response theory (SOR). Existing research will focus on virtual environment aspects like website quality, security, website design and service quality and its impact on customer satisfaction, brand loyalty and brand experience.

Brand experience can be defined as an outcome from series of interactions between brands and consumers during service encounters. The results of the study by Sahin et al. (2017) indicates that there is a significant relationship between brand experience and service quality. Brand experience positively impacts the consumer–brand relationship. Brand experience has been identified as an important factor that influence consumer perception of a brand. Also, pleasant online brand experiences positively impacts satisfaction and brand loyalty towards a brand Brakus et al., (2009). The attributes selected under E-service quality is selected by combining two scales e-SERVQUAL Zeithamal et al. (2002) and E-S-QUAL& E-RecS-QUAL scale items given by Parasuraman et al. (2005). Therefore, following hypothesis is proposed:

H1: E-service quality has significant positive impact on brand experience.

A study conducted by Chang, Hsu and Yang, 2017 show that system quality, information quality, and service quality has a positive impact on customer satisfaction and loyalty. Babakus et al. (2004) found service quality and product quality has substantial impact on customers satisfaction and on store's performance. He further indicated in his study that service quality has a direct positive influence on customer satisfaction. Therefore, we propose:

H2: E-service quality has significant positive impact on customer satisfaction.

Another study by Smith and Rangaswamy, (2002) results indicated Satisfaction builds loyalty, which reinforces satisfaction, which

is stronger online than offline. The study also indicated that in order to develop loyal customer base service providers should develop loyalty-oriented initiatives for customers who prefers online channel to reinforce overall satisfaction. Therefore, we propose the following hypothesis:

H3: Consumer satisfaction has significant positive impact on online brand loyalty

Brand experience defined by Brakus et al. (2009) as sensations, feelings, cognitions, and behavioral responses which are evoked by environment, communication and identity created by brands. Therefore, Brand loyalty has been proposed to be outcome of brand experience. When customers experience unique and memorable brand experiences, they intend to repeat their purchasing behavior and become loyal toward the brand (Brakus et al. 2009). The following hypothesis is proposed:

H4: Brand experience has significant positive impact on online brand loyalty

Also, in previous researches, it has been proposed that superior brand experience increases customer satisfaction with the brand (Brakus et al. 2009). With reference to online shopping behavior it has been found that customer satisfaction is an important outcome of brand experience. (Lee and Jeong 2014; Morgan-Thomas and Veloutsou 2013). Therefore, we propose that:

H5: Brand experience has positive significant impact on customer satisfaction.

Zeithaml (2000) defined Product perceived value particularly emphasizes on the consumer assessment of utility and satisfaction with the product or service of the brand on the basis of monetary costs and non-monetary costs. In online retailing settings factors like website experience, distribution channel and the experience related to purchasing a product like finding, ordering, and receiving products add value to customers (Keeney, 1999). Therefore, we propose the following hypothesis:

H6: E-service quality has significant positive impact on perceived value.

Concept of perceived value has been recognised long ago and its importance and impact with reference to customer preference, satisfaction and loyalty. Also, perceived value

impacts customer satisfaction positively when they experience high value from product or service and also brand loyalty. With this theoretical foundation, we propose a conceptual framework below: 'Fig. 2.1' and we propose following hypothesis:

H7: Perceived value has significant positive impact on customer satisfaction

H8: Perceived value has significant positive impact on brand loyal

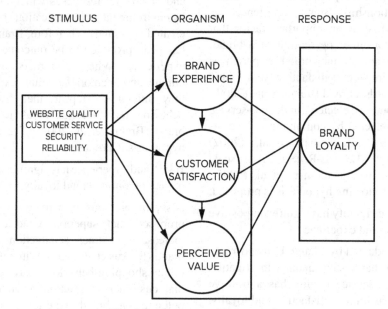

Fig. 2.1 Conceptual framework

Source: Mehrabian and Russell, 1974

4. Conclusion

D2C channel is increasingly adopted by brands with the objective of offering unique and enhanced brand experiences and increase their loyal customer base. This study focused on one of the aspects of changing landscape in retailing and proposed a theoretical framework with the aim of shedding light on factors that can have an impact on consumer behavior with regard to e-commerce and

direct to consumer channel. Future studies should empirically examine the conceptual framework proposed in the paper.

REFERENCES

1. Babakus, E., Bienstock, C. C., & Van Scotter, J. R. (2004). Linking Perceived Quality and Customer Satisfaction to Store Traffic and Revenue Growth*. Decision Sciences, 35(4), 713–737. https://doi.org/1 0.1111/j.1540-5915.2004.02671.

2. Bitner, M. J. (1992). Servicescapes: The Impact of Physical Surroundings on Customers and Employees. Journal of Marketing, 56(2), 57. https://doi.org/10.2307/125204

3. Brakus, J. J., Schmitt, B. H., & Zarantonello, L. (2009). Brand Experience: What Is It? How Is It Measured? Does It Affect Loyalty? Journal of Marketing, 73(3), 52–68. https://doi.org/10.1509/jmkg.73.3.52

4. Chang, Y. W., Hsu, P. Y., & Yang, Q. M. (2018). Integration of online and offline channels: a view of O2O commerce. Internet Research, 28(4), 926–945. https://doi.org/10.1108/intr-01-2017-0023

5. Keeney, R. L. (1999). The Value of Internet Commerce to the Customer. Management Science, 45(4), 533–542. https://doi.org/10.1287/mnsc.45.4.533

6. Lee, S. A., & Jeong, M. (2014). Enhancing online brand experiences: An application of congruity theory. International Journal of Hospitality Management, 40, 49–58. https://doi.org/10.1016/j.ijhm.2014.03.008

7. Morgan-Thomas, A., & Veloutsou, C. (2013). Beyond technology acceptance: Brand relationships and online brand experience. Journal of Business Research, 66(1), 21–27. https://doi.org/10.1016/j.jbusres.2011.07.019

8. Şahin, A., Kitapçi, H., Altindağ, E., & Gök, M. S. (2017). Investigating the Impacts of Brand Experience and Service Quality. International Journal of Market Research, 59(6), 707–724. https://doi.org/10.2501/ijmr-2017-051

9. Shankar, V., Smith, A. K., & Rangaswamy, A. (2003). Customer satisfaction and loyalty in online and offline environments. International Journal of Research in Marketing, 20(2), 153–175. https://doi.org/10.1016/s0167-8116(03)00016-8

10. Zeithaml, V. A. (1988). Consumer Perceptions of Price, Quality, and Value: A Means-End Model and Synthesis of Evidence. Journal of Marketing, 52(3), 2. https://doi.org/10.2307/1251446

Advancements in Business for Integrating Diversity, and
Sustainability – Dimitrios A. Karras et al. (eds)
© 2024 Taylor & Francis Group, London, ISBN 978-1-032-70828-7

A Comprehensive Review on the Implementation of Social Media in Business-to-Business (B2B) Marketing

N. Madhumitha*, G. Nirmala[1], Jayasree Krishnan[2], Monisha[3]

St. Joseph's college of Engineering, Chennai, India

Abstract: Although important components such as media coverage, word-of-mouth, law, and environmental conditions are outside the control of a corporation, they play a vital impact in shaping its brand image. One reason for social media's (SM) delayed uptake in B2B agreements is that firms are unsure how social networking sites may improve their brands. B2B marketers may use SM for data collecting and customer service. Based on 294 publications, this study studied SM in B2B. The impact of SM on B2B was evaluated using bibliometrics and content analysis. Our research shows that, unlike business-to-customer (B2C) companies, many B2B enterprises are unable to fully use the opportunities presented by SM. However, SM may aid B2B marketers in increasing brand awareness and credibility throughout the world, which in turn can aid in the discovery of new consumers and the development of partnerships with international suppliers.

Keywords: Social media, Business-to-business (B2B), B2B brand, Sales management, Innovation

1. Introduction

Constant research and development is being put into the marketing industry in an attempt to make it more efficient and successful at communicating with both direct and indirect customers (Cartwright et al., 2021). In recent years, organisations have been able to co-create value via "consumer involvement", "idea sharing", "networking", and other approaches due to digital platforms, especially SM (Alexander et al., 2015). With SM's growing relevance to B2B companies, the field presents new opportunities and challenges for academics and industry professionals.

Decision-makers and practitioners still aren't looking at this issue critically, despite the rising body of literature on the benefits of SM implementation in the B2B sector

*Corresponding author: madhuphd1316@gmail.com
[1]nirmala.gopinathan@gmail.com, [2]Jayasree.krishnan@gmail.com, [3]monisharamaraj89@gmail.com

DOI: 10.4324/9781032708294-3

and its effect on organisational performance (Pandey et al., 2022). Recent literatures have shown that B2B enterprises' usage of SM is restricted to a few key areas, including marketing and sales (Navaneetha Krishnan Rajagopal et al., 2017). As a result, there is a gap between the research and the reality of companies' struggles to develop and execute SM strategies throughout their core operations (Mention et al., 2019). This highlights the need of refining SM marketing methods appropriate for the B2B setting.

Based on the fact that interest and publications are rising at an exponential pace, we feel it is vital to take account of the results and discoveries from the research and determine how far task has gone in the field of using SM in a B2B context. This objective served as the foundation for the current study, which also provides answers to the following problems and a glimpse into SM research in a B2B environment. 1) How advanced is the study of SM in B2B settings? What topics concerning the use of SM in B2B organisations have been discussed in the literature, and what haven't they? 3. What difficulties and possibilities do academics have when looking at the utilization of SM in B2B settings? We used a review approach based on bibliometric and content analysis to evaluate the research issues. We started by looking at the general direction of the studies. Second, a text-mining technique was applied to the selected research content in the area of SM utilization in B2B firms. We have made the following contributions using this strategy: Two primary things have been accomplished here: 1) research themes have been retrieved throughout a certain time period, symbolising new directions in the chosen study subject, and 2) we have distilled the methodologies identified in the literature into five main takeaways.

2. Related Works

Prodanova et al., (2019) examines the development of SM research in business process management (BPM). After searching for and selecting relevant publications, we conducted a systematic review. Dwivedi et al., (2021) synthesises the related research on SM in B2B by analysing, performing weight analysis, and discussing major results. Itani et al., (2017) explores B2B salespeople's usage of SM for their employment. The authors claim that the attitude of a salesperson on SM utility and learning orientation will influence how much they utilise it for daily work. Holsapple et al., (2018) study conceptual frameworks for Business social media analytics (SMA) and provide a complete model. Zuhdi et al., 2019 mentions that SM marketing includes "running ads", "engaging and listening followers", "assessing outcomes", and posting to SM accounts. "Pinterest", "Instagram", "Snapchat", "Twitter", "Facebook", "LinkedIn", "YouTube", and more are prominent SM sites. These SM platforms are crucial for company growth.

3. Proposed Methodology

The study's purpose was to examine the state of maturity and recurring themes in the field of research dealing with the implementation of SM tactics in a B2B setting. Using the same criteria as Akter and Wamba, we chose the publications shown in figure 3.1. To begin, a database was chosen to investigate for appropriate keywords and corresponding articles. Select scopus because it is the most comprehensive collection of abstracts and citations for academic works, including those published in "scientific journals", "books", and "conference proceedings". Then, we looked for the phrase "B2B" or "business to business" in the article's keywords, heading, and abstract. 8,685 documents were found during the found procedure. Our secondary search for "SM" produced a total of 8685 documents. As a result of this approach, 415 papers were uncovered. Since we wanted a thorough investigation, we didn't include anything except scholarly publications and reviews in our analysis. We next used bibliometric and content analysis on the remaining 298 texts after applying the above procedure of exclusion.

Researchers have utilised a wide variety of approaches to literature reviews. We opted for bibliometric and content analysis techniques within the realm of text-mining strategies due to their adaptability and capacity to offer statistical and contextual data throughout the exploratory stage of our study. This method of literature evaluation is more content-oriented, and it outlines a more topical abstract for arriving at critical judgements in a certain area of research.

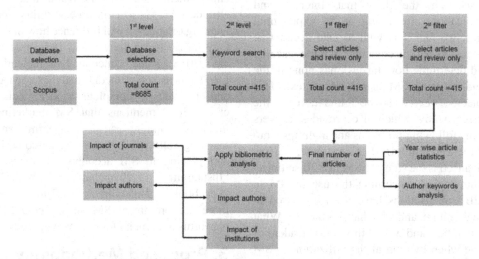

Fig. 3.1 Framework adopted for the research

All abstracts from the 298 publications were analysed using content analysis software (text mining). To demonstrate the evolution of this practise, certain periods were chosen from which themes could be taken.

4. Result and Discussion

Our primary goal was to investigate the level of development and overarching themes in the study area of SM use in a B2B setting. A mature domain is one that has been thoroughly explored by researchers, and this

may be deduced through a statistical study of the no of publications produced each year in the field. The annual article output is illustrated in figure 3.2. After a slow start, interest in this area of study surged in 2008, and it has continued to rise steadily every year thereafter. It demonstrates that 2019 was the apex year for studies of SM deployment in B2B contexts. We performed network analysis on keywords to uncover research trends since keywords represent publication content and help search engines index articles.

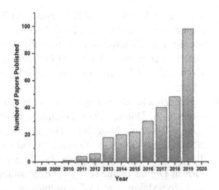

Fig. 3.2 Yearly statistics on articles published on searched keywords

5. Research Profiling

Journal, author, and institution profiles provide insight into the breadth and depth of an investigation's influence. Knowing how well journals fare in the relevant field is also crucial when considering about journals' influence. Therefore, we looked at how many times each paper was cited on average to determine which journals were the most successful. Below are the 15 most prolific writers and their affiliated universities, as measured by both number of publications and total citations.

Content analysis and visualization: We utilised the Leximancer programme to analyse the content. By calculating the distances between each word in the text data (abstract), we may create concept seeds. Then, using either unsupervised or supervised learning, a concept thesaurus is compiled from the source material. We used a constant theme size of 40% throughout the study. Since keywords are primarily concerned with the context of the article, we utilised VOSviewer to filter the keyword co-occurrence network. During the processing phase, Leximancer eliminated these unnecessary stop words, allowing for more relevant topics to emerge.

Contextual and theoretical considerations for the years 2017–2019 are presented here. To fully grasp the significance of journals, one must also be familiar with their standing in the relevant field. To determine the effectiveness of journals, we looked at how many times each article was cited on average.

Thematic Visualization (2017–2018)

Contextual considerations: During these time period, the themes of "customer," "brand," "development," "implications," "social," "industry," "digital," "B2B," and "role" were the focal points of the discussions. These topics came into being as a result of concepts include the customer experience, sales process, brand management, and other similar ideas. During the years 2017 and 2018, authors made great use of phrases that are linked to these ideas. The researchers outlined the important distinctions between the social media communication techniques used by B2C and B2B firms.

Theoretical aspects: During this period, researchers were interested in implementing behavioural theories from either an organisational or an individual viewpoint. B2B enterprises' managerial dedication in international contexts was studied using "reasoned action" and "the theory of planned behavior".

Thematic Visualization (2019)

Contextual considerations: The terms "implications," "use," "social," "engagement," "impact," "online," "model," and "sales" all became as important during the year. Brand content, social impact, online goods, commercial partnerships, etc., were all linked to these concepts. Due to the proliferation of information and the channelling of commerce via the internet, "online" also emerged as a major subject in 2019.

Theoretical aspects: Using the framework of relationship marketing theory, we compared the SM marketing approaches of B2B, B2C, and "business-to-business-to-consumer (B2B2C)" companies on measures such as acquisition orientation and perceived efficacy.

6. Conclusion

Implementing SM in a B2B setting has been a popular area of study during the last decade. A number of aspects, including customer journeys, marketing-finance interfaces, technology adoption, revenue growth, and data analytics, have been highlighted by researchers as being affected by SM implementation. In spite of the increased use of technology, our research revealed that many B2B companies still only make minimal use of SM. Those B2B companies who are contemplating the implementation of SM strategies may find themselves in a difficult position if SM is the only means by which they can engage with their prospective clients. We also discovered that SM may bring possibilities, such as making it possible for micro, small, and medium-sized enterprises (MSMEs) to have access to global resources. In the absence of SM, MSMEs have very limited capacities to gain access to resources owing to a variety of obstacles.

REFERENCES

1. Cartwright, S., Liu, H. and Raddats, C., 2021. Strategic use of social media within business-to-business (B2B) marketing: A systematic literature review. *Industrial Marketing Management, 97*, pp. 35–58.
2. Alexander, M. and Jaakkola, E., 2015. Customer engagement behaviours and value co-creation. In *Customer Engagement* (pp. 3–20). Routledge.
3. Pandey, A.K., Singh, R.K., Jayesh, G.S., Khare, N. and Gupta, S.K., 2022. Examining the Role of Enterprise Resource Planning (ERP) in Improving Business Operations in Companies. *ECS Transactions, 107*(1), p. 2681.
4. Navaneetha Krishnan Rajagopal, Naila Iqbal Qureshi, S. Durga, Edwin Hernan Ramirez Asis, Rosario Mercedes Huerta Soto, Shashi Kant Gupta, S. Deepak, "Future of Business Culture: An Artificial Intelligence-Driven Digital Framework for Organization Decision-Making Process", Complexity, vol. 2022, Article ID 7796507, 14 pages, 2022. https://doi.org/10.1155/2022/7796507
5. Mention, A.L., Barlatier, P.J. and Josserand, E., 2019. Using social media to leverage and develop dynamic capabilities for innovation. *Technological Forecasting and Social Change, 144*, pp. 242–250.
6. Prodanova, J. and Van Looy, A., 2019. How beneficial is social media for business process management? a systematic literature review. *IEEE Access, 7*, pp. 39583–39599.
7. Dwivedi, Y.K., Ismagilova, E., Rana, N.P. and Raman, R., 2021. Social media adoption, usage and impact in business-to-business (B2B) context: A state-of-the-art literature review. *Information Systems Frontiers*, pp. 1–23.
8. Itani, O.S., Agnihotri, R. and Dingus, R., 2017. Social media use in B2b sales and its impact on competitive intelligence collection and adaptive selling: Examining the role of learning orientation as an enabler. *Industrial Marketing Management, 66*, pp. 64–79.
9. Holsapple, C.W., Hsiao, S.H. and Pakath, R., 2018. Business social media analytics: Characterization and conceptual framework. *Decision Support Systems, 110*, pp. 32–45.
10. Zuhdi, S., Daud, A., Hanif, R., Nguyen, P.T. and Shankar, K., 2019. Role of social media marketing in the successful implementation of business management. *International Journal of Recent Technology and Engineering, 8*(2), pp. 3841–3844.

Note: All the figures in this chapter were made by the Authors.

Advancements in Business for Integrating Diversity, and Sustainability – Dimitrios A. Karras et al. (eds)
© 2024 Taylor & Francis Group, London, ISBN 978-1-032-70828-7

4

A Cross Country Analysis of the Opportunities and Challenges in the Banking Sector

Angelin S. Kiruba*
St. Joseph's College of Engineering, Chennai, India

Safeer Pasha M.[1]
St. Claret College, Bengaluru, Karnataka, India

A. Pankajam[2]
Avinashilingam Institute for Home Science and Higher Education for Women, Coimbatore, Tamil Nadu, India

Girish Lakhera[3]
Graphic Era Deemed to be University, Dehradun, Uttarakhand, India

Abstract: This research sought to shed light on key stockholders and their cooperative relationships in providing finance, in addition to gain a better understanding of managers' awareness of AI and the difficulties they face in providing the associated innovations, given their central role in the development and deployment of AI for marketing financial services. The data was acquired via semi-structured interviews with bank managers in industrialised and developing nations, including the Vietnam, UK, Canada, and Nigeria. An AI-based marketing strategy for financial services is also proposed in this study, one that takes into account and highlights the many ways in which customers, financial institutions, outside interests, and government agencies all interact. This research gives empirical insight into the potential, prospects, and limitations of AI in financial sector marketing. It also questions some misconceptions about AI and its function in financial services, and the role of marketing managers in creating AI.

Keywords: Banking, Artificial intelligence, Qualitative, Managers, Financial sector

1. Introduction

Several reasons, such as the increasing need for bank reform, the drive for profit, and the level of competition, have contributed to the rise of AI in the finance sector. Linked to the development of the financial sector and the proliferation of technology sources

---
*Corresponding author: kirubasamraj@gmail.com
[1]safeer@claretcollege.edu.in, [2]ambipankaj@gmail.com, [3]girishlakhera@geu.ac.in

DOI: 10.4324/9781032708294-4

and related innovations. AI draws from psychology, linguistics, mathematics, and philosophy to inform its heavy reliance on computer science applications (Cheng, et al., (2021)). It has been shown to be a useful instrument in the delivery of financial services, and many companies are now making use of a wide range of AI-based analytical tools, such as machine learning, to analyse their data. There has been a 270% increase in the number of companies using AI in their operations over the past four years, and nine out of ten of the most successful companies are making consistent investments in the technology. Insider Intelligence published a research on the use of AI in the banking sector, and it found that 80% of banks see the opportunities given by AI and have already applied it for risk management and revenue creation (Umesh, et al., (2022)). Despite this expanding corpus of study, there are still voids in our understanding of how AI may be used to promote financial services. Firstly, present research has largely ignored other technical breakthroughs brought about by AI in this industry, "such as credit assessment tools, credit score evaluation, and bankruptcy prediction", in favor of focusing on chatbots as the major aspect of AI in this area (Ashish, et al., (2022)). Second, prior research has often zeroed in on a single nation, rather than providing a global perspective on the effects of digitalization on the sector as a whole. Third, previous studies have mainly neglected the viewpoints of managers on the adoption of AI, focusing instead on the adoption and experiences of consumers utilizing AI systems.

The aforementioned represent knowledge gaps that this research seeks to address via the collection and analysis of data from managers working in a wide range of developed and developing world nations and financial services industries. Managers play a significant role in the creation and rollout of intelligent systems, as well as in ensuring that consumers adopt new technology, so it is crucial to comprehend their vantage point and the difficulties they confront when delivering such solutions to clients (Ines, et al., (2020)). As a result, this work contributes significantly to our theoretical knowledge of AI in connection to financial studies, expanding on prior studies by investigating AI from a new angle. The research evaluates the potential, opportunities, and constraints associated with the utilization of AI for marketing banking services and offers a range of major components for banking firms and Fintech companies.

2. Related Works

Using data from over 5,100 banks across 27 countries, Lopez, e al., (2020) analyse the impact that negative nominal interest rates have on bank profitability and behaviour. When negative nominal interest rates are compared to low positive rates, the losses in interest revenue experienced by banks are almost cancelled out by savings on deposit expenditures and increases in non-interest income, which may include capital gains on securities and fees. Omar, et al., (2020) aims to examine the effects of financial inclusion on poverty and income inequality, as well as the factors that contribute to these outcomes, in 116 developing countries. Unweighted yearly panel data from 2004–2016 is used for the study. Chang, et al., (2020) discuss three major obstacles and three ethical concerns with regards to Blockchain technology. The future of Blockchain in banking is the next topic for our discussion. They also detail the genuine reasons for banks to investigate Blockchain, as well as the challenges they confront in doing so. Using data from a large sample of international banks spanning 2003–2016, Forcadell, et al., (2019) empirically investigate the connection between innovation and corporate sustainability. Based on our findings, it seems that service innovation performance improves the corporate sustainability of the banking sector. Akomea-Frimpong, et al., (2022) explore products and factors of green finance and evaluate previous studies on green financing within the banking industry. Forty-six (46) research met the criteria, and their findings were summarised and critically examined using the content analysis method. In-depth, semi-structured interviews with 36 managers at various levels in 12 different public and private Indian banks make up this qualitative research by Sharma, et al., (2022). The financial services industry has a significant part to play in greening the banking system by increasing access to capital and meeting the demands of a "green economy."

3. Proposed Methodology

This study utilised an exploratory and inductive research strategy to provide light on how managers see the application of AI to the promotion of financial services. This strategy was implemented so that researchers could get a more in-depth understanding of the managers' backgrounds, reasoning processes, and relationships with other parties throughout the creation of AI systems for the company's daily operations.

Data collection: Participants should be managers in the financial services business who are tasked with applying AI-based marketing and digital transformation initiatives. Many attempts were undertaken to contact managers in many nations so that a global perspective could be included into the research. "Participants were sought from the United Kingdom (Europe) and Canada (North America) to represent established economies, and from Nigeria (Africa) and Vietnam (Asia) to represent developing nations and emerging markets". Researchers used snowball sampling to first reach out to individuals via their own networks. We received 31 responses from people who said they were willing to take part in our study. All 47 participants were managers from one of the four nations, and 15 more were recruited via personal connections. Tab 4.1 displays demographic information about the study's participants. Semi-structured interviews were used to glean information from the participants that couldn't be captured in a quantitative manner. The interview questions were crafted using the aforementioned material, with an emphasis on the conceptual frameworks. The questions were left open-ended so that the participants could provide their honest feedback and so that more new ideas might be captured. Participants were given similar, broad, open-ended questions on their familiarity with AI in finance, their involvement in building AI systems at their companies, their attempts to promote financial services using AI, and the difficulties they've encountered incorporating AI into their operations.

Table 4.1 Demographic data

Characteristic	Subgroup	Frequency	%
Gender	Male	27	57.4
	Female	19	40.4
	Non-binary	1	2.1
Age	20-49	40	85.1
	50-60+	7	14.9
Country	Canada	10	21.3%
	Nigeria	11	23.4%
	United Kingdom	14	29.8%
	Vietnam	12	25.5%
Years of experiences	0-9	15	31.9
	10-19	25	53.2
	20+	7	14.9

Data analysis: The data transcription was analysed using theme analysis procedures. As a first step, I read the transcripts of the interviews over and over again to get a feel for the participants' reactions. The programme was used to reread the transcripts, and the resulting data was thoroughly analysed to extract relevant themes. In the meanwhile, we also ran Auto-transcribe, a feature of automated transcription technology that may help with the analysis of large datasets, on our data set. After the transcripts were transcribed automatically, they were manually annotated in the programme.

Data credibility: There was a lot of work put in to making sure the data was legit. First, all required steps to ensure participant permission, data protection, and confidentiality were taken, as outlined by the authors' associated institution's ethical standards. Second, we double checked everyone's credentials to make sure they were providing us accurate information in accordance with their positions. Third, participants were given agency over their level of participation, ensuring that they provided only the information that they were willing to provide and were not subjected to coercion or pressure

4. Result and Discussion

Three overarching themes about the managers' perception of AI's potential in marketing financial services emerged from the examination of the qualitative data. Although there were some differences in participants' experiences depending on the sort of financial services they used, their level of expertise, and the nation they were from, the following were the overarching themes: One, an understanding of why AI is important, two, a plan to meet the rising need for AI in their operations, and three, a push to implement AI as quickly as possible to improve those operations. The next section elaborates on these issues using quotations from the management. Tab 4.2 depicts the results of the analysis and the managerial implications.

Table 4.2 Results of the analysis and the managerial implications

Important Consequences	Additional Meanings	Reports
Awareness about AI		
Managers owe it to customers to explain the potential of AI.	The Hype The misconceptions The Chatbot The huge possibilities	Artificial intelligence (AI) is something that everyone uses and speaking on, yet very few really comprehend. Based on one's background and exposure to the topic, many levels of AI comprehension exist.
In order to gain consumer trust, businesses must provide adequate data confidentiality and management.		Many people are unaware of this AI since, like any new technology, it takes time to learn how to use it properly.
Addressing the Business Need		
Managers should consider the moral consequences of their interactions with programmers as well as other vendors.	Addressing AI as a Business Need Evolving naturally Convincing the management team Assembling the right Deploying the systems Managing the team	One common strategy for persuading upper management to use AI is to highlight how the competition is already employing the technology. Keep in mind that no financial institution wants to come out on the losing end of this digital revolution - Director of a Bank in Vietnam
It's crucial for data gathering, storage, and analysis.		The group agreed that it was a good addition and that it was aesthetically pleasing what we already had, but the pricing structure was not making much financial sense; so we finally agreed to get another tech company to work with us – UK Manager
Accelerating AI adoption		
Managers have the responsibility to ensure that data is gathered, compiled, and handled in a fair and ethical manner.	The Regulator's role, The consumers' trust, The managers Knowledge, The manpower, The country of operations	Customers must have faith that we are creating a system that benefits both themselves and financial institutions. The bank's customers may rest certain that the system makes fair and accurate choices, according to the bank's Canadian manager.
Managers who have had formal training and education will be more comfortable with the latest gadgets.		More sophisticated uses of artificial intelligence (AI) are on the horizon for the financial services industry, and customers would be well to keep an open mind. Manager of the UK Operations.

Discussion: According to our qualitative data, banking industry leaders from both developing and developed nations are excited about the potential of AI in the promotion of financial products. Although chatbots get considerable coverage here, the managers emphasised that they are not the only kind of Information system that should be employed when advertising financial services.

5. Conclusion

Managers in the financial services sector would do well to familiarise themselves with the possibilities, opportunities, and problems posed by the AI now being utilised in the sector, given the industry's rapid evolution in response to the digital transformation of business operations. The research specifically aimed to disprove certain commonly held beliefs on the relationship between artificial intelligence (AI) and banking services, chatbots used in the delivery of banking services, and the contribution of marketing managers to AI development. The results of the current research should be evaluated with an awareness of the study's caveats, as is the case with every study. The research used a qualitative approach that relied on managers' self-reporting; as a result, the results should be interpreted with caution. There may be a wide variety of perspectives on how AI has been implemented in corporate operations, depending on the job and degree of expertise of the individual, as well as the country in which they live. In the future, researchers may try to use a more scientific method to determine just how much bank executives know. Finally, the created theoretical framework invites more study and validation to determine the validity and applicability of the components to various business activities.

REFERENCE

1. Cheng, C.Y., Chien, M.S. and Lee, C.C., 2021. ICT diffusion, financial development, and economic growth: An international cross-country analysis. Economic modelling, 94, pp. 662–671.
2. Umesh Kumar Lilhore et al., "A depth-controlled and energy-efficient routing protocol for underwater wireless sensor networks," in International Journal of Distributed Sensor Networks, Volume: 18 Issue: 9, 2022.
3. Ashish Kumar Pandey et al 2022 ECS Trans. 107 2681 https://doi.org/10.1149/10701.2681ecst
4. Inês, C., Guilherme, P.L., Esther, M.G., Swantje, G., Stephen, H. and Lars, H., 2020. Regulatory challenges and opportunities for collective renewable energy prosumers in the EU. Energy Policy, 138, p. 111212.
5. Lopez, J.A., Rose, A.K. and Spiegel, M.M., 2020. Why have negative nominal interest rates had such a small effect on bank performance? Cross country evidence. European Economic Review, 124, p. 103402.
6. Omar, M.A. and Inaba, K., 2020. Does financial inclusion reduce poverty and income inequality in developing countries? A panel data analysis. Journal of economic structures, 9(1), pp. 1–25.
7. Chang, V., Baudier, P., Zhang, H., Xu, Q., Zhang, J. and Arami, M., 2020. How Blockchain can impact financial services–The overview, challenges and recommendations from expert interviewees. Technological forecasting and social change, 158, p. 120166.
8. Forcadell, F.J., Aracil, E. and Úbeda, F., 2019. The influence of innovation on corporate sustainability in the international banking industry. Sustainability, 11(11), p. 3210.
9. Akomea-Frimpong, I., Adeabah, D., Ofosu, D. and Tenakwah, E.J., 2022. A review of studies on green finance of banks, research gaps and future directions. Journal of Sustainable Finance & Investment, 12(4), pp. 1241–1264.
10. Sharma, M. and Choubey, A., 2022. Green banking initiatives: a qualitative study on Indian banking sector. Environment, Development and Sustainability, 24(1), pp. 293–319.

Note: All the tables in this chapter were made by the Authors.

*Advancements in Business for Integrating Diversity, and
Sustainability — Dimitrios A. Karras et al. (eds)*
© 2024 Taylor & Francis Group, London, ISBN 978-1-032-70828-7

5

A Deep Learning Based Analysis of the Human Resource Management and the Organizational Performance

Sujay Mugaloremutt Jayadeva*
JSS Academy of Higher Education & Research, Mysuru, India

Harmeet Matharu[1]
St. Claret College, Bangalore, India

Runumoni Lahkar Das[2]
K. C. Das Commerce College, Chatribari, Guwahati, Assam, India

Rajesh Deb Barman[3]
Bodoland University, Kokrajhar BTR, Assam, India

Abstract: China's tremendous economic growth has benefited small- and medium-sized enterprises (SMEs). This growth is due to worldwide relationships and social-economic development through high-quality services. China's SMEs are smaller and contribute less than in other developing countries. Few organizations are still struggling due to obstacles, lower quality, and a shortage of human resources (HRs). This paper aims to identify the HR issues facing SMOs, their causes, and possible solutions. In this paper, HR data is examined and handled with deep learning (DL) approach called advanced deep belief network (A-DBN). This study collects HR turnover statistics. The DL strategy allows for the realization of HR capabilities while also reducing the business volume to increase HR effectiveness. The performance of the suggested approach is examined, and it is also contrasted with existing methods. By using A-DBN, the suggested model's training and testing accuracy are measured to be 98.74% and 97.06%, respectively.

Keywords: Human resource (HR), Turnover, deep learning (DL), Small- and medium-sized enterprise (SME), Advanced deep belief network (A-DBN)

---
*Corresponding author: sujay.dhsms@jssuni.edu.in
[1]harmeet@claretcollege.edu.in, [2]runulahkardas@gmail.com, [3]rajeshbarman@buniv.edu.in

DOI: 10.4324/9781032708294-5

1. Introduction

Human resource management (HRM) is among the most crucial tools for an organization's growth. Internet and cloud services have assisted HRM systems in development. These solutions are becoming more realistic and successful by integrating data assets and control and enabling information sharing and processing simpler. With expanding innovations and a vast amount of networked devices, a huge volume of data must be effectively handled, preserved, and processed (Wilton, N., 2019). Managing and analyzing such large amounts of data in real time is impossible for a person. An information management system(IMS) includes data collecting, database building, and maintenance. Since data management includes extraction and storage, IMS analyses a lot of data (Calvard, et al., 2018). HRM and IMS provide an effective way to manage and process data. HRM facilitates resource management and data processing. The HRM system aims to normalize HR activities, process information, and improve transparency. HRM systems help the company grow by optimizing business processes, improving management, and boosting work productivity. Process quality affects an organization's performance, growth, and survival (Pandey, et al., 2022). Due to more connected gadgets, companies are collecting more data. The HRM system's inability to analyze large amounts of data prevents frequent data analysis and management. Rich data but low information describes this analytical failure. Data gathering, storage, and management without adequate examination and administration results in unproductive use of a vast amount of data, wasting the organization's limited resources and missing the possibility

to leverage big data to expand rapidly (Rajagopal, et al., 2022). The typical HRM system couldn't meet the organization's big data needs; to function properly, it should automatically explore a large quantity of information to reduce its bulk. So, this paper presents an A-DBN approach to predict payments for HRM.

2. Related Works

Kim, et al., 2019 looked at how sustainable HRM might enhance workers' environmentally friendly behavior and hotels' performance. This study advises that green HRM strategies be implemented by hotel senior management and HR executives.Wei, et al., 2021 used BP neural network (BPNN) to enhance the HRM's usability, chose the dimensions based on the forecasting approach, and created a combined model using an improved GM (1,1) approach and BPNN.Yuan, et al., 2022 suggested an ML-based HR prediction approach. The HR requirements of businesses are predicted using two different forms of neural network models, BPNN and radial basis function neural network (RBFNN). The main goal of Ming, L., 2022 was to determine the actual situation of HR in SMEs, the variables influencing it, as well as the steps that might be taken to successfully address these difficulties. In this research, deep neural networks (DNN) are used to assess and handle HR data. Long-short-term memory (LSTM)was used to assess employees' performance in GULABBHAI, et al., 2019's study.

3. Methodology

This section describes the details of the dataset, data pre-processing and the proposed A-DBN method considered. The IBM database, which includes 1,470 personnel records and 38 attributes wherein 237 people left, is employed (Zhao, et al., 2018). Data cleansing was added, which was essential. Initially, all people who had been identified as temporary employees were taken out of the datasets. Next, any unique-value characteristics that were shared by all personnel records were eliminated. These fundamental data cleaning techniques resulted in 1,470 employees and 31 attributes for IBM information in the finalized statistics. The dataset included typical HR characteristics including age, income, gender, and degree.

Data pre-processing: Employees' turnover forecasting studies generally use pre-processing steps since the datasets frequently have missing data, varied levels of noise, and significant scale discrepancies across features. To ensure that all methods could manage missing data, they were imputed. However, some algorithms may be able to deal with missing variables without imputation. The missing data are restored using the type of data of the missing data to limit the comparative overhead. Converting categorical data to numeric values is among the crucial data preprocessing steps. In this study, label encoding was used to convert data using Python's Scikit-learn module. The variety of attributes is adjusted via feature scaling, which also helps to harmonize various feature scales. Since large-scale differences between attributes are typically not preferred during the algorithm's optimization step, this could assist classifiers to do well. Prediction of payment using A-DBN: Since DBN, a popular deep learning model, is comparable to CNN; it may learn from matching input and develop more conceptual and advanced qualities. The DBN is primarily employed for unsupervised learning, but in actual applications, the A-DBN and the BP method appear to be frequently combined to achieve the unsupervised upwards spreading of sample characteristics through the restricted Boltzmann machine (RBM), and then the opposite okay is achieved through the supervised BP algorithm. The A-DBN can be utilized for reinforcement approaches even though unsupervised learning is where it is most often used.

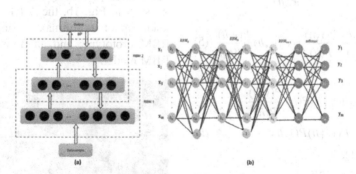

Fig. 5.1 Structures of (a) DBN and (b) A-DBN

As shown in Fig. 5.1a, the majority of the components in a traditional DBN model building diagram are made up of the forward-propagating and back-propagating procedures. The techniques for reconstructing the computer vision-based and hidden units in RBMs, as well as the training procedure for RBMs, are crucial to the A-DBN model structure because the quantum state of numerous RBMs serves as the primary building block of the DBN prototype structure. The model of aDBN demonstrates this.

Using the differences between the data output from every RBM and the training process data, the reconstructing error is determined.

$$R_{error} = \frac{\sum_{i=1}^{n}\sum_{j=1}^{m}P_{ij} - x_{ij}}{nmp_x} \quad (1)$$

Here, n = training data, m = feature, P_{ij} = reconstructed value, x_{ij} = actual value, and P_x = assessment of no. of values.

$$L = N_{RBM} + 1, |R_{error}(k-1) - R_{error}(k)| > \varepsilon,$$
$$L = N_{RBM}, |R_{error}(k-1) - R_{error}(k)| > \varepsilon \quad (2)$$

Here, L = DBN's no. of hidden layers, ε = default value,

As per the law of continuous probability,

$$P - P(v) = P(v_1)P(h|v_1)P(v|h) \quad (3)$$

As per the law of total probability,

$$P(v|h) = \frac{P(v,h)}{P(h)} \quad (4)$$

From (3),

$$P = P(v_1)\frac{P(v_1,h)}{P(v_1)}\frac{P(v,h)}{P(h)} = P(v_1,h)\frac{P(v,h)}{P(h)} \quad (5)$$

As per (4),

$$P = P(v_1|h)P(h)\frac{P(v,h)}{P(h)}$$
$$P(v_1|h)P(v,h) \quad (6)$$

Apply (6) in (1),

$$R_{error} = \frac{\sum_{i=1}^{n}\sum_{j=1}^{m}P_{ij} - x_{ij}}{nmp_x} = P - X$$
$$= P(v_1|h)P(v,h) - P(v_1)$$
$$= P(v_1)[P(v,h) - 1] \quad (7)$$

4. Results and Discussion

The experiment is carried out using a Python tool. The performance of the suggested A-DBN is assessed in this section in terms of sensitivity, f1-score, accuracy, and precision. Additionally, the proposed A-DBN is contrasted with various current BPNN, DNN, and LSTM methods. Fig. 5.2 displays the accuracy and precision results for the proposed and existing approaches. The efficacy of the model is expressed as the percentage of data for which the suggested A-DBN accurately anticipated the outcome. RBM is divided into numerous layers to create DBN. Both the fitting difficulty phenomenon and the insufficient net accuracy rate are influenced by the number of layers. Because DBN learning uses continuous structures, it is referred to as generating pertaining. A Regressed is trained one layer at a time until it is complete, using the activating likelihood of its hidden unit as the data input for the subsequent level. This work adds discriminating and fine-tuning operations based on the characteristics of musical emotion detection chosen aspects based on a producing pertaining approach. As seen in Fig. 1b, the A-DBN network is made up of a Softmax, a single standard RBM prototype, and an n-layer upgraded RBM model.

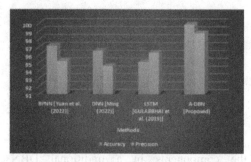

Fig. 5.2 Accuracy and precision outcomes

The degree to which the suggested approach only chooses the most crucial facts for additional analysis is referred to as precision. By dividing the total true positives by the total true and false positives, precision is calculated. According to this graph, the suggested technique outperforms existing techniques BPNN (accuracy = 97.13%; precision = 95.2%), DNN (accuracy = 96.52%; precision = 94.57%), and LSTM (accuracy = 95.1%; precision = 96.3%) in terms of accuracy (99.87%) and precision (98.76%).

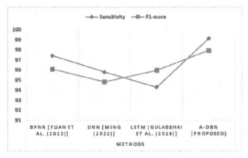

Fig. 5.3   Sensitivity and f1-score outcomes

The findings of sensitivity and f1-score for both suggested and existing approaches are shown in Fig. 5.3. The sensitivity is a metric for how well a model performs accurate estimations across all essential classes. The f1-score combines the sensitivity and precision of the proposed model into a single component by computing the harmonic mean of both. We deduce from this figure that the suggested A-DBN technique outperforms existing approaches [BPNN (sensitivity = 97.43%; f1-score = 96.1%), DNN (sensitivity = 95.81%; f1-score = 94.84%], and LSTM (sensitivity = 94.3%; f1-score = 95.98%)] in terms of sensitivity (99.13%) and f1-score (97.94%).

5. Conclusion

For long-term and adaptable development in the technological advances, every SME must effectively affect structures and remedies from the state, internet, and other SME's .In this study, we aimed to show how the proposed A-DBN can function in terms of payment prediction for HRM. Based on the experimental findings, the suggested A-DBN was the most effective method for payment prediction in terms of accuracy (99.87%), precision (98.76%), sensitivity (99.13%), and f1-score (97.943%) when compared to other methods (BPNN, DNN, and LSTM).

REFERENCES

1. Wilton, N., 2019. An introduction to human resource management. An Introduction to Human Resource Management, pp. 1–632.
2. Calvard, T.S. and Jeske, D., 2018. Developing human resource data risk management in the age of big data. International Journal of Information Management, 43, pp. 159–164.
3. Pandey, A.K., Singh, R.K., Jayesh, G.S., Khare, N. and Gupta, S.K., 2022. Examining the Role of Enterprise Resource Planning (ERP) in Improving Business Operations in Companies. ECS Transactions, 107(1), p. 2681.
4. Rajagopal, N.K., Saini, M., Huerta-Soto, R., Vílchez-Vásquez, R., Kumar, J.N.V.R., Gupta, S.K. and Perumal, S., 2022. Human resource demand prediction and configuration model based on grey wolf optimization and recurrent neural network. Computational Intelligence and Neuroscience, 2022.
5. Kim, Y.J., Kim, W.G., Choi, H.M. and Phetvaroon, K., 2019. The effect of green human resource management on hotel employees' eco-friendly behavior and

environmental performance. International Journal of Hospitality Management, 76, pp. 83–93.

6. Wei, G. and Jin, Y., 2021. Human resource management model based on three-layer BP neural network and machine learning. Journal of Intelligent & Fuzzy Systems, 40(2), pp. 2289–2300.

7. Yuan, S., Qi, Q., Dai, E. and Liang, Y., 2022. Human resource planning and configuration based on machine learning. Computational Intelligence and Neuroscience, 2022.

8. Ming, L., 2022. A Deep Learning-Based Framework for Human Resource Recommendation. Wireless Communications and Mobile Computing, 2022.

9. GULABBHAI, P.P. and GANGIL, M., 2019. Employees Skills Inventory using Deep Learning for Human Resource Management. Research Journal of Engineering Technology and Management (ISSN: 2582-0028), 2(04).

10. Zhao, Y., Hryniewicki, M.K., Cheng, F., Fu, B. and Zhu, X., 2018, September. Employee turnover prediction with machine learning: A reliable approach. In Proceedings of SAI intelligent systems conference (pp. 737–758). Springer, Cham.

Note: All the figures in this chapter were made by the Authors.

*Advancements in Business for Integrating Diversity, and
Sustainability – Dimitrios A. Karras et al. (eds)*
© 2024 Taylor & Francis Group, London, ISBN 978-1-032-70828-7

6

An Innovative Model for Financial Crisis in HR Management

K. Guru*
Takshashila University, Tamil Nadu, India

S. Raja[1]
SRM Valliammai Engineering College. Chennai, India

G. Jitendra[2]
KL Business School, Koneru Lakshmaiah Education Foundation, Andhra Pradesh, India

Navaneetha Krishnan Rajagopal[3]
University of Technology and Applied Sciences, Salalah, Oman

Abstract: As a consequence of difficulties in extracting the features of financial data, the current approaches for predicting financial crises are lacking. Thus, an intelligent financial crisis prediction method for human resources (HR) is suggested using enhanced K-means clustering and fitness scaling improved spider monkey optimization (K-MC+FSISMO). The K-MC+FSISMO technique is used to mine the attributes of financial data using financial index data from publicly traded companies. Following the discoveries made via data feature mining, this study creates an index system for predicting financial crises. CCR measures the effectiveness of publicly listed companies' decision-making units, with a focus on those having the greatest impact on inputs and outputs. Experimental findings show that this technique may significantly shorten the time it takes to foresee financial crises and that its forecast accuracy is comparable to the real status of enterprises, as compared to traditional prediction methods.

Keywords: Human resource (HR), Financial crisis, Enhanced K-means clustering, Fitness scaling improved spider monkey optimization, CCR model

1. Introduction

"Financial asset to management" and "HR" have replaced "work force to the board" in most process summaries. HRM boosts organisational resilience. HRM becomes increasingly crucial to a company's success. HR directors must lead, manage, strategize, mentor, educate, and model in a global economic crisis (Thakkar, et al., (2021)).

*Corresponding author: guruvpm@gmail.com
[1]guruvpm@gmail.com, [2]ksraja22486@gmail.com, [3]gjk.jitendra@gmail.com, [4]bba_rnk@yahoo.co.in

DOI: 10.4324/9781032708294-6

Business and public sector recruiting has faced many challenges, including bias. Due to poor management records and a lack of personal knowledge, organizations and contingent workers lack information (Navaneetha, et al., (2022)). Due to the global economic crisis, commercial entities worldwide are increasing their cash reserves to offset the sharp reduction in demand for various services and products. In today's economy, efficiency matters. Management should prioritise reducing operational costs (Tellez, et al (2022)). Because of the worldwide increase in corporate financial crises over the last decade, corporations everywhere are devoting considerable resources to the study of financial crisis prediction (FCP). It is crucial for a business or financial institution to develop an accurate and timely prediction model in order to foresee the possibility of financial collapse in the future of the business. A rational binary classification model is typical for FCP. The classification model produces two types of results: those that signal a company's failure and those that don't. Financial statement ratios constitute the categorization model's standard input (Navaneetha, et al., (2022)). More classification models for FCP have been built utilizing different types of domain information up to this point.

2. Related Works

Samitas, et al. (2020) examines structured financial network contagion hazards and their implications for "Early Warning Systems" (EWS). Sankhwar, et al. (2020) propose a new FCP model prediction framework using improved grey wolf optimization (IGWO) and fuzzy neural classifier (FNC). Horak, et al. (2020) developed and tested a model to predict corporate insolvency using classification

methods such the Support Vector Machine and artificial neural networks. Uthayakumar et al. (2020) introduce an Ant Colony Optimization (ACO)-based financial crisis prediction (FCP) model with two stages: ACO-FS feature selection and ACO-DC data categorization. Thus, Venkateswarlu et al. (2022) use an oppositional ant lion optimizer to create a feature selection and classification model for FCP in a massive data situation (OALOFS-MLC). A political optimizer-trained deep neural network detects FCC abnormalities (Elhoseny, et al., 2022).

3. Proposed Methodology

This study uses financial index data from chosen publicly traded companies and K-MC+FSISMO to construct a model that can accurately predict their future financial health. Fig. 6.1 shows the method.

Dataset: The "financial data of a Shenzhen and Shanghai-listed organization", including seven companies with stable financials and five in financial crisis, was used for this study since such information is more readily available than for public corporations. 12 publicly traded companies had their five-year financial data analysed. We can estimate each company's financial problem based on their present position and five-year financial data.

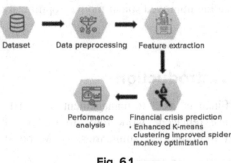

Fig. 6.1

Preprocessing using Min-max normalization: To normalize a property, we scale its values such that they all lie inside a certain range. Assume that the lowest and maximum values for an attribute Y are $\min Y$ and $\max Y$. B value of B, a_w, is "mapped to a_w in the range [new-$\min Y$, new-$\max Y$] by using the following equation":

$$\ddot{B}_w = (b_w - \min Y)/(\max Y - \min Y) *$$
$$(new_{\max Y} - new_{\min Y}) + new_{\min Y} \qquad (1)$$

If the range of future normalization input data for Y is larger than the range of beginning data, the risk of a "out-of-bounds" error rises.

Feature extraction using principle component analysis: In principal component analysis (PCA), the original variables are subjected to a series of orthogonal linear transformations to retain as much data as possible while keeping components while still cutting the number of variables. "Let N be an $m \times t$ data matrix, with n and s standing for the number of factors and occurrences, respectively". Principal component U1 is defined as $U_1 = \sum_{z}^{s} = \alpha_1 z \, N_z$, where $\alpha_1 = (\alpha_{11}, ..., \alpha_1^o)$ O. If we want to increase the dispersion of V1, then we should choose O such that V_1 has the largest possible variance.

$$\alpha_1 = \arg\max_{\alpha} \alpha^O \sum \alpha$$
$$subject \ to \|\alpha_1\| = 1 \qquad (2)$$

The following fundamental components have been defined in sequence, beginning with $\sum = (N^O N)/m$.

$$\alpha_{g+1} = \arg\max_{\alpha} \alpha^O \sum \alpha \qquad (3)$$

Depending on

$$\|\alpha\| = 1 \ and \ \alpha^O \alpha_h = 0, \forall 1 \le h \le g \qquad (4)$$

This specification makes the first h eigenvalues the initial h loading vector.

Eigen decomposition links PCA to N's SVD. Assume M is SVD.

$$N = XKG^O \qquad (5)$$

D is a symmetric matrix with diagonally elements t_1, t_s in decreasing order, while V and G are basis functions matrix of $m \times t$ and $s \times s$ rows and columns, correspondingly. Since H's columns are the eigenvalues, H serves as the loading matrix for the constructs. Since $NG = XK$, we know that X_g is the gth column of, hence $V_g = X_g c_g$. Take into account that the SVL provides a solid low-rank approximation of the data matrix.

In the various geometrical understanding of PCA, straight manifolds are the best fit for information. "This concept aligns with how PCA is built. Make ix the wth row in Y. Take the first g main components together, which equals $L_g = [L_1| ... |L_g]$. L_g is a $s \times g$ orthonormal matrix by definition. Each observation should be projected to the linear region coveged by $\{l_1...l_g\}$". The projected data are $T_h M_x$, $1 \le x \le m$ and the projection operator is $S_g = L_g L^O$.

$$\min_{A_g} \sum_{w=1}^{n} \left\| j_w - A_g A_g^O j_i \right\|^2 \qquad (6)$$

Simple diagrams show the solution's first-generation components. Application parameters can employ many scales and units. Standardized sets each parameter's marginal variance to 1. This principal component analysis method yields the raw data correlation coefficient and the centralized data covariances. *Financial crisis prediction using K-MC + FSISMO:* The clustering method's goal is to classify data into distinct groups; hence, observations assigned to the same cluster have a closer relationship than those assigned to other groups. K-means, a well-known distance-based clustering algorithm, and distance are used to compute similarity; this implies that the objects that are physically closer to one another have a greater degree of similarity. When using the K-means clustering approach, the steps are:

(1) At first, everything is shown. Since N is the total number of main cluster centers, choose a value of K from that large set. Here, K = 2.

(2) Measure how far apart each item is from the centers of the clusters. Following the Eq. (7) the items will be added to the local cluster.

$$T_j^{(s)} = \left\{ \forall_i B_i B_l w_o : \left\| w_o - n_j^{(s)} \right\| \le \right.$$
$$\left. \left\| w_o - n_j^{(s)} \right\| \forall a \le i \le l \right\} \forall i, \forall_i \forall_l \qquad (7)$$

(3) It is necessary to recalculate the centres of all clusters to verify that Eq. (8)

$$n_j^{(s+1)} = \frac{1}{T_j^{(s)}} \sum_{W_j \in T_j^{(s)}} W_i \qquad (8)$$

(4) For the initial cluster centre to look just like the old one, repeat steps 1 and 2. The classification will make use of the cleaned data.

$$Rate = \frac{Remaining\ data}{Sum} \qquad (9)$$

Due to spider monkey behaviour, FSISMO, a swarm intelligence-based programme, was updated. FSISMO is population-based stochastic. The FSISMO algorithm balances exploration and growth well. Spider monkeys are highly gregarious primates that live in groups and have particular foraging and communication routines. A female spider monkey leader harvests for food for her group. The commander divides the group into sub groups to increase their chances of finding food if there isn't enough. Global leaders lead the collective, while local leaders head subgroups.

FSISMO flows in Fig. 6.2. The FSISMO optimises routing from Cluster Heads (CHs) to the Base Station by examining source node, distance, and routing traffic (BS). In hierarchical cluster-based design, intermediary CH data transfer reduces node energy utilisation.

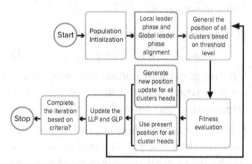

Fig. 6.2 Architecture of FSISMO

4. Result and Discussion

This step tests the financial risk prediction approach for listed corporations after theoretical research is completed.

Financial Crisis Prediction Accuracy: Accuracy in predicting financial crises with this strategy compared to two other ways. This paper's methodology yields as illustrated in Fig. 6.3. This paper's suggested method outperforms the two literature comparison methods. The technique can accurately predict a company's financial future.

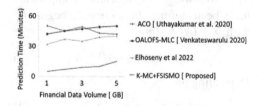

Fig. 6.3 Prediction Accuracy Fig. 1 Proposed Fig. 1

Predicting a financial crisis takes time: Fig. 6.4 displays the labor-intensive comparative findings of the three approaches. The suggested technique is superior. So predicting time is shorter. This method reduces the time needed to predict a financial crisis.

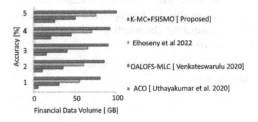

Fig. 6.4 Prediction Time

5. Conclusion

Growing numbers of new entrepreneurs arise as a result of the government's support for what it calls "mass entrepreneurship and innovation." They promote growth in established industries while actively seeking funding from angel investors. Internet plus concept has spread to many products and services, further merging online and offline marketplaces. Businesses need better risk control, real-time financial information, and better management and control to compete in today's market. Therefore, financiers, corporate decision-makers, and expert money organisations must quickly and effectively analyse the latest business data, anticipate future entrepreneurial using current finance data and management strategy, and plan ahead based on these economic projections. That's why a real-time historical analytic system for predicting financial crises is crucial.

REFERENCES

1. Thakkar, A. and Chaudhari, K., 2021. Fusion in stock market prediction: a decade survey on the necessity, recent developments, and potential future directions. Information Fusion, 65, pp. 95–107.

2. Navaneetha Krishnan Rajagopal, Mankeshva Saini, Rosario Huerta-Soto, Rosa Vílchez-Vásquez, J. N. V. R. Swarup Kumar, Shashi Kant Gupta, Sasikumar Perumal, "Human Resource Demand Prediction and Configuration Model Based on Grey Wolf Optimization and Recurrent Neural Network", Computational Intelligence and Neuroscience, vol. 2022, Article ID 5613407, 11 pages, 2022. https://doi.org/10.1155/2022/5613407

3. Tellez Gaytan, J.C., Ateeq, K., Rafiuddin, A., Alzoubi, H.M., Ghazal, T.M., Ahanger, T.A., Chaudhary, S. and Viju, G.K., 2022. AI-Based Prediction of Capital Structure: Performance Comparison of ANN SVM and LR Models. Computational Intelligence & Neuroscience.

4. Navaneetha Krishnan Rajagopal, Naila Iqbal Qureshi, S. Durga, Edwin Hernan Ramirez Asis, Rosario Mercedes Huerta Soto, Shashi Kant Gupta, S. Deepak, "Future of Business Culture: An Artificial Intelligence-Driven Digital Framework for Organization Decision-Making Process", Complexity, vol. 2022, Article ID 7796507, 14 pages, 2022. https://doi.org/10.1155/2022/7796507

5. Samitas, A., Kampouris, E. and Kenourgios, D., 2020. Machine learning as an early warning system to predict financial crisis. International Review of Financial Analysis, 71, p. 101507.

6. Sankhwar, S., Gupta, D., Ramya, K.C., Sheeba Rani, S., Shankar, K. and Lakshmanaprabu, S.K., 2020. Improved grey wolf optimization-based feature subset selection with fuzzy neural classifier for

financial crisis prediction. Soft Computing, 24(1), pp. 101–110.

7. Horak, J., Vrbka, J. and Suler, P., 2020. Support vector machine methods and artificial neural networks used for the development of bankruptcy prediction models and their comparison. Journal of Risk and Financial Management, 13(3), p. 60.

8. Uthayakumar, J., Metawa, N., Shankar, K. and Lakshmanaprabu, S.K., 2020. Financial crisis prediction model using ant colony optimization. International Journal of Information Management, 50, pp. 538–556.

9. Venkateswarlu, Y., Baskar, K., Wongchai, A., Gauri Shankar, V., Paolo Martel Carranza, C., Gonzáles, J.L.A. and Murali Dharan, A.R., 2022. An Efficient Outlier Detection with Deep Learning-Based Financial Crisis Prediction Model in Big Data Environment. Computational Intelligence and Neuroscience, 2022.

10. Elhoseny, M., Metawa, N. and El-hasnony, I.M., 2022. A new metaheuristic optimization model for financial crisis prediction: Towards sustainable development. Sustainable Computing: Informatics and Systems, 35, p. 100778.

Note: All the figures in this chapter were made by the Authors.

Advancements in Business for Integrating Diversity, and
Sustainability – Dimitrios A. Karras et al. (eds)
© 2024 Taylor & Francis Group, London, ISBN 978-1-032-70828-7

Role of Strategic Management in Developing Business Organizations—A Meta-Analysis

E. Hymavathi*, Kalpana Koneru[1]

Vignan's Foundation for Science,
Technology & Research (Deemed to be University),
Guntur, Andhra Pradesh, India

Sanjay Modi[2]

Lovely Professional University, Phagwara, India

Shubhendu Shekher Shukla[3]

SRM Business School, Lucknow, India

Abstract: Beijing was chosen as the location for the research at small and medium-sized firms with the purpose of examining the relationship between sustained competitive advantage and strategic effectiveness. The competitive advantage of small and medium-sized businesses in China is now being studied to determine the effects of strategic absorbency, capacity to modify strategies, and managerial wisdom. The study used a logical thinking process to analyse Chinese Small and medium enterprises, and each regression analysis was performed to measure the influence of each independent variable on organizational performance. A total of 175 questions were filled out, with 152 respondents correctly completing their respective assessments. The study indicated that the absorptive capability had the highest influence on sustainability, whereas the managerial expertise had the least impact.

Keywords: Absorptive, Managerial wisdom, Strategic management, Sustainable competitive advantage (SCA)

1. Introduction

Globalization has transformed industrialised nations. Large organisations are used to a constantly changing, innovative environment. Many governments have focused on small and medium companies (SMEs) as the best way to solve huge commercial problems. Economies affect SMEs. They can also adapt better to global changes (Coban, et al., 2019). Many governments monitor SMEs' business operations and provide assistance

---
*Corresponding author: ehymavathi21@gmail.com
[1]kalpanarao.koneru@gmail.com, [2]saranmds@gmail.com, [3]shubhendusshukla@gmail.com

DOI: 10.4324/9781032708294-7

when needed. SMEs boost economic growth in most developed and developing countries. GDP, salary growth, and job creation raise living standards. Smaller enterprises keep the sector sustainable and creative (Castellanos, et al., 2020). These firms employ many people. SMEs struggle to survive. They face financial issues, technology issues, inefficient human resources, inattention, and harsh policy approach from lawmakers. These obstacles hurt small firms unintentionally. Small and medium-sized firms struggle with administration, business, and infrastructure. Abdullah et al. (2021). This study proposed that self and state subsidies can increase SMEs' competitiveness. Systemic and wealth perspectives underpin it. SMEs' competitiveness depends on managers' skill (Irudayasamy, et al., 2022). SME's would gain from a government programme targeted at boosting their competitiveness as well.

2. Related Works

Managers and executives have a number of responsibilities inside an organisation. Although managers try to alter institutions, managers monitor and sustain them. Cruz, et al., (2018) analyses the U.S. multinational corporations' Canadian affiliates approach strategic planning and management (MNEs). It provides a framework for assessing how they would react to the different World Products Mission policies by the Canadian government. Zerfass, et al., (2018) proposes a new and much more thorough definition of marketing communications based on a year of study in the field and, more specifically, on the papers in this special issue. Bogers, et al., (2019) uses examples from strategy management theory to explain a few possibilities and constraints of this approach. To that end, we construct an agency theory

framework to analyse open innovation's organizational strategies and shed light on the factors that influence its victory or calamity. Shao, et al., (2019), leadership is "the nature of a leader's influencing activity and its effects," factors such as the leader's personality, the followers' beliefs and assumptions, and the setting where the convincing takes place (Samimi, et al., (2022)).

3. Methodology

Dataset: The research was conducted in Fujian Province, China, and its samples were randomly chosen. Only 152 of the 175 questionnaires that were sent out were correctly filled out. Determining the influence of "strategic leadership efficacy (absorptive strategies (AS), capacity to change strategies (CCS), and managerial wisdom (MW))"on gaining a sustainable competitive edge for SMEs in Fujian, China. On a scale out of one (most) essential to five (least) essential, respondents were asked to assess the relative weight of the each item.

Hypotheses development: Hypothesis (1) SCA is significantly and favourably impacted by the ability to absorb as a self-leadership competence. Hypothesis (2) the ability to adapt as a trait of self-leadership positively and significantly affects long-term competitive advantage. Hypothesis (3) SCA is positively and significantly influenced by managerial wisdom as a self-leadership talent.

4. Result and Discussion

This study aimed to determine the extent to which organizational management effectiveness affects the ability of small and SMEs in China's Fujian province to maintain a competitive edge over their rivals over the long term. Pearson correlation (PC) analysis between hypotheses and SCA: Table 7.1 and figure 7.1 displays the results of an Analysis of variance. Table 7.2 displays correlation research that looked at hypotheses as both a self-leadership skill and a real asset for SMEs in China's Fujian province.

Table 7.1 Result of analysis of variance

Analysis of variance						
	Pattern 1	Sum of Squares	df	Mean Square	F	Sig.
H 1	Regression	145.481	1	144.189	222.182	0^b
	Variance	43.9825	785	.046		
	Average	188.0645	786			
H2	Regression	130.178	1	129.649	293.198	0^b
	Variance	39.219	469	.038		
	Average	168.299	472			
H 3	Regression	119.211	1	112.001	117.206	0^b
	Variance	22.582	722	.033		
	Average	138.993	723			

For H1: "DV: SCA, b. Predictors: (Constant), AS"

For H2: DV: SCA, b. Predictors: (Constant), CCS

For H3: "DV: SCA, b. Predictors: (Constant), MW"

Table 7.2 Research outcomes

Correlations											
Hypothesis 1				Hypothesis 2				Hypothesis 3			
Variables	PC	SCA	AS	Variables	PC	SCA	CCS	Variables	PC	SCA	MW
SCA	PC	1	776**	SCA	PC	1	.698**	SCA	PC	1	.747**
	Sig. (2-tailed)	-	0		Sig. (2-tailed)	-	.000		Sig. (2-tailed)	-	0
	N	152	152		N	152	152		N	152	152
AS	PC	.776**	1	CCS	PC	.698**	1	MW	PC	.747**	1
	Sig. (2-tailed)	0	-		Sig. (2-tailed)	0	-		Sig. (2-tailed)	0	-
	N	152	152		N	152	152		N	152	152
**. "Correlation is significant at the 0.01 level (2-tailed)"											

Model Summary					
	Pattern	R	R^2	Adjusted R^2	Std. Error
Hypothesis 1	1	.768[a]	.721	.711	.20711
Hypothesis 2	1	.671	.632	.618	.18625
Hypothesis 3	1	.751	.698	.618	.20154

Coefficients							
		Pattern	**B**		**SB**	t	Sig.
			B	Std. Error	Beta		
Hypothesis 1	1	Constant	.299	.053		3.551	0
		AS	.781	.027	.808	52.126	0
a. "Dependent Variable: SCA"							
Hypothesis 2	1	Constant	.331	.049		5.189	0
		CCS	.713	.029	.717	51.938	0
a. "DV: SCA"							
Hypothesis 3	1	Constant	.252	.089		3.549	0
		MW	.661	.015	.686	32.774	0
a. "DV: SCA"							

Model Summary of hypotheses: Analyzing whether different variables interact is known as regression analysis. Regression analysis' objective is to ascertain how B might influence and change A. Its formula is $B = f(a1,a2,...ac)$ in this section, the managerial wisdom approach, the absorptive approach, and the ability to adapt are all considered as independent variables, while organizational performance is regarded as a dependent variable (DV). Its overall difference will be determined using the comparative advantage's volatility. The variations are calculated by multiplying the projected competitive advantage values by the sum of their squares, it is subsequently proportionally distributed among all participants. By reducing the variation by the complete variation of competitive advantage, by using regression analysis, the study was able to determine the precise aggregate of all distinguishable variables. R Square gives a definition for the number, which has a range of 0 to 1.

Outcomes of ANOVA: There is a substantial correlation between absorption and organizational effectiveness.

Coefficients Analysis of hypotheses and SCA: The implications of the hypotheses are shown in Table 7.1: Based on these results, Absorptive would seem to have a clear positive link with organizational performance.

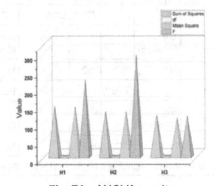

Fig. 7.1 ANOVA results

5. Conclusion

This paper's focus is on how effective strategic leadership contributes to a culture of continuous improvement. Researchers in Beijing focused on SMEs. In order to identify how strategic leadership efficacy affected SMEs in the Fujian area of China, the present research looked at how it affected sustained competitive advantage. "Standard regression analysis was used to estimate the impact of the each independent variable" on the outcomes of SMEs in Fujian, China. The limited data set is the paper's main drawback. This research adds to "the body of knowledge on self-leadership and long-term competitive advantage" by using an established conceptual framework. According to the findings, managerial knowledge had the least effect as a self-leadership strategy for achieving sustained competitive advantage whereas absorptive strategy had the most impact.

REFERENCES

1. Castellanos, J.D. and George, B., 2020. Boardroom leadership: The board of directors as a source of strategic leadership. Economics and Business Review, 6(1), pp. 103–119.
2. Coban, O., Ozdemir, S. and Pisapia, J., 2019. Top managers' organizational change management capacity and their strategic leadership levels at Ministry of National Education (MoNE). Eurasian Journal of Educational Research, 19(81), pp. 129–146.
3. Navaneetha Krishnan Rajagopal, Naila Iqbal Qureshi, S. Durga, Edwin Hernan Ramirez Asis, Rosario Mercedes Huerta Soto, Shashi Kant Gupta, S. Deepak, "Future of Business Culture: An Artificial Intelligence-Driven Digital Framework for Organization Decision-Making Process", Complexity, vol. 2022, Article ID 7796507, 14 pages, 2022. https://doi.org/10.1155/2022/7796507
4. Abdullah, N.N. and Anwar, G., 2021. An Empirical Analysis of Natural Gas as an Alternative Fuel for Internal Transportation. International Journal of English Literature and Social Sciences, 6(1).
5. Irudayasamy, A., Christotodoss, P. R., & Natarajan, R. (2022). Multilingual Novel Summarizer for Visually Challenged Peoples. In J. Zhao, & V. Kumar (Ed.), Handbook of Research on Technologies and Systems for E-Collaboration During Global Crises (pp. 27–46). IGI Global. https://doi.org/10.4018/978-1-7998-9640-1.ch003
6. D'Cruz, J.R., 2018. Strategic Management of Subsidiaries 1. In Managing the multinational subsidiary (pp. 75–89). Routledge.
7. Zerfass, A., Verčič, D., Nothhaft, H. and Werder, K.P., 2018. Strategic communication: Defining the field and its contribution to research and practice. International Journal of Strategic Communication, 12(4), pp. 487–505.
8. Bogers, M., Chesbrough, H., Heaton, S. and Teece, D.J., 2019. Strategic management of open innovation: A dynamic capabilities perspective. California Management Review, 62(1), pp. 77–94.
9. Shao, Z., 2019. Interaction effect of strategic leadership behaviors and organizational culture on IS-Business strategic alignment and Enterprise Systems assimilation. International journal of information management, 44, pp. 96–108.
10. Samimi, M., Cortes, A.F., Anderson, M.H. and Herrmann, P., 2022. What is strategic leadership? Developing a framework for future research. The Leadership Quarterly, 33(3), p. 101353.

Note: All the tables and figure in this chapter were made by the Authors.

Advancements in Business for Integrating Diversity, and
Sustainability – Dimitrios A. Karras et al. (eds)
© 2024 Taylor & Francis Group, London, ISBN 978-1-032-70828-7

Financial Management Procedures: a detailed Analysis of CEOS of Small and Medium-Sized Businesses

Niyati Joshi*

Rajeev Gandhi College of Management Studies, Navi Mumbai, India

Muhammed Shafi M. K[1]

VIT Business School, Vellore Institute of Technology, Chennai, India

Rajesh Verma[2]

Lovely Professional University, Phagwara, India

Shruti Sharma[3]

Graphic Era Deemed to be University, Dehradun, Uttarakhand, India

Abstract: Creating external connections, like interlocks, is a method for acquiring access to limited resources. Creating and preserving these connections may be a resource for the organization that gives Small and Medium Sized Enterprises (SMEs) a competitive edge. It is suggested to use a partial framework of networking approach that takes board diversity, interlocks, entrepreneurial intention, and environmental hostility into account. A survey of 70 local banks provides evidence in favor of the claim those businesses with such a put interests beat those that did not actively promote the formation of networks Chief Executive Officer (CEO) replies.

Keywords: Small and Medium Sized Enterprises (SMEs), Chief Executive Officer (CEO), Organizational strength

1. Introduction

The capacity of a firm to acquire and exercise control over the materials of its surroundings is essential to the industry's ability to continue functioning, based on the resource dependence hypothesis. Studies on entrepreneurship have shown that emerging enterprises look for resources to reduce costs, acquire access to new information, or enhance skills. A method to maximize the benefits of specialization while minimizing the expense of coordinating exchanges is continuous cooperation inside networks (Ashish et al., 2022). This can be accomplished by working together to

*Corresponding author: niyatiloshi.15@gmail.com

[1]mkshafimba@gmail.com, [2]saranmds@gmail.com, [3]shrutisharma.comm@geu.ac.in

DOI: 10.4324/9781032708294-8

achieve a common goal. The implications of a networking strategy on organizational performance in SMEs businesses are the primary topic of investigation in this study (Navaneetha et al., 2022). A board member actively participates in the foundation and development of SMEs. Therefore, board members of small businesses are likely to leverage their existing network connections to grow the company (Soundararajan et al., 2018). This research contributes to the existing body of knowledge by doing the following: (1) using a club's social network connections as a performance predictor (Sanchez et al., 2020) and (3) expanding the consequences of aggressively putting the interests into the environment of entrepreneurship. (2) Adding to the literature in strategic management on board isolators and their performance impacts (Karmaker et al., 2023).

2. Related Works

Morozko and Didenko (2018) intended to pinpoint the prerequisites for small businesses to manage their finances dynamically using a cognitive approach. Anik, (2020) examined how managerial viewpoints, societal interest perspectives, and disclosure-related behaviors may change how management behaves when it comes to providing financial statements without financial facts. Umadia and Kasztelnik (2020) explored the tactics used by industry leaders as the goal of this qualitative multiple-case study. Dalalo and Hunde, (2020) investigated the impact that different financial management strategies have on the level of profitability experienced by SMEs businesses in the KEMBTA TAMBARO Zone of the Southern Nations Nationalities and Peoples Region (SNNPR). Adda, (20200

investigated the capabilities and practices of SMEs businesses regarding their growth. The researchers asked SMEs managers and owners to fill out questionnaires to obtain the necessary information for the study.

3. Methodology

The paper's research was focused on the banking sector. Since bigger banks may have holdings and multiple boards that would make data analysis difficult and time-consuming, community banks were selected as the community to choose banks. The current research focuses on less significant community banks with clear board structures and ownership characteristics. It is simple to research partnerships, or in this instance, networking techniques because community banks are tiny enterprises that typically have a single board and aim to service local community customers. Since community banks frequently cater to local customers, researching coalitions is not too challenging.

4. Results

Even though each of the banks in the study was subject to regulatory oversight, this did not prevent any of them from either performing poorly or very well financially. The interlocking variables and the networking technique variable were both demonstrated to be correlated to varied degrees, which increased the construct validity of the network scale created for this study. Due to the strength of the relationship between the interconnected components and the network approach variable, the networking scale developed in this study has stronger construct validity. With the probable exception of hypothesis 2, Table 8.3 unquestionably confirms the hypotheses. However, the predictive ability of each variable is demonstrated using a simple linear regression model. Table 8.4 displays the regression findings.

Hypothesis 1: This first theory was confirmed. In response to a query regarding the importance of networking, 31 CEOs stated that they thought it was one of the main things board members did.

Hypothesis 2: This was unsupported. In contrast to the premise, it was found that there was a statistically significant negative association between networking approach and environmental hostility. The study was carried out during a time of comparatively stable and abundant conditions in the US economy and financial sector, thus the authors can only speculate that this conclusion may be related to it. Another explanation might be that SME boards tend to add more interlocks when their companies are doing well since doing so reduces the costs of keeping a bigger, more active board.

Hypothesis 3: Although significant at 0.10 points, the innovation capability hypothesis only adds 3% to the variance's explanation. As a result, businesses with an entrepreneurial mindset ought should be more likely to have a robust networking strategy (figure 8.1).

Table 8.1 Standard deviations, Correlations, and Means

	Mean	SD	(1)	(2)	(3)	(4)	(5)
Employees (number)	55.8	48.2	1	0.00	-0.06	0.13	0.24*
Functional activity (factor 1 ± board activity)	-	-		1	0.00	0.55***	0.44***
Relational activity (Factor 2 ± board activity)	-	-			1	0.40***	-0.13
Networking Strategy	3.25	1.32				1	0.35***
Interlocks (average)	1.92	0.91					1
Interlocks (total)	14.52	7.60					
Board size	9.65	2.45					
Environmental hostility	3.02	1.01					
Entrepreneurial orientation	3.95	0.90					
Average ROA	1.08	0.63					
Average ROE	11.25	6.95					

Table 8.2 Results of linear regression

	Support	Adj. R^2	Intercept
Hypothesis 1	Yes***	0.47	4.25
Hypothesis 2	No*	0.03	5.21
Hypothesis 3	Yes*	0.02	3.05
Overall Model	Yes***	0.50	2.21

Table 8.3 Networking technique stepwise regression using performance metrics

Step	Variable	Average ROA		Average ROE	
1	Intercept	0.96	0.40	0.97	3.40
	Employees	0.14	0.11	0.18	0.13
2	Networking Strategy		0.25*		0.28*
	F-value	1.41	3.14*	1.95	3.71*
	Adjusted	0.01	0.06	0.01	0.07

Table 8.4 Analyses of four-item responses

Item	Variable	Means of variables (firms with scored >4)	Means of variables (firms with scored <4)	Levene's test F-statistic
The main activity is networking.	5-year average ROA	1.15 (31,0.38)	1.00 (28,0.85)	3.61
	5-year average ROE	11.28 (30,3.52)	9.09 (27,9.55)	3.92
The bank promotes networking	5-year average ROA	1.17 (48,0.40)	0.66 (9,1.24)	12.81**
	5-year average ROE	12.17 (48,3.65)	6.75 (10.15.01)	23.01***
Gain a competitive advantage by using networks.	5-year average ROA	1.06 (23.0.45)	1.07 (34.0.75)	1.33
	5-year average ROE	12.25 (23.5.85)	9.54 (34, 7.83)	0.01
Recognize networks' previous performance	5-year average ROA	1.24 (18,0.39)	0.98 (38, 0.72)	
	5-year average ROE	13.00 (18,2.33)	10.38 (28, 8.47)	3.85

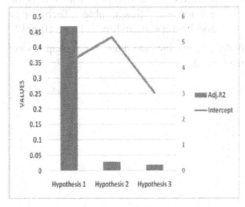

Fig. 8.1 Hypothesis

5. Conclusion

A concerted effort is a networking tactic. Harmony comes through the arrangement of several talents, just like at a performance. Although this study examines board members' networking tactics, creating network links may be a companywide strategy, particularly in knowledge-intensive jobs. For example, network links could be very helpful for researchers and experts in the computing, pharmaceutical, and biotech industries to boost research funding, introduce innovations, advance current technologies, or expand the scope of their applications. These operations will stay diverse if they are integrated into the rm and might give rise to a competitive advantage.

REFERENCES

1. Morozko, N. and Didenko, V., 2018. Financial management of small organizations based on a cognitive approach.
2. AnikYuesti, N.M.D.R., 2020. The behavior of Financial Management for Small and Medium Enterprises in the New Normal Era. Journal of Southwest Jiaotong University, 55(6).
3. Umadia, K. and Kasztelnik, K., 2020. The Financial Management Practice Role of Small to Medium Scale Enterprises From Developing Country and Impact on Global Economy. Journal of Management Policy and Practice, 21(5), pp. 71–88.
4. Dalalo, D.Y. and Hunde, D.A., 2020. Financial Management Practices and Profitability of Small and Medium Enterprises in KembetaTembaro Zone, SNNPR. Journal of the Social Sciences, 48(4).
5. Adda, G., 2020. Financial Management Practices and Growth of Small and Medium-Scale Enterprises: The case of Kassena-Nankana West District. Research in Business and Management, 7(2), pp. 39–58.
6. Ashish Kumar Pandey et al 2022 ECS Trans. 107 2681 Examining the Role of Enterprise Resource Planning (ERP) in Improving Business Operations in Companies. https://doi.org/10.1149/10701.2681ecst
7. Navaneetha Krishnan Rajagopal, Naila Iqbal Qureshi, S. Durga, Edwin Hernan Ramirez Asis, Rosario Mercedes Huerta Soto, Shashi Kant Gupta, S. Deepak, Future of Business Culture: An Artificial Intelligence-Driven Digital Framework for Organization Decision-Making Process, Complexity, vol. 2022, Article ID 7796507, 14 pages, 2022. https://doi.org/10.1155/2022/7796507
8. Soundararajan, V., Spence, L.J. and Rees, C., 2018. Small business and social irresponsibility in developing countries: Working conditions and "evasion" institutional work. Business & Society, 57(7), pp. 1301–1336.
9. Sanchez-Famoso, V., Mejia-Morelos, J.H. and Cisneros, L., 2020. New insights into non-listed family SMEs in Spain: Board social capital, board effectiveness, and sustainable performance. Sustainability, 12(3), p. 814.
10. Karmaker, C.L., Al Aziz, R., Palit, T. and Bari, A.M., 2023. Analyzing supply chain risk factors in the small and medium enterprises under fuzzy environment: Implications towards sustainability for emerging economies. Sustainable Technology and Entrepreneurship, 2(1), p. 100032.

Note: All the tables and figure in this chapter were made by the Authors.

*Advancements in Business for Integrating Diversity, and
Sustainability – Dimitrios A. Karras et al. (eds)*
© 2024 Taylor & Francis Group, London, ISBN 978-1-032-70828-7

An Extensive Survey of the Field of Interactive Digital Marketing Using a Bibliographic Network Analysis

9

Dinesh Gabhane*

Rajeev Gandhi College of Management Studies,
Navi Mumbai, India

A. Celina[1]

College of Management, SRMIST,
Kattankulathur, Chennai, India

Manish Gupta[2]

Lovely Professional University,
Phagwara, India

Deepak Kaushal[3]

Graphic Era Deemed to be University,
Dehradun, Uttarakhand, India

Abstract: Digital technologies and social networking sites are widely used, the way marketers engage with clients has undergone a significant transformation. Businesses can compete by using marketing techniques that are more objective, relational, and interactive thanks to information and communication technology (ICT) technologies and the range of digital platforms that are used. A broad and effective reach is made possible by utilizing cutting-edge technology and data-driven marketing, especially in digital advertising. Consumer groups have consequently become more knowledgeable, powerful, and connected both offline and online thanks to digital marketing (DM). The interaction between DM and improving customer satisfaction is the driving force behind this study. Since improving customer satisfaction is crucial to the survival of educational institutions, educational marketing interactions must begin with meeting both consumer and community needs and wants. This study identifies analysis dynamics in interactive DM by determining the stages of progression of significant articles, topics, co-citation networks, and citations using a variety of computational techniques, including development curve analysis and citation network analysis (CNA) of bi-bliometric data. The research adds to the vast, global field of study known as interactive DM.

Keywords: Information and communication technology (ICT), Digital marketing (DM), Marketing, Citation network analysis (CNA)

*Corresponding author: dtgabhane@gmail.com
[1]celinap@srmist.edu.in, [2]saranmds@gmail.com, [3]dipak.kaushal@geu.ac.in

DOI: 10.4324/9781032708294-9

1. Introduction

DM has become more convenient, has a bigger audience, is more cost-effective, and can now transcend time and space barriers thanks to the adoption of cutting-edge gadgets and methodologies. To achieve retailing goals both in the business-to-consumer and consumer-to-consumer sectors situations, DM makes use of technology of all sorts. DM is a dynamic, multi-disciplinary field that is always changing. It is not only a matter of using electrical technology that may be used for marketing and improvement because of recent advancements in ICT platforms and tools (Krishen, et al., 2021). New methods of reaching out to users, keeping them informed, maintaining their attention, and providing them with goods and services are made possible by DM. Since it performs so admirably, it is projected that marketing will stay at the forefront of technical innovation, and advancement (Ghorbani, et al., 2022). The business has traditionally prioritized analytics in marketing and, in particular, the accurate evaluation of marketing performance (Figueiredo, et al., 2021). Electronic marketing is still a growing system that offers this terrace, making it possible to use internet-based technology to perform all kinds of electronic advertising (Gao, et al., 2021). The internet has grown, and DM has evolved to include a vast network of software, stock trading, consumer behavior research, and other services in addition to just selling items. Today, a very important component of every company, corporation or organization's marketing plan is DM (Verma, S., (2021)). This study uses a range of computational techniques, including as development curve analysis and CAN, to evaluate the phases of development of consider the strength, topics, co-citation networks, and citations in interactive DM. The study contributes to the large-scale, international field of study known as interactive DM.

2. Related works

The internet and DM expanded to provide more than simply product sales, and now encompasses a broad network of software, stock trading, consumer behavior research, and other services. DM is a key element of today's marketing strategies for any business, corporation, or organization (Bramah, et al., 2022). A notable corpus of academic articles on DM that have been published over the last ten years will be analyzed for citation, trend, content, keyword use, and co-citation (Umesh, et al., (2022)).DM, a concept that is still relatively new and describes itself as a medium for communication, was originally known as internet marketing (Rosario, et al., 2019). To find similar themes, divide the specific topics into four groups. They also create graphs to represent coauthor ships, bibliographic coupling, and cogitations (Khan, et al., 2020). Information for academic academics and professionals in the business to help them understand how internet marketing research is developed and how it plays a part in developing marketing strategies (Patrick, et al., 2020).

3. Methodology

Tools for bibliometric-based citation analysis show the flow of information in different substantive study topics via a visual depiction of scholarship networks. Software for social network analysis (SNA), such as gephi and VOS viewer, is used to create the networks for the evolutionary trajectory, citation, co-citation, including co-authorship article using bibliometric data from the selected publications. CNA, which offers a replacement for the expert-based method, is developing as a technological forecasting technique. They undertake a network analysis and temporal analysis of DM-related bibliographic data from the Scopus database using SNA's clustering and main route methodologies. The development of the subject area is then traced using main route analysis, and five phases in the maturity model of the DM development curve are identified. The knowledge burst detection technique provides further confirmation of the findings. Current subjects with potential for future study are identified by doing a main route's leaf nodes' content examination.

Analytic technique: The citation, co-author, and co-citation networks of study papers were used to analyse the bibliographic data of DM research from 1990 to 2019. The 45,260 nodes in the citation network reflect research publications published scholarly publications and conference proceedings, together with the mention that go with them. The biggest node, referred to as the huge component, was taken out of the networks and subjected to further analysis. The phases of DM development are revealed by the global main route for main path analysis method. A topic evolution model is suggested by comparing the Scopus and Web of Science (WoS) data. It was initially suggested to use Search Path Link Count (SPLC) to discover every main route of development of a domain using the citation networks primary route analysis in SPLC. In each literature, several methods are put forward to calculate the traversal count, taking into account both search locally, which utilizes the connections with the greatest SPLC as the exist links, and search globally, which uses the linkages with the greatest total SPLC. They use a global search strategy to identify each primary evolutionary route.

General patterns: The preliminary study pinpoints the typical trends of research in DM. The main multidisciplinary fields that contributed to the dataset are identified, as well as the authors, sources of the publications, institutions connected to the writers, and associated national affiliations. The general knowledge about the main study subjects and their phases of change throughout time is provided by the highly cited publications content analyses arranged by date.

4. Findings

Countries and journals: After going through the pre-processing step, a total of 45,260 records were added to the dataset that was obtained from the Scopus and WoS data repositories by applying the keywords that were mentioned before. We developed a development curve to demonstrate the present level of research maturity as well as the possibility for further development in research that is connected to DM. The advancement of the development curve that is shown in Fig. 9.1 may be utilized to make estimates about the levels of the growth of the research domain.

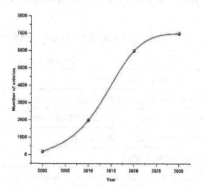

Fig. 9.1 The subject evolution and maturity models for research topics in digital marketing

Topic evolution model: Every development from research subjects in the field is shown by the content examination of significant issues covered in high citation publications that are studied in chronological order. Since more papers have been published during the previous two decades, it is clear that DM is still in its development and dissemination phase and has not yet matured. There are fewer publications in the years before 2000, which may indicate that this is the beginning of evolution.

Main path analysis: Introduced is progression of change revealed by each citation network's major route paper, which concentrated on various theoretical concerns relating to consumer conduct. Their paper further highlighted every possible negative impacts concerning interactive media on politicians' also marketers' ability to make decisions and the issues with regulation they may face. The transition to the new e-Commerce paradigm presented marketing managers and companies with several ethical challenges, most notably privacy difficulties. The first level of development occurs up to the year 2000, as illustrated by the development graph, during which time conversion policies and theoretical difficulties were important to

study topics. During this time, the Internet gained widespread popularity.

Article and journal co-citation networks: For our analysis, networks of publications and journals that have received more than 20 co-citations are constructed utilising bibliographic research. The four main clusters of co-cited publications and relevant topics are depicted by the colours red, green, yellow, and blue in the co-citation networks of articles and journals. Social media marketing is the primary substantive problem with in red.

Cluster, while other topics there deal with research methods, including structural equation modelling. The brand community and social media are two of the major topics of the green cluster. Publications on consumer culture and marketing are represented by the pink cluster, those on interactive marketing by the blue cluster, and those on tourism, management, and hospitality by the violet cluster. Publications on psychology and health are represented by the green cluster. As seen in Table 9.1, articles with many citations cover a wide range of topics, including interactive marketing, business research, tourism, marketing, and advertising.

Table 9.1 The co-citation network's top journals by citation

Journals	Citations	Documents
Journal of Business Research	5646	117
International Journal of Electronic Commerce	1379	33
International Journal of Market Research	360	25
Journal of Interactive Marketing	8335	138
Journal of Marketing	4319	33
Journal of Research In Interactive Marketing	354	80
Tourism Management	5117	47
Journal of Destination Marketing & Management	569	24
Marketing Science	4951	76

Journals	Citations	Documents
International Marketing Review	620	25
Electronic Commerce Research And Applications	800	51
International Journal of Advertising	1261	62
Journal of Travel & Tourism Marketing	1051	39
Business Horizons	3784	50
Psychology & Marketing	1122	43
Computers In Human Behavior	2620	86
International Journal of Information Management	1654	47
Journal of Marketing Research	4829	48
Journal of Advertising Research	1953	76
International Journal of Research In Marketing	2300	34
Journal of Advertising	1832	32
European Journal of Marketing	1444	68

5. Conclusion

The dynamics of research today and the evolution of research trends from a range of perspectives and provides a variety of contributions. It will be able to develop innovative research partnerships in interactive and DM with the subject model and main research agendas that have been defined. Finally, using the two views comparison between citation and co-citation strength, their investigation further reveals the key research works in the DM area. Their paper's last contribution and conclusion in the field of interactive and DM often use one variety about research methodologies. This tendency is particularly noticeable in the most widely referenced publications. Future studies may probe more profound substantive relationships, co-authorships, and subjects as interact.

REFERENCES

1. Krishen, A.S., Dwivedi, Y.K., Bindu, N. and Kumar, K.S., 2021. A broad overview of interactive digital marketing: A bibliometric network analysis. Journal of Business Research, 131, pp. 183–195.
2. Ghorbani, Z., Kargaran, S., Saberi, A., Haghighinasab, M., Jamali, S.M. and Ale Ebrahim, N., 2022. Trends and patterns in digital marketing research: a bibliometric analysis. Journal of Marketing Analytics, 10(2), pp. 158–172.
3. Figueiredo, F., Gonçalves, M.J.A. and Teixeira, S., 2021, October. Information technology adoption on digital marketing: a literature review. In Informatics (Vol. 8, No. 4, p. 74). MDPI.
4. Gao, P., Meng, F., Mata, M.N., Martins, J.M., Iqbal, S., Correia, A.B., Dantas, R.M., Waheed, A., Xavier Rita, J. and Farrukh, M., 2021. Trends and future research in electronic marketing: A bibliometric analysis of twenty years. Journal of Theoretical and Applied Electronic Commerce Research, 16(5), pp. 1667–1679.

5. Verma, S., 2021. Bibliometric analysis of research on digital marketing from 2010-20. International Journal of Modern Agriculture, 10(2), pp. 625–640.

6. Hazela, B., Gupta, S.K., Soni, N. and Saranya, C.N., 2022. Securing the Confidentiality and Integrity of Cloud Computing Data. ECS Transactions, 107(1), p. 2651.

7. Lilhore, U.K., Khalaf, O.I., Simaiya, S., Tavera Romero, C.A., Abdulsahib, G.M. and Kumar, D., 2022. A depth-controlled and energy-efficient routing protocol for underwater wireless sensor networks. International Journal of Distributed Sensor Networks, 18(9), p. 15501329221117118.

8. Rosario, A.M.F.T. and Cruz, R.N., 2019. Determinants of innovation in digital marketing. Journal of Reviews on Global Economics, 8(1), pp. 1722–1731.

9. Khan, M.A., Ali, I. and Ashraf, R., 2020. A bibliometric review of the special issues of Psychology & Marketing: 1984-2020. Psychology & Marketing, 37(9), pp. 1144–1170.

10. Patrick, Z. and Hee, O.C., 2020. A bibliometric analysis of global online marketing research trends. International Journal of Academic Research in Business and Social Sciences, 10(5), pp. 770–787.

Note: The table and the figure in this chapter were made by the Authors.

Advancements in Business for Integrating Diversity, and Sustainability – Dimitrios A. Karras et al. (eds)
© 2024 Taylor & Francis Group, London, ISBN 978-1-032-70828-7

"What Fuels the Employees in Startups?": Hybrid/Colocated/Virtual Working Environment towards Efficiency

Jenifer Esther D.*
Research Scholar, Christ (Deemed to be University)

Rashmi Rai
HOD & Associate Professor, Christ (Deemed to be University)

Abstract: This paper investigates pre- and post-COVID19 working conditions towards work efficiency mediated by job satisfaction. This Study will recognize the elements impacting job satisfaction in the current working condition in Startups. It is a Descriptive Study with the causal research approach. A structured questionnaire framed through an instrument scale has been circulated through Qualtrics (online) to collect the data from 256 employees from Well organized startups in Bangalore, India. Simple random sampling has been used as the sampling method. The respondents found that the Pre-covid working condition impacted positively rather than negatively. Also, the hybrid model leads to Job efficiency because of autonomy and flexibility.Employers must work on individual empowerment in the company to motivate employees, leading to job satisfaction and work efficiency.It was found that few other Extraneous variables could also be considered like the observation method could have been used to understand the present working condition better.

Keywords: Startups, Job expectation, Job satisfaction, Workplace condition, Job efficiency, Employees

1. Introduction

Covid'19 outburst toppled the way of work to an entirely different setting for almost all employees worldwide. (Gallup, 2020). Virtual work has both advantages and disadvantages. Though, it helps easy commuting in flexible work-environment. Employers and employees fail to realize the challenges like Managing workload, lack of proper support, Stress, etc. Human resource professionals are very concerned that the changeover shall affect employees' physical and mental well-being and ultimately affect performance efficiency. Addressing the challenges would enhance and leverage the benefits and performance of the employees. (Graves and karabayeva, 2020).

*Corresponding author: jeniferestherphd@gmail.com

DOI: 10.4324/9781032708294-10

There are numerous Tech startups due to the outgrowth of digital platforms (Ranisari et al., 2020). Startups fail on many grounds, and One of the reasons for the failure of startups is a personal factor(Ganesraman, 2018). Hence, it is essential to satisfy their work expectations.

Pre-COVID'19 Era

Remote working was not so prevalent before covid, but it has become new normal after Covid. (Wang et al., 2020). It is found that there were emotionally intense and comparatively less depression, and the feeling of job security was relatively higher before Covid'19. However, Employees are skeptical about the situation and longevity in the workplace. (Roman, M, and Tomic. p. 2021).

New- Normal the Post-Covid-19

Employers around the world must ensure the company should be safe and productive. Employees must feel safe and enjoy the workspace and should break the inertia to achieve the objective of the Organization (Boland et al., 2020).

Work Expectation

The employee expects clarity in the vision and mission statement from the standpoint of skill development in the startups. Startups must work on employee engagement techniques and tools, which employees expect in the startups. Strategic management practices are effective (Kulkarni et al., 2020)

Job Satisfaction

The leader's characteristic is to nurture a quality workforce with energized employees by satisfying the psychological needs in this new average era. (Men et al., 2021). Emotional intelligence and transformational leadership lead to satisfied virtual team effectiveness (Mysirlaki and Paraskeva, 2020).

Efficiency

As the economic cost of the startup is high, It is essential to maintain the balance between resources and spare capacity for efficiency. (Riani, 2021). Employees prefer a hybrid model over a conventional or virtual setup; they expect the Flexi setting to perform efficiently with the freedom to decide their work environment in the organization(Bahman and Enzi, 2020).

2. Research Design

This paper is a quantitative and descriptive Study. Data collection was conducted through an online questionnaire, and the participants' feedback was gathered through a self-administered questionnaire. This Study followed a Comparative causal approach to find the cause-and-effect relationship between variables.

3. Data and Measures

We analyze the data gathered through Qualtrics and the questionnaire framed through Instrument scales. The sample population is employees from existing startups in Bangalore. Most data were collected through an online questionnaire formulated through Qualtrics. A smaller number of questionnaires were administered through telephone and personnel interviews Response rate is 60-70%. MSQ developed a 20-item "short form." Minnesota Satisfaction Questionnaire (MSQ) (Weiss et al., 1977). In this Study, the short form of the original instrument was used to develop the framework, and questions were split into three realms – job efficiency, job expectation, and job satisfaction – of conditions before the COVID-19 pandemic in comparison to working conditions throughout the COVID-19 pandemic.

The reliability of the questionnaire and the data are measured through Jamovi software, and it was found that Cronbach's alpha is 0.854. The questionnaire is reliable, and the survey is carried over to see the Post COVID'19 efficiency in the workplace.

Table 10.1   Factor analyses - output from Jamovi software

Factor Loadings					
Factor	**Indicator**	**Estimate**	**SE**	**Z**	**p**
Factor 1	Q1_2	0.295	0.0802	3.68	< .001
	Q1_4	0.108	0.0868	1.25	
	Q2_2	0.273	0.0909	3.00	0.003
	Q2_4	0.151	0.0897	1.68	0.093
	Q2_6	0.168	0.0757	2.22	0.027
	Q2_7	0.113	0.0827	1.37	
	Q2_9	0.208	0.0729	2.85	0.004
	Q3_1	0.247	0.0856	2.89	0.004
	Q3_2	0.385	0.0750	5.13	< .001
	Q3_3	0.369	0.0731	5.04	< .001
	Q3_5	0.319	0.0832	3.83	< .001
	Q4	0.213	0.0686	3.11	0.002
Fit Measures				RMSEA 90% CI	
CFI	TLI	RMSEA	Lower	Upper	
0.665	0.591	0.144	0.0914	0.193	

Source: Author's own source

The reliability of the questionnaire and the variables were analyzed, and the goodness of fit index and the p-value is <0.001, which is highly reliable. RMSEA is 0.144, the lower is 0.0914, and the upper value is 0.193.

The data measured is both construct validity and discriminant validity. There is a positive relationship between similar variables.

4. Analysis and Interpretation

Pre Covid-Working Condition

The survey states that five to six work days is too much for 65% of the sample. 69% of the model want their working hours to be minimized, and the same number of people wish their meetings to be converted to emails. 70% of the employees feel the operating hours are too long.

New Normal

58% of Employees working virtually feels that there are comparatively more productive at home. Half of the sample think that work takes less time working from home. 72% of the model find home a comfortable workplace, and 82%   of the piece are pleased to have flexible working hours. 81% of the sample enjoy working from home because they need not commute. 84% of the employees feel they spend more quality time at home, but on the contrary, only 44% of the sample feel that they are resourceful working at home.

Impact of Working Remotely in a Conventional Work Setting

70% of the meetings are being conducted effectively, and 73% of the employees are able to meet the work on time. 63% Employees can share information related to work on time with ease. The issue with team cohesion exist because everything is online, and the personal touch is missing by 46%.

Company Response to Covid

Organization supported the employees to get the job done by 86%. Around 17% of the employees were not paid full salary. More than 50% of the sample is assured that their company does not have any contingency plan during an emergency, but 72% feel that their position is secured because 83% feel that the company motivates them and inquires about their overall well-being, and 97% of the organization has taken proper COVID measures to ensure the safe working environment.

Employees Efficiency

Employees feel that working at the office is more effective than working at home. 71.6% of the employees feel that they perform better in an office environment. Over 67.3% find a hybrid environment works well because they can choose either office or home at their convenience. Moreover, 66.6% of employees feel that working remotely works if there is no option for conventional working space.

Post Covid Work Expectation

Companies expect employees to report to the organization, and the percentage of expected companies falls to 62%. Elsewhere, 83% of the employees prefer to work remotely,

and 93% of employees are happy to work in a hybrid setup. 76% of employees will be satisfied if the number of working days is reduced to four a week. 89% of employees expect flexible working hours.

Comparison between pre-COVID'19 and New normal (Post-COVID'19) work Expectation

Pre-Covid expected working days want to be reduced to four by 65% of the employees, and the prevalence of working remotely tends to increase the % of the desired employee, and it moved to 76% for fewer working days. In-office working hours were also expected to be minimized by 69% of employees before covid, and 89% of Employees in the new normal (Post-COVID'19) expect more flexible working hours and are relatively happy to decide their working hours.

Table 10.2 Using Jamovi Software, Pre- and Post-Covid job expectation and work efficiency

One Sample T-Test		Statistic	df	p
Q1_1	Student's t	29.5	108.0	<.001
Q1_2	Student's t	29.4	108.0	<.001
Q1_3	Student's t	29.6	108.0	<.001
Q1_4	Student's t	29,4	108.0	<.001
Q11_1	Student's t	26.6	87.0	<.001
Q11_2	Student's t	27.9	87.0	<.001
Q11_3	Student's t	37.2	87.0	<.001
Q11_4	Student's t	27.6	87.0	<.001
Q11_5	Student's t	30.8	84.0	<.001

Source: Author's own work

As stated by Herzberg's two-factor theory of job satisfaction, we considered a few factors related to hygiene and motivators to analyze job satisfaction by filling the job expectation thoroughly.

The data analyses through Jamovi software show a significant difference with the P value <0.001.

H0: There is no relation between Good working condition and work Efficiency in the Post Covid workplace.

H1: There is a relation between Good working condition and work Efficiency in the Post Covid workplace.

H0: There is no relation between Autonomy in the workplace and job satisfaction in Startups.

H2: There is a relation between Autonomy in the workplace leads to Job satisfaction in Startups.

It is clearly shown that the Good working condition leads to work Efficiency in the Post Covid workplace and hence we reject the null hypothesis and accept the alternate hypothesis.

H0: There is no relation between Autonomy in the workplace and job satisfaction in Startups.

H2: There is a relation between Autonomy in the workplace leads to Job satisfaction in Startups.

Letting employees decide there working hours and task to complete the work by deciding where and when to work leads to better job satisfaction. Hence, autonomy in the workplace leads to better job satisafaction so we reject the null hypothesis and accept the alternate hypothesis.

It is noted that pre covid working condition was satisfactory to some extent. The expectation of the post covid working condition, which leads to job satisfaction, is on flexibility to choose place and time of work. The statistic value is 30 using one Sample T-test and the p-value is <0.001, which is the maximum. Hence, the flexibility to choose at ease is one of the important motivators which leads to job satisfaction in the new normal era.

It is explicitly stated that only 48% of workplaces already had a contingency plan in case of such emergencies. Though there were issue in transition, still few companies were able to manage it, so the companies must have a CP.

In line with the analysis, it is significant that the statistical value of efficient working in the hybrid(mixed) is effective.

5. Conclusion

As employees expect a hybrid work setup, the employer needs to look at it and ensure they provide a cohesive environment at ease so that employees feel comfortable and satisfied to perform in a comfortable working space. As we live in a new normal era, it is a must to rise with resilience with the keys to running and successful organization with happy employees

It is better to enhance the virtual work set up to be more effective. As employees expect a hybrid work setup, the employer needs to look at it and ensure they provide a cohesive environment at ease so that employees feel comfortable and satisfied to perform in a comfortable working space.

6. Suggestions to HR and Researcher

We hope HR will take corrective actions using the findings in the research. It is vital to practice the results to make positive changes within the organizations. HR or employers must make sure that they create a sustainable environment for a happy and fruitful workplace.

REFERENCES

1. Boland, B., Smet, A. D., Palter, R., & Sanghvi, A. (2020, February 7). *Reimagining the office and work life after covid-19.* McKinsey & Company.
2. Diab-Bahman, R. and Al-Enzi, A. (2020), "The impact of COVID-19 pandemic on conventional work settings", *International Journal of Sociology and Social Policy*, Vol. 40 No. 9/10, pp. 909–927. https://doi.org/10.1108/IJSSP-07-2020-0262 Download as .RIS
3. Esthi, Raniasari & Ekhsan, Muhamad. (2020). The Effect of Millennial Intrinsic Value toward Employee Outcomes with Employee Benefit as Mediating Variable for Strengthening Indonesia's Startup Business. Solid State Technology. 63. 8856–8871. Is working remotely effective Gallup Research says yes? (n.d.). Retrieved August 11, 2022, from
4. Ganesaraman kalyanasundaram (2018). *Why Do Startups Fail? A Case Study Based Empirical Analysis in Bangalore. Asian Journal of Innovation and Policy.* 7.1:079-102, DOI: http//dx.doi.org/10.7545/ajip.2018.7.1.079.
5. Graves, L. M., & Karabayeva, A. (2020). Managing virtual workers—strategies for uccess. *IEEE Engineering Management Review, 48*(2), 166–172. https://doi.org/10.1109/emr.2020.2990386
6. Kulkarni, P., Mutkekar, R. and Ingalagi, S. (2020), *"Role of strategic management for employee engagement and skill development for start-ups"*, Vilakshan - XIMB Journal of Management, Vol. 17 No. 1/2, pp. 79–95. https://doi.org/10.1108/XJM-07-2020-0036
7. Helmold, M. (2021). New Office concepts in the post covid-19 times. *Management for Professionals*, 79–89. doi:10.1007/978-3-030-63315-8_7
8. Mysirlaki, S. and Paraskeva, F. (2020), *"Emotional intelligence and transformational leadership in virtual teams: lessons from MMOGs"*, Leadership & Organization Development Journal, Vol. 41 No. 4, pp. 551-566. https://doi.org/10.1108/LODJ-01-2019-0035
9. Riani, A. (2021, October 22). Why obsessively chasing efficiency in early-stage start-ups could be deadly. Retrieved August 5, 2022, from https://www.forbes.com/sites/abdoriani/2021/10/22/why-obsessively-chasing-efficiency-in-early-stage-startups-could-be-deadly/?sh=228b670e3284
10. Robison, A. H. and J. (2022, July 19). *Is working remotely effective? Gallup Research says yes.* Retrieved August 1, 2022, from https://www.gallup.com/workplace/283985/working-remotely-effective-gallup-research-says-yes.aspx
11. Wang, B., Liu, Y., Qian, J., & Parker, S. K. (2020). *Achieving effective remote working during the COVID-19 pandemic: A work design perspective. Applied Psychology, 70*(1), 16–59. https://doi.org/10.1111/apps.12290

*Advancements in Business for Integrating Diversity, and
Sustainability – Dimitrios A. Karras et al. (eds)*
© 2024 Taylor & Francis Group, London, ISBN 978-1-032-70828-7

Prediction of Customer Default in E-commerce based on Spider Monkey Optimized Scalar Random Forest Algorithm

11

Shashi Kant Gupta*

Eudoxia Research University, USA

Bhadrappa Haralayya[1]

Lingaraj Appa Engineering College, Karnataka, India

Vikas Kumar[2]

School of Applied and life sciences,
Uttaranchal University Dehradun, Uttarakhand, India

Iskandar Muda[3]

Faculty Economic and Business,
Universitas Sumatera Utara, Medan, Indonesia

Abstract: The rising volume of online transactions necessitates more stringent measures to reduce the possibility of non-payment. If a consumer has not paid their bill within 90 days of receiving it, they are said to be in default. Credit scoring (CS) is often used to evaluate a client's potential for non-payment. To update the e-commerce risk management system with a CS model in favor of the pre-risk check, one of the most popular methods to predict the likelihood of customer default. The goal of this study is to use a spider monkey-optimized scalar random forest algorithm (SMO-SRFA) to predict e-commerce consumer default. The data is used in conjunction with exclusion criteria and a standard CS model to conduct the pre-risk assessment. The proposed SMO-SRFA to achieve competitive classificatory accuracy compared to various cutting-edge machine learning techniques, including grey wolf optimization (GWO), genetic algorithm (GA), and particle swarm optimization (PSO).

Keywords: Risk management, Credit scoring, Machine learning, Spider monkey optimized Scalar random forest algorithm (SMO-SRFA)

1. Introduction

A peculiar idiosyncrasy exists in the realm of online shopping. Although popular payment methods like credit cards and PayPal have their place, they don't account for a huge percentage of sales, and open invoicing is used to process the vast majority

*Corresponding author: raj2008enator@gmail.com
[1]bhadrappabhavimani@gmail.com, [2]vikas.mathematica@gmail.com, [3]iskandar1@usu.ac.id

DOI: 10.4324/9781032708294-11

of purchases (Altunan, et al., (2018)). Establishing and maintaining a commanding position while quickly capturing the share market, "the largest e-commerce companies have rapidly increased the rate of annual growth of the total amount of credit and appropriately lowered the terms of credit through e-commerce".Providing people with credit services for every aspect of their life (Saxena, et al., (2021)). This new method of consumption is rapidly gaining traction among consumers at large, but it is especially well-liked by the younger generations that make up today's modern students and the latest generation of industrial workers. Existing specific regulations and laws for e-commerce consumer loans may not be optimal, but the apparent trend in development is for the government to gradually embrace industry standards to encourage the growth of Internet investment instruments (Vivek, et al., (2022)). E-commerce credit failures are widespread since the industry is still in its infancy; as a result, big e-commerce businesses' newly introduced consumer credit products lack useful context from the industry's history. (Ashish, et al., (2022)). When looking at the layout of Chinese online shopping, you can notice an illustration of this uniquely Chinese characteristic. When an E-Commerce building confronts risks or fails to provide the predicted profits, a Strict-Redemption means the government will force third-party organizations to invest, use its cash to pay, or grant investors more make-up. (Vanneschi, et al., (2018)). The information the consumer provides throughout the ordering process is used in this pre-risk assessment. However, in many modern business practices, the pre-risk evaluation is based on an SMO-SRFA. The SMO-SRFA approach is used to identify the consumer default in e-commerce.

2. Related Works

Gan, L., (2022) proposed a novel approach to verifying and contrasting the model using consumer data from a Chinese e-commerce firm. To optimize anticipated return, Yunyan, et al., (2021) uses the consumer credit risk of an e-commerce finance platform as its research object and build a decision tree to do so. Borse, et al., (2021) presents a comprehensive overview of the methods now in use for E-commerce site prediction analysis, as well as a look at some of the most essential concepts and methods in the area of market research. Makinde, et al., (2020) provides a hybrid model for B2B CRM that optimizes decision-making with the use of a Genetic algorithm and Data Mining techniques. The concept divides consumers into two categories: those who often make purchases and those who just browse. Jiang, X., (2022) analyse Urdu Roman evaluations from a widely used and well-known online marketplace. The MATLAB Linux server is used to run experiments. The data set is preserved for research and analysis purposes.

3. Methodology

Dataset: The AFS firm kindly contributed the dataset utilized in this investigation, which comprises order requests handled by RSS between October 2014 and December 2015. There are a total of 56,669 requests for orders, with 15,535 (or around 27%) marked as unsatisfactory and the rest 41,134 marked as excellent. "These requests for orders are randomly divided into a training group of 31,669 (≈56%), a test set of 10,000 (≈18%), and a validation set of 15,000 (≈26%)".

Fig. 11.1 depicts the overall current process of our research work.

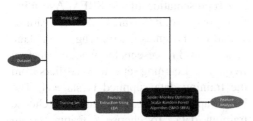

Feature extraction using LDA: Regarding ML issues, the extraction of features is a crucial step. By combining the previous dimensions, feature extraction develops new dimensions. LDA is a form of class-based discrimination. This method helps supervised learning discover a collection of basis vectors. These fundamental vectors are shown as . The proportion of the between and within class disperses from the training instance set which is maximized makes up the vectors. The following generalized eigenvalue issue is resolved for discovering basis vectors.

$$W_{opt} = \frac{\arg\max}{w} \frac{\left|w^T S_c w\right|}{w^T S_v w} =$$

$$[w_1, w_2, \ldots, w_L] \tag{1}$$

Here, L = dubspace's dimension, S_c = between and S_v = within classes, W_s = reducing the within-class dispersion, W_T = distance between the two classes, or scatter between the two classes, W_{opt} = the optimal solution of two classes.

$$S_C = \sum_{k=1}^{a} M_k (\mu_k - \mu)(\mu_k - \mu)^T \tag{2}$$

$$S_V = \sum_{k=1}^{a} \sum_{X_u \in X_k} (x_u - \mu_k)(x_u - \mu_k)^T \tag{3}$$

Here, a = no. of class, $X \in R^N$ = sample, X_k = sample set, M_k = no. of class in k, and μ = mean. First L greatest eigenvalues $\{\psi_k \mid 1 \le k \le L\}$ are the base vectors w_k desired in Eq. (1) if S_v is not singular. Attributed to the reason that the LDA base vectors were orthogonal to one another, it may be projected using a basic linear method, $W^T x$, into the LDA subspace to derive its representations.

Prediction of customer default in e-commerce using ISMO-SRFA: ISMO uses a stochastic approach that is based on the behavior of a population. Exploration and development are often well-balanced using the ISMO algorithm. The foraging habits of spider monkeys reveal that these animals are highly social, group-living primates that use a set of distinct behavior to interact with one another and find food. An adult female often takes charge of a group of spider monkeys and is responsible for ensuring that everyone in the troop has enough to eat. When there isn't enough food for everyone, the leader may split the group up into smaller subgroups to increase their chances of locating food in different areas.

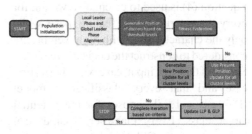

Fig. 11.2 Flow of ISMO algorithm

In Fig. 11.2 we see the ISMO flow. The ISMO takes into account some fitness criteria to determine the optimal routing from the cluster heads (CHs) to the base station (BS), such as the source node, the distance to the CHs, and the routing traffic.

SRFA: Generally speaking, SRFA outperforms the single tree classifier significantly. It offers an effective method for categorizing sets of sparse data. However, because basic SRFA chooses features at random, it's simple to choose irrelevant or distracting characteristics, particularly when the training data is noisy. To use the basic SRFA in search form categorization, it must be improved. By using a weighting system during feature selection as opposed to random selection, we expanded the basic RF. The weighting metrics are set to be Y^2 and are represented as the equation (4).

$$Y^2 = \sum_{j=1}^{n} \sum_{i-1}^{2} \frac{(p_{ji} - f_{ji})^2}{f_{ji}} \quad (4)$$

Here, m = features, The definition of P_{ji} as a measured value, which denotes the number of a joint incident, is equation (5).

$$P_{ji} = count(B = b_i \cap d = d_i) \quad (5)$$

Similarly,

$$expected\ value =$$
$$f_{ji} \frac{count(B = b_j) \times count(D = d_j)}{M} \quad (6)$$

Equation (4) is used to calculate a weight for every characteristic in the feature space, while only the characteristics with high weights are considered to construct the decision tree (DT). Suppose that the input case x is the testing case and that every classification model (DT) $g_i[i = 1...l]$ chooses for the potential target class. Every classifier's output can be estimated as $O(J(z) = d_j \mid g_i)$. The final categorization results are then calculated by adding the probability values as equation (7):

$$O(J(z) = d_j) = \frac{1}{l} \sum_{i=1}^{l} O(j(z) = d_j \mid g_i) \quad (7)$$

Y input vector belongs to d_j if and only if d_j has the highest likelihood. Algorithm-1 is a representation of the SRFA. Assuming that there are n features, $[\beta. \ m]$ features would be chosen as the training set in stage 3, wherein β represents the feature selection frequency. Learning separate classifiers from the training data supplied is stage 4. The bootstrapping approach is used to choose training data. To choose t features from n' features, sampling with replacement is employed (Here, $t = [\log_2 n + 1]$). Equation (4) is employed to categorize the unlabeled cases, and after every round, the trained DT is inserted into the forest N*.

Algorithm-1: SRFA's procedure
Stage-1: Estimate weights using equation (4)
Stage 2: Sorting features as per weight (U) in decreasing order;
Stage-3: Allowing n' to equal $[\beta. \ m]$, choose $[\beta. \ m]$ features with higher Ws as training sets.
Stage-4: for i = 1 to k do
Bootstrapping approach is used to choose training data (c').
When t features are chosen at random, the choice is biased in favor of features with high Ut.
Create a C4.5 DT using the d data and chosen features.
Trained DT is added to N*.
End for
Stage-5: Perform classification with M* relying on equation (7).

4. Result and Discussion

The proposed SMO-SRFA performs well with 95% accuracy, PSO has the lowest accuracy of 65%, GWO has the 77%, and GA has the 83% depicted in Fig. 11.3.

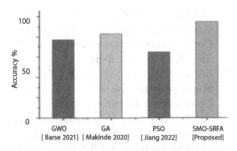

Fig. 11.3 Comparison of accuracy and precision

The proposed SMO-SRFA well with 93% of precision and GA has the lowest precision of 66%, GWO has the second-highest precision of 83%, and PSO has the 73%. The proposed SMO-SRFA is well with 95% of recall and GWO has the lowest recall of 66%, GA has the second-highest precision of 74%, and PSO has the 85%. The precision and recall outcomes for the existing and proposed methods are presented in Fig. 11.4.

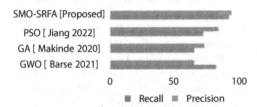

Fig. 11.4 Comparison of precision and recall

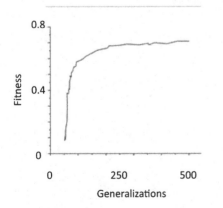

Fig. 11.5 median overall runs for fitness

Typical fitness development in SMO-SRFA, as seen in Fig. 11.5, involves great development early in the evolution change, accompanied by a more gradual increase later on rapidly during the first 200 generations but slowly throughout the subsequent 300 generations.

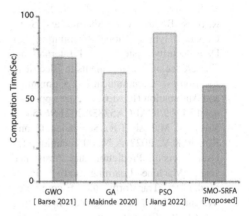

Fig. 11.6 comparison of computation cost

Figure 11.6 denotes the comparison of computation costs. Our suggested SMO-SRFA has a superior efficiency when measured against other existing approaches.

5. Conclusion

As one of the most popular methods for estimating the likelihood of a client defaulting on their payment. The biggest threat to the survival of the spider monkey optimization is the degradation of tropical rainforests and the risks from hunting. This project aimed to create an SMO-SRFA model to replace the e-commerce risk management system's pre-risk assessment. The suggested SMO-SRFA outperforms some state-of-the-art machine learning methods in terms of classification accuracy, precision, recall, and fitness function.

REFERENCES

1. Altunan, B., Arslan, E.D., Seyis, M., Birer, M. and Üney-Yüksektepe, F., 2018, August. A data mining approach to predict E-Commerce customer behavior. In The International Symposium for Production Research (pp. 29–43). Springer, Cham.

2. S. Saxena, D. Yagyasen, C. N. Saranya, R. S. K. Boddu, A. K. Sharma, and S. K. Gupta, "Hybrid Cloud Computing for Data Security System," 2021 International Conference on Advancements in Electrical, Electronics, Communication, Computing and Automation (ICAECA), 2021, pp. 1–8, doi:10.1109/ICAECA52838.2021.967549.

3. Vivek, V., Mahesh, T.R., Saravanan, C. and Kumar, K.V., 2022. A Novel Technique for User Decision Prediction and Assistance Using Machine Learning and NLP: A Model to Transform the E-commerce System. In Big data management in Sensing (pp. 61–76). River Publishers.

4. Ashish Kumar Pandey et al 2022 ECS Trans. 107 2681 https://doi.org/10.1149/10701.2681ecst

5. Gan, L., 2022. XGBoost-based e-commerce customer loss prediction. Computational Intelligence and Neuroscience, 2022.

6. Yunyan, H., Weiwei, W. and Qiuju, Z., 2021. Prediction of Credit Risk in Electronic Commerce Financial Industry Based On Decision Tree Method. In Advances in Smart Vehicular Technology, Transportation, Communication and Applications (pp. 227–236). Springer, Singapore.

7. Borse, S.S. and Kadroli, V., 2021, March. Comparative Analysis Grey Wolf Optimization Technique & Its Diverse Applications in E-Commerce Market Prediction. In International Conference on Machine Learning and Big Data Analytics (pp. 160–174). Springer, Cham.

8. Makinde, A.S., Vincent, O.R., Akinwale, A.T., Oguntuase, A. and Scheme, I.D., 2020, March. An Improved Customer Relationship Management Model for Business-to-Business E-commerce Using Genetic-Based Data Mining Process. In 2020 International Conference in Mathematics, Computer Engineering and Computer Science (ICMCECS) (pp. 1–7). IEEE.

9. Jiang, X., 2022. A Sentiment Classification Model of E-Commerce User Comments Based on Improved Particle Swarm Optimization Algorithm and Support Vector Machines. Scientific Programming, 2022.

10. Vanneschi, L., Horn, D.M., Castelli, M. and Popovič, A., 2018. An artificial intelligence system for predicting customer default in e-commerce. Expert Systems with Applications, 104, pp. 1–21.

Note: All the figures in this chapter were made by the Authors.

An Empirical Analysis of Critical Success Factors for E-Commerce Applications

12

Mahesh Singh*
Kebri Dehar University, Kebri Dehar, Ethiopia

Veer P. Gangwar[1]
Lovely Professional University, Punjab, India

Vikas Kumar[2]
School of Applied and life sciences,
Uttaranchal University Dehradun, Uttarakhand, India

Iskandar Muda[3]
Faculty Economic and Business,
Universitas Sumatera Utara, Medan, Indonesia

Abstract: This investigation concentrates on the links between entrepreneurial characteristics (accomplishment focus and networking), e-commerce elements (trustworthiness, response), governmental assistance, and also the achievement of e-commerce entrepreneurs. Findings demonstrate that the performance of e-commerce entrepreneurial endeavors in China is positively associated with entrepreneurs' accomplishment oriented and location of control as well as their company' attention on the trustworthiness and accessibility of e-services. Governmental assistance, founder communication and taking risks, and e-service response and self-service are all determined to be insignificant.

Keywords: e-commerce, Entrepreneurs, Communication, e-service, Critical success factors

1. Introduction

E-commerce and entrepreneurship both have a big impact on economic development and wealth generation, according to research. E-commerce is expanding incredibly quickly. Electronic commerce is feasible for SMEs due to the Internet's availability (Li, et al., 2020). The worth of goods, companies, and data transferred via the Internet appears to increase each year all over the world as the volume of business conducted online expands. Internet is business-enabling technology that enables

*Corresponding author: mahesh300@gmail.com
[1]veer.23954@lpu.co.in, [2]vikas.mathematica@gmail.com, [3]iskandar1@usu.ac.id

DOI: 10.4324/9781032708294-12

organizations to improve the precision and effectiveness of transaction processing (Choshin, et al., 2017). The process of purchasing and selling or transferring goods, services, and information using computer systems, particularly the Internet, is known as e-business. The word refers to an expanded concept of e-commerce that involves working with trading partners and providing customer service. As evidenced by the 2021 E-commerce and Development Report from the United Nations Conference on Trade and Development (UNCTAD), there is currently increasing evidence on the significant benefit of information and communication technology (ICT) towards increased productivity. ICT is used to reach new markets, increase the competitiveness of businesses, and provide new job possibilities (Pandey, et al., 2022). All of this will lead to the creation of wealth and long-term economic expansion. The Global Entrepreneurship Monitor (GEM) has found a link between entrepreneurship and economic expansion. The majority of nations that have successfully adopted and modified a technology to support their high rates of economic growth are those that had rapid growth. The rise of Southeast Asia as a dominant power is the most important change in global competitiveness (Jayesh, et al., 2022). Southeast Asia, which contributed about 45% of the global GDP during 2021, is quickly rising in popularity as a location for foreign investment (Tsironis, et al., 2017). Already, Asia receives over than 65% of the direct investments from abroad undertaken in developing countries. This research focused on the links between the characteristics of IT entrepreneurs, assistance from the government, and e-commerce success in business.

2. Related Works

Varela, et al. (2017) suggested the "multi-perspective critical success factors (MPCSF)" strategy for internet shopping. Raut, et al., (2017) evaluated the CSFs promoting cloud application in micro SMEs. The methodology for directly assessing and looking into the effects of different factors on the e-commerce's success was proposed by Choshin, et al., 2017. To examine the interactions between e-commerce achievement and certain other customer-oriented specific goals, Sharma, et al., 2019 suggested a structural model. The goal of Nurchayo, et al., 2021 was to pinpoint crucial aspects as the key factor in joint decision-making between partners and e-commerce enterprises.

3. Methodology

Data samples: 1800 internet entrepreneurs are surveyed for this research. They were asked to self-administer surveys and return it in a prepaid package. 485 people responded, or 32%. After removing surveys with incomplete data and participants without a two-year-old business, 350 or 25% replies fulfilled all requirements. Table 12.1 depicts the participants' data.

Questionnaires: Nearly 5 e-commerce entrepreneurs were first interviewed in-depth. And 5 respondents were individually interviewed in order to discover and fix the survey instrument's faults. In-depth survey opinions and data were employed to further enhance the questions; certain variables were removed and others were included. The initial questionnaire was edited into Chinese by professionals before being back-translated into English by a different expert who was skilled in both languages and capable to ensure accuracy. The information was gathered in China. Ten senior students can take a degree in business management in the international business scheme at Tsinghua University were required to fill out the survey in the English version as a pre-test, as well as ten more senior students can take entrepreneurialism at Peking University were arbitrarily provided ten questionnaires in the Chinese edition. Due to the uniformity between the English and China versions, the findings of the translation of the original English survey into China were acceptable. The pre-test question initially had 65 items. Following comments from the e-commerce entrepreneurs' pre-test, certain questions were clarified and some elements were removed. 50 items made up the complete questionnaire survey.

Table 12.1 Participants' data

Features		n=350 Frequency
Gender	Men	225
	Women	125
Age	18-25	25
	26-45	205
	46-60	120
Education level	High school	22
	Diploma course	117
	Bachelor courses	158
	Master courses and high-level	53

Hypotheses development:

Hypothesis-1 (H1): The accomplishment focus of the founder is related to the achievement of e-commerce entrepreneurs.

Hypothesis-2 (H2): The networking of the founder is related to the achievement of e-commerce entrepreneurs.

Hypothesis-3 (H3): The innovative venture's e-service trustworthiness has a direct

impact on the achievement of e-commerce entrepreneurs.

Hypothesis-4 (H4): The innovative venture's e-service response has a direct impact on the achievement of e-commerce entrepreneurs.

Hypothesis-5 (H5): The government's assistance of innovative e-commerce businesses is linked to the achievement of e-commerce entrepreneurs.

Dependent variable: The participants were asked to assess the effectiveness of their organizations on a 5-point Likert scale (1 being extremely low and 5 being very high) based on growth score, sales, business stability, customer engagement, and total self-happiness. Another variable called "Achievement" is created by adding the results from the study factors.

Independent variables (IVs): There are 9 variables as follows, IV-1: accomplishment focus; IV-2: networking; IV-3: trustworthiness; IV-4: response; IV-5: governmental assistance.

4. Results and Discussion

The dependability of this study is assessed using the Cronbach alpha test, while the authenticity is evaluated by principal component analysis (PCA). When an eigenvalue exceeds one, all factors are regarded as significant. This demonstrated that the ranges of measurements for every concept accurately captured the concepts, so confirming that the article's tests attained authenticity. The results of the correlation, multiple linear regression (MLR) analyzes are shown in Table 12.2. The Cronbach's alpha test is used to evaluate the dependability of scales. An appropriate and dependable construct value . The findings show that the majority of the indicators are dependable. The H1 is confirmed by the data provided in the table, demonstrating that the achievement of China's e-commerce entrepreneurs is positively correlated with the desire for accomplishment.

Table 12.2 Results of correlation, MLR analyzes

Variables	Dependability Cronbach's A test	Mean	Std. Dev.	Authenticity Items' value	Eigenvalue
Achievement	0.815	3.54	0.69	5	2.87
IV-1	0.789	3.58	0.61	8	3.30
IV-2	0.67	3.2	0.69	5	2.17
IV-3	0.861	3.67	0.32	4	3.51
IV-4	0.79	3.92	0.7	5	2.75
IV-5	0.66	3.64	0.54	5	2.38
Correlation analysis					
IVs	IV-1	IV-2	IV-3	IV-4	IV-5
IV-1	0.43**				
IV-2	0.0	−0.05			
IV-3	0.6**	0.43**	0.17**		
IV-4	0.2**	0.05	0.08	0.33**	
IV-5	0.01	−0.03	0.02	0.13*	0.01

Note: $p<0.05$ for (*) and $p<0.01$ for (**)

MLR analysis Hypotheses	B	SB
H1	0.093	0.042
H2	0.018	0.05
H3	0.315	0.037
H4	−0.08	0.052
H5	0.024	0.015

Note: $R^2 = 0.57$ and Adjusted $R^2 = 0.51$

The outcomes show that the H2 is indeed not statistical significance in a similar manner. H3 is validated and statistically significant. H4 is statistically significant, although. But according to the MLR analysis's findings, this component is negatively linked. H4 is therefore not supported. That H5 is also not statistically significant is demonstrated by this table. It follows that H5 is not accepted. Given the significance of the government's significant support for developing IT companies, this result is a little unexpected.

Two of the hypotheses developed for this research are significant statistically, according to analyzes' findings. These findings demonstrate that founders with a strong accomplishment focus are related with the achievement of e-commerce firms. Business models that highlight e-service dependability are likewise linked to the achievement of innovative IT ventures. The research also demonstrates the relative importance of the critical factors that influence the competitive achievement of e-commerce business owners.

5. Conclusion

Global marketplaces make it crucial to be competitive. To develop a successful and reliable e-commerce business, we must understand the CSFs. This study analyzed the CRFs for e-commerce purposes. The researchers created a survey with 50 items depending on the report's variables. 1800 Chinese internet business owners provided the data that was gathered. This study looked into the effect of five factors on e-commerce achievement. This research will inspire experts to explore the CRFs in various e-commerce's applications.

REFERENCES

1. Li, Y., Pinto, M.C.B. and Diabat, A., 2020. Analyzing the critical success factor of CSR for the Chinese textile industry. Journal of Cleaner Production, 260, p. 120878.
2. Choshin, M. and Ghaffari, A., 2017. An investigation of the impact of effective factors on the success of e-commerce in small-and medium-sized companies. Computers in Human Behavior, 66, pp. 67–74.
3. Pandey, A.K., Singh, R.K., Jayesh, G.S., Khare, N. and Gupta, S.K., 2022. Examining the Role of Enterprise Resource Planning (ERP) in Improving Business Operations in Companies. ECS Transactions, 107(1), p. 2681.
4. Jayesh, G.S., Novaliendry, D., Gupta, S.K., Sharma, A.K. and Hazela, B., 2022. A Comprehensive Analysis of Technologies for Accounting and Finance in Manufacturing Firms. ECS Transactions, 107(1), p. 2715.
5. Tsironis, L.K., Gotzamani, K.D. and Mastos, T.D., 2017. e-Business critical success factors: toward the development of an integrated success model. Business Process Management Journal.
6. Varela, M.L.R., Araújo, A.F., Vieira, G.G., Manupati, V.K. and Manoj, K., 2017. Integrated framework based on critical success factors for e-Commerce. Journal of Information Systems Engineering & Management, 2(1), p. 4.
7. Raut, R.D., Gardas, B.B., Jha, M.K. and Priyadarshinee, P., 2017. Examining the critical success factors of cloud computing adoption in the MSMEs by using ISM model. The Journal of High Technology Management Research, 28(2), pp. 125–141.
8. Choshin, M. and Ghaffari, A., 2017. An investigation of the impact of effective factors on the success of e-commerce in small-and medium-sized companies. Computers in Human Behavior, 66, pp. 67–74.
9. Sharma, H. and Aggarwal, A.G., 2019. Finding determinants of e-commerce success: a PLS-SEM approach. Journal of Advances in Management Research.
10. Nurcahyo, R. and Putra, P.A., 2021. Critical factors in indonesia's e-commerce collaboration. Journal of Theoretical and Applied Electronic Commerce Research, 16(6), pp. 2458–2469.

Note: All the tables in this chapter were made by the Authors.

*Advancements in Business for Integrating Diversity, and
Sustainability – Dimitrios A. Karras et al. (eds)*
© 2024 Taylor & Francis Group, London, ISBN 978-1-032-70828-7

Role of Customer Relationship Management in Marketing Decision Making: Predictive Analytics Approach

13

Sathish A. S.*
VIT Business School, VIT Vellore, India

Neha Jain
Department of Languages, Presidency University, India

Somya Choubey
Department of Commerce, Manipal University Jaipur, India

Priyank Kumar Singh
Doon University, India

Abstract: Customer Relationship Management (CRM) is the technique of continuous interaction with customers to attract and retain them in the business. This paper aims to identify various dimensions of CRM that significantly affect marketing decision making. These dimensions have been extracted from the existing literature and tested through a predictive technique – Multiple Regression Analysis. Data were collected from 216 respondents from customer-centric businesses such as retail and financial services. The results indicated that the dimensions such as 'understanding, communicating, and fulfilling the needs, retaining, and generating value, engaging customers, Individual marketing, 'maintaining loyalty have a significant impact on 'Marketing Decision Making'. The results may be suitably applied by the CRM managers to sharpen and customise their decisions. The study is limited to the conclusions derived from primary and numerical study. A qualitative validation of these results by future researchers may add more value to the results of this study.

Keywords: Customer relationship Management, Marketing decision making, Predictive analysis, Customer-centric businesses, Customised decisions

1. Introduction

Customer Relationship Management (CRM) is a wide-ranging approach and process to acquire, retain and associating with selective users to generate qualitative value for customers and company. It engages in amalgamation of customer service, sales, marketing and supply chain role of companies to attain more effectiveness and efficiencies

*Corresponding author: sathish.as@vit.ac.in

DOI: 10.4324/9781032708294-13

in providing customer value (Wali, 2018). In the present economic environment, it is impossible for any business to survive without an understanding of its customers and positive association with them. CRM is as old an approach as business itself and along with monetary growth, CRM is need is growing rapidly. Companies that want to enhance their performance must apply or use CRM in their business strategies. Product or services provided to the customer help companies through CRM to understand their expectations and need in future (Hitka, Pajtinkova-Bartakova, Lorincova, et al. (2019). Initially, CRM focus was on to alter the market i.e., firstly at mass marketing that provide the path to focus on target marketing and segment marketing and lastly individual. Afterward companies recognize that to maintain loyal customer and retain them are more profitable as compared to focus on only new customers. CRM implementation affects the entire process of a company and formulates alterations in technology, process as well as people. CRM system support in collection of information related to customers and this information is imperative for not only present customers but also for potential customers. Customers are analyzed and categorized based on their association with companies. It follows a proper procedure for sales, marketing and business function and backs it up with collection of data and evaluates it at every stage.

2. Literature Review

Lu (2021) explored that Customer behavior management is not a new model for any business, it considers customer as the midpoint with the main objective to share information and communication. Due to the increase in competition, many changes have taken place in dealings with customers and enterprises, and lots of other factors have also enhanced the complication of relations with customers.

Juanamasta, Ni, Wati et al. (2019) examined that as there is fast development in network and ecommerce marketing, companies are participating actively in designing and evaluation of behavior of customers and relationship management. Hence, the behavior of customer and relationship management has turned out to be a modern tool for marketing management. CRM supports companies to gather information of customers, offer tools for data mining, evaluate information of customer, respond timely to changes in market and realize sharing information and business intelligence. Krasniqi, Vlahna and Krasniqic (2021) explored that due to widespread of social media, internet and association among seller and buyer is getting bigger. A variety of choices are available to customers, so companies are trying to customer to loyal from casual. This is the foremost objective of customer relationship management. Modern CRM and marketing has now become sophisticated and provides golden opportunity to all types of companies with the objective to get share in business world. Gil-Gomez, Guerola-Navarro, Oltra-Badenes and Lozano-Quilis (2020) found that innovation and customer information management are the two main factors to attain successful growth and development, survival, improving efficiency of business, performance and sustainable viable benefits in modern world. CRM is defined as a process of integration of workforce and technology looking for better understanding of customers of company. Additionally, when a company wants to focus mainly on retention of customers and making better relationship with them, CRM is the most important approach for the same. Krizanova, Gajanova and Nadanyiova (2018) explored that successful companies are now aware of the way to drive efficiently their efforts of marketing by giving propriety to their customers and generating high amount of revenues. They make strategies based on customer centered. Companies based on CRM implement strategies that manage personalized relations with customers with the support of database of customers and interactive mass communication technologies. Kunasekaran, Zheng and Wan (2020) found that CRM system examines the potential association from huge amount of information of customers and then manage the customers and achieve true customer relationship management. Nowadays, enterprises are customer based and can serve customers accordingly to sustain relations with customers. Jiaoyang (2016) examined that as the needs of customers are becoming diverse day by day, they are also becoming wide-ranging day by day. Hence it is important for companies to have strategies or processes to fulfill all the needs of customers. Customer relationship management is one such system and support in achieving company's objective of increase in profits and retaining customers at maximum. It also supports in providing better quality service to customers. Toriani and Angeloni (2011) explored that CRM is not a service or product that is it doesn't bring revenue directly, it supports as a strategy for business to maintain the association with customers to maintain and retain relationship, generates indirect and long-term outcomes. To have a successful strategy, the enterprise must consider a set of factors as its execution needs an experienced workforce, well-defined process, new attitude and cultural changes from employees. Navarro, Gomez,

Badenes and Acosta (2022) explored that an important benefit of globalization is that it provides great opportunity to customers to access information as well as purchase of products and services available even outside of countries. This reflects that desires, needs and customer expectations are changing and demand is increasing. Therefore, the market has become so dynamic that only companies that are able to adopt these changes can survive. Marketing management along with entrepreneurial marketing and CRM supports in promoting the economic development of society. Chen and Wu (2016) found that "Customer relationship management (CRM)" is an important foremost strategy for business and tool of business management, and reflected crucial in enhancing marketing, sales, and strategies for production planning. CRM is a technological solutions and philosophy that supports companies to make policies or strategies to make healthy relations with their customers. Retention of customers is as important as attracting new customers. The loyalty of customers also plays a significant part in generating revenue for organizations. El-Gohary, Edwards and Huang (2013) explored that there must exist some principles or regulations that must be pursued by decision makers of business of flourishing companies that look to attain high level of performance of business and undergo ultimately as representative company and exclusive shining example of successful business. Therefore, the existence and significance of CRM and marketing as part of successful business is important for any business management methodology. CRM is important for every management as it supports collecting customer management information and its usage in sketching strategies.

Garrido-Moreno, Lockett and Garcia-Morales (2015) explored that the main part of CRM is the result obtained from CRM with the help of different CRM source values. It provides overall impact on companies with adequate information of customer need and services. Innovation and knowledge management powered by solutions of CRM technologies has huge implications for marketing. Therefore, entrepreneurial marketing consequences do not directly lead to decisions related to management but also the result of culture and entrepreneurial processes. Customer relation management is observed as an important tool of business to manage sales, entrepreneurial services and marketing. Bojanowska (2017) found that Marketing is a regulation that is related to study the market behavior and consumer's needs. Customer Relationship management is an important tool of modern business management to setup effective method and channel of customer-based information management, in combination of "Enterprise Resource Planning solutions." Its main objective is to enhance the performance of the company to enable companies to attain better results for business. The focus of CRM role is not only to its possibility to enhance existing management but also to develop capacity for innovation. This prospective establishes CRM as an important powerful technology for management solutions in today's business management. Chang and Zhang (2016) explored that there is association among CRM technology solutions, association marketing on the basis of focus on customer and success of business. To attain the anticipated advantages of relationship marketing, CRM is important for business management. It's a technology that has gained popularity and attracted the interest of many academics and researchers. Additionally, its scope for further development is linked closely to relationship marketing. CRM is also found as most significant solution to obtain the main information for management to develop strategy for marketing.

3. Objective

To ascertain the impact of Customer Relationship Management on Marketing Decision Making.

4. Methodology

The study was conducted with the help of a survey method where people from the marketing sector were considered to take part in the survey. The questionnaire was filled to know the role and impact of Customer Relationship Management in Marketing Decision Making. The research design was descriptive, and the data were collected from 216 respondents from customer-centric businesses such as retail and financial services. Data were analyzed with the help of a predictive technique - multiple regression analysis (Paul et al., 2016).

Findings

In this study, to measure the Role of CRM on "Marketing Decision Making," multiple regressions were applied. Table 13.1 shows that the model explained 85% of the variance (R Square = .845). Table 13.2 shows that more than 1 or more IDVs have significant impact on the DVs as the significance value is less than 0.05 (0.000).

Multiple Regression analysis

Table 13.1 Model Summary

Model	R	R Square	Adjusted R Square	Std. Error of the Estimate
1	.919a	.845	.841	.31949

Predictors: CRM provide platform to companies understand, communicate and fulfil need of customers, Help to get, retain and associate with selective users to generate qualitative value, Help to engage in merger of customer service, sales, marketing and supply chain role of companies, Provide the path to focus on target, segment and individual marketing, Maintain loyal customer and retain them for more profitability, CRM support companies to gather information of customers and offer tools for data mining

Source: Author (SPSS output)

Table 13.2 ANOVA[a]

	Model	Sum of Squares	df	Mean Square	F	Sig.
1	Regression	116.370	6	19.395	190.007	.000[b]
	Residual	21.334	209	.102		
	Total	137.704	215			

DV: **Overall impact of CRM on Marketing Decision Making**

Predictors: CRM provide platform to companies understand, communicate and fulfil need of customers, Help to get, retain and associate with selective users to generate qualitative value, Help to engage in merger of customer service, sales, marketing and supply chain role of companies, Provide the path to focus on target, segment and individual marketing, Maintain loyal customer and retain them for more profitability, CRM support companies to gather information of customers and offer tools for data mining

Source: Author (SPSS output)

Table 13.3 Coefficients[a]

Model	Unstandardized Coefficients		Standardized Coefficients	t	Sig.
	B	Std. Error	Beta		
(Constant)	.016	.136		.120	.905
CRM provide platform to companies understand, communicate and fulfil need of customers	.077	.036	.080	2.139	.034
CRM Helps to get, retain and associate with selective users to generate qualitative value	.124	.035	.131	3.503	.001
CRM Helps to engage in merger of customer service, sales, marketing and supply chain role of companies	.182	.061	.182	2.964	.003
CRM Provides the path to focus on target, segment, and individual marketing	.671	.062	.651	10.858	.000
CRM Maintains loyal customer and retain them for more profitability	.154	.043	.156	3.623	.000
CRM support companies to gather information of customers and offer tools for data mining	.044	.020	.063	2.245	.026
DV: Overall impact of CRM on Marketing Decision Making					

Source: Author (SPSS output)

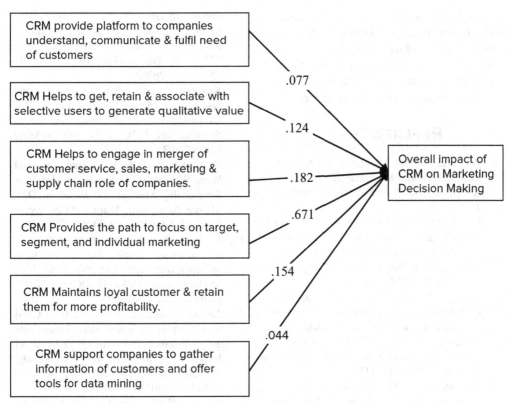

Fig. 13.1 Role of customer relationship management in marketing decision making

Source: Author

Table 13.4 shows that all the 6 statements regarding the role of customer relationship management have a significant impact on Marketing Decision Making. The Beta value of all the variables is positive. Highest Beta value 0.651 is shown by the variable "CRM Provides the path to focus on target, segment, and individual marketing" and lowest Beta variable is shown by "CRM support companies to gather information of customers and offer tools for data mining (Fig. 13.1).

5. Conclusion

The study had analyzed the role and impact of customer relationship management in marketing decision making and found some of vital roles such as CRM provides platform to companies understand, communicate and fulfil need of customers and generate qualitative value. It helps to engage in merger of customer and shows path to focus on target marketing, maintain loyal customer and retain gather information of customers and offer tools for data mining. The study concludes that there is a significant impact of customer relationship management in marketing decision making. Organizations should provide mock-drills, end-to-end consumer issues resolution and customer feedback and reconciliation training to make their CRM team expert in query handling. In the present era customers are well-connected through digital media (Kudeshia and Mittal, 2015), hence digital marketing, automation through well-established CRM software such as Zendesk, Trailhead and Mailchimp etc. are the ways to handle customer queries and communicate them to the management.

REFERENCES

1. Wali, A.F. (2018). Customer Relationship Management and Marketing Effectiveness: A Comparative Consumer Study. Paradigm 22(2), 1–24.

2. Lu, J. (2021). The Role of Customer Behavior and Relationship Management in Modern Enterprise Marketing. Advances in Economics, Business and Management Research, 203, 2998–3002.

3. Hitka, M., Pajtinkova-Bartakova, G.; Lorincova, S., et al. (2019). Sustainability in Marketing through Customer Relationship Management in a Telecommunication Company. Marketing and Management of Innovations, (4), 194–215.

4. Juanamasta, I. G., Ni, M., Wati, N., et al. (2019). The Role of Customer Service Through Customer Relationship Management (CRM) To Increase Customer Loyalty and Good Image. International Journal of Scientific and Technology Research, 8 (10), 2004–2007.

5. Krasniqi, D., Vlahna, K. and Krasniqic, B. (2021). Customer Relationship Management in the Purchase Decision Process. Journal of Accounting, Finance and Auditing Studies, 7(4), 151–168.

6. Gil-Gomez, H., Guerola-Navarro, V.; Oltra-Badenes, R. and Lozano-Quilis, J.A. (2020). Customer relationship management: digital transformation and sustainable business model innovation. Economic Research-Ekonomska Istrazivanja, 33(1), 2733–2750. https://doi.org/10.1080/133167 7X.2019.1676283

8. Krizanova, A., Gajanova, L., and Nadanyiova, M. (2018). Design of a CRM level and performance measurement model. Sustainability,10(7), 1–17. doi:10.3390/su10072567

9. Kunasekaran, K.K.H., Zheng, Y. and Wan, W. (2020). Research on Customer Relationship Management Based on Data Mining. Asia-pacific Journal of Convergent Research Interchange, 6(5), 61–77.

10. Jiaoyang, Z. (2016). Analysis of the role of customer relationship management in enterprise marketing, Shopping Mall Modernization, 20, 87–88, DOI: 10.14013/ j.cnki.scxdh.2016.20.052

11. Toriani, S. and Angeloni, M.T. (2011). CRM as A Support for Knowledge Management and Customer Relationship. Journal of Information Systems and Technology Management, 8(1), 87–108. DOI: 10.4301/ S1807-17752011000100005

12. Paul, J., Mittal, A., and Srivastav, G. (2016). Impact of service quality on customer satisfaction in private and public sector banks. International Journal of Bank Marketing, 34(5), 606–622. doi: 10.1108/ ijbm-03-2015-0030

13. Kudeshia, C., and Mittal, A. (2015). Social Media: An Eccentric Business Communication Tool for the 21st Century Marketers. International Journal of Online Marketing, 5(2), 37–57. doi: 10.4018/ ijom.2015040103

Advancements in Business for Integrating Diversity, and
Sustainability – Dimitrios A. Karras et al. (eds)
© 2024 Taylor & Francis Group, London, ISBN 978-1-032-70828-7

Impact of Artificial Intelligence in Effective Knowledge Management: An Application of Stepwise Multiple Regression

R. Indradevi*
VIT Business School, VIT Vellore, India

P. Horsley Solomon
SRM Arts and Science College, India

Shankar Ramamoorthy
School of CSE&IS, Presidency University, India

Ity Patni
Department of Business Administration, Manipal University Jaipur, India

Abstract: Artificial Intelligence is considered as foundation stone for Knowledge Management (KM) as it includes gaining, developing, and sharing of knowledge along with successful consumption within companies. Artificial Intelligence (AI) supports computers to carry out everyday jobs that usually need human intelligence. AI performs many jobs which were earlier carried out by human beings. Applications of AI support in processing data and discover pattern after that automatically. This study aims to find the impact of various dimensions of AI on KM effectiveness. The data were collected from 192 respondents and analyzed with stepwise multiple regression technique. It was found 'KM processes and performance is improved by AI tools', 'Knowledge is enlarged and utilized in very effective way through AI', 'The process becomes effective and make knowledge available any time everywhere by AI', 'KM makes better proficiency', sensitivity, innovation and efficacy by AI have a significant impact on overall effectiveness of KM.

Keywords: Artificial intelligence, Knowledge management, Proficiency, Efficacy, Sensitivity, Stepwise multiple regression

1. Introduction

In present times, with the development of Artificial Intelligence and Information Technology, Knowledge Management (KM) was found to be more sophisticated and advanced. In addition, many companies that are leading all over the world have accepted various practices of knowledge management to make sure that they stay in the lead of

*Corresponding author: rindradevi@vit.ac.in

DOI: 10.4324/9781032708294-14

their competitors' companies in the present competitive world of business. Therefore, organizations keep on looking for methods to enhance their practices of knowledge management. "Knowledge Management" term is not a straightforward concept to describe as it is comprehensive and adopted in diverse situations by diverse people. For example, knowledge management involves the methods used to recognize, collect and highlight knowledge. Knowledge management enriches methodically know - how and comfortable to make better proficiency, sensitivity, innovation and efficacy in a company.

Usually, knowledge management involves three major constituents that are process, technology and people. Process shapes all works to be done in physical management of knowledge like creation, storage, sharing, transfer and use of knowledge. Human factors, i.e., people, are the major constituent of knowledge management and lead to more than 70 percent success. It is due to the truth that human beings are the main source of knowledge as they develop and circulate it. Third component technology supports people to make the process effective and make knowledge available any time everywhere (Mansoori, Salloum and Shaalan, 2021).

With the improvement in technologies, knowledge management leads to less expensive, ever-present, and homogeneous and are more efficient in respond to need of individual. The tools of Artificial Intelligence capabilities support effectively to take knowledge management to further level. It helps the workforce to get concerned or needed information in seconds and increase real time in making decisions. It also supports companies to enhance their capability to follow documents and processes in an effective way. Technologies of Artificial Intelligence are used to enhance the process

of knowledge management in most modern companies to enhance their performance.

Alterations made in knowledge management may come about improving work environment, management, and operating activities. Improvement of artificial intelligence advances will impact future modifications made in knowledge management. KM will play significant part in companies continuously in coming future, along with dependence of economy is on expert knowledge and exchange of information. Consequently, digitization and the increase of new advancements in technologies in different areas will gulp down many daily routines works, leaving complicated jobs for highly professionals, i.e. workers, white-collar workers. At the same time, novel types of knowledge are formed with the use of new technologies, leading to the need of new requirements to handle and manage knowledge. Technologies implement various types of functions related to knowledge, that support the computer guided processing of knowledge, the implementation of knowledge technically, its presentation, storage and visualization of knowledge.

2. Literature Review

Jarrahi, Askay, Eshraghi and Smith (2022) explored that companies must evaluate the possible role for new systems of AI in supporting companies' activities of knowledge management due to spontaneous association between two. The main KM function is to generate and sustain a company's memory that generated tracks and acquire knowledge resources. The purpose of Knowledge management is to unite the knowledge workforce with correct people or knowledge resources at correct time to take decisions better. The enhancement of capabilities of AI and its hopeful functions to achieve these objectives may request for different types of work division among intelligent machines and workers.

Jallow, Renukappa and Suresh (2020) found that innovative pattern of business and work practices is still in development phase to make better KM with the help of advancement in technologies in which all companies refer it as 4th industrial revolution. The Industrial revolution involves advancement of technologies like Artificial Intelligence (AI) that is considered to make possible tasks particularly at managerial level along with manual employees to undergo a simple process and have effective output. The present process of knowledge, i.e., from development of knowledge to its storage and supervising must be re-evaluated with the discovery of helpful knowledge with the use of learning algorithms. For example, sharing of knowledge among AI and humans may vary through common process of sharing knowledge among humans. Companies must make strategies to consider all involved actors in accessing knowledge.

Sandhya and Balaji (2022) examined that the Knowledge management (KM) function is to allow human beings and concerned parties to work together, generate, share, and utilize knowledge. It increases performance, boost innovation and cultivates the competence support for both business enterprises and human beings. AI with the help of studying gadgets supports machines to attain, approach and utilize experts to perform tasks and to release understanding that may support people to increase their process of decision making. AI helps in understanding the way knowledge ships to individual who need it. Artificial Intelligence is utilized to balance the effectiveness and volume of distribution of knowledge.

Leoni, Ardolino, Baz, Gueli and Bacchetti (2022) found that machines enabled with AI support in practices such as learning, gathering, processing and using knowledge to carry out tasks, reveal or unlock the knowledge that can be provided to people to enhance process of decision making in their companies. Artificial Intelligence takes out new knowledge from various amounts of information, portray complicated mappings on the basis to make decisions. AI and KM involves close mutual association among them. Knowledge management supports in making the possibility of understanding knowledge whereas AI provides the tools to enlarge and utilize knowledge along with new knowledge in very effective way.

Mageswari, Sivasubramanian and Dath (2017) examined that modern companies rapidly depending on AI tools to increase knowledge management processes and performance with the capability to inductively find out association and trends in companies knowledge repositories to generate new knowledge. It supports in searching of knowledge and distribute knowledge who call for it. AI can enhance productivity of companies by making data management process automatic and eliminates the requirement for intermediaries.

Mittal and Kumar (2019) explored that adoption of AI support companies to get a competitive benefit and increase their performance by providing better efficiency, profitability and productivity. In the case of manufacturing companies, AI applications provide decision making in real time and improvement of performance by facilitating project maintenance, enhanced quality control and improved safety. Artificial intelligence allows significant ability to develop better controlling tools and look areas of disturbance as it supports companies in collecting information and process data more effectively and hence facilitates companies resource orchestration and process information, making the coordination in real-time and teamwork processes.

Rhem (2021) found that Artificial Intelligence support in ranging the quantity and effectiveness of distribution of knowledge. The adoption of AI in providing knowledge relies on information that is applied to instruct the algorithms of machine learning.

Pai, Shetty, Shetty, Bhandary, Shetty, Nayak, Dinesh and D'souza (2022) found that AI has the capabilities to highlight the recognized concepts, context and meaning that emerge up with stimulating new mutual methods among machines and knowledge workers. Knowledge management tries to merge various discipline concepts such as human resources management, organizational behavior, information technology and artificial intelligence. These machines can support the enhancement of competencies of human beings and generate new experts. Organizations must update and redesign the flows, proficiency and job of knowledge workers to use AI at the best completely. Patterns used in AI make the future predictions and these patterns develop an innovative type of knowledge. Fteimi and Hopf (2021) found that AI and it's fast advancement in technologies considerably influence the future work and the way companies manage their process of Knowledge Management. Knowledge shared by AI and human beings differs using common process of knowledge sharing among humans. Companies must form a strategy that involves all stakeholders to access knowledge. Standard access of knowledge and its retrieval is obtained from using AI technology, but overall monitoring

tools and control may make the information biased. Hence, adoption of AI in working environments may lead to change in fundamentals of companies.

3. Objective

To examine the Impact of Artificial Intelligence in Effective Knowledge Management.

4. Methodology

The study was conducted with the help of a survey method where people from different occupational sectors were considered to take part in the survey. The questionnaire was used to know the Impact of Artificial Intelligence in Effective Knowledge Management. Sample of 192 respondents were surveyed to collect the data and stepwise multiple regression was applied to get the results (Paul et al., 2016).

5. Findings

In this study, measurement of the Impact of Artificial Intelligence in Effective Knowledge Management has been done. The IDVs (Independent Variables) are 'Knowledge management processes and performance is improved by AI tools (V1). Knowledge is enlarged and utilized in very effective way through AI (V2), AI can replace the other IT support (V3) 'The process becomes effective and make knowledge available any time everywhere by AI' (V4), 'Knowledge management makes better proficiency, sensitivity, innovation and efficacy by AI (V5), stepwise multiple regressions were applied. The DV is "Overall impact of Artificial Intelligence in Effective Knowledge Management" Model 1 explains 81% of the variance with R Square 0.818, model 2 has explained 83% of the variance and R square is 0.832, model 3 has shown 83% of variance with 0.837 R square and model 4 is showing 84% variance and value of R square is 0.844 (Table 14.1).

Multiple Regression analysis

Table 14.1 Model Summary

Model	R	R Square	Adjusted R Square	Std. Error of the Estimate
1	.905[a]	.818	.818	.34317
2	.912[b]	.832	.830	.33122
3	.915[c]	.837	.834	.32735
4	.919[d]	.844	.841	.32060
"a. Predictors: (Constant), V4"				
"b. Predictors: (Constant), V4, V5"				
"c. Predictors: (Constant), V4, V5, V2"				
"d. Predictors: (Constant), V4, V5, V2, V1"				

Source: Author (SPSS output)

Table 14.2 ANOVA[a]

	Model	Sum of Squares	df	Mean Square	F	Sig.
1	Regression	100.875	1	100.875	856.579	.000b
	Residual	22.375	190	.118		
	Total	123.250	191			
2	Regression	102.515	2	51.258	467.215	.000c
	Residual	20.735	189	.110		
	Total	123.250	191			
3	Regression	103.104	3	34.368	320.724	.000d
	Residual	20.146	188	.107		
	Total	123.250	191			
4	Regression	104.029	4	26.007	253.026	.000e
	Residual	19.221	187	.103		
	Total	123.250	191			
DV: Overall impact of Artificial Intelligence in Effective Knowledge Management						
IDV: See Table 14.1						

Source: Author (SPSS output)

Table 14.3 Coefficients[a]

Model		Unstandardized Coefficients		Standardized Coefficients	t	Sig.
		B	Std. Error	Beta		
1	(Constant)	.282	.127		2.215	.028
	V5	.935	.032	.905	29.267	**.000**
2	(Constant)	.110	.131		.840	.402
	V4	.806	.045	.780	17.787	**.000**
	V5	.168	.044	.170	3.867	**.000**
3	(Constant)	.195	.134		1.452	.148
	V4	.840	.047	.813	17.839	**.000**
	V5	.185	.044	.186	4.236	**.000**
	V2	−.080	.034	−.083	−2.345	**.020**
4	(Constant)	.122	.134		.915	.361
	V4	.817	.047	.791	17.474	**.000**
	V5	.171	.043	.173	3.993	**.000**
	V2	−.136	.038	−.142	−3.557	**.000**
	V1	.111	.037	.119	3.000	**.003**
DV: Overall impact of Artificial Intelligence in Effective Knowledge Management						

Source: Author (SPSS output)

Table 14.2 and 14.3 shows that all the 4 models show an impact of Artificial Intelligence in Effective Knowledge Management. The Beta value of all the model and its variables is positive except one variable "Knowledge is enlarged and utilized in very effective way through AI" of model 3 and one variable "Knowledge is enlarged and utilized in very effective way through AI" of model 4.

6. Conclusion

The study had analyzed the Impact of AI in effective KM, and found that knowledge management processes and performance increases by AI tools, Knowledge is enlarged and utilized in very effective way through AI, The effectiveness and volume of knowledge management is balanced by AI, The process becomes effective and make knowledge available any time everywhere by AI, Knowledge management makes better proficiency, sensitivity, innovation and efficacy by AI and AI in knowledge management lead companies in present competitive world of business. The study concludes that there is a significant Impact of Artificial Intelligence in Effective Knowledge Management.

References

1. Mansoori, S.A.; Salloum, S.A. and Shaalan, K. (2021). The Impact of Artificial Intelligence and Information Technologies on the Efficiency of Knowledge Management at Modern Organizations: A Systematic Review. Recent Advances in Intelligent Systems and Smart Applications, Studies in Systems, Decision and Control

295, https://doi.org/10.1007/978-3-030-47411-9_9

2. Jarrahi, M.H.; Askay, D.; Eshraghi, A. and Smith, P. (2022). Artificial intelligence and knowledge management: A partnership between humans and AI. Business Horizons, 66(1), 1–13. DOI:10.1016/j.bushor.2022.03.002

3. Jallow, H.; Renukappa, S. and Suresh, S. (2020). Knowledge Management and Artificial Intelligence (AI). 21st European Conference on Knowledge Management (ECKM 2020), 1–9.

4. Sandhya, C. and. Balaji, R. (2022). Artificial Intelligence in Knowledge Management. Specialusis Ugdymas/Special Education, 1(43), 6373–6382.

5. Leoni, L.; Ardolino, M.; Baz, J.E.; Gueli, G. and Bacchetti, A. (2022). The mediating role of knowledge management processes in the effective use of artificial intelligence in manufacturing firms. International Journal of Operations and Production Management, 42(13), 411–437. DOI 10.1108/IJOPM-05-2022-0282

6. Mageswari, S.U., Sivasubramanian, R.C. and Dath, T.S. (2017). A comprehensive analysis of knowledge management in Indian manufacturing companies. Journal of Manufacturing Technology Management, 28(4), 506–530.

7. Mittal, S. and Kumar, V. (2019). Study of knowledge management models and their relevance in organizations. International Journal of Knowledge Management Studies, 10(3), 322–335.

8. Rhem, A.J. (2021). AI ethics and its impact on knowledge management. Springer, 1, 33–37. https://doi.org/10.1007/s43681-020-00015-2

9. Pai, R.Y.; Shetty, A.; Shetty, A.D.; Bhandary, R.; Shetty, J.; Nayak, S.; Dinesh, T.K. and D'souza, J. (2022). Integrating artificial intelligence for knowledge management systems–synergy among people and technology: a systematic review of the evidence. Economic Research-Ekonomska Istraživanja, 35(1), 7043–7065. https://doi.org/10.1080/1331677X.2022.2058976

10. Fteimi, N. and Hopf, K. (2021). Knowledge Management in The Era of Artificial Intelligence—Developing an Integrative Framework. Adaptive AI-oriented Knowledge Management, 1–10.

11. Paul, J., Mittal, A., and Srivastav, G. (2016). Impact of service quality on customer satisfaction in private and public sector banks. International Journal of Bank Marketing, 34(5), 606–622. doi: 10.1108/ijbm-03-2015-0030

Advancements in Business for Integrating Diversity, and
Sustainability – Dimitrios A. Karras et al. (eds)
© 2024 Taylor & Francis Group, London, ISBN 978-1-032-70828-7

15

A Study on the Performance of the Banking Industry During the COVID-19 Crisis

Bhadrappa Haralayya[1]
Lingaraj Appa Engineering College, Karnataka, India

Amit Mishra[2]
University of Lucknow, UP, India

Mahesh Singh*
Kebri Dehar University, Kebri Dehar, Ethiopia

Iskandar Muda[3]
Faculty Economic and Business,
Universitas Sumatera Utara, Medan, Indonesia

Abstract: This study looks at how global bank stocks were affected by financial sector policy pronouncements during the COVID-19 crisis' early stages. They conclude that borrower assistance programs and liquidity support are important. Reduced the crisis's negative effects, while their effects differed greatly between institutions and nations. Contrarily, countercyclical prudential measures caused bank stocks to see negative anomalous returns, a sign that markets have already priced in it the potential negative effects of these actions. The banking system is significant in this situation since it is an important component from an economic perspective. In recent years, the banking industry has experienced continuous reinvention and adaptation to meet changing customer needs and the need for cost reductions. The COVID-19 pandemic has accelerated the digitalization of the financial sector, although innovation and a digital strategy were essential to banking even before the pandemic started.

Keywords: Government announcements, COVID-19 pandemic, Bank stock returns, Liquidity premium.

1. Introduction

The COVID-19 pandemics' direct and indirect economic effects on numerous nations and sectors have had negative effects on the world economy. (Baldwin et al. (2020)). All areas of activity have been affected by the global economic slowdown brought on by

*Corresponding author: mahesh300@gmail.com
[1]bhadrappabhavimani@gmail.com, [2]amitmishralko1308@gmail.com, [3]iskandar1@usu.ac.id

DOI: 10.4324/9781032708294-15

the containment measures taken to combat COVID-19. International scholars right now scrambling to evaluate each consequence that COVID-19 on its actual economy and generate conclusions to find the best remedies. This stand particularly true of economists (Beraich et al. (2022)). The offshore dollar finance markets experienced severe difficulties in March 2020 as a result of the COVID-19 issue. Similar to each "Global Financial Crisis" (GFC) of 2008, these stresses showed themselves as deviations from neo-classical arbitrage requirements, such as departures from "covered interest parity" (CIP) (Aizenman et al. (2022)). Financial literacy makes it easier for families, particularly those belonging to underprivileged groups in developing nations, to obtain financial inclusion, which refers to access to diverse financial services that are readily available and equitable in all respects (Nguyen et al. (2022)). As collateral coverage decreases and borrowers struggle to make payments, access credit, and get liquidity, asset price declines put a strain on bank balance sheets, which is represented by a rise in "Non-performing loans" (NPLs) (Arner et al. (2022)).

2. Related Works

The imposition of societal limitations brought on by the COVID-19 pandemic has decreased worldwide production. Small enterprises also saw a sharp decline in revenue (Riadi et al. (2022)). Focused policy assistance and easing the reorganization of businesses that have been negatively affected by COVID-19. Evaluates enterprise sector risks and weaknesses as well as country readiness for a significant business reorganization (Araujo et al. (2022)). The resilience of the financial system, particularly banks, between COVID-19 and the global financial crisis is compared and contrasted in this paper. They demonstrate that banks are now a part of the solution rather than a part of the issue as a result of institutional and regulatory changes over the last ten years (Giese and Haldane (2020)). The crisis is moving from the liquidity phase to the solvency phase. All of this presents challenging short- and long-term problems. The biggest problem facing policy in the next ten years will likely be rebuilding policy buffers across the board (Muthukumaran et al. (2022)). An economic and medical disaster has been brought on by the COVID-19 pandemic. They are now facing difficulties that are comparable in size to both the Spanish flu outbreak and Great Depression, as has been mentioned by (Shashi et al. (2022)).

3. Methodology

Data samples: Refinitiv data from May 2, 2018, through May 12, 2020, which covers all 52 nations' publicly listed banks. The data collection includes information on state ownership, quarterly financial reports, and daily stock prices. They exclude 242 equities from the data set's 1590 bank stocks that were traded for less than 30% of each country's business days during the sample period. They also take 208 institutions under the management of businesses whose primary activity is not banking out of the dataset. They chose 896 commercial banks for their final sample.

Bank's risk premium during the crisis: In this part, they demonstrate that asset pricing models cannot explain the underperformance of bank stock prices. Furthermore, given we are taking into account bank of possibility that the appropriate asset pricing model varies across nations or even between banks within one country based on results from all around the globe and banks of different sizes.

The results of bank b alone are not included in the value-weighted domestic market component to prevent spurious correlation AA, the model is shown in equation (1):

$$R_{b,t} = \alpha b + \beta_G R_l^G + \beta UR_t^{D/b} + u_{b,t} \qquad (1)$$

The empirical investigation described is a panel regression in equation (2). Links several bank attributes to weekly abnormal bank returns. The error term AAA3 is clustered at the national level, while the coefficients AAA and AAA are fixed effects on the country and week, respectively. These are the details of our final specifications:

$$ARET_{b.e.t} = \alpha_0\alpha_1 Liquidity + \alpha_2 Oil\ exposure_b +$$
$$\alpha_3 Size_b + \alpha_4 Public\ bank_b + \alpha_5 Capita;\ ratio_b +$$
$$Covid_{c,t} + \gamma_c + \delta_t + u_{b,c,t} \qquad (2)$$

Endogeneity: The COVID-19 shock is exogenous, and a nation's choice of policies is not arbitrary. Their estimates would be skewed to the degree that chosen policies exactly are comparable to those that financial authorities determined to be also effective as respective jurisdictions, accounting for consideration of regional monetary circumstances, bank both stock performance and features.

Cross-border banks: The response of these banks' stock prices on days when the nation of the subsidiary's fiscal and regulatory authorities enact financial sector policies.

Drivers of policy adoption: The degree to which both internal and external factors such as a jurisdiction's banking sector characteristics and a neighboring country's adoption of comparable policies may be used to forecast the implementation in a given jurisdiction of certain policies.

Cross-country announcements: Euro region broad cross-country policy indicators to see if each endogeneity of policy measures affects our results. One may argue that national-specific issues are less likely to have an impact on the "European Central Bank's (ECB)" operations.

4. Results and Discussion

Impact of policy announcements: We depict the average anomalous returns for each policy category during the event window using banks from all countries as a benchmark to determine the severity of stock market effects.

Liquidity support: There is a decrease in the liquidity premium after announcements of liquidity assistance. In other words, when regulators announce financing and liquidity measures, the shares of banks having a lower proportion of liquid assets perform better.

Prudential measures: Prudential actions seem to hurt the overall value of bank stocks and do not appear to be linked to a noticeable decline in the liquidity premium.

Borrower assistance: The abnormal returns on bank equities was significantly correlated with announcements of borrower help. Some nations enhanced their public liability guarantees systems, with government guarantees up to 90% of loan values, in response to the shock's impact, particularly on small, non-essential businesses that wouldn't be able to fund operational expenses during prolonged lockdowns.

Table 15.1 and Fig. 15.1 illustrate the findings on how financial sector reforms affected cross-sectional behavior. Even though we give results for both the complete sample and the limited example, their favored explanation, and discussion center on particular action objectives. Every finding supports our earlier discovery that borrower assistance programs have a significant impact on how banks' stock prices react.

Table 15.1 Policy initiatives' effects

	Liquidity Support		Prudential Meas		Borrower Assist.	
	0	**3**	**0**	**3**	**0**	**3**
Panel A. Complete sample: days with several announcements about domestic policy						
Oil exposure	0.057	−0.085	0.002	0.282	0.124	−0.347
	[0.190]	[0.324]	[0.158]	[0.263]	[0.222]	[0.444]
Public bank	0.675	0.425	−0.696	0.383	−0.010	0.869
	[0.592]	[0.996]	[0.621]	[1.020]	[0.815]	[1.530]
Size	0.136	−0.612	0.513***	0.212	1.665***	0.735
	[0.223]	[0.378]	[0.171]	[0.282]	[0.254]	[0.484]
Constant	1.554***	0.292	0.560***	−0.333	2.108***	1.976***
	[0.224]	[0.377]	[0.205]	[0.334]	[0.210]	[0.419]
Capital ratio	0.206	−0.212	−0.049	−0.541	−0.081	0.092
	[0.233]	[0.402]	[0.206]	[0.344]	[0.295]	[0.657]
Liquidity ratio	−1.002***	−1.684***	−0.492*	−0.403	−0.385	−0.386
	[0.350]	[0.589]	[0.286]	[0.468]	[0.348]	[0.665]
R-squared	0.297	0.506	0.371	0.489	0.451	0.234
Observations	718	707	1,143	1,124	368	357
Panel B. Restricted sample: days with one announcements about domestic policy						
Liquidity ratio	−0.816	−2.101**	0.096	−0.030	−0.274	−0.389
	[0.494]	[1.013]	[0.366]	[0.605]	[0.465]	[0.846]
Oil exposure	−0.398	−1.283**	−0.194	0.347	0.127	0.040
	[0.290]	[0.591]	[0.227]	[0.380]	[0.272]	[0.534]
Size	−0.764*	−1.565*	0.662***	0.630	1.807***	1.090**
	[0.427]	[0.874]	[0.231]	[0.385]	[0.294]	[0.529]
Public bank	1.522**	0.523	−1.041	−1.275	−0.164	−1.224
	[0.740]	[1.508]	[1.033]	[1.705]	[1.356]	[2.409]
Capital ratio	−0.014	1.254	−0.856**	−0.574	0.120	0.254
	[0.445]	[0.910]	[0.336]	[0.558]	[0.346]	[0.758]
Constant	−0.393	0.324	−1.266***	−1.601***	3.476***	3.269***
	[0.405]	[0.830]	[0.262]	[0.431]	[0.321]	[0.614]
Observations	172	171	557	548	270	259
R-squared	0.277	0.385	0.289	0.425	0.341	0.188

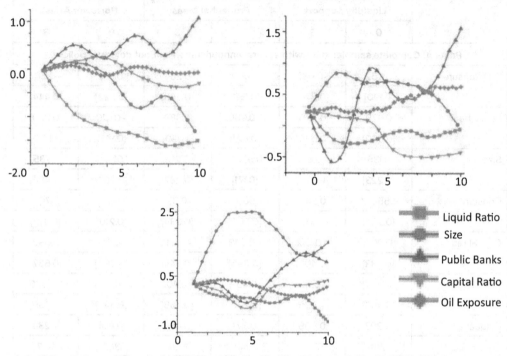

Fig. 15.1 Policy announcement's cross-sectional effects

5. Conclusion

The spread of COVID-19 is a sudden shock that has affected the whole globe, and both the sickness itself and the measures used to combat it such as social isolation and partial or complete lockdowns have had a big effect on the economy. Globally, central banks and governments have tried a wide range of policy initiatives to boost liquidity and promote the flow of credit. The crisis and the countercyclical lending role they are required to perform have pressured banking systems, depending on their characteristics and pre-crisis vulnerabilities throughout each globe to varying degrees.

References

Riadi, S.S., Hadjaat, M. and Yudaruddin, R., 2022. bank concentration and bank stability during the COVID-19 pandemic. Emerging Science Journal, 6, pp. 262–274.

2. Beraich, M. and El Main, S.E., 2022. Volatility Spillover Effects in the Moroccan Interbank Sector before and during the COVID-19 Crisis. Risks, 10(6), p. 125. doi:10.21511/ppm.19(3).20

3. Aizenman, J., Ito, H. and Pasricha, G.K., 2022. Central bank swap arrangements in the covid-19 crisis. Journal of International Money and Finance, 122, p. 102555.

4. Nguyen, M.H., Khuc, Q.V., La, V.P., Le, T.T., Nguyen, Q.L., Jin, R., Nguyen, P.T.

and Vuong, Q.H., 2022. Mindsponge-Based Reasoning of Households' Financial Resilience during the COVID-19 Crisis. Journal of Risk and Financial Management, 15(11), p. 542.

5. Arner, D.W., Avgouleas, E. and Gibson, E.C., 2022. COVID-19, Macroeconomic and Sustainability Shocks, Moral Hazard and Resolution of Systemic Banking Crises: Designing Appropriate Systems of Public Support. European Business Organization Law Review, pp. 1–40.

6. Mohammed, K.U., Fatima, N. and Imran, M., 2022. The moderating role of COVID-19 on determinants of bank spread. Pakistan Social Sciences Review, 6(2), pp. 538–553.

7. Araujo, J.D., Garrido, J., Kopp, E., Varghese, R. and Yao, W., 2022. Policy Options for Supporting and Restructuring Firms Hit by the COVID-19 Crisis. Departmental Papers, 2022(002).

8. Giese, J. and Haldane, A., 2020. COVID-19 and the financial system: a tale of two crises. Oxford Review of Economic Policy, 36(Supplement_1), pp. S200–S214.

9. Muthukumaran, V., Natarajan, R., Kaladevi, A.C. et al. Traffic flow prediction in inland waterways of Assam region using uncertain spatiotemporal correlative features. Acta Geophys. (2022). https://doi.org/10.1007/s11600-022-00875-8

10. Shashi Kant Gupta et al 2022 ECS Trans. 1072927 https://doi.org/10.1149/10701.2927ecst Faster as well as Early Measurements from Big Data Predictive Analytics Model.

Note: The figure and the tables in this chapter were made by the Authors.

Advancements in Business for Integrating Diversity, and Sustainability – Dimitrios A. Karras et al. (eds)
© 2024 Taylor & Francis Group, London, ISBN 978-1-032-70828-7

16

An Analysis of Commercial Bank Customers' Intentions to Utilize Online Banking Services to Identify its Influencing Elements

Veer P. Gangwar[1]
Lovely Professional University, Punjab, India

Mahesh Singh*
Kebri Dehar University, Kebri Dehar, Ethiopia

Amit Mishra[2]
University of Lucknow, UP, India

Iskandar Muda[3]
Faculty Economic and Business,
Universitas Sumatera Utara, Medan, Indonesia

Abstract: Online banking requires e-commerce and e-business because of the global economy. In this modern age, the banking sector's prosperity depends on encouraging customers to use online banking. This survey aims to identify commercial bank customers' intentions to use online banking services. In this research, convenience sampling was used. For data collection, 250 bank customers were requested to participate. The sample size was n = 180 and the response rate was 72%. SPSS 27.0 was used for correlation and hypothesis testing. The research found that "perceived security risk (PSR), perceived usefulness (PU), perceived ease of use (PEU), social influence (SI), and consumer innovativeness (CI)" affect the intention to embrace online banking services. To improve bank customers' willingness to accept general banking services online, the bank management committee should use "PU, PEU, SI, and CI". This report presents numerous important implications for future research and gives bank management committee guidance.

Keywords: online banking services, social influence, perceived ease of use, and perceived security risk

1. Introduction

Online banking is a financial service that enables bank customers to carry out a wide range of online banking tasks, including bill payment, online transfers, account data inquiries, financial investments, currency conversion, simple transaction verification,

*Corresponding author: mahesh300@gmail.com
[1]veer.23954@lpu.co.in, [2]amitmishralko1308@gmail.com, [3]iskandar1@usu.ac.id

DOI: 10.4324/9781032708294-16

and worldwide connection (Xiong et al. (2022)). Online banking relies heavily on e-business, which is the key component of the global economy and a key driver of a nation's economic growth. The development of future banking, business, and financial services sectors in particular depend on this technological advancement (Sihotang et al. (2022)). Rapid technological advancement has given the financial services industry, particularly banking, a new opportunity. This development continuously alters how businesses operate in the cutthroat market. information and communications technology (ICT) include generally one key component of online funding that makes it possible to supply services via the use of technical tools including Credit cards, electronic cards, mobile banking, and automated teller machines (ATMs) (Sambaombe (2022)). In the current web-based technology age, when people prefer utilizing the online for both their everyday and commercial needs, businesses must contend with strong competition. The most recent technological advancement that gives customers instant online access to their financial activities and data is online banking (Arif et al. (2020)). The concept of online banking has various advantageous opportunities for the banking system to meet the needs of the contemporary financial industry by attracting and retaining a fresh set of banking customers from the already-present online user base. Updated financial services have been offered to clients by the banking industry by using online-based technologies in banking procedures (Rahi et al. (2021)). The bank authorities should identify the key influencing elements that would contribute to a level of client acceptance of online banking services. Also, the rising growth of

the online banking business relies on bank customers increased comprehension. The contributing elements that lead to intention among banking consumers need to be studied by financial organizations.

2. Related Works

The purpose of this paper is to identify the variables that commercial bank customers have in their propensity to utilize online banking services (Bramah et al. (2022)). Global economic integration and the development of banking services based on technology is a natural and objective tendency (Shashi et al. (2022)). Online banking is a must for the growth of e-business globally. Examining elements that affect how privately owned commercial banks utilize their online banking services is the paper's main goal ((Hapuarachchi and Samarakoon (2020)). The components of online banking service quality and how they affect client happiness. The research is based on a theoretical model that contains five aspects of online bank service quality and one exogenous variable (Vetrivel et al. (2020)). Because online banking is the fastest-growing banking service, the chapter on consumer confidence in commercial banks must pay particular attention to it. The paper investigates variables impacting online banking trust and calculates its effect in the Baltic republics (Skvarciany et al. (2018)).

3. Methodology

Due to the uncertain number of bank users, a convenience sample approach was adopted in this research, and bank customers with one or more bank accounts were the intended population. The main data set was used in this investigation, which may be seen as an exploratory quantitative study. A web-based survey questionnaire that had been used in earlier research was modified for this one. The questionnaire was delivered via email to the selected bank customers along with a cover letter using a Google form. The users' email addresses were gathered from commercial banks. To understand the responses most completely, the survey questionnaire included explanations of "PSR, PU, PEU, SI, and CI". In the end, 210 answers were given; however, 30 of these had to be rejected because of incorrect or missing data. Thus, an analytical sample made up of 180 respondents was chosen. Thus, n = 180 constitutes the study's sample size. The survey questionnaire included two sections. The one part of the questionnaire is made up of the respondents' demographic data, such as their age in years, sexual orientation, marital status, income, educational background, and frequency of online banking usage. Another part of the questionnaire is made up of study variables, such as "perceived security risk, perceived usefulness, and perceived ease of use, social influence, and degree of consumer innovation".

4. Results and Discussion

Demographic findings: The sample size was 180, and the intended respondents were online bankers from private banks who had one or more bank accounts. Out of 250 online survey questions, 180 were completed, and 180 were determined to be the final sample size a result. Male bank customers made up 53% of the total respondents, while female bank users made up 47%, as seen in Table 16.1 demographic data.

Table 16.1 Demographic information

Description	Frequency	Percentage (%)
Gender		
Men	94	53.3
Women	88	46.9
Income (BDT)		
< 20,000 Taka	36	18.7
20000 - 30,000 Taka	39	20.5
30000 - 40,000 Taka	41	21.9
40000 - 50,000 Taka	44	23.1
> 50,000 Taka	31	15.4
Age		
< 30 years	33	16.5
30 - 40 years	71	38.1
40 - 50 years	45	23.6
Marital Status		
Unmarried	83	45.3
Married	97	55.8
Online banking usage experience		
< 1 month	72	41.3
1 - 6 months	45	26.4
6 - 12 months	54	28.6
> 1 year	5	3.5
Education		
UG	33	20.4
Graduate	84	47.6
PG	40	23.7
Doctorate	16	7.3

Hypotheses testing and regression analysis: The test value for this study was determined to be 1.689, which is considered to be an acceptable value, and a fair value range of 1.5 to 2.5 was discovered in the research in Table 16.2.

Table 16.2 Regression analysis

Independent variables	Sig.	Tolerance	t-value	VIF	β value
PU	0.007**	0.537	3.467	3.233	0.287
CI	0.003**	0.563	3.746	3.413	0.269
PEU	0.009**	0.459	3.155	2.439	0.243
SI	0.000***	0.637	3.543	2.655	0.297
PSR	0.043**	0.343	3.549	2.348	0.273

According to Table 2, the tolerance values were dropped within the allowable range of 0.1-1.0, and the "variance inflation factor (VIF)" values were dropped in the range of 1.00–5.00. This implies that the research model proposed for this study has no multicollinearity problems. Fig. 16.1 and Table 16.2 show the analysis of intention to use online banking channels (IUOBS)

the outcome of the regression coefficient, with an R^2 value of 0.635 accounting for 63 percent of the variation. This reveals that the roughly 63 percent variation in identifying consumers' tendency to utilize online banking channels within the setting of the research has been provided by five independent variables: "PSR, PU, PEU, SI, and CI".

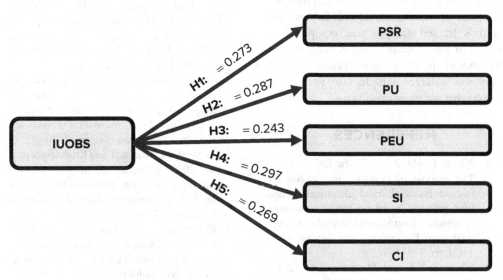

Fig. 16.1 Regression analysis results

Discussion: This paper examines a factor that "PSR, PU, PEU, PEU, SI, and CI" about bank users' purpose to use commercial banks' online net banking services. According to

the paper's findings, people's propensity to use online banking services is statistically influenced by how much security risk they perceive. This outcome agrees with previous study results. Bank customers' behavioral inclination to utilize online banking services is influenced by a perceived security risk.

5. Conclusion

An economy's primary service sector, the banking industry, plays a crucial role in fostering economic progress. Modern technology is used by the financial industry to lower costs, boost efficiency, and minimize competition. However, the users or clients of financial organizations are their most important resources. Future scholars have been provided with several essential future research directions by this work. First off, there are certain limits in this owing to the use of quantitative research; thus, in the future, scholars may turn to qualitative research to get more discoveries and increase the body of literature reviewed. Second, the study's limited sample size compared to others of a comparable kind is likely one of its limitations. As a result, future research may use a larger sample size to provide results that are more explicative.

REFERENCES

1. Xiong, T., Ma, Z., Li, Z. and Dai, J., 2022. The analysis of influence mechanism for internet financial fraud identification and user behavior based on machine learning approaches. International Journal of System Assurance Engineering and Management, 13(3), pp. 996–1007.

2. Sihotang, E.T. and Murdiawati, D., 2022. Acceptance of internet banking services: The role of demographic factors as moderating variables. Jurnal Ekonomi dan Bisnis, 25(1), pp. 153–176.

3. Sambaombe, K., 2022. An analysis of online banking on customer satisfaction in commercial banks based on the TRA model: a case study Stanbic main branch (Doctoral dissertation, The University of Zambia).

4. Arif, I., Aslam, W. and Hwang, Y., 2020. Barriers in the adoption of internet banking: A structural equation modeling-Neural network approach. Technology in Society, 61, p. 101231.

5. Rahi, S., Mansour, M.M.O., Alharafsheh, M. and Alghizzawi, M., 2021. The post-adoption behavior of internet banking users through the eyes of self-determination theory and expectation confirmation model. Journal of Enterprise Information Management.

6. Bramah Hazela et al 2022 ECS Trans. Securing the Confidentiality and Integrity of Cloud Computing Data 107 2651 https://doi.org/10.1149/10701.2651ecst

7. Shashi Kant Gupta et al., 2022 ECS Trans. 1072927 https://doi.org/10.1149/10701.2927ecst

8. Hapuarachchi, C. and Samarakoon, A., 2020. Drivers affecting online banking usage of private commercial banks in Sri Lanka. *Asian Journal of Economics, Business, and Accounting*, pp. 1–10.

9. Vetrivel, S.C., Rajini, J. and Krishnamoorthy, V., 2020. Influence of internet banking service quality on customer satisfaction-an Indian experience. Journal of Critical Reviews, 7(2), pp. 546–551.

10. Skvarciany, V. and Jurevičienė, D., 2018. Factors influencing individual customers' trust in internet banking: Case of Baltic states. *Sustainability, 10*(12), p. 4809.

Note: All the tables and the figure in this chapter were made by the Authors.

Advancements in Business for Integrating Diversity, and Sustainability – Dimitrios A. Karras et al. (eds)
© 2024 Taylor & Francis Group, London, ISBN 978-1-032-70828-7

17

Credit Risk Assessment in Banking Industry Using Optimization Based ML Algorithm

Manoj Kumar Rao[1]

S.B. Jain Institute of Technology, Nagpur, Maharashtra, India

Bhadrappa Haralayya*

Lingaraj Appa Engineering College, Karnataka, India

Amit Mishra[2]

University of Lucknow, UP, India

Iskandar Muda[3]

Universitas Sumatera Utara, Medan, Indonesia

Abstract: Lending cash to individuals who require it is the typical strategic of the banking sector. The depositor banks collect the interest received through chief lender to repay the capital borrowed from them. Credit risk assessment (CRA) is attracting attention in the management of financial risks. For customer dataset' CRA, numerous CRA methodologies are employed. The difficult task that necessitates a thorough consideration of the customer's credit history or the data that the customer has provided is the CRA databases, which determines whether to accept the loan or deny the customer's request. In this article, we present seagull optimized naive Bayes (SONB) algorithm for CRA in banking industry. For this research, German credit dataset is gathered. The proposed SONB's performance is analysed in terms of accuracy, sensitivity, precision, and root mean square error (RMSE), and the suggested SONB approach is contrasted with traditional techniques.

Keywords: Credit risk assessment (CRA), Banking, Machine learning (ML), Seagull optimized naive Bayes (SONB)

1. Introduction

With the help of data, input in the kind of exchanges and observations from the actual world, ML permits computers to operate and study like people do while also enhancing their learning capacity. However, one field is finance and banking (Leo, et al., 2019).

*Corresponding author: bhadrappabhavimani@gmail.com
[1]manojrao6611@gmail.com, [2]amitmishralko1308@gmail.com, [3]iskandar1@usu.ac.id

DOI: 10.4324/9781032708294-17

There is a huge amount of work underway to integrate ML approaches with the banking sector in order to identify defaulters or scams. For proper supervision of financial firms, ML's capacity to spot abnormalities and trends is often used (Pandey, et al., 2022). The CRA of loan borrowers, however, is the focus of this research.

Before classifying borrowers as favorable or unfavorable, the banking sector evaluates the accuracy of the data used to make the determination. Candidates with strong academic records have a greater chance of making good on their promise to return the loan. Applicants with low GPAs are a high risk for the bank because they are unlikely to be able to repay the loan. CRAs use a wide range of strategies to lower the defaulter chance. Sometimes even a minor increase in credit assessment accuracy can significantly mitigate losses. The advantages of using an accurate credit risk data include lower credit scoring costs, quicker decision-making, and reduced risk associated with loan recovery (Jayesh, et al., 2022). Accuracy is crucial in the categorization of credit information to prevent economic loss since CRA plays a major part in the banking industry and is one of the main challenges that banks encounter (Bussmann, et al., 2021). The rise in the defaulter's ratio in the unreliable credit risk data set inspires research in this area.

2. Related Works

The use of various well-known contemporary machine learning algorithms for predicting business failures, such as company bankruptcy, was examined by Chow, J.C., 2018. To estimate the likelihood of a loan default, Addo, et al., 2018 developed binary classifiers depending upon machine learning and deep learning architectures on actual data. A model of CRA that beats the methods presently in use was presented by Moradi, et al., 2019. The approach integrates a fuzzy inference system (FIS) that takes into account credit risk indicators, particularly during economic crises, and a dynamic engine that evaluates the behaviour of problematic clients on a monthly basis. Kou, et al., 2019 review the literature and approaches for measuring and assessing financial systemic risk in conjunction with machine learning algorithms, such as sentiment classification, big data analysis, and network analysis. Ma, et al., 2019 sought to model and analyse actual user data from the network credit framework using machine learning, and they suggested recommendations for the design and prediction of credit risk on the E-banking framework while taking into account all computational capabilities and the need for real-time responses.

3. Methodology

The suggested SONB approach is explained in relation to CRA in this section. Here, the naive Bayes (NB) method's analytical effectiveness is enhanced by the seagull optimization (SO) method.

CRA using SONB: Techniques from NB and SO are incorporated into the suggested method.

NB: The Bayes principle is applied with significant (naive) independence hypotheses in Bayes, a basic probability-based analysis. Based on the Bayes Rule and using equation (1), NB's analysis is done:

$$P(A \mid Y) = \frac{P(A \mid Y)P(A)}{P(Y)} = \frac{P(Y \mid A)(A)}{P(Y)} \quad (1)$$

Here, Y denotes data;

   $A = assumption\ that\ Y\ is\ class\ data$

Assuming that every variable or deciding variable is autonomous (independence), NB can alternatively be described as a classifier using probability concept and the Bayesian principle. This means that the presence of one variable has no consequence on the presence of other features.

SO algorithm: The fundamental idea behind SO is to develop optimization rules by observing seagull populations' migration and foraging patterns. Foraging behavior refers to the activity of the seagull population feeding in their residence, whereas migratory behavior relates to migration of seagull communities through one residence location to another. The SO optimization model is as below, and Fig. 17.1 depicts the procedure of SO method.

Migration process: Three requirements should be met by seagull migration behavior: avoid collisions, travel in the path of the greatest neighbor, and stay near to the greatest search agent.

Preventing collisions: SO uses variable H to modify the seagulls' positions to prevent collisions among seagull populations.

$$\vec{X}_s = H \times \vec{B}_s(d) \qquad (2)$$

Here, $\vec{X}_s$ denotes a new position distinct from other seagulls, $\vec{B}_s$ denotes the seagull's existing position, and H denotes the seagull's travel patterns inside a particular search area.

$$H = l_c - l_c(d/D_{max}) \qquad (3)$$

Here, l_c equals 2, d represents the amount of iterations in progress, and D_{max} equals the maximum amount of iterations.

Moving in the direction of the greatest neighbor: After making sure that no seagulls were going to collide, they all began to move in the path of their greatest neighbors.

$$\vec{N}_s = P \times \left(\vec{B}_{best}(d) - \vec{B}_s(d) \right) \qquad (4)$$

Here, $\vec{N}_s$ shows that the seagulls are migrating to $\vec{B}_{best}$, the seagull which is in the best position. A random number with the potential to examine a balanced procedure is called P.

$$P = 2 \times H^2 \times random \qquad (5)$$

Maintain a relationship with the greatest search agent: Every seagull begins its movement after establishing its path of convergence.

$$\vec{T}_s = \left| \vec{X}_s + \vec{N}_s \right| \qquad (6)$$

A seagull that has moved is represented by in its new location.

Attacking process: As per information obtained through migration behavior, the seagull population engages in foraging behavior. In migration, the seagull population frequently modifies both attack positions and flying rates. To attack prey, seagulls spiral through the air.

$$\begin{cases} xx' = r \times \cos(c) \\ yy' = r \times \sin(c) \\ zz' = r \times c \\ r = u \times e^{cv} \end{cases} \qquad (7)$$

Here, c is the random inclination within $(0, 2\pi)$, u and v are indeed the correlation coefficients of the helix structure, and r is indeed the helix radius that is governed by these variables. The position updating equation for the seagull population was created using the updated seagull position.

$$\vec{B}_s(d) = \left(\vec{T}_s \times xx' \times yy' \times zz' \right) + \vec{B}_{best}(d) \qquad (8)$$

The latest seagull population is located at $\vec{B}_s(d)$.

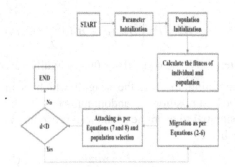

Fig. 17.1 Procedure of SO algorithm

4. Results and Discussion

The accuracy, precision, RMSE, and sensitivity of the suggested SONB's performance are assessed in this section. Additionally, the suggested SONB is contrasted with other methods currently in use, including the decision tree (DT), support vector machine (SVM), and adaptive neuro-fuzzy inference system (ANFIS). The Python software is used to perform this research. The suggested SONB method's effectiveness is examined using a German credit sample. The data was gathered from the UCI repository (Pandey, et al., 2017). The dataset has 2 classes that represent the creditors who the loans are granted and not granted, respectively. These classes are labelled "desirable" and "undesirable." 1000 instances and 20 characteristics comprise this dataset.

Findings for accuracy and precision for both suggested and traditional technologies are shown in Fig. 17.2. The percentage of samples for which the suggested SONB correctly predicted outcomes is presented as the effectiveness of the system. The degree to which the suggested approach only chooses the most crucial facts for additional analysis is referred to as precision. By dividing the total true positives by the total true and false positives, precision is calculated. The suggested technique, compared to existing techniques [ANFIS (accuracy = 95.69%; precision = 93.12%), SVM (accuracy = 97.15%; precision = 96.7%), and DT (accuracy = 96.05%; precision = 95.3%), provides the highest effectiveness in accuracy (99.81%) and precision (98.33%).

The outcome of sensitivity for both existing and suggested approaches is shown in Fig. 17.3. The ability of the suggested model to recognise each significant sample in a data collection is known as sensitivity. It is determined statistically by dividing the percentage of true positives by the total of true positives and false negatives. This figure shows that the proposed SONB technique has a higher level of sensitivity (98.96%) than existing techniques [ANFIS (sensitivity = 96.42%), SVM (sensitivity = 96.98%), and DT (sensitivity = 93.11%)].

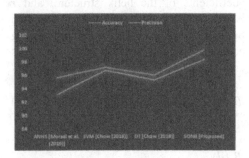

Fig. 17.2 Accuracy and precision outcomes

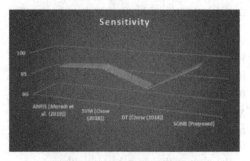

Fig. 17.3 Sensitivity outcome

Fig. 17.4 depicts the result of RMSE for both proposed and existing methods. RMSE illustrates the degree to which estimations deviate from actual measurements. The recommended SONB technique exceeds existing techniques [ANFIS (RMSE = 2.55), SVM (RMSE = 1.12), and DT (RMSE = 2.31] in rates of RMSE (1.002).

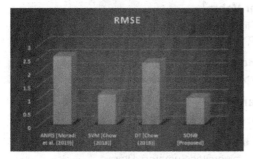

Fig. 17.4 RMSE outcome

5. Conclusion

This study looked into CRA in the banking industry using the SONB technique. For this study, the German credit dataset was compiled. The empirical results revealed that the suggested SONB approach had the maximum efficiency when compared to other methods in terms of accuracy (99.81%), precision (98.33%), sensitivity (98.96%), and RMSE (1.002). We solely use the German credit dataset in this investigation. However, if we go on and use more datasets, the CRA performance of our suggested method will be 100%.

REFERENCES

1. Leo, M., Sharma, S. and Maddulety, K., 2019. Machine learning in banking risk management: A literature review. Risks, 7(1), p. 29.

2. Pandey, A.K., Singh, R.K., Jayesh, G.S., Khare, N. and Gupta, S.K., 2022. Examining the Role of Enterprise Resource Planning (ERP) in Improving Business Operations in Companies. ECS Transactions, 107(1), p. 2681.

3. Jayesh, G.S., Novaliendry, D., Gupta, S.K., Sharma, A.K. and Hazela, B., 2022. A Comprehensive Analysis of Technologies for Accounting and Finance in Manufacturing Firms. ECS Transactions, 107(1), p. 2715.

4. Bussmann, N., Giudici, P., Marinelli, D. and Papenbrock, J., 2021. Explainable machine learning in credit risk management. Computational Economics, 57(1), pp. 203–216.

5. Chow, J.C., 2018. Analysis of financial credit risk using machine learning. arXiv preprint arXiv:1802.05326.

6. Addo, P.M., Guegan, D. and Hassani, B., 2018. Credit risk analysis using machine and deep learning models. Risks, 6(2), p. 38.

7. Moradi, S. and Mokhatab Rafiei, F., 2019. A dynamic credit risk assessment model with data mining techniques: evidence from Iranian banks. Financial Innovation, 5(1), pp. 1–27.

8. Kou, G., Chao, X., Peng, Y., Alsaadi, F.E. and Herrera-Viedma, E., 2019. Machine learning methods for systemic risk analysis in financial sectors. Technological and Economic Development of Economy, 25(5), pp. 716–742.

9. Ma, X. and Lv, S., 2019. Financial credit risk prediction in internet finance driven by machine learning. Neural Computing and Applications, 31(12), pp. 8359–8367.

10. Pandey, T.N., Jagadev, A.K., Mohapatra, S.K. and Dehuri, S., 2017, August. Credit risk analysis using machine learning classifiers. In 2017 International Conference on Energy, Communication, Data Analytics and Soft Computing (ICECDS) (pp. 1850–1854). IEEE.

Advancements in Business for Integrating Diversity, and
Sustainability – Dimitrios A. Karras et al. (eds)
© 2024 Taylor & Francis Group, London, ISBN 978-1-032-70828-7

Analysis of the Integration of Digital Marketing and the Business Strategy of the Organization

Sunil Kumar Vohra[1]

Amity Institute of Travel and Tourism, Amity University,
Noida, UP, India

Bhadrappa Haralayya*

Lingaraj Appa Engineering College, Karnataka, India

Veer P. Gangwar

Lovely Professional University, Punjab, India

Iskandar Muda

Faculty Economic and Business, Universitas Sumatera Utara,
Medan, Indonesia

Abstract: This research examined digital marketing's influence on corporate strategy formulation. This applied research used a survey to gather data and was correlational, examining the impacts of numerous factors. Random sampling chose 272 marketing and IT managers from SMEs in Tehran, Iran. The Digital Marketing Questionnaire collected data. Validity of the Business Strategy Scale was assessed. "Cronbach's alpha coefficient" (α) and "composite reliability" (CR) were also computed. As surveys were completed and returned, the data were analysed using SPSS (version 22) descriptive statistics and Smart PLS inferential statistics and structural equation modelling (SEM). All study hypotheses that assessed the variables' substantial impacts on each other were supported. The research findings may help company managers and strategy practitioners understand how DM affects BS creation.

Keywords: Digital marketing, Cost leadership strategy formation, Differentiation strategy formation

1. Introduction

The fast development of "Information and Communication Technologies" (ICT) in both the commercial and public sectors in recent years has resulted in the establishment of a new environment for digital marketing (DM) (Miklosik et al. 2019). As a natural

*Corresponding author: bhadrappabhavimani@gmail.com

[1]sunilvohra2002@yahoo.co.in, [2]veer.23954@lpu.co.in, [3]iskandar1@usu.ac.id

DOI: 10.4324/9781032708294-18

reaction by businesses, this sort of marketing emerged for further management and promotion in response to the rising usage of the internet by customers. This was done in an effort to attract more customers. As a component of their marketing strategies and deployment plans, various organizations, such as entities ranging from corporations to hospitals to schools to councils to professional groups and even non-governmental organizations (NGOs), are currently putting DM into practice. These organizations include councils, professional associations, and schools. Even if some businesses are able to initiate their very own platforms for conducting electronic commerce (e-commerce), the vast majority of companies use the internet as a conduit or medium as part of their corporate communication plans (Miklosik et al. 2019). Consumers' usage of digital media platforms has grown rapidly in the last decade. Companies use DM to reach target audiences. Since 2010, internet users have risen past two billion and are expected to grow yearly. Due to fast-paced competition and changing expectations, DM has become essential for promoting new goods and services. DM involves delivering electronic messages to prospective consumers online (Nuseir et al. 2020). Due to rising competition, digital technologies have changed the operational operations of firms, notably communication and information exchange. Such technologies and applications are seen to be the best way to start early consumer connection (Yoga et al. 2019). In this setting, there is limited research on the link between DM and business strategy (BS), hence this study investigated the interrelationships. A firm is a value chain that combines manufacturing, marketing, sales, and service with HRM, R&D, and information technology. This research examined DM and BS's connections (Ashish et al. 2022).

2. Related Works

The time in which digital marketing is employed impacts the choice of DM tools, how its success is monitored, and managers' impression of its cost-effectiveness. (Melović et al. 2020) studied digital marketing was most successful when it was done via social networks, and Google Analytics was the most prevalent tool for analysing the effects of digital marketing. The more a firm depends on DM, the more it impacts promotion and brand positioning. (Saura et al. 2019) offered a study to identify significant participants in the business environment about innovative business models and DM tactics used to them to boost corporate advantages. Their paper defines the key players of the "electronic commerce", ecosystem, their typologies, and the primary DM strategies utilized in this industry. The exploratory study's findings may be utilized for future research and to strengthen the bibliography in that topic. Internet marketing methods disrupted the corporate landscape. We examine these difficulties from the perspectives of explorers, analysts, reduced defender, and distinguished defenders. (Olson et al. 2021) showed marketing managers how organizations with different strategies address digital marketing difficulties to help them execute their firm's plan efficiently and effectively. Digital transformation is driving digital marketing via technical breakthroughs and evolving client needs. (Peter et al. 2021) aims to bridge the knowledge gap and give SMEs with a literature-based overview of the most essential DM tools in order to exploit digital technology in marketing and shorten the distance to LE. Nineteen related articles were found. Digital business is transforming people's business behaviour. That explains why customers buy business technology. (Hamdani et al. 2022) analysed an applied hypothesis that digital promotion and marketing processes impact customer purchase choices in the fashion sector, particularly shoes. Influence was 56.0%. This study helps businesses increase marketing success by using technology as a promotion or sales technique. Digital marketing reaches a bigger clientele and is more flexible in time and location. Social media is becoming a regular component of millennials' digital lives. (Piranda et al. 2022) explained how to utilize Facebook marketplaces as a digital marketing tool. This library-based study is descriptive. According to the results, Facebook's social media has comprehensive functionality since users may interact, post videos, form a group or association, and more. Facebook marketplace is also a popular digital marketing platform for buying and selling. FB marketplace may be used as a DM tool via advertising, sales promotions, individual sale posting, and aesthetically appealing packaging.

3. Methodology

The current research studied DM's impact on BS in small and medium-sized enterprises (SMEs), as shown in Fig 18.1. In this study, which was a cross-sectional investigation using a quantitative design, all of the variables were investigated using a questionnaire that had a Likert-type scale with a point value ranging from one to five in order to determine how they were

related to one another within the research framework.

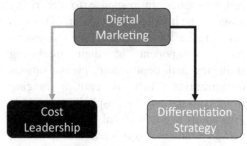

Fig. 18.1 Research model

The questionnaire that was recruited here was divided into four sections; the first one dealt with the participants' demographic data, while the next three parts concentrated on DM and BS respectively.

In order to do this, a standardised Digital Marketing Questionnaire consisting of six questions and a Business Strategy Questionnaire including eight questions were given to the respondents. On the basis of the data that had been obtained, the Smart PLS software was used to conduct an analysis of the data using the measuring model and the structural equation modelling (SEM).

4. Findings

The interrelationships between the study components were investigated using both structural equation modelling and the data that was obtained. The results of the reliability test were provided in the following manner after the first investigation was carried out using the partial least squares (PLS) regression technique.

Table 18.1 Evaluation Scale ((Reliability test)

Variables	Cronbach's alpha coefficient (α)	AVE	CR
DF	0.704	0.501	0.778
DM	0.871	0.611	0.903
CL	0.845	0.685	0.896

The values for, CR, and AVE are shown in Table 18.1. For this particular line, the value should not be lost more than 0.7, and CR should be greater than 0.7. while the AVE value should be more than 0.5 in order for the data collecting instrument to be recognised as being statistically reliable. In this case, the statistically acceptable results demonstrated the construct's validity and dependability.

The discriminant validity index, which demonstrates the extent of the association between the variables, is shown in Table 18.2. It is strongly suggested that the value of the square root of the AVE be higher than the correlation value with the various other factors. Due to this fact, the square root of the AVE may be found written in italics at the very top of the table. This suggests that the first value in each column is higher than the values that continue to satisfy the discriminant validity criteria.

Table 18.2 Evaluation Scale (Discriminant validity)

Variables	CL	DM	DF
DF	0.562	0.593	0.707
DM	-	0.781	-
CL	0.827	0.379	-

SEM

We investigated and analysed the interrelationships between the various suggested model constructs. After then, the data that had been obtained were put through the bootstrap technique of analysis.

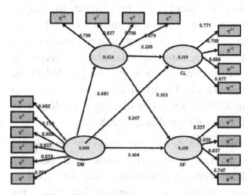

Fig. 18.2 Measurement model

5. Discussion and Conclusion

In this research, the interrelationships between DM as well as their influence on BS were explored. If the research hypotheses are shown to be correct, the findings of this study may be of use to corporate executives and strategy practitioners in determining the interrelationships between the organizational capabilities, namely DM, and the influence those capabilities have on BS development. The outcomes of the research analyzed that there is a substantial positive association between DM strategy development and CL strategy creation. According to this point of view, the CL approach required organisational characteristics to achieve efficiency and productivity, which included optimality in terms of both time and cost, in addition to flexibility. In addition, a strong and favourable association was shown to exist between the development of DM and DF strategies. The conclusions of the research might be stated as follows: the given system has the potential to play a leading role in the development of marketing strategies. Additionally, the study discovered that the flow of operational information and resources may be subject to change once things become more capable and connected. As a direct consequence of this, the interactions that take place between the two business models will be molded at the micro level. The implications of the "Internet of Things" on various business models were investigated in this research.

The findings of the research revealed a considerable positive association between DM strategy formulation and DF level of critical thinking, calling into question the role that BS plays in achieving a competitive advantage. As a result, the conclusion that was reached was that Digital Marketing as an effective tool might enable a company to enhance its profits, perform better on the market, and sometimes even increase the competitive edge that its firm had. In addition, the components of the Internet of Things may play three distinct functions throughout the integration of goods or services. This differentiation in roles was thus essential in order to comprehend how the IoT may alter everything for the purpose of accomplishing certain business growth objectives that are monitored by a corporation.

Despite the fact that this research presented a significant number of implications for the advancement of multidimensional measurement. In this regard, it is suggested that the marketing and IT managers of the SMEs operating in the city of Tehran, Iran, should take action by forming DM values, and then the process of amassing, going through, and evaluating information about their surroundings, competitors, customers, and suppliers, as well as a variety of industry trends and expected patterns of behaviour for market and environmental components in the future. In this regard, the city of Tehran is located in Iran.

In conclusion, it is advised to boost the motivation of workers who are active in the marketing and sales departments in order to assist them in the production of original and innovative ideas that will distinguish their goods and services. Because all of the information for this study came from "Small and Medium-sized Enterprises" (SMEs) that were functioning in the city of Tehran in Iran, it is strongly advised that academics and researchers proceed with caution when attempting to generalise the results.

REFERENCE

1. Miklosik, A., Kuchta, M., Evans, N., & Zak, S. (2019). Towards the adoption of machine learning-based analytical tools in digital marketing. Ieee Access, 7, 85705–85718.

2. Nuseir, M. T., & Aljumah, A. (2020). The role of digital marketing in business performance with the moderating effect of environment factors among SMEs of UAE. International Journal of Innovation, Creativity and Change, 11(3), 310–324.

3. Yoga, I. M. S., Korry, N. P. D. P., & Yulianti, N. M. D. R. (2019). Information technology adoption on digital marketing communication channel. International journal of social sciences and humanities, 3(2), 95–104.

4. Ashish Kumar Pandey et al 2022 ECS Trans. 107 2681 Examining the Role of Enterprise Resource Planning (ERP) in Improving Business Operations in Companies https://doi.org/10.1149/10701.2681ecst

5. Melović, Boban, Mijat Jocović, Marina Dabić, Tamara Backović Vulić, and Branislav Dudic. "The impact of digital transformation and digital marketing on the brand promotion, positioning and electronic business in Montenegro." *Technology in Society* 63(2020): 101425.

6. Saura, Jose Ramon, Pedro R. Palos-Sanchez, and Marisol B. Correia. "Digital marketing strategies based on the e-business model: Literature review and future directions." *Organizational transformation and managing innovation in the fourth industrial revolution* (2019): 86–103.

7. Olson, Eric M., Kai M. Olson, Andrew J. Czaplewski, and Thomas Martin Key. "Business strategy and the management of digital marketing." *Business horizons* 64, no. 2 (2021): 285–293.

8. Peter, Marc K., and Martina Dalla Vecchia. "The digital marketing toolkit: a literature review for the identification of digital marketing channels and platforms." *New trends in business information systems and technology* (2021): 251–265.

9. Hamdani, Nizar Alam, Rio Muladi, and Galih Abdul Fatah Maulani. "Digital Marketing Impact on Consumer Decision-Making Process." In *6th Global Conference on Business, Management, and Entrepreneurship (GCBME 2021)*, pp. 153–158. Atlantis Press, 2022.

10. Piranda, Dea Resti, Dessy Zulfianti Sinaga, and Erga Eka Putri. "Online Marketing Strategy In Facebook Marketplace As A Digital Marketing Tool." *Journal of Humanities, Social Sciences and Business (JHSSB)* 1, no. 3 (2022): 1–8.

Note: All the figures and tables in this chapter were made by the Authors.

*Advancements in Business for Integrating Diversity, and
Sustainability* – Dimitrios A. Karras et al. (eds)
© 2024 Taylor & Francis Group, London, ISBN 978-1-032-70828-7

19 Green HR Techniques: A Sustainable Strategy to Boost Employee Engagement

Navaneetha Krishnan Rajagopal*
University of Technology and Applied Sciences,
Salalah, Oman

L. Anitha[1]
Saveetha Engineering College (Autonomous),
Thandalam, Chennai, India

Pooja Nagpal[2]
International School of Management ISME,
Bangalore, Karnataka, India

G. Jitendra[3]
KL Business School, Koneru Lakshmaiah Education Foundation,
Vaddeswaram, Andhra Pradesh, India

Abstract: The sustainable consumption practises of consumers have an influence on the growth of society. Customers' pro-environment behaviour ensures the environment grows sustainably, which helps society economically. This research makes a noteworthy addition to the process of moving toward sustainability by empirically evaluating the mediating role played by employee engagement in green activities among green HRT practises and personalized green behaviour. The conventional idea of person-organization-fit was used in this study to evaluate the influence that specific personality types play in altering the correlations between HRT practices and organizational support for environmental efforts. 366 staff members of five and six hotels running in Qatar were contacted using a qualitative methodology and a suitable sampling strategy. The study's original data shows that staff involvement somewhat mediate the relationship between environmentally friendly HRT practises and personal environmental behaviours. This research also emphasises the value of employee engagement in encouraging motivation in environmental projects.

Keywords: Green HRT, Employee engagement, Individual green behavior, Environmental sustainability

*Corresponding author: bba_rnk@yahoo.co.in
[1]anithal@saveetha.ac.in, [2]pooja.nagpaal@gmail.com, [3]gjk.jitendra@gmail.com

DOI: 10.4324/9781032708294-19

1. Introduction

Organizations are now under intense social, legal, ethical, and ecological pressure to quickly join the environmental-sustainability bandwagon. Because of worries about climate change, the depletion of environmental assets, and environmental preservation, corporate pressure on companies to act swiftly to implement the necessary adaptations of environment protection systems and practises. (Chung (2020)). An organization's human resources division should be equipped to contribute significantly to the development of a sustainable culture. Many authors have said that their HR, particularly in the area of HRT, must be of high calibre in order for management innovations and strategic tools to be effective (Han et al. (2019)). To encourage sustainable practices and boost employee engagement and responsiveness to sustainability issues, green HRT refers to utilizing every employee. Utilizing each employee to promote the sustainable application and boosting employee responsiveness and dedication to sustainability issues is referred to as green HRT (Grobelna (2019)). Corporate social responsibility and sustainability are causing organizations more and more anxiety. A sustainability plan may be developed and implemented with the help of the HR department. To create corporate values and sustainability strategies, the HR department might serve as a coworker in defining what is required or what is feasible. Organizations' human resources divisions have the potential to influence how their company's sustainability culture is designed (Wu et al. (2018)). Green management is the process through which businesses create environmental management plans

to control their impact on the environment. This idea becomes a strategic priority for companies, especially multinational ones that do business abroad (Tang et al. (2018)). In conclusion, in term of green management is the management of an organization's interactions with the environment and its effects on it. It must now include theoretical concepts like pollution control, green purchasing, and social responsibility for businesses since it must go beyond just meeting statutory criteria.

2. Related Works

Mostly in past, an organization's monetary efficiency was likely to assure success in corporate for the corporation and its shareholders. However, this is not the case; instead, financial and economic outcomes must be accompanied by improved attention to social and environmental factors as well as the reduction of environmental footprints Ali et al. (2021)). Therefore, corporate environmentalism, also known as green management, became a new strategic issue in the 1990s, and it also became a catchphrase in the 2000s all over the world (Bramah et al. (2022)). Utilizing new technology might help the environment by, for instance, creating biotech goods and looking for alternate sources of energy to lessen the usage of scarce natural resources (Shahand Soomro (2022)). To reduce the effects of environmental degradation by developing goods that are safe and cause less pollution to the environment, corporations should invest more time and energy in the development of new technologies (Jayesh et al. (2022)). Many scholars, mostly in the field of HRT, argued that the usefulness and effectiveness of any organization's innovation and strategy initiatives depend on the availability and aptitude of its HR when used in strategic ways (Darban et al. (2022)).

3. Methodology

It takes genuine contributions from all corporate domains and sectors to achieve the ultimate sustainability goals. As a result, it makes sense for the hotel sector to consider environmental challenges. This study's goal is to investigate the suggested conceptual model's effects on workers who are knowledgeable about environmental management ideas and practices and who have experience using them. As a result, participants working in IV- and V-star hotels were specifically targeted using a quantitative research approach with useful sampling. As a result, the use of intentional sampling facilitates the main goal of focusing on individuals who match the environmental quality criteria.

Participants and procedures: According to the 71 four-five-star hotels, all 71 websites were personally checked and only 21 communicated their environmental commitment. Each hotel's HR manager was contacted, and a letter inviting them to participate in the research was sent to them, stressing their involvement, and ensuring information confidentiality. Eight managers invited their employees to participate in the research. The rate of response was 24.1%, with 366 usable surveys. Table 19.1 shows the research sample's demographics.

Table 19.1 Demographic characteristics

		Sample (N)	Sample (%)
Gender	Male	162	49
	Female	215	59.7
Department	Housekeeping	119	33.5
	Food and beverage	39	7.7
	Sales and marketing	21	4.1
	Front desk	132	33.7
	Human resources	41	8.6
	Maintenance	10	3.9
	Others	21	4.4
	Missing	45	12
Tenure	<3 years	80	21
	4-10 years	132	33.7
	11-20 years	112	31
	>20 years	91	26.6
	Missing	3	6
Age	18-27 Years	62	36.7
	28-37 Years	96	29.5
	38-45 Years	132	5.2
	>45 Years	112	41.6
	Missing	21	5.6

4. Results and Discussion

Hypotheses testing:

The direct and mediation effects: Employee involvement in environmental efforts is a channel via which P1 and P2 represent direct and indirect correlations between environment conscious HRT and eco sustainable behavior displayed by workers. According to the present study's suggested model, there were substantial direct impacts of green HRT on employee green behavior,

green HRT on Employer Support of Environmental Initiatives, and the impact of employee green behavior on environmental objectives.

The influence of personality traits in moderation: The hypotheses (H3a, b, and c) claimed that the conscientiousness, positive effect, and proactive personality traits given in table 19.2 would function as moderators of the connection among green HRT and employee involvement with environmental activities.

Table 19.2 Utilizing path analysis to test hypotheses

	β values	Level of significance	R^2
H3a:			0.36
Green HRT Engagement	0.41	0.006***	
Positive affect Engagement	0.12	0.08**	
Green HRT × Positive affect	0.10	0.06**	
H3b:			
Green HRT × Engagement	0.34	0.007***	
Proactive personality Engagement	−0.06	0.13*	
H3c: Green HRT × Proactive personality	0.09	0.11*	
H3c:			
Green HRT Engagement	0.39	0.006***	
Conscientiousness Engagement	0.41	0.001***	
Green HRT Conscientiousness	0.21	0.08**	

Figure 19.1 demonstrates that when the level of perfectionism was high, the effect of environmentally sustainable HRT on employee satisfaction was substantially larger than when the level was low. Similarly to this, when the positive affect was high, green HRT had a higher impact on employee support for environmental measures, and it had a smaller impact when the positive affect was low. Discussion: As a result of the growing interest in HRT behavioral literature,

in this research, an attempt is made to fill in the knowledge vacuum about the underlying psychological processes that support how organizational structures and practices might influence employee green behavior. According to the present research, there is a mediator among green HRT practices and employee green behavior: employee involvement in environmental efforts. It was also suggested that certain personality traits may alter the intensity of this connection.

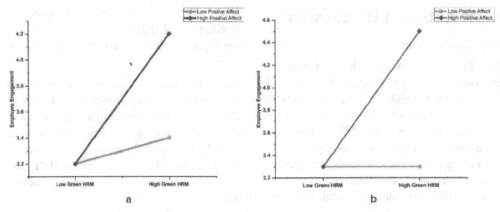

Fig. 19.1 Consciousness and good emotion act as moderators

5. Conclusion

Finally, the use of a variety of models that take into account an increased number of underlying processes would provide a more comprehensive perspective and expand our understanding of the factors that go into the selection of environmentally friendly activities. This is because employee environmental behavior is complicated. The moderating impact of style of leadership on the relationship between green HRT employees and organisational support for environmental activities is one particular example of a likely mechanism. The utility of this report will rise if, in the future, its findings can be applied to additional market segments.

REFERENCES

1. Chung, K.C. 2020. Green Marketing Orientation: Achieving Sustainable Development in Green Hotel Management. Journal of Hospitality Marketing & Management 29 (6): 717–722

2. Han, H., J. Yu, J.-S. Lee, and W. Kim. 2019. Impact of Hotels' Sustainability Practices on Guest Attitudinal Loyalty: Application of Loyalty Chain Stages Theory. Journal of Hospitality Marketing & Management 28 (8): 905–921.

3. Grobelna, A. 2019. Effects of Individual and Job Characteristics on Hotel Contact Employees' Work Engagement and Their Performance Outcomes: A Case Study from Poland. International Journal of Contemporary Hospitality Management 31 (1): 349–369.

4. Wu, H.-C., C.-C. Cheng, and C.-H. Ai. 2018. An Empirical Analysis of Green Switching Intentions in the Airline Industry. Journal of Environmental Planning and Management 61 (8): 1438–1468.

5. Tang, G., Y. Chen, Y. Jiang, P. Paille, and J. Jia. 2018. Green Human Resource Management Practices: Scale Development and Validity. Asia Pacific Journal of Human Resources 56 (1): 31–55.

6. Ali Ababneh, O.M., Awwad, A.S. and Abu-Haija, A., 2021. The association between green human resources practices and employee engagement with environmental initiatives in hotels: The moderation effect of perceived transformational leadership. Journal of Human Resources in Hospitality & Tourism, 20(3), pp. 390–416.

7. Bramah Hazela et al 2022 ECS Trans. Securing the Confidentiality and Integrity of Cloud Computing Data 107 2651 https://doi.org/10.1149/10701.2651ecst

8. Shah, N. and Soomro, B.A., 2022. Effects of green human resource management practices on green innovation and behavior. Management Decision, (ahead-of-print).

9. G. S. Jayesh et al 2022 ECS Trans. 107 2715 A Comprehensive Analysis of Technologies for Accounting and Finance in Manufacturing Firms https://doi.org/10.1149/10701.2715ecst

10. Darban, G., Karatepe, O.M. and Rezapouraghdam, H., 2022. Does work engagement mediate the impact of green human resource management on absenteeism and green recovery performance? Employee Relations: The International Journal.

Note: All the tables and the figure in this chapter were made by the Authors.

Advancements in Business for Integrating Diversity, and Sustainability – Dimitrios A. Karras et al. (eds)
© 2024 Taylor & Francis Group, London, ISBN 978-1-032-70828-7

20 Work Satisfaction and Green HRM Mediate the Effect of Corporate Ecological Culture on Employee Performance

B. Sakthimala*, G. Deepalakshmi[1]

Marudhar Kesari Jain College for Women,
Vaniyambadi, Tamil Nadu, India

Abstract: Work satisfaction and green human resource management (GHRM) have seldom been investigated. Green human capital's mediation role is also overlooked in the study. This study extends the ability-motivation-opportunity (AMO) hypothesis in order to analyse the until unnoticed indirect and direct effects of GHRM on dairy enterprises. In 287 self-administered questionnaires, convenience sampling was used. The structural and measurement model was analysed by Smart Partial Least Square (Smart-PLS) (3.2.9). The results demonstrate that green training and recruiting increase business commitment. Green human capital (GHC) influences organisational commitment through green hiring, selection, training, and development. According to this study, GHRM practises are essential for putting into practise an environmental strategy that encourages green workplace practises. The research helps managers and policymakers improve workplace environmental culture and employee green behaviour.

Keywords: Green human resource management (GHRM), Work satisfaction, Ability-motivation-opportunity, Employee performances, Environmental culture

1. Introduction

As part of green management, every facet of a company must be made environmentally friendly, including its operations, human resources, accounting and finance, retailing, and marketing. In each and every one of these functional areas, employees are included under the corresponding term. Empower will increase if these workers are given a voice in the decisions that affect them and are actively encouraged to contribute to the process of resolving issues and finding solutions. Green human resource management involves a broad variety of practises, one of which is "green

---
*Corresponding author: sakthi.lbk@gmail.com
[1]deepasenthil1979@yahoo.com

DOI: 10.4324/9781032708294-20

employee empowerment," which is the practise of giving workers the freedom to participate in environmentally responsible activities at their place of employment (Chen et al., 2022). People are "as fundamental to the running of a business as neurons are to the functioning of the brain," and this significance is only growing, making greening HR and empowering green employees increasingly crucial. People as fundamental to the running of a business as neurons are to the functioning of the brain (Rajagopal et al., 2022). Green human resources are characterised by their emphasis on preserving the natural environment as well as the company's intellectual property. In order to provide this information asset the attention it requires and eventually achieve organisational wellness, green employee empowerment across all of these pillars is required.

Many organisations are coming to the realisation that ecological dedication and a fresh approach to environmental management are necessary for their continued existence. Today's organisations need to strike a balance between their environmental impact and their financial success. Therefore, in order for businesses to attain sustainability, they need to examine the consequences they have on the environment. The human influence on climate change must be acknowledged, and the success of the corporate sustainability strategy is contingent on employees' green habits in the workplace that are congruent with the organization's green aims. Research on the micro and macro factors that determine work green practises has risen in recent years as a result of the positive impact it has had on the long-term viability of businesses (Pandey et al.,

2022). These behaviours are beneficial to society because they slow the progression of climate change. The purpose of this study was to attempt to explain the influence that a corporate ecological culture has on employee performance by using GHRM and job satisfaction as mediators in the relationship.

2. Related Works

Gila, et al., 2019 analysed on data collected from colleges and universities, looks at that green HRM practises affect organisational effectiveness in terms of environmental sustainability. Úbeda-García, et al., 2021 analyzed expands connections between Corporate Social Responsibility and HRM, two emerging fields of study in the field of management GHRM. Awan, et al., 2022 evaluated SMEs' environmental performance using GHRM, green transformational leadership (GTFL), and green innovation (GI). Pham, et al., 2020 examined the AMO hypothesis to examine GHRM practises' direct, indirect, and interaction effects. Amjad et al., 2021 examined how training and development, performance assessment, and incentive and pay affect organisational sustainability via environmental and employee performance.

3. Research Methodology

It was suggested that study be carried out making use of an explanation framework in order to gain a better understanding of the ways in which the various components interact with one another. In keeping with idealism, researchers have also made use of deductive reasoning in order to construct a research model and testable hypotheses.

Data sample:

There were 77% men and 21% females in the whole sample. Importantly, 37.6% of the research participants were under the age of 3029, while 10.7% were above the age of 45. Additionally, those between the ages of 40 and 50 made up 34.1% of the total. When broken down by function, 25.6% of those surveyed worked in human resources and were involved in sustainability initiatives. Research has also made use of deductive approach in line with idealist to create a study design and verifiable hypotheses.

Research hypothesis:

H1: Relationships between green HRM and corporate ecological culture are expected to improve.

H2: An organization's hard work will increase in tandem with the use of GHRM.

H3: Human resources that is invested in environmentally friendly practices can boost employee loyalty.

H4: Relationship between GHRM and work engagement is influenced by corporate ecological culture.

Table 20.1 Workforce characteristics of the dataset

Demographic variable	Characteristic	Frequency	Percentage (%)
Gender	Men	223	74
	Women	62	22
	Total	282	97
Age	Under 35	30	10.8
	35-45	105	35.7
	45-55	97	33.2
	Above 55	47	15.4
	Total	286	98
Unit	Funding	48	16.2
	Concerning matters of public safety, security, and the environment	28	9.3
	HRM	73	24.7
	Selling a product	37	13.2
	QEC	31	10.2
	Other	62	21.1
	Total	286	95
Work experience	Less than 1	26	8.39
	1-4	35	11.3
	5-7	74	25.3
	8-15	53	17.6
	Above 15	92	327
	Total	286	97

4. Results and Discussion

The Smart PLS 3.2.9 statistical program was used to perform PLS-SEM tests. As "co-variance based structural modelling (CB-SEM)" necessitates based on averages data, "PLS-SEM"" was used instead. "PLS-SEM", on the other hand, does not presuppose anything about the form of the data. Therefore, the PLS-SEM method has been selected so that the overall findings are not skewed by extremes.

SME-Hypothesis Experiment: The suggested model's "correlations, confidence intervals, t-qualities, and data suggests" were determined by a bootstrapping procedure of 4000 iterations (p). After a complete examination of the model's fitness has been conducted, a path analysis is necessary. At this stage, we investigate and establish the links between the constructions we're studying. The findings show that GHRM procedures have had both immediate and long-term effects on employee dedication within processing industry.

Direct effect: Throughout the course of this research, we came to the conclusion that GHRM practises have a statistically significant correlation with GHC "($\beta = 0.374$, $t = 7.32$)". There is a significant positive relationship between GHRM and devotion to the organisation "($\beta = 0.332$, $t = 5.82$)". The GHC has a significant and beneficial influence on identification and involvement "($\beta = 0.416$, $t = 6.65$)" (see Table 20.2).

Table 20.2 Path hypothesis correlation

Hypotheses		P	Status	Beta	t
H1	GHRM GHC	0.00	Supported	0.374	7.32
H2	GHRM work organization	0.00	Supported	0.332	5.82
H3	GHC	0.00	Supported	0.416	6.65
Hypotheses		Total effect	Indirect effort	Status	VAF
H4	GHRM GHC work organization	0.485	0.155	Supported	32%

Indirect effect (Mediating effect): The "variance account factor (VAF)" medol was utilised to investigate the mediating effect. This method involved determining the ratio of the mediated influence to the total effect. The computed result of 32% pointed toward the possibility of partial mediation (Fig. 20.1).

Discussion: GHRM was found to significantly increase organisational dedication "($\beta = 0.333$, P = 0.0001)". The result suggested that HRM that emphasises environmental sustainability might boost employee loyalty. The results show that GHC is positively affected by GHRM "($\beta = 0.374$ and P = 0.000)". According to this research, GHRM is a potent predictor of GHC (Piwowar-Sulej. K, (2022)). The findings of this research are consistent with the theory underlying the concept. The next step that this investigation takes is to test a hypothesis regarding the connection that exists between environmentally conscientious human capital and organisational dedication. This research found that "($\beta = 0.416$, P = 0.000)"; see also GHC and Organizational work, the existence of GHC significantly affects the level of commitment to the organisation. In this model, it is suggested that GHC is an effective predictor of organisational, and the findings are consistent with the theory that behind this assertion. This argument is supported by the theory that underpins this model (Al-Swidi et al., 2021). The purpose of developing this model was to study the connection between GHC and the performance of organizations.

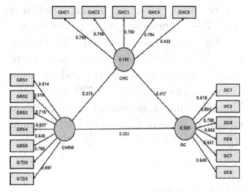

Fig. 20.1 Adapted from Smart-PLS 3.2.9

5. Conclusion

The primary objective of this research was to investigate the effects that GHRM processes have on the level of organizational devotion displayed by dairy companies. During the course of this inquiry, a GHC mediation analysis was put through its paces. Our research makes a contribution to the existing body of knowledge by employing the AMO theory's conceptual framework to investigate the subject of environmentally responsible behaviour in the workplace. In order for the researchers to achieve the objectives of the study, they utilised a technique that was based on surveys and analysed the data using SmartPLS software. The findings of this research point to a connection between an organization's overall commitment to sustainability and environmentally responsible employment practises, as well

as training and development practises. GHC acts as a moderator for a number of different impacts, including those associated with green recruiting and selection, green training and development, and green organisation commitment. In addition, our findings are consistent with the AMO paradigm of greening the dairy business. The findings of the study might be used by policymakers, supervisors, and upper management to develop human resource policies that encourage a culture of environmental stewardship in the workplace.

REFERENCES

1. Chen, Y.S. and Yan, X., 2022. The small and medium enterprises' green human resource management and green transformational leadership: A sustainable moderated-mediation practice. Corporate Social Responsibility and Environmental Management.

2. Rajagopal, N.K., Saini, M., Huerta-Soto, R., Vílchez-Vásquez, R., Kumar, J.N.V.R., Gupta, S.K. and Perumal, S., 2022. Human resource demand prediction and configuration model based on grey wolf optimization and recurrent neural network. Computational Intelligence and Neuroscience, 2022.

3. Pandey, A.K., Singh, R.K., Jayesh, G.S., Khare, N. and Gupta, S.K., 2022. Examining the Role of Enterprise Resource Planning (ERP) in Improving Business Operations in Companies. ECS Transactions, 107(1), p. 2681.

4. Gilal, F.G., Ashraf, Z., Gilal, N.G., Gilal, R.G. and Channa, N.A., 2019. Promoting environmental performance through green human resource management practices in higher education institutions: A moderated mediation model. Corporate Social Responsibility and Environmental Management, 26(6), pp. 1579–1590.

5. Úbeda-García, M., Claver-Cortés, E., Marco-Lajara, B. and Zaragoza-Sáez, P., 2021. Corporate social responsibility and firm performance in the hotel industry. The mediating role of green human resource management and environmental outcomes. Journal of Business Research, 123, pp. 57–69.

6. Awan, F.H., Dunnan, L., Jamil, K. and Gul, R.F., 2022. Stimulating environmental performance via green human resource management, green transformational leadership, and green innovation: a mediation-moderation model. Environmental Science and Pollution Research, pp. 1–19.

7. Pham, N.T., Thanh, T.V., Tučková, Z. and Thuy, V.T.N., 2020. The role of green human resource management in driving hotel's environmental performance: Interaction and mediation analysis. International Journal of Hospitality Management, 88, p. 102392.

8. Amjad, F., Abbas, W., Zia-UR-Rehman, M., Baig, S.A., Hashim, M., Khan, A. and Rehman, H.U., 2021. Effect of green human resource management practices on organizational sustainability: the mediating role of environmental and employee performance. Environmental Science and Pollution Research, 28(22), pp. 28191–28206.

9. Piwowar-Sulej, K., 2022. Environmental strategies and human resource development consistency: Research in the manufacturing industry. Journal of Cleaner Production, 330, p. 129538.

10. Al-Swidi, A.K., Gelaidan, H.M. and Saleh, R.M., 2021. The joint impact of green human resource management, leadership and organizational culture on employees' green behaviour and organisational environmental performance. Journal of Cleaner Production, 316, p. 128112.

Note: All the tables and the figure in this chapter were made by the Authors.

*Advancements in Business for Integrating Diversity, and
Sustainability – Dimitrios A. Karras et al. (eds)*
© 2024 Taylor & Francis Group, London, ISBN 978-1-032-70828-7

21

Analysis on the Impact of Mediating role of Human Capital on the HR Management Practices

Brijendra Singh Yadav[1]

Quantum School of Business, Quantum University,
Roorkee, Uttarakhand, India

Bhadrappa Haralayya*

Lingaraj Appa Engineering College, Karnataka, India

Vikas Kumar[2]

School of Applied and life sciences,
Uttaranchal University Dehradun, Uttarakhand, India

Iskandar Muda[3]

Faculty Economic and Business,
Universitas Sumatera Utara, Medan, Indonesia

Abstract: The aim of this research is to conduct a comprehensive literature review to better understand the connection among human resource analytics (HRA), organizational performance (OP) and human capital management (HCM). HR analytics were used as a mediator between HCM constituent parts and the impact of HCM has on performance of organization. The study is based on a thorough review of the existing research. The systematic research indicated HRA to assist firms and analyze HCM and improve performance of organization. This study provides substantial additions to the current body of knowledge about HCM and the implementation of innovative tools for HRA. Based on the results, various practical implications may be drawn. The study is particularly relevant to organizations in the early stages of applying HRA to improve performance of organization.

Keywords: Human capital management (HCM), Human resource (HR), Organization performance

1. Introduction

Organizational development is aided by human capital since it fosters innovation and new ways of thinking among employees. Human resource analytics, which manages intellectual capital, is a fundamental driver of organisational success. Academics engaged

*Corresponding author: bhadrappabhavimani@gmail.com
[1]brijendra.coer@gmail.com, [2]vikas.mathematica@gmail.com, [3]iskandar1@usu.ac.id

DOI: 10.4324/9781032708294-21

in management approach organisational performance. Employees play a growing role in an organization's capacity to grow and achieve a competitive advantage (Rajagopal et al., 2022). Therefore, businesses are investing heavily in human capital development programmes that use HR data to boost employee productivity. This will help corporate goals and long-term sustainability. HRA examines that HCM influences company performance. A survey of relevant research article led to the establishment of a conceptual architecture for a full assessment. HCM and its effect on outcome of organization are examined using a descriptive study approach (Rajagopal et

al., 2022). The results of this research suggest that increasing both customer satisfaction and service quality in an organization may be achieved through objective performance evaluation and attentive hiring practises. Integrating HR data into HCM helps organization perform better. It is a novel method that improves HR practises and the efficiency of organizations.

2. Conceptual Architecture

Incorporating academic research with practitioner recommendations in the areas of HCM, HRA, and OP, the authors created a framework as shown in Fig. 21.1.

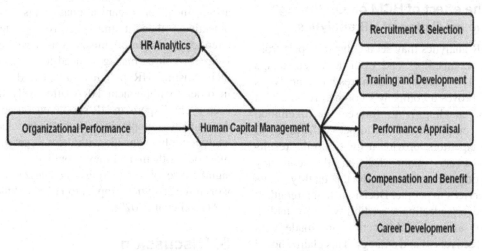

Fig. 21.1 Conceptual architecture

Source: Authors

3. Hypothesis Development

The below mentioned point shows that the hypothesis point which is developed for the HRA to assist organization and to analyze HCM and improve performance of organisation

H1 (a): The elements of HRM have a substantial impact on an organization's performance.

H2 (b): HCM and organisational performance are mediated by HR analytics.

4. Related Works

According to Hallaj, Y. (2018) examining the strategic ramifications of HR practises such job analysis, creation, discovery, recruiting, selecting, performance appraisal, training, benefits and compensation structure, labour relations, and aiding issue management in organisations was covered.The aim of Alnoor, A. (2020) was to determine how different human capital factors affected form survival. The mediating function of knowledge management in the aforementioned connection was also studied in the study.

The goal of Channa, et al., 2019 research by employing the regular incident concept was to identify the connection among strategic HRM and crisis management. Organizational resilience was used as a mediator in this study to determine the strength of various associations.

The effect of HCM on OP through the mediation of HR analytics

HR analytics may set a company apart from its competitors and offer it an advantage in the market. Human resource analytics improves a company's competitive position by enabling it to foresee the likelihood of employee or customer defections to competitors, provide insight into the results of every major decision the company produces, and maximise the quality of its services to people. Decisions that strengthen the organization's credibility and establish HR as a central function are made with effectiveness and strategy. This claim should be backed up by studies focusing on things like return on investment, cost savings, and efficiency (Gaur, B. (2020)).

Big data is increasingly being embraced by businesses, providing new insights that aid in decision-making. Sentiment analysis, network analysis, and machine learning have made significant contributions to the management of people and organisations. HR departments might benefit from positioning itself as strategic business partners by using this approach.

HRA is a specialised field that calls for skills not often used by HR professionals. Since HRA is the result of collaboration between business and technology, having a dedicated HR analytics group within a company could be extremely interesting. Data collection, processing, and transformation would be the purview of this suggested team or unit, which would serve to both aid HR decision-making and inform broader strategic business choices for the organisation (Gurusinghe et. al., 2021).

The HR industry is experiencing a dramatic upheaval due to the increased use of HR Analytics. If the department wants to play a more strategic role and contribute to the achievement of organisational goals and objectives, then it must receive greater attention from the organisation as a whole. Human resource managers need to evaluate their existing HR policies and procedures in order to implement HRA effectively in each cycle. Experts in HR should encourage departments employing technology and analytic tools to engage with them to get the most out of them, and they should stress the significance of scheduling when assessing workforce analytics' impact to HRA and the OP (Jyoti et al., 2020).

5. Discussion

The metadata analysis by Cayrat et al., 2022 highlights the importance of HCM in achieving organisational success in today's modern era of intense competition among organizations. The study demonstrates how businesses should priorities employee knowledge to find the optimal solution. The knowledge base of a company's employees is represented by human capital management, which also serves as a vital source of innovation. Therefore, HCM may be regarded as one of the most significant intellectual resources of a business that offers creative resources. According to Guru et al., 2021 study utilising their model, a higher level of organisational HCM will emerge from a higher level of individual HCM. They also found that the HCM is positively and directly related to "aggregated individual human capital." The framework developed by Ployhart is presented as a tool for managing HC. The report explained that adding HR analytics into HCM affects firms' performance.

A measurement of the efficacy, quantity, cost, and quality of HR operations is currently necessary in every organisation. These indicators are used by businesses to assess, improve, and adjust effective HR procedures. Performance is positively impacted by HRA because it increases employees' motivation to perform at a higher level and their satisfaction with the performance review process. When HCM strategies are successful, companies realise the value of HRA. HRA and performance have not been sufficiently linked. Consequently, the authors' proposed conceptual research framework will guide future studies of HCM and the ways in which it boosts organisation performance through the mediation of HR analytics. There are possibilities for further study and implementation presented in this research.

6. Conclusion

The study offers implications for researchers as well as practitioners in the field of HCM by integrating the novel tool of HRA for the purpose of increasing the performance of organisations. In addition to this, it provides suggestions for upcoming researchers to empirically experiment with the provided conceptual framework and generated

hypothesis in a variety of organisational settings. The paper presents evidence that HR analytics may increase corporate performance by enabling more effective management of HR. In addition, the study offers a helpful contribution to firms who are looking to strengthen their HR technology skills or to expand their present activities with HR analytics.

REFERENCES

1. Rajagopal, N.K., Saini, M., Huerta-Soto, R., Vílchez-Vásquez, R., Kumar, J.N.V.R., Gupta, S.K. and Perumal, S., 2022. Human resource demand prediction and configuration model based on grey wolf optimization and recurrent neural network. Computational Intelligence and Neuroscience, 2022.

2. Rajagopal, N.K., Qureshi, N.I., Durga, S., Ramirez Asis, E.H., Huerta Soto, R.M., Gupta, S.K. and Deepak, S., 2022. Future of business culture: an artificial intelligence-driven digital framework for organization decision-making process. Complexity, 2022.

3. Hallaj, Y. (2018). The strategic role of human resources management in managing organizational crises - a fieldstudy on city councils in Lattakia Governorate. PhD Thesis, Business Administration, Tishreen University, Syria. (in Arabic).

4. Alnoor, A., 2020. Human capital dimensions and firm performance, mediating role of knowledge management. International Journal of Business Excellence, 20(2), pp. 149–168.

5. Channa, N.A., Shah, S.M.M. and Ghumro, N.H., 2019. Uncovering the link between strategic human resource management and crisis management: Mediating role of organizational resilience. Annals of Contemporary Developments in Management & HR (ACDMHR), Print ISSN, pp. 2632–7686.

6. Gaur, B. (2020). HR4.0: An Analytics Framework to redefine Employee Engagement in the Fourth Industrial Revolution. 2020 11th International Conference on Computing, Communication and Networking Technologies, ICCCNT 2020. https://doi.org/10.1109/ICCCNT49239.2020.9225456.

7. Gurusinghe, R. N., Arachchige, B. J. H., &Dayarathna, D. (2021). Predictive HR analytics and talent management: a conceptual framework. Journal of Management Analytics, 8(2), 195–221. https://doi.org/10.1080/23270012.2021.1899857.

8. Jyoti, J., Sharma, P., & Rani, A. (2020a). Assessing the impact of human resource management practices on teachers' performance through HR analytics. In Sustainable Business Practices for Rural Development: The Role of Intellectual Capital. Palgrave Macmillan. https://doi.org/10.1007/978-981-13-9298-6_11.

9. Cayrat, C., & Boxall, P. (2022). Exploring the phenomenon of HR analytics: a study of challenges, risks and impacts in 40 large companies. Journal of Organizational Effectiveness: People and Performance, ahead-of-print(ahead-of-print). https://doi.org/10.1108/JOEPP-08- 2021-0238.

10. Guru, K., Raja, S., Umadevi, A., Ashok, M., & Ramasamy, K. (2021). Modern approaches in HR analytics towards predictive decision-making for competitive advantage. Artificial Intelligence, Machine Learning, and Data Science Technologies: e ISBN 9781003153405.

Advancements in Business for Integrating Diversity, and
Sustainability – Dimitrios A. Karras et al. (eds)
© 2024 Taylor & Francis Group, London, ISBN 978-1-032-70828-7

22 Impact of Financial Management Practices on SMEs Profitability with Moderating Role of Agency Cost

Raseem Abdul Khader P*

Ansar Arabic College, Affiliated to the University of Calicut,
Valavannur, Kerala, India

Nawal Mohammed P. K.[1]

Malabar College of Advanced Studies,
Affiliated to the University of Calicut, Vengara, Kerala, India

Vishnuprasad T.[2]

Government College, Affiliated to the University of Calicut,
Kodancherry, Kerala, India

P. Nissar[3]

PSMO College, Affiliated to the University of Calicut,
Tirurangadi, Kerala

Abstract: The growth and development of the economy are significantly influenced by Small and Medium Sized Businesses (SMEs). Some SMEs are unable to grow as a result of financial resources and managerial skills. This study's purpose is to investigate the agency costs affect small and medium-sized firms' profitability as well as the relationships between those activities' financial management techniques. Most of the study's data come from primary sources. The structural equation model's Partial Least Squares Method (PLS3) is used for descriptive analysis, while SPSS 23 is used for hypothesis testing. The study's findings show a correlation between effective financial management and SMEs' profitability; however, agency cost does not moderate this association in any way. The report is going to discuss greater adherence to financial management practices.

Keywords: Techniques for financial management, Agency fees SMEs, Small and medium-sized businesses managing finance

1. Introduction

The Micro, Small, as well as Medium-Sized business (MSME) sector, is extremely important to the overall social and economic environment of the world. As a result, small and medium businesses are considered to be the backbone of both industrialized countries

*Corresponding author: raseempoongadan@gmail.com
[1]najadv86@gmail.com, [2]vishnure21@gmail.com, [3]nissarkdp@gmail.com

DOI: 10.4324/9781032708294-22

and growing economies (Mwavu et al., 2018). The department's revenue, expense, asset, and liabilities management framework, processes, internal controls, and practices, as well as any unpredictable circumstances that might occur, all are included in the financial management framework. Jayesh et al., (2022). To perform better and more effectively compete, businesses of all sizes, particularly those with owners with less education, invest a lot of tangible and intangible resources. Their most valuable resources for operating a firm are education and work experience. Low management abilities are the majority of the major reasons why SME businesses fail (Ashish et al., 2022). SMEs typically interact with a single interlocutor, the bank, in the financial system, which gives them less negotiation strength (Sensini, and Vazquez et al., 2021). It is necessary to prioritize further research on the relationship between the budgeting techniques utilized and the profitability of SMEs in the Philippines. In addition, additional factors that serve as a gauge of profitability is provided, including ROI, ROE, and EVA (Fortuna et al., 2021).

2. Related Works

Nguyen et al., (2023) investigated the effect that the financial crisis had on the accuracy of bankruptcy forecasting models. More than 90,000 small and medium-sized enterprises had their data collected from 2015 to 2019, and prediction models were developed for three distinct periods: two times when there was no crisis, and one time when there was a crisis. Nketsiah et al., (2018) investigated the effect that the financial crisis had on the accuracy of bankruptcy forecasting models. More than 90,000 small and medium-sized

enterprises had their data collected from 2015 to 2019, and prediction models were developed for three distinct periods: two times when there was no crisis, and one time when there was a crisis. Mohanty and Mehrotra et al., (2018) make a modest attempt to examine the connection between liquidity and profitability in 28 SMEs that were listed and traded on the Bombay Stock Exchange between 2011 and 2016. Veeraraghavan, et al., (2018) evaluated the financial performance of small and mid-sized enterprises in Puducherry, India, to understand how financial management methods impacted this performance. Bismark et al., (2018) explore how financial management practices in the Birim Central Municipality of Ghana affect the expansion of small and medium-sized businesses.

3. Methodology

The efficiency of the financial management strategies utilized by SMEs in Faisalabad was assessed in this research using primary data. In this study, the independent variables Accounting, Financing Information System, and Present Capital Management will be studied together with the predictive variable, Firm Growth, with agency cost acting as a moderator. Target population responses are collected via survey questionnaires. 300 SMEs from the city of Faisalabad constitute the study's sample. The SMEs were given a total of 300 questionnaires, and 200 responses were received. Twenty surveys were missing or deemed unnecessary during data entry. The analysis took into account the 180 unfinished surveys. Partial least squares are used in SEM, which is used to test the hypothesis. Figure 22.1 displays the theoretical framework.

Fig. 22.1 Theoretical frame work

Hypotheses development:

Hypothesis-1 (H1):

H1: The profitability of SMEs is favorably correlated with Accounting Information Systems (AIS).

H1a: The profitability of SMEs is not positively correlated with Accounting Information Systems (AIS).

Hypothesis-2 (H2):

H2: The profitability of SMEs is favorably correlated with Financial Information Systems (FIS).

H2a: The profitability of SMEs is not positively correlated with Financial Information Systems (FIS).

Hypothesis-3 (H3):

H3: Working capital management (WCM) and SMEs' profitability are closely related.

H3a: Working capital management and SME profitability do not have a strong correlation.

Hypothesis-4 (H4):

H4: The agency problems moderator has an impact on the revenue of SMEs.

H4a: Agency costs have no moderating impact on SMEs' profits.

4. Results and Discussion

The present study's reliability and validity were assessed using Cronbach's alpha, concurrent validity, and Average Variance Extracted (AVE). Cronbach's alpha values of 0.50 and less are not acceptable, 0.50 and 0.60 are considered average though acceptable, and any number over 0.70 is considered to be excellent, stating George and Mallery (2003). Results show that the information is accurate.

Table 22.1 Intrinsic validity (Measurement Model Quality Criteria)

	Cronbach's Alpha	Composite Reliability	AVE
systems for keeping track of finances	0.878133	0.906154	0.617016
system for financial data	0.768343	0.831899	0.582577
working capital administration	0.772220	0.828645	0.639078
Agency expense	0.674858	0.779431	0.616230
Firm efficiency	0.552710	0.653922	0.563824

Techniques for Financial Management and the Performance of a Firm's Structure

A three-item measure was used to assess the business' effectiveness. Working capital Management (Q3 = .112), the financial information system (Q2 = .238), and the accounting information system (Q1 = .515) were used to gauge the performance of the business, and these features constituted the overall business performance (Q5 = .654).

Table 22.2 All Independent Variables Summary for the Model

Hypothetical relationship	Path coefficient	Absolute t-statistical values	Values of R2	Values of Q2
Q1- Q5	0.515***	6.402		
Q2-Q5	0.238***	2.882		
Q3-Q5	0.112**	1.976		
Q5			0.654	0.231

Company Performance Agency Cost and Structural Mode (Moderator)

Agency cost serves as the study's moderator; the model below utilizes Agency Cost (Q4) as an Independent Variable (IV) to Investigate how it affects firm performance. Its findings demonstrate that overall company performance is at a very low level (R2 = −.076, 0.191, and 0.216). Because it should be more than 0 C ronbach's, the value of R2 is insignificant (1951). Four hypotheses were investigated in the current investigation. The final findings showed that three hypotheses (H1, H2, and H3) were validated. The results show a strong correlation between SMEs' profitability and their use of working capital management (WCM), financial information systems, and accounting information systems. When a certain theory was confirmed (H4a). This indicates that the research's conclusions, which were based on information from Faisalabad, Pakistan, show the relationship between (IV) and (DV).

Table 22.3 Model Summary

Hypothetical Relationship	Path Coefficient	Absolute t-statistic value	Value of R2	Moderator
Q1-Q4	−0.078	0.733		
Q6			0.642	Not moderator
Q2-Q4	0.192	0.945		
Q6			0.683	Not moderator
Q3-Q4	0.218	0.938		
Q6			0.565	Not moderator

5. Conclusion

One of the main objectives of the research was to investigate how financial management practises affected the profit of small and medium-sized enterprises in Pakistan's Faisalabad city. To examine agency cost behaviors as a mediator of the association between personal finance and SME profit in Faisalabad, Pakistan, they were also evaluated in the present research. Agency problems may significantly affect the performance of businesses. This study also demonstrates how agency costs, which are independent variables, have an impact on SMEs' profitability. Most companies in Faisalabad city regularly produced their revenue report, income statement, and financial statements. The majority of organizations employ accountants on staff to manage the accounting department. Medium-sized businesses had a robust accounting system, whereas small businesses tended to use computers less often.

6. Limitations of the Research Study

Lack of financial and non-financial resources, time restraints, and the scope of the study's investigation forced researchers to set a limitation on the number of objectives, which was one of the study's key constraints.

7. Implications for the Further Research

The results of this research may be utilized to enhance capital requirements administration, permanent asset tracking, and current asset-management practices in other Pakistani cities.

REFERENCES

1. G. S. Jayesh et al 2022 ECS Trans. 107 2715 A Comprehensive Analysis of Technologies for Accounting and Finance in Manufacturing Firms https://doi.org/10.1149/10701.2715ecst.Mwavu, V.M., 2018. The Effects of Financial Management Practices on the Financial Performance of the Top 100 Small and Medium Enterprises in Kenya (Doctoral dissertation, University of Nairobi).

2. Ashish Kumar Pandey et al., 2022 ECS Trans. 1072681 Examining the Role of Enterprise Resource Planning (ERP) in Improving Business Operations in Companies https://doi.org/10.1149/10701.2681ecst

3. Sreenu, N., 2021. Financial Management Practices of Indian Small and Medium Enterprises (SMEs): A Study of the Food Processing Sector. South Asian Journal of Management, 28(3).

4. Sensini, L. and Vazquez, M., 2021. Effects of Working Capital Management on SME Profitability: Evidence from an emergent economy. International Journal of Business and Management, 16(4), pp. 85–95.

5. Fortuna, C.P.A., 2021. Budgeting Practices: Its Impact on the Profitability of Small and Medium Enterprises in Isabela. Universal Journal of Accounting and Finance, 9(3), pp. 336–346.

6. Nguyen, N.T., 2023. How does adopting occupational health and safety management practices affect outcomes for employees? The case of Vietnamese SMEs. International Review of Economics & Finance, 83, pp. 629–640. Technologies for Accounting and Finance in Manufacturing Firms. ECS Transactions, 107(1), p. 2715.

7. Nketsiah, I., 2018. Financial management practices and performance of SMEs in Ghana: The moderating role of firm age. Open Journal of Economics and Commerce, 1(4), pp. 8–18.

8. Mohanty, B. and Mehrotra, S., 2018. Relationship between liquidity and profitability: An exploratory study of SMEs in India. Emerging Economy Studies, 4(2), pp. 169–181.

9. Srinivasan, Veeraraghavan, K., 2018. Effect of financial management practices on the financial performance of small and medium enterprises in Pudhucherry, India. International Journal of Management Studies, 4(8), p. 51.

10. Bismark, O., Kofi, A.F., Kofi, O.A. and Eric, H., 2018. Impact of financial management practices on the growth of small and medium scale enterprises in Ghana: The case of Birim Central Municipality. International Journal of Innovation and Research in Educational Sciences, 5(2), pp. 177–184.

Note: All the tables and the figure in this chapter were made by the Authors.

Advancements in Business for Integrating Diversity, and Sustainability – Dimitrios A. Karras et al. (eds)
© 2024 Taylor & Francis Group, London, ISBN 978-1-032-70828-7

23

Human Resource Development Equity: A Serious Awareness for Businesses

V. Vidya Chellam*
Directorate of Distance Education, Madurai Kamaraj University, Madurai, Tamil Nadu, India

S. Praveenkumar[1]
Madurai Kamaraj University, Madurai, Tamil Nadu, India

Amit Dutt[2]
Lovely Professional University, Phagwara, Punjab, India

KVB Ganesh[3]
Koneru Lakshmaiah Education Foundation,
(KL Deemed to be University), Vaddeswaram, Andhra Pradesh, India

Abstract: Organizational learning fostered by teamwork, innovation, and personal dedication characterizes Corporate Entrepreneurship (CE). Therefore, HRM procedures are often believed to play a significant role in a company's performance. While HRM has been shown to increase risk-taking, creativity, and initiative in the workplace, more research is needed to quantify these effects. Employment diversity and equitable management are discussed, along with the structural and labor market factors that contribute to these processes. Here, we take a look at the empirical literature that connects Human Resource Management (HRM) practices to CE. Researchers discovered that while everyone agrees that CE benefits from HRM, the data is contradictory and rarely provides a coherent theoretical reason. As we look for a theoretical explanation for this crucial relationship, this analysis highlights two key themes: the promotion of discretionary entrepreneurial contributions, and the individual's acceptance of risk. The two problems are supposedly intertwined.

Keywords: Corporate entrepreneurship, Human resource management (HRM), Empirical research, Employment equity, Labor market factors

*Corresponding author: vvidyachellam@gmail.com
[1]s.praveenkumarus@gmail.com, [2]saranmds@gmail.com, [3]kvbganesh@kluniversity.in

DOI: 10.4324/9781032708294-23

1. Introduction

In academia, Human Resource Development (HRD) is still in its infancy, but in practice, it has been around for quite some time Swanson, R, (2022). It seems practically inherent to the human condition to work on one's personal development to better one's living situation Margherita, A. (2022). Both the theory and practice of HRD are firmly based on this expanding and maturing worldview (Rajagopal, et al., 2022). The emergence of business analytics as a core skill has led to the development of data-driven human resource management and advanced analytics solutions that link employee performance to business value drivers and corporate success. It's common knowledge that the level of economic and non-economic (political, religious, cultural, social, and psychological) elements, as well as the quality of human resources, have a major bearing on output (del-Castillo, et al., 2022). Therefore, the value of people can be assessed periodically Mahapatro, B. (2022). There are many facets to building an institution, but some of the most important are strategy development, organizational structure, leadership and performance management, labor-management interactions, coordinated marketing and sales, and sound financial management. Affirmative action and diversity appreciation are two procedures that are integral to a strategic HRD strategy, rather than being treated as separate concepts.

2. Related Works

Yong, et al., 2020 examined the impact of green HRM practices on sustainability from the resource-based view of the organization using cross-sectional data from 112 large manufacturing firms. Karman, A., (2020) developed a notion that correlates Strategic Human Resource Management (SHRM's) value creation with its focus on employees' needs and wants. Amrutha, et al., 2020 examined how Green HRM might help businesses accomplish social sustainability goals, and highlighted both emerging trends and lingering questions in the sector. Pandey, et al., 2022 employed a thorough literature analysis to develop the hypotheses for an integrative theoretical framework connecting HRM practices, entrepreneurial orientation, and business performance (Hamid, et al., 2022). When it comes to human resource disclosures, training for employees is the most discussed topic in annual reports. It is suggested that organizations improve their HR reporting and transparency practices.

3. Methodology

HRD refers to the process by which members of society gain the understanding, competence, and motivation to carry out their individual and collective responsibilities as productive members of society. Within the context of the organization, this calls for a unified strategy that defines human resource development as Overcoming racial, gender, and class discrimination in the workplace through resolving historical imbalances resulting from an organization's overall strategy and inextricably linked to its human resource goals. It's an expense that pays for itself. As a part of the overall strategic planning process, human resource planning can be used to assess both immediate and long-term staffing needs. Connecting back to the larger goal of succession planning, this opens the door to training future leaders. The steps in this procedure give a systematic framework for determining areas of growth and subsequently implementing coaching and career development programs.

A unified national, industry, and organized human resource development strategy that takes into account the demand for skilled, managerial, and professional entry is necessary to meet the short- and long-term objectives of institution creation. To this purpose, business organizations and the trade-union movement have recently begun talking about human resource development policies. For corporatist structures to be credible, especially in supporting the new RDP, such HRD accords must be given effect at the organizational and community levels.

4. Results and Discussion

The necessity for thoughtful, organization-specific answers is more crucial than the possibility of affirmative action laws. Affirmative action may need to be accompanied by the carrot of legislation or industrial action to get through to obstinate employers who fail to see the value in investing in their employees' growth.

If implemented correctly, HRD has the potential to boost economic competitiveness. At whatever level of an organization, training and development programs must be funded, and managers who do a great job in this area must be recognized and rewarded. Taking on more responsibility and learning the ins and outs of the business on the job are both necessary for professional development, which points to a company that offers a variety of career pathways. To establish a culture of progress, institutional prejudice must be completely eradicated. Businesses will need to examine their present HR and organizational practices and gain a better understanding of diversity management if they are to achieve this goal.

Data on human resources and performance comparisons

Information that is both timely and relevant is essential for strategic planning, tactical execution, and talent development in organizations. Assessing, monitoring, and adjusting an organization's performance is impossible without access to crucial data that can't be acquired, processed, or communicated.

Both the domestic and international labor markets should be covered by this information. HRD with a strategic lens is depicted in Fig. 23.1.

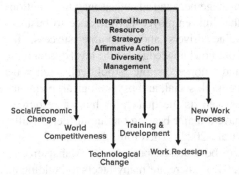

Fig. 23.1 Human resource development with a focus on strategy

It offers data specific to the company, comparing it to both the national sample and its industrial sector. Organizational strategy, human resource planning, and human resource development all share a need for up-to-date and relevant data. Assessing, monitoring, and adjusting an organization's performance is impossible without access to crucial data that can't be acquired, processed, or communicated. The project intends to continue providing trustworthy and insightful data, longitudinal trends, and a productivity metric (labor income gap) to HR decision-makers. Data from the HRD Survey of the Labor Market is displayed in Table 23.1 below.

Table 23.1 Human resource development information on the labor market

Internal labor market	External labor markets
Realistically defined job entry and structural change performance criteria	
Mobility flows (upwards and lateral)	Structured alteration and the resulting makeup of the labor market
Skills flexibility and mix	Education and relevant experience
Relevant experience profile	Shifts in employment patterns
Capacity potential of individuals	Skills availability in individuals
Skills availability profile	Aptitudes and the Distribution of Professions

5. Conclusion

Strategic human resource development must think ahead to factors like less trade protection and increased global competition. Affirmative action (AA) and diversity management are useful tactics in this regard. However, they should be viewed as HRD devices rather than as standalone initiatives. Internal and external benchmarking, in addition to constant monitoring and evaluation, are essential components of accountable human resource strategies. In this respect, the Breakwater Monitor has been a significant tool. Human resource professionals can advance their field by using comparative analysis to make educated decisions.

REFERENCES

1. Karman, A., 2020. Understanding sustainable human resource management–organizational value linkages: The strength of the SHRM system. Human Systems Management, 39(1), pp. 51–68.

2. Yong, J.Y., Yusliza, M.Y., Ramayah, T., Chiappetta Jabbour, C.J., Sehnem, S. and Mani, V., 2020. Pathways towards sustainability in manufacturing organizations: Empirical evidence on the role of green human resource management. Business Strategy and the Environment, 29(1), pp. 212–228.

3. Amrutha, V.N. and Geetha, S.N., 2020. A systematic review on green human resource management: Implications for social sustainability. Journal of Cleaner Production, 247, p. 119131.

4. Swanson, R.A., 2022. Foundations of human resource development. Berrett-Koehler Publishers.

5. Margherita, A., 2022. Human resources analytics: A systematization of research topics and directions for future research. Human Resource Management Review, 32(2), p. 100795.

6. Mahapatro, B.B., 2022. Human resource management. PG Department of Business Management.

7. Del-Castillo-Feito, C., Blanco-González, A. and Hernández-Perlines, F., 2022. The impacts of socially responsible human resources management on organizational legitimacy. Technological Forecasting and Social Change, 174, p. 121274.

8. Rajagopal, N.K., Qureshi, N.I., Durga, S., Ramirez Asis, E.H., Huerta Soto, R.M., Gupta, S.K. and Deepak, S., 2022. Future of business culture: an artificial intelligence-driven digital framework for the organization decision-making process. Complexity, 2022.

9. Pandey, A.K., Singh, R.K., Jayesh, G.S., Khare, N. and Gupta, S.K., 2022. Examining the Role of Enterprise Resource Planning (ERP) in Improving Business Operations in Companies. ECS Transactions, 107(1), p. 2681.

10. Hamid, Z., Muzamil, M. and Shah, S.A., 2022. Strategic human resource management. In Research Anthology on Human Resource Practices for the Modern Workforce (pp. 1–16). IGI Global.

Note: The table and the figure in this chapter were made by the Authors.

*Advancements in Business for Integrating Diversity, and
Sustainability – Dimitrios A. Karras et al. (eds)
© 2024 Taylor & Francis Group, London, ISBN 978-1-032-70828-7*

24

A Statistical Analysis of the Effect of E-Commerce in the Banking Industry

S. Praveenkumar*
Madurai Kamaraj University, Tamil Nadu, India

K. Madhavi[1]
VR Siddhartha Engineering College, Vijayawada,
Andhra Pradesh, India

K. Kavita[2]
BVRIT HYDERABAD College of Engineering for Women,
Hyderabad, Telangana, India

P. Krishna Priya[3]
KL Business School, Koneru Lakshmaiah Education Foundation,
Andhra Pradesh, India

Abstract: The rise of internet banking in Pakistan's financial sector over the past few years represents one of the sector's most momentous paradigm shifts. The purpose of this study is to investigate the efficiency of various types of online transactions, including those between businesses, between businesses and consumers, and between businesses and governments (Business operation, Job performance, and Customer satisfaction). This inquiry's sample was collected from the banking industry in Pakistan over six to eight months using 55 different forms that were filled out online between the years 2020 and 2021. The years 2020 and 2021 were used for the forms that were used for this investigation. The results demonstrate a favorable relationship between e-commerce and the success of businesses, suggesting that organizations may boost their operations, employee output, and client pleasure by adopting e-commerce practices.

Keywords: E-commerce, Banking industry, Online transactions correlation analysis, Regression analysis

*Corresponding author: s.praveenkumarus@gmail.com
[1]madhavi.aditi@gmail.com, [2]kavitha.k552017@gmail.com. [3]parvathanenikrishnapriya@gmail.com

DOI: 10.4324/9781032708294-24

1. Introduction

The word "electronic commerce" is now ubiquitous in all business, industrial, and governmental settings throughout the globe. (NUGROHO, L. et al., (2020) exhibit that e-commerce is a relatively new development in IT, and many businesses and governments have adopted it as a cutting-edge strategy for staying agile by digitizing their operations. Haq, S. (2018) says that the number of electronic transactions is growing and that the world is heading toward becoming a cyber world where everyone is linked via the internet. This is all because of the dramatic shift brought about by the expansion of electronic commerce. Alzoubi, H. et al (2022) state that E-commerce, or electronic commerce, is the practice of buying and selling tangible items through the Internet, where they may be paid for conveniently and quickly by both the buyer and seller. Whoever has the right to engage in commercial transactions in any market at any moment. Rahi, S. et al (2016) establish the benefit of their clients, banks engage in a wide range of financial dealings, including receiving, transferring, paying, lending, investing, and the value perception by buyers as a crucial factor in online shopping success. Wang, P. et al (2021)., While network finance has several benefits, such as reduced transaction times, lower costs, and better access to information, it also has certain drawbacks. Applications of e-commerce businesses includes online selling and buying websites, android and apple applications like amzon, flipkart, zebpay, bitcoin apps for trading and mutual funds, which enabled the door of managing funds online by trading and it affects the economy as well in terms of growth and welfare.

2. Related Works

A wide variety of businesses are actively using technological initiatives. Navaneetha Krishnan Rajagopal, et al., (2022) examine the potential effects of banking systems on company results by combining consumer choice with the matching principle. Vinoth, S. et al., (2022)   It is now crucial for all cloud operations to find the best solution guidelines to boost cloud security. Here, we look at and evaluate the major threats to a cloud network and data security. Li, L. et al., (2020) The purpose of this research was to examine how e-commerce enables financial institutions to become more agile and competitive. Mutuku, M.K. et al., (2019) examined the role of competitive advantage as a moderator between commercial banks' e-commerce capabilities and their financial results. A company's operations may benefit greatly from the use of an ERP system. Ashish Kumar Pandey et al (2020) more than that, this study will identify problems with ERP system rollouts and provide solutions to those problems in the form of strategies and recommendations. The following are the goals, by which the banking and commercial sectors will be improved in E-commerce.

3. Proposed Methods

Research indicates e-commerce doesn't affect company performance. Operational, customer, and staff efficiency determine efficiency. E-commerce includes B2B, B2C, and C2C. E-commerce impacts business. E-commerce and organizational performance are studied. E-commerce improves business. E-commerce enhances quality, profitability, and morale. E-commerce increased profits, market share, and customer service. Finance, production, sales, and administration improved. Pakistani banking combined e-commerce and OP. Businesses without e-commerce may lose. Fig. 24.1 shows banking e-commerce.

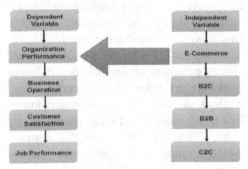

Fig. 24.1 Flowchart of e-commerce in the banking industry

Research hypothesis

H1: Organizational effectiveness increases as e-commerce expands.

H2: Electronic commerce and business performance have a strong correlation.

H3: There is a favorable correlation between e-commerce and the contentment of the buying public.

H4: E-commerce boosts a company's productivity.

H5: The effect of electronic commerce on the efficiency of businesses.

Table A shows the sample name with alpha values.

Table 24.1 Described the sample name and alpha value

Sl. No.	Scale name	Alpha value	No. of items
1	B2C	.727	8
2	B2B	.726	4
3	C2C	.758	3
4	Business Operation	0.707	5
5	Customer Satisfaction	0.737	5
6	Job Performance	0.711	5

Data collection: Lahore, the second biggest city in the nation, is the location of the study since it is home to nearly all bank branches and has a wealth of enterprises. Probability sampling was the sampling method employed in this study as a selection criterion. Participants in this study were managers and operations managers from commercial banks located in Lahore. Out of 55 mail-order surveys, 22 were returned,

Table 24.2 Statistical expressive

Gender			
	Number	Valid Percent	Cumulative Percent
Women	77 (76.2)	76.2	76.2
Men	24 (23.8)	23.8	100.0
Total	101 (100.0)	100.0	
Occupational Index			
	Number	Valid (%)	Cumulative (%)
Administrative Positions	63 (62.4)	63.4	63.4
Managerial level	36 (36.5)	36.6	100.0
Total	101 (100.0)	100.0	

representing a 45% response rate from the respondents. Of the 81 questionnaires filled out by managers and operations managers, 77 were used in this study. Table 24.2 depicts the statistical expressive dataset.

4. Result and Discussion

Correlation analysis: Then, each theory was examined. The answers to the first four hypotheses were revealed via the correlation coefficients. Table 24.3 depicts the correlation analysis H1: E-commerce performance is connected. The E-commerce and organizational performance 0.54 correlation support this idea (p<0.001). H2: using e-commerce software would enhance corporate procedures. E-commerce and company operations have a "positive association of 0.503 (p<0.001)" H3: E-commerce has nothing to do with customer

pleasure, thus banks' e-commerce apps won't affect client contentment. E-commerce and consumer happiness have a "0.103 (p<0.001) correlation". H4: E-commerce and work happiness are linked. According to this idea, e-commerce and work performance correlated "0.553 (p<0.001)". Limitation of this research is that its only applicable to some specific sectors of the other industries, such as education, telecommunications, textile, entertainment, etc.

Regression analysis: The companies' performance is compared to e-commerce. The results, which are shown in table D, seem to corroborate this notion as well. This signifies that the three control variables, b2b, b2c, and c2c, substantially accounted for 56% of the variance in organizational performance, as shown by the "R square value of 0.563 at a significant level of "P<0.001" with df (3)".

Table 24.3 Correlations

		FINAL ORG PERFORMANCE	Ecommerce	C-satisfaction	BOPR	FINLJOBPER
FINAL ORG PERFORMANCE	Pearson Correlation	1	.541**	.355**		.909**
	Sig. (2-tailed)		0	0	0	
	N					
Ecommerce	Pearson Correlation	.355**	103	1	.034	.043
	Sig. (2-tailed)	0	.306		.738	.670
	N	101	101	101	101	101
C.satisfaction	Pearson Correlation	.355**	.103	1	−.034	.043
	Sig. (2-tailed)	0	.306		.738	.670
	N	101	101	101	101	101
BOPR	Pearson Correlation	.911**	.503**	.034	1	.95**
	Sig. (2-tailed)	0	0	.738		.000
	N	101	101	101	101	101
FINLJOBPER	Person Correction	.909**	.553**	.043	.955**	1
	Sig. (2-tailed)	0	0	.670	0	
	N	101	101	101	101	101

Table 24.4 Description methods and ANOVA analysis

Model	R	R Square	Adjusted R Square	Std. The error of the Estimate
1	.750	.563	.550	.28108

Model		Some of Squares	df	Mean Square	F	Sig.
1	Residual	7.663	97	.079		
	Regression	9.879	3	3.293	41.683	.000
	Total	17.543	100			

This shows the overall level of association among corporate strategy and e-commerce platforms such as "B2B, B2C, and C2C." Table 24.4 depicts the description methods and ANOVA analysis.

5. Conclusion

This study's primary goal was to aid in the comprehension of how E-commerce affects business success, particularly in Pakistan's banking industry. This study shows a significant positive relationship between e-commerce adoption and organizational performance in Pakistan's banking sector. It helps managers see the importance of e-commerce in raising the efficiency of Pakistan's banking sector. The results of this study support previous research indicating e-commerce improves organizational effectiveness. This research is only applicable to the banking industry, albeit it may be conducted in other industries as well, such as education, telecommunications, textile, entertainment, etc.

REFERENCES

1. NUGROHO, L. and NUGRAHA, E., 2020. The Role of Islamic Banking and E-Commerce for The Development of Micro, Small, and Medium Entrepreneur Businesses. Business Economics and Management Research Journal, 3(1), pp. 11–24.

2. Haq, S. and Khan, M., 2018. E-banking challenges and opportunities in the Indian banking sector. Innovative Journal of Business and Management, 2(4), pp. 56–59.

3. Alzoubi, H., Alshurideh, M., Kurdi, B., Alhyasat, K. and Ghazal, T., 2022. The effect of e-payment and online shopping on sales growth: Evidence from the banking industry. International Journal of Data and Network Science, 6(4), pp. 1369–1380.

4. Rahi, S. and Abd Ghani, M., 2016. Customer's perception of public relations in e-commerce and its impact on e-loyalty with brand image and switching cost. The Journal of Internet Banking and Commerce, 21(3).

5. Wang, P. and Han, W., 2021. Construction of a new financial E-commerce model for small and medium-sized enterprise financing based on multiple linear logistic regression. Journal of Organizational and End User Computing (JOEUC), 33(6), pp. 1–18.

6. Navaneetha Krishnan Rajagopal, Naila Iqbal Qureshi, S. Durga, Edwin Hernan Ramirez Asis, Rosario Mercedes Huerta Soto, Shashi Kant Gupta, S. Deepak, "Future of Business Culture: An Artificial Intelligence-Driven Digital Framework

for Organization Decision-Making Process", Complexity, vol. 2022, Article ID 7796507, 14 pages, 2022. https://doi.org/10.1155/2022/7796507

7. Mutuku, M.K., Muathe, S. and James, R., 2019. Mediating effect of competitive advantage on the relationship between e-commerce capability and performance: Empirical evidence from commercial banks in Kenya. European Journal of Business and Management, 11(17), pp. 48–57.

8. Vinoth, S., Vemula, H.L., Haralayya, B., Mamgain, P., Hasan, M.F. and Naved, M., 2022. Application of cloud computing in banking and e-commerce and related security threats. Materials Today: Proceedings, 51, pp. 2172–2175.

9. Li, L., Lin, J., Turel, O., Liu, P. and Luo, X.R., 2020. The impact of e-commerce capabilities on agricultural firms' performance gains: the mediating role of organizational agility. Industrial Management & Data Systems.

10. Ashish Kumar Pandey et al., 2022 ECS Trans. 107 2681 https://doi.org/10.1149/10701.2681ecst

Note: All the tables and the figure in this chapter were made by the Authors.

Advancements in Business for Integrating Diversity, and Sustainability – Dimitrios A. Karras et al. (eds)
© *2024 Taylor & Francis Group, London, ISBN 978-1-032-70828-7*

25

Big Data-based System Enhancement for Corporate Financial Management and Decision-Making

Naila Iqbal Qureshi*

College of Business Administration,
Princess Nourah Bint Abdulrahman University, Riyadh, KSA

Abhay Arvind Bedekar[1]

IAS, PhD Economics, Addl Collector, Indore,
Govt of India, India

Ginni Nijhawan[2]

Lovely Professional University, Phagwara, Punjab

Dinesh Chandra Pandey[3]

Graphic Era Deemed to be University,
Dehradun, Uttarakhand, India

Abstract: Corporate financial management can better drive business development by achieving the integration of business and finance. It can also raise management standards inside the company, which helps boost core competitiveness. We hope the research we offer in this post will help other companies in a related field that want to leverage big data for making financial decision-making. Big data enables previously impractical techniques for procurement management, factory controls, budgetary control, and financial decision-making to become more efficient and affordable. It is indicated that in the age of big data, enormous information can be used to encourage business judgments in detail, lowering financial and commercial barriers, enhancing decision efficacy and quality, improving organizational structure and personnel, and improving the capacity for forecast and early detection. The use of big data technologies is now essential for supporting financial judgment and increasing corporate value.

Keywords: Big data, Corporate financial management, Decision-making

---

*Corresponding author: nailaiqbal@rediffmail.com
[1]bedekar.abhay@gmail.com, [2]saranmds@gmail.com, [3]dineshchandra@geu.ac.in

DOI: 10.4324/9781032708294-25

1. Introduction

Big data has a revolutionary effect on financial management in several key ways, including the following: (i) Processing financial data is increasingly complicated as a result of big data, and (ii) The depth and breadth of financial management are altered by big data; (iii) Big data substantially boosts financial management effectiveness. (iv) Big data substantially enhances the capacity of financial management to control risk. In a nutshell, using the potential of big data may improve the accuracy of forecasting while lowering the danger of systemic financial threats to businesses (Shamim, et al., (2019)). The widespread promotion of big data's use in financial management choices is a difficult task. In actuality, there are a plethora of challenges, including financial managers' antiquated ideas, their reluctance to embrace change, a lack of internal communication and collaboration, an absence of an understanding of the risks associated with financial transactions, and the inadequacy of Fostering widespread adoption of big data for use in financial management decisions is a challenging task. There are a lot of difficulties (Irudayasamy, et al., (2022)). Financial managers, for instance, often have antiquated views, resist new ideas, and refuse to invest in data storage and analysis. Furthermore, internal information procedures are often flawed, and information exchange is subpar. Obtaining commercial opportunities, developing markets, lowering costs, raising revenues, and creating new business models are all facilitated by the wealth of information made available by big data. It is challenging to successfully tap into traditional data management and data analysis approaches, which may lead to a failure to recognize

the value of information and an increase in the complexity of acquiring and using that information (Ranjan, et al., (2021)). Big data is not without flaws in its current implementation. At this time, financial decision systems are only being used by major online corporations. Most businesses are still on the fence about whether or not to use data mining online analysis, despite the obvious benefits (Navaneetha, et al., (2022)). We must demonstrate the big data in the business decision at every level, from blueprint generation to front-end presentation, to improve organizational efficiency, cut costs, and solidify the advantages of the company's core competitiveness.

2. Related Works

To enhance insightful organizational performance and analysis of decisions, Niu, et al., (2021) offer a paradigm for Optimized Data Management with Big Data Analytics (ODM-BDA). Singh, et al., (2022) gives a thorough analysis of the developments and uses of Deep Learning (DL), Reinforcement Learning (RL), and Deep Reinforcement Learning (DRL) approaches for data-driven decision-making in the financial industry. Elia, et al., (2022) the relationship between big data analytics capabilities (BDAC) and four goals were examined in the first empirical research to directly investigate the theoretical model via the mediation supplied by four value creation mechanisms. This paper discusses the advantages of big data and the challenges of constructing a micro. Moharm, K. (2019) outlines the fundamentals of big data analytics. The recommended informatization approach provides a theoretical framework for data sharing and compatibility among corporate management and project management. (You, et al., (2019)). Sun, et al., (2020) because it aims to ascertain the advantages, dangers, and long-term repercussions of big data in the finance system, research in this area are innovative. The goal is to identify areas of differentiation in terms of the tangible benefits that big data may provide, while also drawing attention to the difficulties that may arise in this area.

3. Methodology

Design of Big Data Personal Finance and Decision-Making Systems: Management accounting is a vital component of modern accounting progress, and informatization is a technology mechanism for efficiently putting these concepts and procedures into practice. The firm's business and financial operations may be linked via the intelligent financial system, with each connection being monitored in real-time so that the internal and external management of the enterprise have access to data that will allow them to make better-informed decisions. Enterprises place a premium on internal control as a

means of mitigating and resolving risks, but this emphasis may result in unnecessary redundancies when it comes to approving purchases, payments, withholdings, contracts, and other similar transactions. Intelligent finance helps streamline the approval procedure, which saves time and money for the finance department. In addition, consumers may utilize the data presented in financial statements to stay abreast of the company's progress, better grasp the company's perspective, and even play a small but important part in bolstering the company's decision-making processes via quantitative analysis. The primary goal of this software is to improve fundamental company operations; it is being adopted first by manufacturers and thereafter by other sectors.

Figure 25.1 illustrates how the properties of this software architecture vary across market segments, how it often caters to a subset of sectors, company sizes, or business models, and how it falls short of offering comprehensive coverage for any sector. Management accounting capabilities are still underutilized in most corporate management

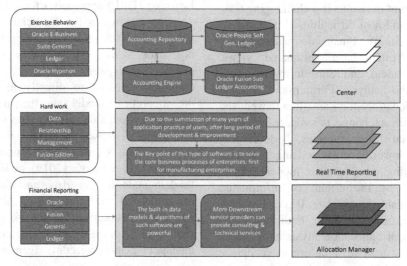

Fig. 25.1 Big data financial management and decision-making framework

accounting information systems, despite their central importance in accounting. In the process of operating and managing firms, accounting management processes are underused, and management accounting is rarely used.

$$tab = tab_R \cap tab_M,$$

$$\rho = \lim_{\Delta f \to 0} \frac{x(f - \Delta f) - x(f)}{R(f) + \Delta f} \qquad (1)$$

The data warehouse, which is comprised of several data marts, is the result of the preceding four stages of processing. The portal for financial and strategic analysis is the primary source of the data layer and data processing layer technologies used in the system. Indicators may be presented in a variety of formats including charts, tables, text, and dashboards. Therefore, the pre-prediction, during-event control, and post-event analysis phases of management are all materialized and visualized, completing the integrated company performance evaluation and control plan.

$$I = \sum_{yn}^{r} \frac{j_{yn} + j_{yn\,min}}{j_{yn\,max} - j_{yn}}$$

$$\overrightarrow{RW} = \sum_{0}^{j} r^j w^2 \qquad (2)$$

The theory of control must underpin a management accounting information system, which must then chunk the enterprise's overall goal into more manageable pieces and provide each management topic with its information interaction terminal and information transmission route. The management accounting information system cannot function without continuous input from the management topics.

$$R^* = \arg\max \left\{ \sup | e(f^3) + L^K P(f^2) | \right\}$$

$$R(f) = l_2 \sigma^2 (l_1 f_2)$$

$$N = R\left(f^2, \{l_y^2\} \right) - f \qquad (3)$$

The primary goal is to improve a company's market competitiveness by analyzing the issues plaguing its management in the context of its present business process from a variety of angles. When managing a company's budget thoroughly, it's important to keep in mind not only the day-to-day operations but also the long-term goals of the company, all to strengthen internal controls and guarantee the smooth operation of all business operations. Budget management helps clarify the roles and responsibilities of each division within organizations, while also setting up a system of effective and scientific communication between them, all of which contribute to a positive work environment and the successful completion of the company's goals. The value network model, the explicit value store model, as well as the supply chain model. In the classic value chain model, conventional or fully integrated producers are largely responsible for the creation of value in the form of physical commodities, whereas linear manufacturing processes are responsible for the creation of value in the form of intangible goods.

$$sS = \min_{S} \sum_{y=1}^{j} \frac{1}{2} f_y + F_{S,2}^2 - FS_{2,1}$$

$$G_W(l) = \lim_{j \to \infty} \sum_{y,n=1}^{J} \frac{1}{yn} (S_y + S_n)^2 S_{yn}^3 \qquad (4)$$

Companies within a group may save time and effort by centralizing their ERP systems to streamline and improve the accuracy of their internal financial operations. Financial Management and Decision Design: The first benefit is that it facilitates the integration of the company's finance department into the front lines of operations. In the past, a bachelor's degree in accounting, finance, or a similar field was the bare minimum for hiring financial staff, and a junior or intermediate position was preferred.

$$S_{yn}^J = 1 - S_{yn}^2$$

$$x^j(k) \lim_{j \to \infty} \frac{1}{d^y} \sum_{r=0}^{j} (-1)^r n \binom{j}{r} x(k^2 + f^2 d^2) \quad (5)$$

The group's data management office, together with representatives from other business units, and developers, make up the project team.

$$X_y^h(k) = \sum_{n \in T} rand_n X_{yn}^h(k_{yn}^2)$$

$$QN_{yt}^{nyjk} = \sum_{y=1}^{j} Q_n^n N_{yt}^{nyjk} \quad (6)$$

The massive amount of business data, the inability to target a particular report, the absence of a complete presentation, and other factors are all represented in the limitations of the management decision-making process, which are exposed by the conventional sense of aggregated analysis reports. To be ready for a potential integrated call from the business system, the data management that can be reused goes through the usual cleansing of all crucial business data. Finally, the issue of data silos may be addressed and supported by an optimal storage structure for indicator data.

Clothing manufacturers, e-commerce businesses, department store chains, and payment processing companies are just a few of the industries that have benefited from using intelligence in their financial management. As illustrated in Fig. 25.2, the financial intelligent subject is comprised not only of the application subject, the system's central object, but also of the appropriate governmental agencies, industry associations, and big data platforms that are required for the system to evolve. Because of the financial shared service center, we can consolidate our fund accounting, streamline our company operations, and do away with redundant bureaucracy.

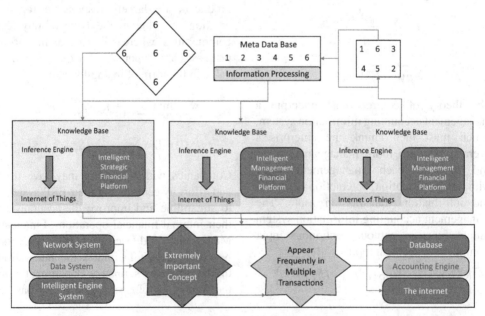

Fig. 25.2 Smart financial system decision

4. Performance Analysis

Both the insightful financial analysis report and the comparison of the Bureau of Reclamation to other reclamation businesses in the same province provide a thorough depiction of the institution's industry benchmarking role. As can be seen in Fig. 25.3(a), the most important metrics are net profit, operational income, assets, liabilities, owner's equity, gearing ratio, current ratio, and quick ratio. After sections of the index have been examined,

the benchmarking warning assessment index system is created by the economic risk early warning mechanism. Finally, the overall evaluation and score of the business operation are provided as shown in Fig. 25.3(b).

To achieve coordination and federalization, a unified platform of bank accounts for business operations and transaction details must be established, allowing the information of both to be automatically matched and bound in Fig. 25.4(a). Due to the transition from finance to management accounting, the financial shared service center may be

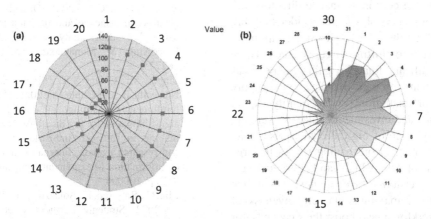

Fig. 25.3 (a) Group industry benchmarking ranking, (b) review of benchmarking advanced warning in

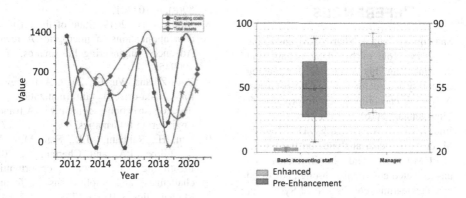

Fig. 25.4 (a) Group industry benchmarking ranking, (b) Overall evaluation of benchmarking early warning

optimized by retaining just the accounting specialists, technical workers, financial officers, etc. Several crucial business processes have been shown in their before and after optimized states in Fig. 25.4 (b).

5. Conclusion

With the advent of big data, businesses can examine massive amounts of information and fine-tune their financial strategies. To meet the difficulties posed by big data, finance professionals will need to acquire a deeper understanding of cutting-edge tools, while corporate finance directors and decision-makers should reconsider how big data affects their job and learn to adapt more effectively to shifting circumstances. There are significant financial gains in the areas of human resource management, supply chain administration, product quality, capital planning, and investment choice. To sum up, in today's age of big data, enterprises may benefit greatly from having access to large amounts of data, which can help them make better decisions, save money, streamline operations, maximize the effectiveness of their workforce, and boost their capacity for foresight and foresight.

REFERENCES

1. Shamim, S., Zeng, J., Shariq, S.M. and Khan, Z., 2019. Role of big data management in enhancing big data decision-making capability and quality among Chinese firms: A dynamic capabilities view. Information & Management, 56(6), p. 103135.

2. Irudayasamy, A., Ganesh, D., Natesh, M. et al. Big data analytics on the impact of OMICRON and its influence on unvaccinated community through advanced machine learning concepts. Int J Syst Assur Eng Manag (2022). https://doi.org/10.1007/s13198-022-01735-w

3. Ranjan, J. and Foropon, C., 2021. Big data analytics in building the competitive intelligence of organizations. International Journal of Information Management, 56, p. 102231.

4. Navaneetha Krishnan Rajagopal, Naila Iqbal Qureshi, S. Durga, Edwin Hernan Ramirez Asis, Rosario Mercedes Huerta Soto, Shashi Kant Gupta, S. Deepak, "Future of Business Culture: An Artificial Intelligence-Driven Digital Framework for Organization Decision-Making Process", Complexity, vol. 2022, Article ID 7796507, 14 pages, 2022. https://doi.org/10.1155/2022/7796507

5. Niu, Y., Ying, L., Yang, J., Bao, M. and Sivaparthipan, C.B., 2021. Organizational business intelligence and decision-making using big data analytics. Information Processing & Management, 58(6), p. 102725.

6. Singh, V., Chen, S.S., Singhania, M., Nanavati, B. and Gupta, A., 2022. How are reinforcement learning and deep learning algorithms used for big data-based decision making in financial industries–A review and research agenda. International Journal of Information Management Data Insights, 2(2), p. 100094.

7. Elia, G., Raguseo, E., Solazzo, G. and Pigni, F., 2022. Strategic business value from big data analytics: An empirical analysis of the mediating effects of value creation mechanisms. Information & Management, 59(8), p. 103701.

8. Moharm, K., 2019. State of the art in big data applications in microgrid: A review. Advanced Engineering Informatics, 42, p. 100945.

9. You, Z. and Wu, C., 2019. A framework for data-driven informatization of the construction company. Advanced Engineering Informatics, 39, pp. 269–277.

10. Sun, H., Rabbani, M.R., Sial, M.S., Yu, S., Filipe, J.A. and Cherian, J., 2020. Identifying big data's opportunities, challenges, and implications in finance. Mathematics, 8(10), p. 1738.

Note: All the figures in this chapter were made by the Authors.

26 Factors Determining the Efficiency in Indian Banking Sector—An Empirical Analysis

N. Saranya Devi*
School of Management Studies,
Tamil Nadu Open University, Saidapet, Chennai, India

R. Meenambigai[1]
School of Continuing Education,
Tamil Nadu Open University, Chennai, India

Namita Kaur[2]
Lovely Professional University, Phagwara, Punjab

Rupa Khanna[3]
Graphic Era Deemed to be University, Dehradun,
Uttarakhand, India

Abstract: This specialization identifies cost-efficiency factors in India's account management business. These research findings give tips for improving efficiency. After analyzing each bank's efficiency, the current study employed an econometric model to evaluate the influence of bank-specific attributes utilizing inefficiency ratings as the dependent variable. The most prior study employed ordinary least squares (OLS) to analyze the influence of factors on the efficiency of basic leadership units in various countries. This method has drawbacks. If OLS happens, efficiency scores would presumably fall between zero and one; in this scenario. We need to do some Multi-tobit estimations for the study. We would accept change for the decision-making unit (DMU) with efficiency scores of one and deduct a little amount from those with lower scores. There's also another option. Relapse analysis is used to analyze external stressors' influence on dependent variables.

Keywords: Banking sector, Ordinary least squares (OLS), DMUs, Multi-tobit estimates, Regression

*Corresponding author: saranyan19@gmail.com
[1]rmeenambigai@gmail.com, [2]saranmds@gmail.com, [3]dr.rupakhanna@geu.ac.in

DOI: 10.4324/9781032708294-26

1. Introduction

Insight into the optimal and productive allocation of assets across a wide variety of holdings and income generators may be gained by perusing the net-premium edge to resources portion of the section on sustaining money. The retaining money structure will function more effectively overall if the percentage is lower (Smets, F., (2018)). The size of the Net interest margin (NIM) in the savings sector was bigger before the modifications, but following the budgetary deregulation, competition among banks has successfully increased their net premium edge. As a result, the weight of NIM or spreads has been adjusted downward (Jha, S. (2018)). An indicator of the connection between NIM and the efficiency dimension is the negative and statistically significant correlation between NIM and the cost inefficiency dimension and its related segments (Navaneetha Krishnan Rajagopal, et al., 2022). Based on these findings, we may deduce that the NIM has been steadily declining over time and that as the spread has shrunk, the level of cost inefficiency has correspondingly decreased, pushing the Indian monetary system closer to the cost-effective fringe (Ashish Kumar Pandey et al., 2022). Reducing the measure and, as a consequence, emphasizing maintaining the money component for decreasing weight on spreads is the outcome of increased competitiveness between different bank business owners after continuous shift arrangements introduced by RBI (Pradhan, J.P., 2017). Consequently, in the concentrated and deregulated market in India, the net premium advantage would generally diminish as a result of the nearness of more global engagement in the accounting sector. Competition has increased in India's banking sector, prompting banks to give customers a greater rate of interest on deposits while reducing the premium they charge on loans (Basu, U.K. (2018)).

2. Related Works

Using panel data from 2005 to 2020, Haralayya, B. et al., (2021) analyze the determinants influencing the performance of 18 public sectors, 13 private, and 16 foreign sector banks in India. Eren, B.M. et al., (2019) to evaluate the presence and direction of causality between variables, the Granger causality test was used inside a vector error correction model. Fernandes, F.D.S. (2018) analyses domestic banks in the periphery of Europe from 2007 to 2014 to determine their level of efficiency and the impact of bank-risk variables on their overall performance. Sahoo, P. et al., (2021) exhibit to add the continuing policy discussion of whether or not OFDI complements or substitutes for domestic investment and, by extension, economic development.

3. Multi-tobit Regression Analysis

No defined method exists for determining crucial bank efficiency drivers; therefore choosing logical parts is risky. Previous literary works are utilized as guidance for such problems. Illustrative elements are relapsed on bank efficiency scores to evaluate likely causes. This sub-section combines cost, specialized, and allocative inefficiency models (AIE). This explains 1-16 inefficiency vs. efficiency. Positive slope coefficients signify inefficiency or efficiency decline, whereas negative coefficients imply the opposite. Fig. 26.1. shows the importance of ROE, An/OE, COM/OE, PS/AD, BD, MGT, Size, SP, NPA/NA, NIM, MS, DPub, DPrv at 1%

individual level. This validates our prior results on markers and ownership in the Indian monetary system. Fig. 26.1. shows that the ordinary value for detail-related factors is repeated across all components, which helps compare pointer effects. An/OE, NPA/NA, and possession sham coefficients are inefficient. Fig. 26.1. details Model 14-17 options. Model 14's multi-tobit findings are analyzed since they are comparable to other models. Revenue-to-value conversion measures productivity and growth potential. Value-to-resources analyses capital quality in all models. ROE helps investors measure risk and evaluate CEOs and banks. Negative ROE indicates banks can save capital, safeguarding India's financial stability. Low coefficient values show good and terrible periods in India's saving business. The unstable relationship may be owing to the financial collapse, decreasing saving rates, and increased oil costs from the global fiscal crisis. The factor suggests that Indian banks are getting more efficient as their earnings grow. Studies spanning several money divisions yield comparative findings.

4. Indian Banking Performance Measures

The proportion of marketing combined attentiveness to operating costs is factually essential at 1 percent with a positive coefficient; expanding the proportion would lower cost efficiency and associated segments. These results may be due to banks' strong competition to attract and retain customers through an innovative mix. Banks in India should focus more on their products and services than on advertising and attention. The percentage of an ad to operating expenses is a determinant of efficiency using the multi-tobit Model. In each model, the coefficients are factually

significant, leading to cost efficiency for Indian banks.

The coefficient shows an expected relationship between correspondence expenses and working costs. The results show that banks may reduce inefficiency by increasing their share. As a key component of account management costs, it's important to focus on it. 5% of regional and Tier 1 urban individuals must contribute 30% of spare income over the coming decade. White-collar family groups earning $90,000 to $200,000 per year would be India's greatest clientele. These clients will be supplied with an easy action plan and cost-effective branches with a good structure. In the meanwhile, mobile and broadband access in India has grown quickly, creating a possibility for online and telephone stations. The category will change during the next decade due to money-saving innovations. The account management sector in India will focus on technological advances to move the next generation toward saving. Consequently, the substantial correlation between this fraction and efficiency suggests that focusing on communication expenses would help boost account efficiency and profitability. Prior research predicts these consequences PSBs and PrSBs must lend 40% of their net bank credit or shaky sheet exposures. The variable requirement segment progresses to add up and is factually important at 5% centrality and is in sign with previous wants. Giving additional loans to the needy may increase banks' risk or non-performing assets, reducing profits. It may also increase the client base and interest in account exchanges.

When banks develop, they get access to resources like credit offices, scale efficiency, and the possibility to better control inputs. However, small banks must also enhance their performance through improved administration, expansion, and size competition. Studies revealed similar findings. Both large and small banks have benefits and disadvantages, as seen in Fig. 26.1. While defining returns to scale, the results showed banks' difficulties expanding them, proving their size is too small. The data suggest that Indian banks may improve cost efficiency by expanding. Banks must maintain steady returns for economies of scale. Relapse study shows small-size activity. Shifting activities to a greater scale, through organic development or tightening cash management, can provide significant savings. Indian banks must be small while pursuing large projects to maximize efficiency.

The board compensates its personnel handsomely to boost efficiency and bank development. Banks may make less money with more workers. Khandelwal Committee (2010) detected HR concerns in Indian PSBs. Lack of human capital pushed t behind competitors, according to studies. They worry about pay, age, skills, and restrictions. The inquiry comprises an estimator to assess the Indian account area (stores + propels) persons. Higher staff efficiency will assist minimize bank inefficiency since employee profitability is negative and critical at 1 percent noteworthiness. As employee motivation grows, their working capacity increases, allowing the administration and the entire organization to operate better. Since bank personnel in India best represent bank service excellence, they should be constantly improved. According to estimates, a bigger share will help banks expand and

Model	x²		LL	oE	DPrv	/oE	Pub	/OE	S	S/AD	IM	D	PA/NA	GT	Size
	11.18	0.46		0.002											
			1.1												
		0.01		0.001											
	3.5	0.46	0.14			410									
		0.02				0.02 10									
	65.1	.510				0.85									
			110.5												
		0.02						0.232							
	46.9								0.0.55						
			142.1												
		0.027						0.002							
	28.0s	0.46	0.125								.135				
		0.215									0.028				
		0.46	0.139												
	48.5	0.465												0.138	
			141.3												
		0.022												0.11	
	17.5	0.845													0.105
			57.84												
		0.035													0.009
	41.95	0.739													
			111												
		0.035													
	54.9	0.419											-3		
			130.1												
		0.02											0.002		
0	17-8.5		122.1								0.612				
		0.012									0.18.5				
1	21.5		-49.5						0.02						
			23.80												
		0.03							0.23						
2	34		.295		0.217		.215								
			30.45												
		0.003			0.022		0.015								
3	17.05	0.445	56.38	0.001		0.78		0.92	0.015	0.027	0.165	0.05	0.005	0.97	0.077
			0												
		0.043		0		0.190		0.222	0.001	0.047	0.132	0.16			0.01
4	96.9	0.21	87.6	0	0.190	0.155	0.18	0.187	0.120	0.101	0.3.50	0.311	0.007	0.273	0.05
		0.057		0.001	0.025	0.194	0.032	0.04.5	0.003	0.049	0.127	0.060	0	0.140	0.01
0.5	21.85	0.069		0.002	0.052	0.16	0.06	0.16	0.04	0.223	0.118	0.462	0.006	0.38	0.09
			91.07												
		0.095		0.001	-0.01	0.14	0.02	0.095	0.001	0.0ss	0.003	0.18	0	0.2	0.022
6	31.87	0.144	61.210	0.002	0.198	0.170	0.233	0.153	0.216	0.007	0.348	0.308	0.002	0.168	0
		0.082		0.00t		0.154	0.028	0.225	0.018	0.002	0.00t	0.06			0.011

Fig. 26.1 Multi-tobit Calculations

Source: Authors

flourish. Positive results for representational efficiency correspond to strong economic growth, albeit this may be attributed to relatively static staffing levels, especially for PSBs involved in over 80% of India's money exchanges.

NPA-to-net-loan ratios are good credit indicators. Reduced NPAs boost Indian bank efficiency. NPAs affect bank profitability over time, and there's no quick fix. RBI has tried many NPA-reduction measures. Securitization and Reconstruction of Financial Assets and Enforcement of Security Interest Act, 2002 and Asset Reconstruction Company foundation help banks with NPAs. According to earlier studies, NPAs killed banks in various economies. As non-performing net advances reduce, the board expects banks' financial efficiency to drop. Higher NPAs for net advances mean higher Indian bank inefficiency. Banks must recover bad assets swiftly and monitor nonperforming assets and risk practices to manage an account's financial record and reduce NPAs over time. Poor governance and CEO quality boost operational expenses and NPLs. Banks must reconsider how the board handles NPAs. Our findings are similar to those of a prior study, which found that non-performing assets and the percentage of issue advances cause considerable cost inefficiencies, showing that banks in many nations are far from ideal practice.

These methods helped banks lower net-premium edge and boost performance, but the 2008-09 crises made the market more competitive. A growing economy expanded global expertise, and a focused market has reduced India's net premium advantage since finance cost subordinates are not being produced and there are fewer opportunities to profit from shaky exercises. India's NIM saves money. The share coefficient for all models in the present investigation was 1%. The analysis shows merchants' share has grown, and most contributors feel competition has increased despite a restricted market for saving money. The pie size shows Indian account management. The negative cost coefficient is large. Parts confirm a big industrial account. Growing bank share decreases inefficiencies and costs. Control variable: high market share.

5. Conclusion

The multi-tobit findings reveal that advertising expenses, bank enhancement, the executives' soundness, measure, nonperforming resources, and inefficiency are decisively linked to gen inefficiency and possession effects in gen inefficiency. Based on what we know about how banks in the developing world and the developed world compare, it seems that banks in the latter operate more efficiently than those in the former. The use of such creative strategies has given the field an advantage over nations that have bankers that are less open to change. Positive and important coefficient estimates were found between inefficiency and the public and private sectors. Deregulation exacerbated open and private bank inefficiency. Indian governmental and private banks are lucrative, according to the results. In the Indian family banking sector, efficiency and ownership are strongly correlated. Higher communication costs, net premium edge to resources, and bank expansion in other salaries suggest higher cost efficiency for Indian banks following deregulation.

REFERENCES

1. Smets, F., 2018. Financial stability and monetary policy: How closely interlinked? 35th issue (June 2014) of the International Journal of Central Banking.
2. Navaneetha Krishnan Rajagopal, Naila Iqbal Qureshi, S. Durga, Edwin Hernan Ramirez Asis, Rosario Mercedes Huerta Soto, Shashi Kant Gupta, S. Deepak, "Future of Business Culture: An Artificial Intelligence-Driven Digital Framework for Organization Decision-Making Process", Complexity, vol. 2022, Article ID 7796507, 14 pages, 2022. https://doi.org/10.1155/2022/7796507
3. Fernandes, F.D.S., Stasinakis, C. and Bardarova, V., 2018. Two-stage DEA-Truncated Regression: Application in banking efficiency and financial development. Expert Systems with Applications, 96, pp. 284–301.
4. BASU, U.K., 2018. NPA, Interest RateSpreed, NIM, Base Rate, MCLR, and Efficiency of monetary Transmission in India. Hyperion International Journal of Econophysics& New Economy, 11(2).
5. Jha, S., 2018. Performance appraisal of commercial banks and linkage financial indicators with economic growth in Nepal (Doctoral dissertation).
6. Haralayya, B. and Aithal, P.S., 2021. Performance affecting factors of the Indian banking sector: an empirical analysis. George Washington International Law Review, 7(1), pp. 607–621.
7. Ashish Kumar Pandey et al 2022 ECS Trans. 107 2681 https://doi.org/10.1149/10701.2681ecst.
8. Eren, B.M., Taspinar, N. and Gokmenoglu, K.K., 2019. The impact of financial development and economic growth on renewable energy consumption: Empirical analysis of India. Science of the Total Environment, 663, pp. 189–197.
9. Sahoo, P. and Bishnoi, A., 2021. Impact of outward foreign direct investment: Evidence from Asia. Journal of Policy Modeling, 43(5), pp. 1131–1148.
10. Pradhan, J.P., 2017. Indian outward FDI: a review of recent developments. Transnational Corporations, 24(2), pp. 43–70.

Advancements in Business for Integrating Diversity, and Sustainability – Dimitrios A. Karras et al. (eds)
© 2024 Taylor & Francis Group, London, ISBN 978-1-032-70828-7

27

Adoption of Artificial Intelligence Technology for Effective Human Resource Management

Anchal Pathak[1]

UPES, School of Business, Dehradun, India

Priyanka Tyagi[2]

Sharda University, Greater Noida, India

Bhavana Sharma[3]

Birla Global University, Bhubaneswar Odisha, India

Rajesh Natarajan*

University of Technology & Applied Sciences, Shinas, Sultanate of Oman

Abstract: The use of artificial intelligence (AI) has been shown to be a very successful method of simplifying problems and arriving at the best possible conclusions quickly. AI is a new field with rapid development. It has been effectively used to many different areas. Therefore, this research examined a variety of factors that have a role in advancing AI in the human resource management (HRM). To determine the most important factors in determining whether or not AI would be adopted, a poll of 350 respondents utilized. Analysis shows that "Organization use AI to bring effective business innovation," "Organization use AI to align with its business plan," and "Organization use AI to increase the levels of production" are the most important drivers of AI adoption. Additionally, the data was verified using reliability and normality tests. This research has important implications for the adoption of AI and the formation of efficient managcmcnt.

Keywords: Artificial intelligence (AI), Reliability and normality, Human resource management (HRM)

1. Introduction

Robust data sets and advanced computer infrastructure have helped define AI. The processing and interpretation of data may now be done more quickly, making it possible to do both regular and non-routine jobs with greater ease. Technology

*Corresponding author: rajesh.natarajan@shct.edu.om

[1]anchal.pathak@ddn.upes.ac.in, [2]priyanka.tyagi@sharda.ac.in, [3]sharmabhavana44@gmail.com

DOI: 10.4324/9781032708294-27

based on AI has recently received a lot of attention in the field of energy production, and it holds tremendous promise for the design of energy systems of the future. By collecting and assessing the data, AI technology helps make the energy sector more safe and efficient. The spread of information technology and its effect on the HRM function is one of the primary focuses of academic study. Transportation, human contact, service robots, healthcare, education, public safety, and security are just few of the areas where experts believe AI will have a significant impact in the near future. The public has high expectations on the dependability and security of AI systems used in the transportation sector. HRM has undergone significant change in recent years, and one important contributor to this is the advent of new information technology. Early Human Resource Information Systems (HRIS) or Digital HR Systems dramatically aided a firm's capability to electronically analyse, save, and disseminate HR-related data among internal and external parties. Initially beginning with the successful implementation of e-government services, digitalizing public services has now progressed to a mobile government platform, marking the third stage of its evolution. Human resources (HR) processes like talent acquisition have grown more dependent on AI based solutions, connectivity, and automation, and this trend is only increasing. Understanding the elements that influence the adoption of any technology in the field is crucial. Therefore, the purpose of this research was to rank the several HRM elements that might potentially influence the energy firm's adoption of AI.

2. Related Works

Bag, et al., (2021) makes use of institutional theory and resource-based perspective theory to shed light on how automotive companies set up their material resources and personnel skills to allow technology, enhance sustainable production methods, and forge forward into the circular economy. Enholm, et al., (2022) presents a comprehensive literature analysis that seeks to clarify the value creation processes of AI technologies and how they might be used by businesses. Vrontis, et al., (2022 to compile the current literature on automated processes and to determine its primary advantages and disadvantages for HRM. Grover, et al., (2020) examines job-fit, level of complexity, impacts over time, real impact on usage, social obligations, and apparent simplicity for different facets of OM are just some of the six factors that determine whether or not AI can be successfully implemented inside an organisation. It does this by tapping into the accumulated understanding of experts on Twitter as well as scholarly journals. Tambe, et al., (2019) highlights four obstacles to using data science techniques for HR tasks: the complexity of HR phenomena, the limitations of using small data sets, the potential for unfavourable employee responses to management choices made using information methods, as well as the responsibility concerns related to fairness as well as other legal and ethical limitations.

3. Proposed Methodology

Our goal in writing this piece was to examine how HRM and IT factors affect the use of AI in HRM sector initiatives. Fig. 27.1 shows

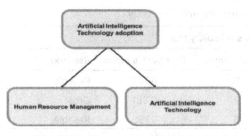

Fig. 27.1 Proposed methodology

how HRM and AI technologies influence one another in terms of adoption. In order to obtain meaningful results in such a large data set, the present research used a quantitative approach to data collecting, which is why a quantitative analytic strategy was used. The information was gathered using a questionnaire.

Likert scale: It is expected that respondents would use an asymmetric disagrees/agrees on scale to rate their degree of agreement with a series of items while answering Likert scale questions. Five-point Likert scales were utilized for data collection, "with 1 indicating extreme disagreement, 2 indicating disagreement, 3 indicating neutral agreement, 4 indicating agreement, and 5 indicating strong agreement. The information was analysed using SPSS (Statistical Package for the Social Sciences)".

Cronbach's alpha: Data validity was assessed with the use of Cronbach's alpha, which measures internal consistency. The RII method was used to examine the data and rank the parameters in order of importance. The data's normalcy was also evaluated since it must conform to the normality assumption. Errors and incorrect conclusions might be drawn from abnormal data. The skewness and kurtosis criteria is used to determine whether or not the calculated values are normal by making a comparison to a magnitude of 2. If

the value is more than 2, then the normality assumption has been broken; if it is less than 2, then the distribution is assumed to be normal, or at least approximately so.

4. Result and Discussion

Dataset: The questionnaire was administered through "email, in-person meetings, LinkedIn, Facebook, a Google form, and WhatsApp". Therefore, an excellent 86.25% response rate was achieved, as 350 filled forms were returned from a total of 400 sent out (Pazzaglia, et al., (2016)). Tab 27.1. summarizes the demographic information that was acquired about the respondents before any analysis was performed. A reliability test was conducted to ensure the steadiness of the data obtained from these respondents. The study instruments' internal consistency and quality were confirmed by the reliability test. The reliability test known as Cronbach's alpha is often utilized.

Table 27.1 Backgrounds of respondents

Items	Frequency	%
Qualification		
Undergraduate	175	50%
Postgraduate	140	40%
Doctorate	35	10%
Working Experience		
Less than 5 years	87	25%
6 – 10 years	175	50%
11 – 15 years	35	10%
Above than 15 years	53	15%
Working Position		
Executive	175	50%
Department heads	140	40%
Managers	35	10%

Table 27.2 Outcomes of reliability and normality

Data from the survey's reliability test				
Name of construct	Code of construct	No of items	Cronbach's alpha	Remarks
AI technology adoption	AIE	9	0.744	Reliable
Technology	AIT	9	0.881	Great
Human resources	HRM	11	0.795	Reliable

The normality test's findings				
	Kurtosis		Skewness	
	Stat	Variation	Stat	Variation
AIE	−0.724	0.260	−0.342	0.130
AIT	−0.871	0.260	−0.239	0.130
HRM	−0.805	0.260	−0.277	0.130

If Alpha is more than 0.7, then the data is reliable. Cronbach's alpha for each factor group in this analysis is shown in tab 27.2. That's why this information is trustworthy and fine for future study. Skewness and kurtosis were used to determine whether the data were normal. As can be seen in tab 27.2, the skewness and kurtosis values for all parameter sets are within the acceptable range of 2. What this implies is that we may safely make conclusions based on the data provided since they satisfy the normalcy assumption. Organizations that embrace AI tend to excel in three key areas: providing effective business innovation, aligning with their strategic goals, and raising output levels, as shown in tab 27.3.

Table 27.3 Respondent's demography

Code	Attribute	Scale /Frequency					N	RII	RANK
		1	2	3	4	5			
AI Technology adoption in UAE									
AIE8	AI innovates enterprises	17	39	111	110	73	350	0.705	1
AIE2	AI strategy alignment	34	54	75	79	108	350	0.699	2
AI Technology (AIT)									
AIT7	AI is intuitive	16	45	86	102	101	350	0.730	1
AIT3	AI improves job quality	12	36	104	121	77	350	0.723	2
Human resources management (HRM)									
HRM6	AI training for employees	12	59	76	81	122	350	0.738	1
HRM7	AI issues need a referral.	7	67	67	120	89	350	0.724	2

5. Conclusion

AI-based solutions make it easier to make choices that take into account interactions with the environment. Around three hundred and fifty samples of data were taken and analysed using descriptive statistics. "The data's accuracy and internal consistency were confirmed by a reliability test". Skewness and kurtosis of the data were used to evaluate the normality of the data. The study's results may be used as a visual aid to comprehend the variables influencing energy players' adoption of AI in HRM and their willingness to do so, given the many hurdles that lie ahead.

REFERENCES

1. Shneiderman, B., 2020. Human-centered artificial intelligence: Reliable, safe & trustworthy. International Journal of Human–Computer Interaction, 36(6), pp. 495–504.
2. Navaneetha Krishnan Rajagopal, Mankeshva Saini, Rosario Huerta-Soto, Rosa Vílchez-Vásquez, J. N. V. R. Swarup Kumar, Shashi Kant Gupta, Sasikumar Perumal, "Human Resource Demand Prediction and Configuration Model Based on Grey Wolf Optimization and Recurrent Neural Network", Computational Intelligence and Neuroscience, vol. 2022, Article ID 5613407, 11 pages, 2022.
3. Ghobakhloo, M. and Ching, N.T., 2019. Adoption of digital technologies of smart manufacturing in SMEs. Journal of Industrial Information Integration, 16, p. 100107.
4. Navaneetha Krishnan Rajagopal, Naila Iqbal Qureshi, S. Durga, Edwin Hernan Ramirez Asis, Rosario Mercedes Huerta Soto, Shashi Kant Gupta, S. Deepak, "Future of Business Culture: An Artificial Intelligence-Driven Digital Framework for Organization Decision-Making Process", Complexity, vol. 2022, Article ID 7796507, 14 pages, 2022.
5. Bag, S., Pretorius, J.H.C., Gupta, S. and Dwivedi, Y.K., 2021. Role of institutional pressures and resources in the adoption of big data analytics powered artificial intelligence, sustainable manufacturing practices and circular economy capabilities. Technological Forecasting and Social Change, 163, p. 120420.
6. Enholm, I.M., Papagiannidis, E., Mikalef, P. and Krogstie, J., 2022. Artificial intelligence and business value: A literature review. Information Systems Frontiers, 24(5), pp. 1709–1734.
7. Vrontis, D., Christofi, M., Pereira, V., Tarba, S., Makrides, A. and Trichina, E., 2022. Artificial intelligence, robotics, advanced technologies and human resource management: a systematic review. The International Journal of Human Resource Management, 33(6), pp. 1237–1266.
8. Grover, P., Kar, A.K. and Dwivedi, Y.K., 2020. Understanding artificial intelligence adoption in operations management: insights from the review of academic literature and social media discussions. Annals of Operations Research, pp. 1–37.
9. Tambe, P., Cappelli, P. and Yakubovich, V., 2019. Artificial intelligence in human resources management: Challenges and a path forward. California Management Review, 61(4), pp. 15–42.
10. Pazzaglia, A.M., Stafford, E.T. and Rodriguez, S.M., 2016. Survey methods for educators: Analysis and reporting of survey data (part 3 of 3). Applied Resarch Methods. Search in.

Note: All the tables and the figure in this chapter were made by the Authors.

Advancements in Business for Integrating Diversity, and Sustainability – Dimitrios A. Karras et al. (eds)
© 2024 Taylor & Francis Group, London, ISBN 978-1-032-70828-7

28

Low-cost Technology Diffusion: How WhatsApp is used by Small Retailers

Chakshu Mehta, Naveen Nandal*
Assistant professor, Sushant University Gurugram

Parul dhaka
Research Scholar, Sushant University Gurugram

Nisha Nandal
Assistant professor, Sushant University Gurugram

Abstract: The increase in internet penetration and the Digital India campaign movement initiated by the government of India. With more internet penetration and change in customer preference, Smartphone users are no longer unfamiliar with the word WhatsApp. It is now a crucial tool that enables small firms to react immediately to opportunities. The study focuses on how small retailers are using WhatsApp as part of their business marketing strategy in these circumstances. Even though WhatsApp is one of the most widely used messaging apps on smartphones, little research has been done on how it is used by small retailers as a marketing tool to reach out to a wide range of customers. This study aims to investigate the social media marketing tactics used by small retailers through WhatsApp. This paper has used the wheel in retailing theory that discusses that, Prior to now, location and space are essential components of retailer strategy and how due to the advent of technology stores, space and places have become less dominating.

Keywords: Retailing, Small retailers, WhatsApp

1. Literature Review

About WhatsApp

Social networking tools up to the early 1900s were telephones and radios. According to the study, the online revolution would connect gadgets like TVs, cell phones, cars, and even microwaves, all of which could be managed by a single person over the internet. The market's dynamic and international pressures have been addressed by retailers. Changing lifestyles of customers, changing marketing activities and a globalized way to do business

---

*Corresponding author: Naveennandal@sushantuniversity.edu.in

DOI: 10.4324/9781032708294-28

have changed the dynamics of retailing. Adequate retail management has changed the system of doing business and has also changed the way to face challenges (M. N. Rudrabasavaraj, 2010). The same revolution we all can see in form of WhatsApp. WhatsApp is a social media platform used for communication and information sharing with the quickest rate of growth, which was created by Brian Acton and a Ukrainian immigrant to the United States named Jan Koum. the SMS service of WhatsApp has reduced global barriers. WhatsApp is a flexible communication tool that may be used on internet-connected smartphones, tablets, and PCs. In order to acquire WhatsApp from its creators, Facebook paid around US$19 billion in January 2014. A rags-to-riches tale, the acquisition was signed and completed at the welfare office that Koum had once visited in his youth (Olson, Parmy, 2014b). The expansion of internet retailing in India has been fueled by the speed, convenience, and accessibility of a wide range of merchandise at competitive rates. Even in small towns customers are preferring online purchases. The public and private sector have been working to promote the use of digitization in recent years because they offer advantages such cost savings brought on by increased performance and power, visibility and security, accountability, and equitable growth. In some cases, the fear of tax repercussions and increased bank fees imposed on digital transactions, as well as the prospective investment required to use the technologies, have a significant impact on kirana owners' attitudes toward digital technology. Companies including Google, and Facebook have made investments in ventures to automate India's grocery retail sector. Although the trade ministry has suggested a viable strategy to combine kirana outlets and e-commerce (Kapuria, P, 2021).

Small retailers and the Use of WhatsApp

Retailing is a social economic system that helps in interaction with people and the exchange of goods and services. Professor Malcolm P. McNair's key theory regarding trends in retail development is known as "THE WHEEL of retailing." According to this theory, new retail kinds typically enter the market as low-status, low-margin, low-price operators. New forms of commercial activities usually get out to a rough start with subpar facilities, minimal status, and a track record of slashing prices and profits. As the activities increase the process become more expensive with higher margin and new competitors also enters. The author also explains the different personalities of entrepreneurs that always wish for higher profits and great success and adjust quickly to the changes in the environment. Retailing is linked to Imperfect competition. Due to the impact of retaining trade groups the retailers try to avoid any type to competition whether it is related to price or location. But the author defines that place and location is not important parameter in competition (S.C. Hollander, 1960). Typically, we have considered the "store" to be the site of the transaction—a particular place where the trade takes place. The transaction typically takes place in a designed store format, which is offered to potential customers as a branded version of the format. The importance of the physical location of the transaction is diminished in e-retailing. India is a nation of merchants where the dominant position is held by small retailers. They frequently operate on a small scale, are owner-managed, have a very limited selection of items, and employ very few people. The Covid-19 crisis has had a significant negative impact on SMEs, and some of them have been left unable to meet their obligations to their suppliers, employees, or customers. This effect is particularly important to know because many small and medium-sized businesses were expected to fail following the pandemic event. SMEs that have implemented e-commerce are anticipated to function better than ordinary firms, but this may not be enough to fully alleviate the effects of a pandemic-related economy that is shattered. The Sustaining Competitive and Responsible Firms (SCORE) program of the International Labor Organization (ILO) draws attention to the crucial fact that micro, small, and medium-sized enterprises (MSMEs) now matter more than ever. It is indisputable that MSMEs account for more than 70% of global employment and 50% of GDP. Due to the advent of social media platforms, this sector is facing a lot of challenges and competition due to changes in customer preference toward online purchases (M. N. Rudrabasavaraj, 2010). WhatsApp was acquired by Facebook, used by billions of customers and millions of videos and photos shared on this platform are becoming a powerful tool for communication and interaction by organizations. The biggest feature of WhatsApp is that virtually everyone uses it and that no special required training is required. Another perk is that since the team is already using WhatsApp, I don't need to expressly ask them to check it. As per the various studies, the direct call method has fewer advantages than the SMS service on WhatsApp. 40% of the response is more than the previous method. WhatsApp feature check on Status gives more quick response than at direct calling. Nowadays small retailers are using and making the best thereof advantage by using WhatsApp and sharing offers and discounts through WhatsApp. WhatsApp is considered a direct communication tool. Loyalty is a more powerful tool to reach new customers. WhatsApp features have a main focus on gaining the loyalty of customers than engaging with new customers. The success of WhatsApp is in being more creative and updated. Food and beverage businesses are using WhatsApp to keep their customers on high priority. Family physicians are increasingly providing consultations over WhatsApp. However, texting your doctor to ask a typical medical question cannot take the place of a face-to-face consultation (**Profit books. Net (2015).** In the field of marketing, "content marketing" has garnered a lot of recognition. As per the author all over the world, entire businesses are changing their ways of marketing. The study is conducted in Pakistan where a maximum part of the population is involved in social networking platforms. Kirana's may face some risks from the expanding organized grocery retail industry in terms of revenue and earnings. The lockout had essentially stopped customers from visiting businesses' storefronts, directly reducing the revenue of the company. This is typically the reason that most businesses are hurrying or ready to adopt e-commerce, particularly during the pandemic. Within Less than a year of the pandemic, my company started implementing e-commerce. The study stated that they only utilized WhatsApp and Telegram to connect with their clients and that this was their favourite method of communication. In India, there has been a significant shift toward digitalization in the past few years due to several reasons. India is the 73rd most ready country (out of 152) to embrace online shopping. Due to rising internet and smartphone use, the fashion and clothing sectors are expected to lead this expansion

(Kumar Siddhartha, et al; 2018). The author has considered both service and service sectors in the study. Service is considered as part of both tangible and intangible parts of our business system. The service sector is considered aa s major part of European countries and plays a very dominant role in its growth and GDP. Now a day with changing roles of providing services and the way companies provide services to customers has changed. Nowadays companies are capable to provide services without having face-to-face interaction with customers. This provides an independent way to interact with customers and the main objective behind is to provide independent value creation for the customers. Due to the increase in complexity of the business environment, increase in online reviews, more applications based on mobile, and services based on the location that creates the best value for both customers and industries. The advancement in the service sector and the way the service is provided is becoming an integral part to reach out to customers. But it is required that customers are on the Web. Discussing on importance of service the author has also highlighted some drawbacks. The author said that with the advancement of technology, there is a decrease in personnel contact. But if it is done in strategic manner companies can be at the best advantage. As opposed to using traditional or conventional techniques, consumers are browsing the internet more and more to discover the best bargain from suppliers all over India. It is confirmed that firms can gain significantly from digital marketing. Facebook and WhatsApp have made all more connected, and the rising popularity of social media is giving digital marketers new ways to reach consumers. Comparing young students to their older peers, social networking sites' online

marketing have a significant impact on how they choose their clothing. Social media has altered the potential of marketing. It has attracted the interest of businesses, public figures, artists, and creative professionals who utilize social networking sites to influence people and expand their businesses (J. G. Miles, 2014). Both production and process of marketing are supported by social media for both small, medium and large-scale organizations. During the pandemic, WhatsApp has become a great support for business. WhatsApp has become a way to communicate. With numerous applications used in WhatsApp. Its application is popular among all businesses. More than a chatting app it has become a formal way to communicate in business, social networks help small firms with their marketing and manufacturing processes. As small organizations are not technically strong and get less support from the government and financial institutions, WhatsApp has become one of the major support for them. Small business has started making small WhatsApp groups they chat privately and try to solve problems in a few minutes. During covid pandemic, WhatsApp has tried to reduce the challenge in the business. WhatsApp has reduced the problem of face-to-face communication. The pandemic which has become an obstacle in day-to-day communication WhatsApp has reduced that problem, therefore, social media is supported by effective communication. The author has also highlighted some of the drawbacks of WhatsApp as this application is based on internet connectivity and if one network is lost the application is failed (N. L. A. Sugiyantoro, et al; 2022). There is no reason that WhatsApp is a familiar app among all age groups and provides real-time opportunities for businesses. With the effectiveness of WhatsApp is used for marketing, socializing and interactivity with customers. Both vendors, customers and suppliers are using this technology that is providing flexibility in their work. WhatsApp is a mobile application with easier use of a smartphone WhatsApp is low-cost technology and become most popular among all age groups. The author has highlighted that WhatsApp is being used by small organizations also to internally communicate within the business. In India, small business has used WhatsApp in a more creative and economical way. WhatsApp as an important tool of social media is used by both small and large organizations for both internal and external communication with customers and stakeholders. Earlier productivity and connectivity was the main challenge for small retailers now which is resolved with the WhatsApp application use. Social media's rapid development has expanded its significance to the point where corporations increasingly view it as essential for achieving marketing objectives. The study's smartphone usage statistics demonstrate how much of our daily lives are dominated by smartphones. Smartphone users are no longer unfamiliar with the phrase WhatsApp. It is now a crucial tool that enables small firms to react immediately to opportunities. The consumer base is constantly engaged in using WhatsApp; thus, distance and time zones are no longer an obstacle. Users in both developing and advanced economies benefit from this. WhatsApp is used by multinational organizations to communicate with their clients around the world WhatsApp a wireless protocol that enables the sending and receiving of brief 160-character text messages to and from any mobile phone is compatible with all mobile phones. It is a dynamic alternative because it enables the

sharing of images, audio, and video. WhatsApp is a smartphone-only mobile instant messaging (MIM) program that is optional and not a default standard. WhatsApp requires a mobile internet connection. WhatsApp uses spatial location and colour to differentiate between sent and received messages in chats, which appear as threaded messages on a wall (A. Modak, et al.; 2017). New and creative approaches to the strategic placement of small firms are required as the market environment becomes more complex (Begam, M. S. 2020). As per the studies, it's critical that retail companies adapt their operational procedures through the use of WhatsApp in order to survive the COVID-19 pandemic. As a result, the study advises companies who presently sell their products through physical storefronts to adopt WhatsApp rather than creating online channels while the pandemic is underway. The study reveals that Since social media has a lower entry barrier than e-commerce platforms, which may have stricter standards or be more complicated, SMEs often choose social media as their initial e-commerce alternative because they have already likely used it. According to reports, all 100 of the largest corporations in the world as of 2017 are active on various social media sites. It is because of this tendency that several SMEs have begun using various social media platforms as a social media marketing tools. However, a substantial portion of the research done in the past concentrated on social media strategies for big businesses and organizations. The usage of social media marketing, which has been shown to encourage growth, foster positive customer relationships, and give SME owners a clear idea of how their consumers may be served, is one such tactic that is crucial for SMEs to grasp and benefit from. The current study will help in finding the features of WhatsApp that are best suitable particularly for small store retailers and this study also intends to assess WhatsApp's advantages as a social network communication tool used by small store retailers.

Attractive features of WhatsApp for small retailers

The modification in patterns of the retail institutional structure must be addressed by the theory of retail transformations and changes with time. Although the process is ubiquitous, it happens at various rates and in various ways. Wheel of retailing: from a simple, low-margin retailer to adding value through additional services and going on to a premium store.

Cost efficient Marketing Tool for its user

1. Due to limited resources, it makes sense for small enterprises to embrace manageable, reasonably priced technologies, Considered as prospects at a cheaper cost. enabling small enterprises to use manageable, reasonably priced technologies. Began has also highlighted the use of WhatsApp by small businesses and strategies used by them in their business growth through WhatsApp. From the age of using traditional marketing and towards the web site. There are a lot of challenges in keeping oneself updated. Websites include continuous updating otherwise companies may lose it, customers. opinion of people towards WhatsApp marketing has changed in the last few years. It is helping customers to give their valuable inputs connection to being close to customers. Only an

internet connection makes WhatsApp a low-cost application nowadays used by small retailers. The article focuses on small retailers and strategies used by them using WhatsApp features in their business. The study reveals the result that any change in business strategy by small retailers using WhatsApp brings in great advantage (Begam, M. S. 2020).

2. WhatsApp is considered a device to communicate with one another for free and with nearly impenetrable security, It saves time and money for both customers and service providers, Used to take orders over the phone and deliver them as needed, WhatsApp is quick in Sending sales alerts through the phone.

3. No training cost Since everyone currently uses it, there is no need for training. WhatsApp is a formidable tool for communication. Due to its simplicity, it has gained a large following. WhatsApp can be used for your organisation in a variety of ways beyond than for interactive interaction. It is cheap, inexpensive and affordable and you may start using it immediately and right away (Profit books. Net (2015).

WhatsApp advantage as a social network communication too

1. Using a profile of your past purchases and interests, WhatsApp Marketing enables you to tailor your offers to customers, WhatsApp is also used for better strategic placement

2. Used by small enterprises to manage sales, marketing, and other business-related activities, gives small businesses flexibility in their interactions

with their vendors and suppliers, Using WhatsApp for Customer Communication and Using WhatsApp for Customer Support. WhatsApp provides Competitive Advantage to small retailers and help in developing more customer engagement and trust.

Reasons why stores utilize WhatsApp

1. WhatsApp let retailers develop relationships with their clients. Begam also highlighted that WhatsApp messaging will be at a disadvantage if there is an increase in unwanted SMS by the organization. That loses the customer focus. There are lot of hidden costs incurred by the organization that can bring a negative impact on the organization. The success of WhatsApp is only possible when customers are at top priority and customers' queries and concerns are met on time. Small businesses use this to stay in touch with the community as well, WhatsApp is used by small businesses For Marketing & Promotion purposes. A shopping cart feature that WhatsApp has added makes online purchasing even simpler. With WhatsApp Business's portfolio feature, users can explore and add items to their grocery baskets (Begam, M. S. 2020).

The strategies small retailers must employ to utilize WhatsApp

1. Frequent personalized communication that captures the bulk of your marketing abandonment, Businesses should offer compelling generic content frequently each day to keep the community lively, enjoyable, and amusing, content should appeal to a wide audience and be easy for people to consume and share with others.

2. Customized service through faster response from clients (A. Modak, et al.; 2017).

3. Quick response to customer queries, Regular blogging, and messaging to customers.

WhatsApp is a crucial tool that enables small firms to react immediately to opportunities. WhatsApp is used for business promotion and meeting day to day needs of customers and is utilised for sales and marketing as well as customer service WhatsApp has become a secret weapon for small businesses nowadays.

2. Conclusion

E-commerce has significantly impacted India's retail sector; by 2025, 220 million people are anticipated to buy online, and by 2027, it is anticipated that the industry will be worth INR 13,97,800 crore (US$200 billion). However, neighborhood kirana (grocery) stores and small-format vendors still account for about 90% of India's retail grocery commerce. These kirana establishments must quickly adopt digital technologies due to the changing retail landscape and shifting consumer preferences. This unorganized sector fears going out of business if they don't use digital technologies to streamline its operations as India's retail sector grows more organized. This paper encourages the use of digitization and the incorporation of WhatsApp networking in the retail system. However, particularly in developing nations, little is known about how small enterprises are implementing this marketing. The majority of small firms haven't yet used WhatsApp marketing to its full potential

(Begam, M. S. 2020). The studies show that Small retailers are less likely to benefit from such a new marketing strategy without the right understanding of how social media platforms can be used to improve business performance. There are studies that claimed that small retailers are persuaded to embrace social media in their marketing efforts because they perceived it as a fresh way to make quick cash but business owners may take the initiative to regularly blog and communicate with their clients to improve their business performance. Further, there is a need to address how social media marketing, particularly through WhatsApp, may impact the performance of the retail sector.

REFERENCES

1. Begam, M.S. (2020). Analyzed View Of Factors That Determine The Marketing Of Small Sized Enterprises By WhatsApp Marketing. Editorial Board, 9(5), 62.

2. Kumar Siddhartha, D. K. Dubey and Neeraj Singh, "Survival Strategies of Unorganized Food & Grocery (Kirana) Stores in Bhopal City,"Anusandhan 7, no. 13(2018); 30–36, http://aujournals.ipublisher.in/p/56355.

3. Modak, A., & Mupepi, M. G. (2017). Dancing with WhatsApp: Small businesses pirouetting with social media. In Conference Proceedings by Track (Vol. 51).

4. Olson, Parmy (2014b). Inside The Facebook-WhatsApp Megadeal: The Courtship, The Secret Meetings, The $19 Billion Poker Game. Forbes March 4, 2014.

5. Profitbooks. Net (2015). How to Use WhatsApp for Business – 5 Tips With Examples Accessed 5/31/2016 http://www. profitbooks.net/how-to-use-whatsapp-for-business/.

6. Sugiyantoro, N. L. A., Wijaya, M., & Supriyadi, S. (2022). Benefits of WhatsApp as a Communication Media on Small Business Social Networks. The Journal of Society and Media, 6(1), 1–16.

7. Miles, J. G. (2014). Instagram power: build your brand and reach more customers with the power of pictures. New York: McGraw-Hill Publishing.

8. Swallehe Rudrabasavaraj M. N., (2010), "Dynamic Global Retailing Management", Himalaya Publishing House, 1st Edition.

9. Hollander, S. C. (1960). The wheel of retailing. Journal of marketing, 25(1), 37–42.

10. Kapuria, P., & Nalawade, H. S. (2021). Digitising Indian Retail: Analysing Challenges and Exploring Growth Models. Observer Research Foundation, 304, 2–31.

Advancements in Business for Integrating Diversity, and
Sustainability – Dimitrios A. Karras et al. (eds)
© 2024 Taylor & Francis Group, London, ISBN 978-1-032-70828-7

29 Challenges of Green Marketing in the Indian Context

Parul Dhaka
Research scholar, Sushant University, Gurugram

Naveen Nandal*
Sushant university, Gurugram

Neeraj Sehgal
Research scholar, Sushant University, Gurugram

Aarushi Kataria
Assistant Professor,
Bharati Vidyapeeth University, New Delhi

Abstract: Going "green" and purchasing environmental friendly products is indeed more popular than ever, but it is still a relatively new sensation in the consumer market. Environmentalists perceive the industrial sector as the primary source of resource depletion. As a result, there is more pressure on the industrial sectors to fulfil consumer demand and move ahead with caution in these scenarios. This paper analyses the concept of green marketing and its implications for businesses. Further, This paper also discusses 4P's of green marketing and SWOT Analysis of green marketing. Green marketing is a worldwide phenomenon that is gaining popularity, including in India. This paper also explores the purpose of green marketing and the challenges that businesses encounter when it comes to green marketing in India. The paper also examines recent developments in green marketing in India and explains why organizations' should do so.

Keywords: Green marketing, Environment, Eco-friendly

1. Introduction

The idea of "green marketing" emerged between the 1960s and early 1970s in response to worries about how purchasing and manufacturing behaviors could affect the environment (Konar & Cohen, 2001). Green marketing entails a series of activities that take into account the social interest in protecting the natural environment in

*Corresponding author: Naveennandal@sushantuniversity.edu.in

DOI: 10.4324/9781032708294-29

addition to the current requirements of customers. Green marketing encompasses a variety of initiatives that go above and beyond the existing needs of the consumers in order to consider the social interest in safeguarding the natural environment (Chamorro & Bañegil, 2006). Additionally, Green marketing has been defined in a variety of ways by other researchers such as It was defined as All endeavors that aimed at generating and streamlining transactions that fulfil human needs and desires while having the minimum possible adverse impacts on the environment (Polonsky, 1994). Further, Green marketing is defined as the advocacy of items that are believed to be environmentally safe by American Marketing Association. When dealing with customers, suppliers, dealers, and employees, businesses adhere to environmentally friendly and ethical practices. Companies have embraced a green marketing inclination due to a handful of factors which includes Competitive environment, peer pressure, environmental protection, politics, and legal initiatives. Not only environment is impacted by global warming and ozone layer depletion but it also lead to major health problems such as skin conditions, cancer, sunburns, cataracts, rapid ageing, and weakened immune systems to humans. It is high time to have made sustainability as high priority by everyone including customers. Customers should frequently opt for products that are economical, of great quality, and principally eco-friendly. Green marketing must culminate in transformation of customer perceptions as well as a push among businesses and organizations to reap the benefits of the green market segment in order to achieve a competitive edge.

2. Objectives of the Study

To understand the idea of green marketing and purpose of green marketing. To investigate the challenges Indian businesses encounter when implementing green marketing strategies. To investigate the current development and potential future of green marketing in India.

3. Literature Review

Since the outset of green marketing, It has been a significant academic research topic .This subject gained attention when American marketing association organized its first ever workshop on ecological marketing in 1975 that further contributed in publication of first book on the subject named as Ecological marketing in 1976 by Henion and Kinnear (Shrikanth et al., 2012) .It was observed from a survey of the literature that end-users and industrialists exhibit a concern for environmentally friendly products. The demand for organic food, clothing, cosmetics, electronics, and electrical goods has surged with time and as a consequence of the burgeoning popularity of green products among consumers. Products with green elements are more appealing to consumers. The concept, need, and significance of green marketing have garnered the most attention .Further, Study anlysised the current situation of Indian market and also examined the difficulties faced by green marketing (Tiwari and jaya, 2014). Further, Researchers have focused on green marketing in India .Such as One of the Study intends to analyze how green marketing programmes are being implemented in Indian businesses. Further, the concepts of green products, the green marketing mix, and the complications affecting green marketing pioneers were highlighted by some of previous literature. According to one of research, concern for the environment and engagement in environmental behavior are high in priority for Indian consumers (Jain and Kaur, 2004). Since Green marketing in high priority for all the stakeholders including customer, government and business. There is huge significance of this topic. Further other researchers have shed light on purpose and challenges of green marketing. One of researcher has also accentuated brief overview of green marketing and its operation and its avenues in India (Madhumita, G. & Sara, 2014).

4. Research Methodology

This study is exploratory in nature and it incorporates secondary data for its findings. Secondary sources include literature review from various articles, journals, research papers and books. The company websites has been mined for valuable information regarding green marketing strategies.

Purpose of Green Marketing

All individuals, rich or poor, would prefer to spend a healthy and vigorous life, including the corporate class. Every corporate company has its primary purpose as financial gain and economic profit. However, it has only lately been focused that how much destruction businesses operating globally are causing to the environment. Therefore, Green marketing is gaining popularity in corporate world.

Green marketing can aid in capitalizing on market opportunities. Enterprises see green marketing as opportunity to gain competitive advantage. It is desire of around 30% of Indian population to purchase eco-friendly goods. It is viewed as a chance to seize and gain an advantage by Progressive companies

and organizations over others who have not embraced green marketing. Due to elevated public concern over the manufacturing of polystyrene and ozone depletion, McDonald's switched from clam shell packaging to waxed paper. A "PREMIUM" recycled photocopier paper was introduced by Xerox in an effort to accommodate industry needs for fewer environmentally perilous products. It is understood by organizations that they are component of a broader society so they have started acting in an environmentally responsible manner. Green marketing can be utilized by business units and institutions to track cost and profit issues. Companies associations enterprises that can minimize their grievous wastes scraps can save a considerable quantum of money, lower expenditures, and boost gains. Organizations additionally face stress from government. Main goal of government is to safeguard consumers and society that has huge significance for green marketing. The Indian government has enacted a set of laws to protect consumers and the general public, limiting the production of harmful products. The need for organizations to remain competitive has been a significant driving force in the domain of environmental marketing (Sharma et al. 2015). It is noticed by firms that competitors advocate their environmental activities and also attempt to imitate this behavior. Revive 100% Recycled paper was launched a few years ago and became Xerox's effort to introduce recycled copy paper which also led to different manufacturers following suit. As research shows that Indian population are more concerned towards eco-friendly products. It is important for organization to consider this change.

Many businesses throughout the world have embraced green marketing because of the following reasons:

- Perceive it as opportunity
- Moral obligation to be more socially responsible
- Peer pressure
- Pressure from Government's Side
- Companies Cost and Profit Issues

Green Marketing Mix

Businesses utilise a green marketing mix to use marketing factors to generate the desired reaction from target customers and audiences. 4P's of green marketing are:

- **Green Product:** The products should be produced in such a fashion that they require fewer resources, use recycled materials, save water and energy also which have a modest environmental impact, and do not contain any toxics whose use can be detrimental and deadly.
- **Green Price:** Green pricing implies taking care of both employees and customers, as well as manufacturing products in an effective fashion. The buyers will spend the additional cost for receiving the high quality products in terms of design, performance, attractiveness, quality, or anything else however that higher price should be justified.
- **Green Place:** The marketers should opt for measures like handling the storage in such a fashion that lessens the total transportation time and therefore reduces the emission of overall harmful gases.
- **Green Promotion:** Promotion should be done in such a manner that it does not harm environment and humans such as less use of paper and promoting the product digitally.

Like traditional marketing, Green marketing mix also has 4P's which looks at not only producers and consumers perspective but also considers environment perspective.

Green Marketing Strategies

- Engagement of people in your campaign can give them feeling of attachment. So,An organization should publicise their plan and encourage individuals to support campaign. For instance, Starbucks leveraged the Facebook social media network to persuade people to contribute in their programme to plant trees and paint streets.
- One of the best and most affordable green marketing techniques is recycling. Recycling has been embraced by several major organizations, such as Apple, to strengthen their credibility. Both the carbon footprint and the proportion of waste on the globe can be reduced by recycling.
- Renewable energy is another economical way of green marketing. This also aids in the conservation of non- renewable resources. For instance, you can generate solar energy by installing solar panels on your store's rooftops and investing in wind energy.
- Packaging is also one of attractive green market strategy. In today's world, wherein everything is sold online, adopting eco-friendly packaging to minimize paper waste and plastic consumption is also a smart idea. Furthermore, it will contribute in the creation of a favorable image of your organization in the perspective of your clients.

Green Marketing: Swot Analysis

SWOT ANALYSIS is a preliminary tool for determining a company's strategies and plans. Things become a little trickier when a company views the SWOT analysis from the perspective of its social and green marketing. In addition to the market and revenue growth, the marketer will also need to analyze the company's social and environmental repercussions.

STRENGTHS:

- Marketing professionals enjoy exposure to new markets and have an edge over competitors who do not prioritize "greenness."
- Companies that embrace green marketing are perceived to be more socially responsible.
- Products that are perceived as being more environmentally friendly can fetch a higher price.

WEAKNESS:

- The majority of customers would rather focus on their own requirements than the environment.
- Many consumers steer clear of products with the "Green" label because they see such labelling to be a marketing ploy, and they may lose trust in a company that suddenly professes to be green.

OPPORTUNITIES:

- These customers are looking for products that reflect their changing attitude. Therefore, companies can take it as opportunity as customers have inclination towards eco-friendly products.
- In a response, companies endeavor to improve their societal consciousness. This supports the rise in socially conscious customer behavior and will offer them an edge over rivals who do not cover these concerns in their advertisements.

THREATS:

- There are apprehensions over green marketing initiatives which are appropriate from the standpoint of the government.
- The likelihood of consumer or government reaction due to existing green marketing promises made, risks one and two above, may culminate in repercussions.

Key Principles of green marketing:

- It is very important to educate the customer about benefits of eco-friendly products otherwise people will not pay attention towards environmental friendly products unless they know the repercussions.
- Companies should be genuine and they should be selling what they are claiming otherwise it will destroy the trust of customer and it will not tarnish the image of company but also customer will not take serious other companies who are making claim of selling green products.
- Company selling green products should also consider affordability of the product to customers as customer can pay extra for premium products but up to a point after that people will not purchase the products.
- Consumers must be convinced that the product does what it is promised to do; they will not compromise product quality for the sake of the environment.
- Suggestion should also be taken from customers about improving the quality of products and simultaneously making it environmental friendly .With this customer will value the product more.

5. Challenges

Green marketing is yet to reach its recognition stage and it faces hurdles for recognition especially in India where people are price sensitive. One of researcher found that Indian consumers are price conscious that is either they are unable to pay or reluctant to pay high prices for green products. Only 5% of green campaign marketing copy is completely true, lacking evenness to validate these claims for now, there is no standardization for certifying products as organic. Some regulatory bodies are required to provide the certifications. Businesses won't be able to make money right away since it will take time for the production of green products to attain economies of scale. One of researcher laid down that green marketing incorporation and compliance to green practices by organizations was due to government pressure and legislation (Singh and panday, 2012). As a consequence of this, these regulations provide businesses with a competitive advantage because they foster environmentally friendly marketing strategies and practices.

Therefore, Green marketing should be combined as a critical and operational component. Business, rather than as a backlash to societal and regulatory pressures. Organizations continue to produce largely the same item, while adding some "new" environmental benefits in their progression fights to capitalize on the burgeoning customer base in the environment. When green marketing is practiced in this manner, organizations are only concerned with promotional activity, with really no effort being made to create items that are genuinely green. From above literature, It can be extracted that Indian consumer being more price sensitive and lack of standarisation

are main challenges in adoption of green marketing.

Some other challenges ahead are:

*   In the initial years, Cost will be higher and also company will have to spend on research and development. Many firms may not survive in this challenging situation.
*   Companies may not be able to earn sufficient profit in beginning however they will attain economics of scale in long run.
*   Companies may go beyond fair means to survive in the market when they are not earning sufficient profits.

Green Initiatives Taken in India

*   To create, identify, and maintain an eco-friendly management framework, "H.C.L." developed a plan termed as "H.C.L. Eco safe."
*   The leading oil producer in our nation, O.N.G.C., is one of ten major Indian corporations that have taken on the mission of developing energy-efficient "green crematoriums" that will soon substitute conventional hardwood fires across the nation.
*   The first company in India to manufacture eco- or environment-friendly products is Wipro.
*   The push for transformation in the Indian construction sector has been triggered by Godrej green buildings.

Future of Green marketing in India

Organizations have realized that Consumers are becoming more and more environmental friendly and they are incorporating environmental friendly products in their lifestyle and customers are king of market therefore organizations are producing green products. However, there is lot to be done for future generation therefore companies should pay more attention to produce environmental friendly products. The C.S.R. idea has been embraced by numerous businesses to improve their company image. Businesses are facing pressure to modify their sustainability policies due to their competitors' behavior, and government bodies are pressuring companies to embrace more ecologically friendly practices. However, the issue of green marketing's future still needs to be addressed. Businesses are therefore required to apply their creativity and commitment for the development of eco-friendly products that will ultimately benefit society.

6. Suggestions

To fully explore the potential of green marketing, which is yet to reach its recognition stage, there needs to be a lot of research done. There are some suggestion which should be considered to successfully implement green marketing. These suggestions are:

Green marketing is still in its youth and it has long way to go however customers are not fully aware of its benefits therefore companies and government should create awareness among customers of all ages. Infact Green marketing and promotion are solid moves in that direction. Most important role is played by government. Governemnt should have stringent laws for those companies which do not sell what they promise in a product. Some companies make fake claims because of which customers do not trust others companies also. Companies should also pay attention to price they charge because customers will

not be **willing to very high** prices for eco-friendly products. Company should produce green products which are affordable to customers. Future research should also focus on customers expectations from green products. As rightly said that customers are king of market therefore they should be center of attention while producing products and producer should be aware of their expectations.

7. Conclusion

Today, consumers are much more concerned about climatic changes. There is a radical change in consumer preferences and lifestyles. Adopting green marketing may be Inaccessible for businesses in the short run, however it will positively impact business undertakings in the long run. Green marketing to some extent strengthen company's image in the mind of respondents that is very much clear from trustworthiness of green claims and certainly it do have positive image of the organization in the minds of the respondents. It should not be a matter of choice to adapt to green marketing rather it should be compulsory for the consumers, industrial buyers and suppliers. Government should make the strict rules to save the world from pollution and its negative effects In emerging nations like India, green marketing has an even greater significance and relevance. Moreover, companies' "Ethical Approach" must be a reality, not merely a promotional tool for better implementation. Furthermore, the government needs to take stringent measures to protect the environment in the best interests of humanity, as well as develop and implement laws that will make the environment safer. Moreover, the king of the market, the customer, must comprehend that it is their obligation to build green patronage and illustrate their green credentials by purchasing green products and services, even if they are costly. All that is required is dedication and commitment from all of the companies' stakeholders. Marketers are also liable for making consumers comprehend the value and advantages of green products over non green ones, as well as the rewards they can reap in the long term. The government will wholeheartedly endorse green marketers, and consumers will not bother spending extra for a cleaner and greener environment.

REFERENCES

1. Konar, S., & Cohen, M. A. (2001). Does the Market Value Environmental Performance? Review of Economics and Statistics, 83(2), 281–289.

2. Chamorro, A., & Bañegil, T. M. (2006). Green Marketing Philosophy: A Study of Spanish Firms with Ecolabels. Corporate Social Responsibility and Environmental Management, 13(1), 11–24.

3. Sharma, M. K., Pandey, N., & Sajid, R. (2015). Green marketing: A study of emerging opportunities and challenges in Indian scenario. International Journal of new technology and research, 1(4), 263679.

4. Polonsky, M. J. (1994). An introduction to green marketing. Electronic green journal, 1(2). *Howe, J., Bratkovich, S., Bowyer, J., Fernholz, K., & Stai, S. (2010). Green Marketing-Growing Sales in Growing Markets. Dovetail Partners INC.

5. Tiwari Jaya (2013) Green marketing in India: An Overview IOSR Journal of Business and Management, pp. 33–40.

6. Jain S. K. and Kaur G., (2004), Green Marketing: An Attitudinal and Behavioral Analysis of Indian Consumers? Global Business Review, Sage Publications, 5:2 187–205.

7. Singh, P. B., & Pandey, K. K. (2012). Green marketing: policies and practices for sustainable development. Integral Review, 5(1), 22–30.

8. Vural, C. A. (2015). Green marketing: A conceptual framework and suggestions for industrial services marketing. In Handbook of Research on Developing Sustainable Value in Economics, Finance, and Marketing (pp. 63–85). IGI Global.

9. Madhumita, G.& Sara. (2014). Green Marketing – Companies Urging Towards Green Revolution. Asia Pacific Journal of Research, Vol: I, Issue XIII.

10. Shrikanth, R., & Raju, D. S. N. (2012). Contemporary green marketing– brief reference to Indian scenario. International Journal of Social Sciences & Interdisciplinary Research, 1(1), 26–39.

Advancements in Business for Integrating Diversity, and
Sustainability – Dimitrios A. Karras et al. (eds)
© 2024 Taylor & Francis Group, London, ISBN 978-1-032-70828-7

30

Customer Perceived Value of Luxury Brands with a Perspective of Price Sensitivity and Aesthetics

Ritika Malik

Bharati Vidyapeeth (Deemed to be) University, Pune,
Institute of Management and Research, New Delhi

Swati Luthra

Assistant Professor, Bharati Vidyapeeth (Deemed to be) University, Pune,
Institute of Management and Research, New Delhi

Naveen Nandal*, Chakshu Mehta

Assistant Professor, Sushant University, Gurugram

Abstract: Purpose - The study has been conducted for the purpose of reviewing the customer perceived value of luxury brands from the year 2017 from the perspective of Price Sensitivity and Aesthetics as main variables. Various articles from top journals published including from ABDC, Web of Science and Scopus were reviewed from 2017 via google scholar and other online modes with a focus on two constructs - Symbolic value to customers and Exclusivity of the brand. The two unidimensional constructs - Price sensitivity and Aesthetics of the brand have been studied to understand the Customer Perceived Value for luxury brands.

Keywords: Customer Perceived Value, Customer Value, Luxury, Luxury brands, Marketing

1. Introduction

Luxury goods have been labeled as goods only for the wealthy. These goods are not required for a simple living but do work as status symbols that show the wealth of the owner. In Economics, luxury goods have been understood as goods for which the demand grows according to the growth in the incomes of potential buyers i.e., for which the growth in demand is directly proportional to the growth in incomes. China serves as a great example in this regard. Chinese middle class has grown rapidly with the double digit domestic growth numbers in the past few years' pre-pandemic. The middle class incomes were

---

*Corresponding author: Naveennandal@sushantuniversity.edu.in

DOI: 10.4324/9781032708294-30

estimated to be USD 2600 to USD 3900. Due to this jump in income levels, the luxury brands started flocking to this part of the world and capitalized on the opportunity. Today, Chinese luxury consumers are one of the biggest contributors to the high number of sales of such luxury brands. Today, even after the pandemic, Chinese consumers have contributed to a whopping 21% of the total global luxury market. Americans have been embracing the personal luxury and own the biggest share of 31% in the global luxury market. Europe, Japan and rest of Asia is expected to recover from the pandemic impact to the pre-crisis level by 2024. Luxury goods include mainly the personal luxury goods, luxury cars, luxury hospitality, fine wines and spirits, gourmet food and fine dining, high quality design furniture and homeware, fine art, private jets and yachts and luxury cruises.

Indian Luxury Market

Indian luxury market is highly made up of luxury cars segment then luxury jewelry, then super premium beauty and personal care followed by fine wines/champagne and spirits. As per Euromonitor International, the beauty and personal care segment of luxury goods in India was approximately $313 million in the year 2019. Mercedes Benz showed a sales number of 4101 cars in the third quarter of 2021. The Indian luxury market is expected to grow to $8.4 billion by the year 2024.

Price Sensitivity in Luxury Market

The luxury business is highly dependent on the principle of rarity where the rare items are sold at high prices. Their limited supply is the key to maintain the image of luxury. Luxury Brands like Ferrari, which sells high-end luxury cars at high price-points, sold less than a total of 7,000 units in the year 2013. However, this also works as a barrier in achieving sales numbers and restricts growth in profits. To combat this problem, luxury brands usually indulge in launching a number of products which are priced lower, for example, accessories, which are much less costly compared to the main products the luxury brands are focused on. Surprisingly, these additional product varieties bring most of the profits for such brands. The brands are, therefore, able to maintain their "luxury" status and able to grow their profits at the same time. This increase in product portfolio is known as "abundant rarity" strategy as given by Jean-Noël Kapferer.

In the wake of the pandemic, the luxury brands pivoted to new strategies to bring in revenues and make up for the losses incurred due to lockdown situation. In India, Taj Hotels launched an app called "Qmin" to service clients with online gourmet food services. Mercedes-Benz India focused on its e-platform "Merc from Home" for ordering and serving the customers with car delivery at home. These e-stores were created to give an immersive experience to the customers willing to purchase online. Indian fashion designers launched their reusable face masks under their label names. Due to restrictions on gyms, the brands embraced the fitness segment and launched several products like Louis Vuitton came up with fitness equipment including skipping rope and dumbbells.

The luxury brands are slowly embracing the e-commerce with the increase in influx of the online platforms. However, the brands are putting their product prices on display due to this, which has long been considered a negative move in the luxury segment since the idea is to preserve the exclusive status of the product. But displaying the price quickly forms a picture in the mind whether one is able to afford the product or not. Since there are laws regarding disclosing the prices online, luxury businesses are bound to do so. Disclosing product price draws attention to the value proposition, as to if the product is worth the price or not. Power Distance Belief (PDB) influences the price sensitivity of consumers as it makes consumers accept and endorse the hierarchy. Consumers are more willing to pay a higher price if slogans are used to activate a high-PDB, for example, "you deserve to reach the top". Low PDB consumers show a lower price sensitivity as compared to high PDB consumers providing better scope for acceptability if brands wish to increase the prices of products in low PDB zones. Indian customers are highly price sensitive due to factors – perceived risk, perceived usefulness, perceived ease of use, perceived enjoyment and satisfaction and personal innovativeness when it comes to using mobile shopping applications for purchasing goods. The Study conducted for Airbnb confirmed that price is a critical factor that impact the consumer's perceived value. Perceived risk negatively affects the price sensitivity. The perceived authenticity and e-word-of-mouth also serve as important factors.

The millennials exhibit a slight disregard to price changes when it comes to consumption as they value product attribute over price. The millennial consumer behavior is to give preference to ethical consumption over price when companies are engaged in Corporate Social Responsibility. The pricing of a luxury product is to be done through the psychological pricing or prestige pricing technique as consumers who purchase luxury items often believe that the price of luxury item reflects its quality. They are willing to purchase exorbitantly high priced goods as they perceive the goods to be of supreme quality. The high price helps create an image of the luxury item as a symbol of reputation, power, glamour and influence. High price of the luxury item enhances both- perceived value and real value. The result of the study conducted for Apple computer owners among the students confirmed that they would prefer purchasing apple computer which is much costlier than other brands because of peer influence. There is a strong word-of-mouth, brand loyalty and brand trust in terms of product's quality, reliability and its consistency.

Aesthetics in Luxury Market

Aesthetics play an important role when it comes to consumers looking for pleasant experiences in the moment of consumption for hotel industry. Such hedonistic consumer groups tend to positively respond to the store aesthetics and design which can be effectively used for marketing purposes. It affects the customer experience and can directly have an impact on customer loyalty and building word-of-mouth. The aesthetics of a store affects the affective and cognitive attitudes of the consumers when it comes to window displays. Aesthetic experience is basically one which is easily distinguishable from the everyday experience. It has the power to engage the subject's interest with the given object, suppressing all other surrounding objects. Aesthetics are the principles concerned with the nature and appreciation of beauty. Store aesthetics would mainly consist of the Layout planning and Hygiene maintenance. The stores pay attention to the walking space so that it can accommodate flow of traffic into the store. Then the focus is on the flow of the store to ensure customers enter the store and are encouraged to walk up to the back of the store and discover all merchandise on display without human intervention. Products must be placed at an eye level that improves visibility of all products to convert into better sales numbers. Products should be displayed in such a manner that they are highlighted and draw attention. Also, store cleanliness plays an important role. A properly lit store, with comfortable temperature, clear path and clean display of products serves as an encouragement. The design of store aesthetics serves as a positive influence on customer loyalty and customer satisfaction. Customers perceived the offerings to be of higher value which in turn enhanced the image of the store and product. The consumers' perceived brand image was also affected due to lighting and colour of the flagship stores. In addition to this, the store layout, fitting rooms, store area and furniture also contributed towards a more pleasurable experience of customers and their friends and family while shopping. Aesthetics are not only limited to the traditional product design, but it extends its relevance and presence in its embodiment for example through dresses of the dancers in the salsa event. Aesthetics play a major role in experiential luxury as well as they provide consumers with a more engaging and immersive experience. Consumers also evaluate the product aesthetics on the basis of their attributes to derive their satisfaction. Consumers prefer products with appealing product aesthetics over the non-appealing aesthetics. The price factor also has lesser influence in case of attractive product aesthetics. East Asian Luxury markets are still a lot to do with showing off. Therefore, a high price works as a signifier of high quality

for these consumers and motivates towards the conspicuous consumption. However, on the other end, any reduction in prices is perceived negatively. Any price drop due to sale on luxury items is unwelcomed as the consumers on this side of the globe cannot take pride while telling their peers that the purchase was made on sale prices.

2. Research Methodology

The paper adopts a method of systematic literature review of previous years' research papers from the year 2017 to 2021 to understand the luxury market from the perspective of price sensitivity and aesthetics particularly as there is limited study in this aspect. The previous research has mentioned the two constructs – price sensitivity and aesthetics merged with others. The study drew out previous research undertaken to build a further understanding of the subject. The paper is concerned with building a better understanding related to the price sensitivity and aesthetic value in relation to luxury consumption. Below is a description of the variables explained further in this paper using the systematic literature review method.

Price Sensitivity

The high priced brands have an inverse relationship between the variables- price and demand. Therefore, the price elasticity is low and with a temporary reduction or discount in prices there are very less chances to achieve larger sales. Situations of higher importance are linked to consumption of products that have low price elasticity, for example, high-priced champagne is linked to important occasions (Ava Huanga, 2017). Customers are willing to pay higher prices showing low price sensitivity if they are more sensitive for the quality of the product (Ana Paula Graciola, 2018).

Journal Name	Title	Keywords	Objectives	Findings	Data Analysis Tech.
Journal of Retailing and Consumer Services	Does price sensitivity and price level influence store price image and repurchase intention in retail markets?	Customer Repurchase Intention, Price Image, Price Sensitivity	The objective of the study is to find out how the showcasing of prices in stores impact the repurchase intention in the context of South Brazil	The study resulted in showing that customers were positively impacted for repurchasing goods when price images were available in stores.	PLS-SEM
Journal of Retailing and Consumer Services	Consumer response to price changes in higher-priced brands	Price Elasticity, Consumer, Elasticity	To Understand how the consumers respond to high-priced branded goods (wine) when they are aware the quality would be better than those regular packaged goods	The study showed that price elasticity was 2.6 where the consumption situation was considered to be highly important, for those who purchase and consume expensive wines and for brands with starting prices higher than regular brands. The price elasticity was 1.8 for expensive brands.	Online choice experiment conducted to study the situational, contextual and consumer factors
Journal of Business and Behavioral Sciences	Brand Loyalty, Brand Trust, Peer Influence and Price Sensitivity as influencers in Student Computer Purchase	Price sensitivity, brand trust, peer influence	To study the how brand loyalty, price sensitivity, brand trust and peer influence in affect the choice of brand of computers for purchasing among university students	Price sensitivity had a negative influence by peer influence and brand trust. Brand loyalty serves as an important factor in the student choice when buying an expensive branded computer.	Survey method analysed through confirmatory factor analysis and reliability analysis
Journal of Marketing	Price No Object!: The Impact of Power Distance Belief on Consumers' Price Sensitivity	Social density, Price search, Price sensitivity	To understand how PDB (Power Distance Belief) cultural dimension influences the consumers' price sensitivity	Social density lowers the price sensitivity for bw PDB consumers. PDB is to be treated separately from "culture" as Indians proved by showing they are more willing to pay premium prices signalling they are more price sensitive	Scanner Panel data, consequential measure, field study
Journal of Travel & Tourism Marketing	Understanding repurchase intention of Airbnb consumers: perceived authenticity, electronic word-of-mouth, and price sensitivity.	Airbnb, Repurchase intention, peer-to-peer economy	To further the research on the consumer intention for repurchasing, consumer perceived value and risk perceived from the viewpoint of peer-to-peer economy - Airbnb	the results show that perceived risk of consumers was not bwered by price sensitivity but improves the consumer preceived value. It also has a positive impact on the perceived value. It also showed that repurchase intention was positively affected by E-WOM but negatively affected the perceived risk.	Survey method
Journal of Marketing Analytics	Price sensitivity versus ethical consumption: a study of Millennial utilitarian consumer behavior	Price sensitivity, Millenials, Ethical con-sumption	The aim of the study is to find how millenials are affected by price sensitivity and ethical consumption and whether they prefer to purchase from companies invested in CSR efforts	The researchers developed two separate models focused on utility of products to study the consumer behavior of millenials regarding their price sensitivity and ethical consumption showing that millenials prefer to consume products made ethically and have bw price sensitivity	Semi-structured survey method
Journal of Retailing and Consumer Services	Understanding the intention to use mobile shopping applications and its influence on price sensitivity	Price sensitivity, Technology Acceptance Model, Mobile shopping applications	To build a further understanding of customer intentions being influenced due to price sensitivity while using mobile phone shopping apps	The study concluded that customer perceived risk and personal innovativeness of customers play a role in decision making.	Structural Equation Modeling approach

Source: Author's Source

Journal Name	Tite	Keywords	Objective	Findings	Data Analysis Tech.
International Journal of Business and Globalisation	International flagship stores: an exploration of store atmospherics and their influence on purchase behaviour	In-store experience. Luxury retail, flagship store	To analyse how the luxury flagship stores affect purchase behaviour of consumers	Results show that the design features and atmospheric cues play a role on the perceived brand image. The store layout, product displays and fitting room experience also are considered important by customers.	Qualitative study through semi-structure d interviews
Journal of Retailing and Consumer Services	Price image and the sugrophobia effect on luxury retail purchase intention	Sugropho-bia, SOR model, Price image	Sugrophobia is a psychological feeling where one feels taken advantage of. The study aimed at exploring how this foling and price image influence the consumers' behavioural intention in the future	The findings show that the price image of the retailr positively affects the consumer perceived vahe, their trust and attitudes along with the consumer perceptions. On the other hand, sugrophobia weakens this relationship of price image with consumer perceptions.	SEM-PLS
Journal of the Association for Consumer Research	The Influence of Product Aesthetics on Consumer Inference Making	Design, aesthetics. Comumer	To examine how aesthetics exert influence on estimating the missing attribute information regarding the aesthetically superior product	The results show that aesthetics influence help form biased inferences of consumers regarding the functionality.	Survey method
Journal of Business Research	Moments of huxury: Hedonic escapism as a luxury experience	Hedonism, Luxury, Experience	The objective of the study is to further the limited research of huxury which has been product centric to luxury experiences by studying hedonism and escapism as luxury characteristics	The comumer experiences take form of luxury when they are exclusive, exhibit aesthetic value and attached with authentic history.	Ethnographic method
Creativity and Marketing The Fuel for Success	Creative Art-based Initiatives Enabling Value Co-creation in the Lucary Fashion Industry.	Artification, Luxury fashion brand, service logic	To study the linakge between huxury and art from the perspective of co- creation of value	Luxury brands deploy initiatives which are art-based for value co-creation for the brand and customers	
Fashion & Textil Research Journal	Artification in Flagship Stores of Luxury Fashion Brands	A rtification, flagship store, exclusivity	The study is to understand how artification of flagship luxury brand stores help communicate the brand identity and value	The artification of flagship stores is divided into pursuance of band permanency and maintainence of brand exclusivity.	Literature review
Journal of Asian Finance, Economics and Business	The Concept of Luxury Brands and the Relationship between Consumer and Luxury Brands	Comsumer Behaviour, Brand Personality. Luxury brand	The aim of the study is to define what luxury brand means and propose a frame work for relationship of luxury and consumers by providing an empirical evidence.	The study conducted in Portugaland United States gave a holistic perspective on constructs of luxury brands and defined huxury with the point of view of symbolism.	Factor analysis and internal consistency reliability test
Journal of Fashion Marketing and Management: An International Journal	Exploring the rok of visual aesthetics and presentation modality in luxury fashion brand communication on Instagram	Visual aesthetics, Instagram Luxury brand	To examine how important the prsentation and visual aesthetics are in terms of huxury fashion brand content which is posted on instagram	The study reveald that instagram videos received more engagement from the audience compared to pictures posted. Expressive aesthetics abngwith video and audio brand content posted got more response from the audience.	Content analysis
Journal of Marketing Management	Store artification and retail performance	Art, store artification, consumer experience	To explore the impact of artification of the retail store on the performance of the retail	the results showed that the store artification enhanced the perceived differentiation of the store and value of what the store was offering, ako enhancing the customer satisfaction and product image.	Survey method

Source: Author's Source

Aesthetics

In the context of fashion brand communications through platforms like Instagram, consumers prefer expressive visual aesthetics as it fosters pleasure and arousal. Expressive aesthetics are more pleasing to consumers as compared to the classical aesthetics as they work as mood enhancers and motivate self-indulgence (Kusumasondjaja, 2020). In the physical world, (Bargenda, Luxury heritage brands between tradition and modernity, 2021) as the consumers involved in the constant value creation, affective response is generated to serve a phenomenological brand experience through aesthetics including the lighting of the store, goods on display, floor and wall art, furniture, etc.

3. Conclusion

Aesthetics features including the design of brand logo, store architecture, services capes, etc, help project the heritage of a luxury brand (Bargenda, Aesthetic heritage and corporate branding, 2021). Aesthetics and rich heritage of a brand are two important factors, among many others, which many customers in the luxury segment seek. The "ratification" technique of luxury brands helps create value and ensures better customer engagement in cognitive, emotional and imaginal activities as art experiences are a source of co-creation practices (Huiru Yang, 2021). The result is reflective in the aesthetics of luxury brand stores, their products and experiences offered. This ratification process is actively being used by the luxury flagship stores to convey the brand identity and brand value (Hwang, 2020). The aesthetics must be interesting in order to open a "mental space" making the customers fascinated with the aesthetics for a longer time (MarkoviÄ‡, 2012).

REFERENCES

1. Ana Paula Graciola, D. D. (2018). Does price sensitivity and price level influence store price image and repurchase intention in retail markets? Journal of Retailing and Consumer Services, 201–213.
2. Ava Huanga, J. D. (2017). Consumer response to price changes in higher-priced brands. Journal of Retailing and Consumer Services, 1–10.
3. Bargenda, A. (2021). Aesthetic heritage and corporate branding. In C. D. T C Melewar (Ed.), Building Corporate Identity, Image and Reputation in the Digital Era. Routeledge.
4. Bargenda, A. (2021). Luxury heritage brands between tradition and modernity. In Building Corporate Identity, Image and Reputation in the Digital Era. Routledge.
5. Blazquez, M. B. (2019). International flagship stores: an exploration of store atmospherics and their influence on purchase behaviour. International Journal of Business and Globalisation, 22(1). doi:10.1504/ijbg.2019.097392
6. Blotnicky, S. K. (2020). Brand Loyalty, Brand Trust, Peer Influence and Price Sensitivity as Influencers in Student Computer Purchase. Journal of Business and Behavioral Sciences, 32(1), 131–150.
7. Cheah, J.-H. W.-J. (2020). Price image and the sugrophobia effect on luxury retail purchase intention. Journal of Retailing and Consumer Services. doi:10.1016/j.jretconser.2020.102188
8. Markovic, S. (2012). Components of aesthetic experience: aesthetic fascination, aesthetic appraisal, and aesthetic emotion. i-Perception, 3(1), 1–17. doi:10.1068/i0450aap
9. Natarajan, T. B. (2017). Understanding the intention to use mobile shopping applications and its influence on price sensitivity. Journal of Retailing and Consumer Services, 37, 8–22. doi:10.1016/j.jretconser.2017.
10. Nobbs, V. M. (2013). Form and function of luxury flagships. Journal of Fashion Marketing and Management: An International Journal, 17(1), 49–64. doi:10.1108/13612021311305137

Advancements in Business for Integrating Diversity, and Sustainability – Dimitrios A. Karras et al. (eds)
© 2024 Taylor & Francis Group, London, ISBN 978-1-032-70828-7

31 Marketing Approach to Boost Contemporary Businesses' Performance

Sunil Kumar Vohra*

Amity Institute of Travel and Tourism,
Amity University, Noida, UP, India

Manoj Kumar Rao[1]

S. B. Jain Institute of Technology, Management and Research,
Nagpur, Maharashtra, India

Manoj B Pandey[2]

Central India College of Business Management and Studies,
Nagpur, Maharashtra, India

Abstract: Small- and medium-sized enterprises (SMEs) use marketing methods to improve performance. This research investigates how marketing methods affect SME's profitability, brand recognition, and share price in Ghana. Questionnaire data were obtained. Stratified random sampling selected 363 SMEs from 900. Marketing strategy and performance hypotheses were examined. Strategic marketing drives organizational position in a complicated situation and helps generate new products/services for existing markets, according to this research. According to the survey, SMEs in Ghana employ traditional marketing to attract new clients and build their brands. SMEs should employ more sophisticated technological marketing strategies to boost their success. The results offer policymakers and SME owners significant insights into marketing strategy and SME performance in a worldwide growing economy.

Keywords: Small- and medium-sized enterprises (SMEs), Marketing strategy, Technological marketing, Performance

1. Introduction

Organizations, including Small and Medium Enterprises (SMEs), have come to realize the necessity of establishing strategies that will assist them in gaining a comprehensive understanding of the market, particularly of their competitors and customers. These strategies will support them in achieving this goal. According to (Akindoju 2016),

*Corresponding author: sunilvohra2002@yahoo.co.in
[1]manojrao6611@gmail.com, [2]manojpandey07@gmail.com

DOI: 10.4324/9781032708294-31

the aspects that are most important to the success or failure of a small firm include financial restrictions, managerial experience, leadership abilities, marketing, and planning. Education is also an important component. Nevertheless, the emphasis of our investigation is on the marketing side of success or failure. After extensive marketing research has been completed, the next step in developing a marketing plan is to formulate a marketing strategy to implement. It assists a company in directing its resources, which are often limited, to the most productive work feasible to boost its sales. In the current highly competitive business world, promoting can be defined as a collection of firm activities that are meant to plan, produce, value, promote, and distribute goods, services, and concepts with the intention of pleasing appropriate customers and clients. This suggests that many different marketing actions are engaged in the chain of distribution that takes place between the supplier and the customer in the process of distributing items. The marketing strategy of a company is an essential factor in determining how successful it will be in expanding its share of the market and reducing the negative effects of the presence of rival companies (Kenu 2019). It is impossible to understate the importance of small and medium-sized businesses to economic growth. According to (Tetteh et al. 2022) Small and medium-sized businesses (also known as "SMEs") are widely acknowledged to be the most important factor contributing to overall economic expansion by policymakers, economists, and business professionals alike. Because they have contributed to more than fifty percent of the gross domestic product and provided more than sixty percent of the total employment in countries that are considered to be developed and have high incomes. The significance of

small and medium-sized businesses (SMEs) to a number of economies throughout the globe has been the subject of several academic discourses (Magd and El Gharib, 2021) In the majority of economies across the globe, the role the SME sector fulfills is both important and strategic. (Deku et al. 2022) discussed how it has been universally formed that the SME sector has played a significant role in incredibly quick economic growth and achieving quick modernization in most developing nations. They said that this is because the SME sector is comprised of SME businesses. It is general knowledge that small companies play an important part in the lives of all people since a significant portion of the economic activities that we engage in daily are dependent on small enterprises. The major purpose of this research is to investigate the connection that exists between the marketing approaches used by SMEs and the level of success that they enjoy in the relevant market. The results of the research are intended to serve as a guide for political leaders to take actions that will aid in the growth of businesses in the sector. The findings are also intended to contribute to the expansion of the existing body of knowledge concerning the application of marketing strategy to the SME sector.

2. Related Works

(Khalayleh et al. 2022) examined how digital content marketing mix affects marketing performance. Digital advertising information, social networking sites, digital pricing, and digital advertising were parts of the marketing mix for digital content. Study results were evaluated using a structural equation model. All marketing mix parameters for digital content improved marketing success, according to the research. (Kerdpitak et al. 2022) investigated herbal medicine company performance in Thailand. The research was quantitative. Data were collected by questionnaire. 340 herbal entrepreneurs provided data. SEM was used to investigate the real herbal economic performance of the firms examined across all operational connections in the promotional strategy, competitive advantage, logistical integration, and inventive management. (Zhang et al. 2022) examines the influence of green marketing and financing on company success in Ethiopia's Chinese textile industry. 237 respondents in Ethiopia's Chinese textile industries provided main and secondary data for the study. Green investment, marketing, and company performance were studied using an SEM and multivariate regression analysis. The ability of the digital market to provide clients with the goods and services they want is one factor contributing to the expansion of the service sector. For this purpose of this (Nuseir et al. 2022) analyzed the data-gathering strategy consisting of a cross-sectional survey questionnaire. The partial least square-structural equation modeling approach was used in this research project to provide empirical validation of the hypothesis that digital marketing skills have a substantial influence on the improvement of company performance. The conclusions of this research will be beneficial for regulators and policymakers as they build a strategy to boost corporate performance via the use of various methods of digital marketing, which can be aided by the information provided by the study. When businesses want to acquire a competitive edge, they often build solutions that are more creative and original. The relationship between Porter's classifications and the levels of business performance in Micro, Small, and medium firms is the focus of this research (MSMEs). (Knezović et al. 2022) the approach of cross-sectional

surveying was used to gather data from 118 different managers as samples. According to the findings, some typologies are more beneficial to the operation of a firm than others. Multiple regression was used so that we could evaluate our hypotheses. As a result, the findings of this research lead to a better understanding of the connection between Porter's typologies and the success of businesses.

3. Methodology

This study used a survey research approach to investigate the influence that marketing strategies had on the levels of performance of small and medium-sized enterprises (SMEs) in Ghana. The small and medium-sized businesses located in Ghana's Eastern Region are the focus of this study's population. The NBSSI Regional Office was consulted to get the database. Nine hundred (900) Eastern Region SMEs were selected as the population for the research after the database was screened using the definition of SMEs based on revenue and the number of people employed. These SMEs were selected from a wide range of economic sectors, including, but not limited to, fishing, agro-processing, industry, telecommunications, finance, tourist industry, and import and export, to name a few.

To ensure that every member of the target demographic had an equal opportunity to be chosen, a simple random sampling technique was used to choose three hundred sixty-three responders from the pool of candidates. It was decided to use a standardized questionnaire, which had both open-ended and closed-ended items. For analysis, three hundred and twenty copies of the questionnaire that was distributed were collected, which represented 88.88%

of the replies. Interviews were conducted with thirty-two (32) of the respondents who filled out the questionnaire to acquire a more in-depth understanding of the factors that were assessed. To aid in the process of deciphering the real meaning of what the study indicates, the statistical methods that were outlined above were used. This further indicates that the statistical approaches were helpful in finding and evaluating correlations and effects in circumstances when the results could not be similarly duplicated due to the inherent variability in the measures of interest.

4. Discussion of Result

Traditional Marketing Strategies

Table 31.1 illustrates that SMEs promote through conventional media. 29.3% of respondents market on TV and radio. They also utilize newspapers (23.8%), banners and billboards (11.5%), and branded items (14.0%). SMEs also utilize trade fairs and exhibits (12.3%) and door-to-door and word-of-mouth (12%) to get client feedback. This face-to-face meeting allows SMEs to obtain valuable consumer information, which they rely on to assure customer happiness SMEs employ discount sales (10%) to sell outdated stock and promote new items. Discounts and promotions are used to keep and attract clients.

Non-traditional strategies

According to the survey, SMEs utilize non-traditional marketing tactics to contact current and new clients. SMEs use sophisticated marketing technology to compete in the global market. SME goods and services were heavily promoted on social media (33%). Facebook was the most popular social network. SMEs may build a Facebook account or page for 56% less than

a corporate website. A company website in Ghana costs roughly US$600, which SMEs find more costly than social networking. SMEs chose Facebook over email for interactivity (23%). Table 31.2 shows the media for non-tradition.

Table 31.1 Media tradition

Communications	FQ	P
Tv & radio	80	29.3
Newspaper and Magazine	55	23.8
Banner and Billboards	48	11.5
Branded paraphernalia	41	14.0
Trade fairs and Exhibitions	35	12.3
Door-to-door and word-of-mouth	62	12.0
Discount Sales and Promotions	25	10.0
Total	346	112

Table 31.2 Media non-traditional

Communications	FQ	P
Internet sites	152	33
Mails	53	23
Facebook	141	56
Total	346	112

SMEs' market performance

The ANOVA table reveals 0.657 is larger than 0.5(0.5). Each advertising method helps SMEs contact prospective clients.

Table 31.3 Customers' media access

	Total of the Squares	Df	Mean Square	FQ	Sig.
Between Groups	2.266	6	568	.610	.659
Within Groups	313.431	364	934		
Total	315.697	370			

Table 31.4 shows that SME marketing methods affect profitability (36%), brand recognition (20%), and market share (56%). "I advertise on the radio since more people listen now." When I began my company, I sold 50 cartons. My product's demand has grown following local promotion. I sell 5000 cartons every week in Ghana and Nigeria. Good sales!

Table 31.4 SMEs performance

	FQ	P
Profitability	155	36
Brand Awareness	52	20
Market Share	139	56
Total	346	112

Examination of the Hypotheses

Difference between the Marketing performance and Strategies

Null Hypothesis: Traditional marketing strategies help SMEs.

$$HP_0 = \varepsilon_1$$

Alternative Hypothesis: SMEs' performance is affected by non-traditional marketing strategies.

$$HP_1 \neq \varepsilon_1$$

Table 31.5 shows that conventional marketing methods are more linked to SME success than non-traditional ones.

Table 31.5 Traditional and non-traditional media

	Total of the Squares	Df	Mean Square	FQ	Sig.
Between Groups	4.090	9	.684	.830	.551
Within Groups	262.337	321	.835		
Total	266.427	330			

5. Conclusion

Overall, the findings imply that strategic marketing campaigns promote organizational positioning in a changing environment and assist generate new products/services for current markets. The research found that neither method traditional or non-traditional is better than the other; finding the correct blend may generate the best communication/marketing plan for SMEs. Traditional marketing methods affect SME performance more than non-traditional ones. This reveals that SMEs utilize conventional marketing – principally TV and radio, newspapers and magazines, banners and billboards, and branded paraphernalia – to attract clients. Non-traditional marketing methods were less associated with SMEs' success. Few SMEs use technology-based marketing to reach clients. FB was the most popular marketing platform above company websites and E-mails. Social media interaction attracts SMEs. Social media pages are easier and cheaper to put up than business websites.

REFERENCES

1. Akindoju, O. O. (2016). Exploring small business strategies in Halifax, Nova Scotia. Walden Dissertations and Doctoral Studies, Walden University

2. Kenu, A. Z. (2019). Effect of Marketing Mix Strategy on Performance of SMEs Evidence from Selected Manufacturing Enterprises in Southern Region, Ethiopia. International Journal of Science and Research (IJSR). Volume 8 Issue 12, December 2019. 1129–1133.

3. Tetteh, Lexis Alexander, Amoako Kwarteng, Emmanuel Gyamera, Lazarus Lamptey, Prince Sunu, and Paul Muda. "The effect of small business financing decision on business performance in Ghana: the moderated mediation role of the corporate governance system." International Journal

of Ethics and Systems ahead-of-print (2022).

4. Magd, H. & El Gharib, A. (2021). Entrepreneurship and SMEs Sustainable Development through Business Incubators: The case of Oman.

5. Deku, Wisdom Apedo, Jiuhe Wang, and Narain Das. "Innovations in entrepreneurial marketing dimensions: evidence of Halal food SMEs in Ghana." *Journal of Islamic Marketing* (2022).

6. Khalayleh, M., and S. Al-Hawary. "The impact of digital content of marketing mix on marketing performance: An experimental study at five-star hotels in Jordan." *International Journal of Data and Network Science* 6, no. 4 (2022): 1023–1032.

7. Kerdpitak, C. "Business performance model of herbal community enterprise in Thailand." *Uncertain Supply Chain Management* 10, no. 2 (2022): 345–352.

8. Zhang, Youtang, and Hagos Mesfin Berhe. "The Impact of Green Investment and Green Marketing on Business Performance: The Mediation Role of Corporate Social Responsibility in Ethiopia's Chinese Textile Companies." *Sustainability* 14, no. 7 (2022): 3883.

9. Nuseir, Muhammed, and G. Refae. "The effect of digital marketing capabilities on business performance enhancement: Mediating the role of customer relationship management (CRM)." *International Journal of Data and Network Science* 6, no. 2 (2022): 295–304.

10. Knezović, Emil, and Aida Hamur. "Porter's Business Strategies and Business Performance in SMEs." In *Entrepreneurial Innovation*, pp. 7–23. Springer, Singapore, 2022.

Note: All the tables in this chapter were made by the Authors.

Advancements in Business for Integrating Diversity, and
Sustainability – Dimitrios A. Karras et al. (eds)
© 2024 Taylor & Francis Group, London, ISBN 978-1-032-70828-7

32 Factors Influencing Investor's Wealth Management Behaviour in Delhi NCR

Naveen Nandal*

Assistant professor, Sushant University Gurgaon

Chakshu Mehta

Assistant professor, Sushant University Gurgaon

Aarushi Kataria

Assistant Professor, Bharati Vidyapeeth University, New Delhi

Shevata Singhal

Faculty, Institute of Banking Personnel Selection, Mumbai

Abstract: Market performance and fluctuations bring a lot of uncertainties in the behaviour of investors and in that situation financial institutions play a dominant role in the wealth management of investors The purpose of this study is to explore the factors that influence an investor's behavior towards wealth management services in India. Factors investigated in the current study are Attitude, Risk Appetite, subjective norms, beliefs, investment behavior and financial literacy of investors. The study was conducted on investors living in Delhi/NCR. The respondents consist of a mix of both males and females falling in the age group of 21 and above. The study covers financial institutions and banks that provide wealth management services. The analysis was conducted by applying Bartlett's Test of Sphericity and Kaiser-Meyer-Olkin Measurement is used to know Sampling Adequacy. After the data was checked with help of Bartlett's Test of Exploratory Factor Analysis (EFA) was conducted. Exploratory Factor Analysis (EFA) is normally conducted to examine the association between the observed and latent variables which is unknown or uncertain. The article provides novel insight into the role of various factors that influence wealth management behavior. Further, it enhances the body of knowledge in understanding wealth management in investment decisions of investors in an emerging market. The survey includes banks and financial firms that offer wealth management services.

Keywords: Investor, Wealth management, Behavior

*Corresponding Author: Naveennandal@sushantuniversity.edu.in

DOI: 10.4324/9781032708294-32

1. Introduction

For any person living on this globe, money has its own significance. Merely earning money is no longer enough for a person to become rich; it is equally crucial to manage money in a careful manner. In other words, the creation of wealth must be followed by protecting it. This is possible only if money is managed in a proper and organized way. A secure future for oneself and one's family is possible only when one follows a suitable saving and investment plan that utilizes wealth in an organized way. At present, there are varied investment plans that an individual can choose from. An investor makes investment decisions based on various factors. He makes use of fundamental and technical analysis and also relies upon market information to make an informed judgment about his investment. But he might not be able to completely comprehend the information and analysis. This is where financial institutions come into the picture. They help an individual by providing professional services to manage his wealth. Wealth management is not merely providing investment recommendations but includes all aspects of the financial life of an individual or a company. It refers to the facilities provided by financial organizations or individuals to assist investors in protecting and enhancing their wealth. It encompasses various kinds of services including the planning of finances, managing investments, planning tax returns, handling the cash flow in addition to management of debts. Wealth management can thus be defined, as an activity that aims to maximize, safeguard and handle the financial well-being of a person, family or firm. This field has immense potential and is amongst of the rapidly growing industries

of the financial sector. It deals with every facet of a customer's financial life and provides consultation in a personalized/ tailored manner. It includes employment of varied kinds of goods, services and tactics. It is wealth managers that assist people to recognize their financial aims and take steps to attain them. Previously, setting of the goals was considered to be beyond the scope of wealth management; this however has become an intrinsic part of wealth management services in the current times. This sector is becoming more prominent and significant because of the increasing number of rich & super rich people.

Apart from individuals, several private and public sector banks have also begun to offer wealth management services to assist their clients especially the High Net-worth Individuals (HNW) to safeguard and enhance their wealth. HNW individuals are the people who have assets worth more than USD1 million including investable and liquid financial assets but excluding personal assets and real estate. This classification enable banks to provide personalized services to the individuals. In India, wealth management services include providing information and assistance in investing in equity-linked portfolio management services, distinct products tailor-made for a class of people, mutual funds and also insurance. Furthermore, the services have also been extended to provide information and assistance in tax evaluation and planning, investment in real estate, advisory services related to art by varied firms. For High-net-worth individuals (HNWIs), the owner and families of small firms, who desire the help of a credentialed financial specialist, implore the wealth managers to organize estate planning, retail banking, tax professionals, investment management and legal resources. Wealth managers can encompass backgrounds as independent certified financial planners in the USA and UK, chartered financial consultants, chartered strategic wealth professionals in Canada or any professional like MBA (professional money managers) who work to improve the income or profit, growth and tax preferential action of long term investors. One should already have accumulated several quantity of wealth for strategies of wealth management to be very effective. Private wealth management is distributed to High Net-worth Investors. Commonly this includes opinion based on the utility of different business succession, stock option planning, estate planning vehicles and occasional use of hedging for huge amount of stock. A professional service is the combination of investment or financial advice, accounting or tax services and estate planning for a fee.

The wealth management firms offer a wide array of options to an investor to invest. The investment strategy of every investor is distinct. The global wealth management scenario has considerably improved over a year. The new global regulations, changing investor's behavior, rapid advancement of digitization have changed the way a business is done. It is imperative for the wealth managers to adapt quickly to the changing rules and the changing scenario. The rapid advancement in digitization is influencing the expectations of investors towards wealth management. As more and more individuals are becoming technology savvy and aware, they are looking for alternatives to manage their wealth. Thus, it has become important for wealth mangers to track their behavior and step-up the ladder of success. Investment behavior is referred to as how investors

predict, review, judge and analyze the decision making procedures that encompass information gathering.

2. Literature Review

The idea of Wealth Management originated in the US in the 1990's. In the beginning, it encompasses investment advisory which in turn included financial planning that offered people with services like private banking, portfolio and asset management, taxation advisory etc. Majority of these services are extremely personal and portfolio management being the most common among them. These services include products like stocks, equity linked and structured savings products, mutual funds and alternative investments.

The Wealth Management Services can be availed by High Net-worth Individuals (HNWIs), small entrepreneurs and other individuals who want their hard earned money to be professionally managed by specialists known as Wealth Managers. After China, India is considered to be the second most appealing market for Wealth Management. According to a research conducted by one of the Asia's leading wealth manager firm, Barclays Capital, a known Investment Banking firm, "China and India persist in being the most appealing Asian markets, both in context of ability to expand businesses and anticipated growth rate of revenues."

According to Evensky (1997), in wealth management, everything is client-centric; in fact, this process commences only when an official association is set up between the wealth manager and the customer. Evensky (1997) further opines that the task of a wealth manager is to successfully develop and personalize the procedure of wealth management to encompass the personal experiences of the customer. Thus, wealth management can be regarded as an association between a customer and an advisor referred to as a wealth manager. Wealth management is currently one of the most demanding and competitive industries in the world. It also faces numerous current issues, such as promoting its services, expanding its range of customer support, and fostering client trust. Current wealth management clients are interested in using mobile applications to access and manage their accounts due to the growing use of technology. In order to protect the wealth of their investors, wealth managers must have a solid and secure IT infrastructure. Clients are now reluctant to trust their wealth managers due to concerns about their integrity following the significant financial setback suffered by wealth management organisations (Kumar et al., 2011).

India's economic growth and promising future make it a desirable market for wealth management companies. India's GDP has consistently hovered around the 9% mark. This trend is forecast to continue, and by 2030, India's economy is projected to be the third largest in the world. Given that India's economy is expanding at an enormous rate and is expected to be ranked third among all economies by 2030, potential new entrants in the wealth management sector are drawn to this market, which motivates them to establish a strong foundation and increase their market revenues (Cognizant Report, 2011).

The wealthy population of India is significantly younger than their global counterparts, and as a result, they have different perspectives on wealth management.

The change in the demographics offers an opportunity to create new plans to address the needs of the younger population and have an impact on emerging technologies, such as social media and mobile-based applications, which enable investors to bring investment opportunities at their fingertips and these advancements have turned out to be key differentiators in this industry.

Wealth management service industry in India is widely fragmented which is not astonishing because this sector is still in its early years of growth and is still not mature. A fifth of the population of high net worth individuals (HNI) in India are now untapped because the majority of organised businesses have focused mostly on those who live in metro areas. India is thought of as one of the wealth management markets that is rapidly expanding.

In contrast to its large populace, the Indian HNW market is quite small; with 153,000 HNWIs India ranked 16th in the world by the HNI Population (Asia-Pacific Wealth Report, 2014). However, it is growing quickly all around the world, giving wealth managers a lot of room to grow. The development of the HNW population is a result of the Indian economy's strong financial performance, which has increased the proportion of HNW business owners and entrepreneurs. A study by Data Monitor (2011) found that a guy over the age of 65 who has mostly amassed wealth through entrepreneurship is the most likely description of an Indian high-net-worth individual. He has a preference for real estate in his portfolio and prefers to allocate the largest majority of his fortune to real estate investment funds since he views real estate as a reliable investment.

The growing volatility in Indian markets makes a shift in the focus of clients to low risk products with the expectation of higher returns at competitive prices. This poses a challenge for wealth managers to redesign their business models in order to sustain and maintain their market share in the evolving market.

Objective

This study aims to explore the factors that influence an investor's behavior towards wealth management services

Sample:

The survey's participants were HNWI investors who reside in Delhi/NCR, India. They were mostly evaluated if they were between the ages of 21 and older. They had a range of educational and professional experiences. The study's sample size could include both males and females. The survey includes banks and financial organizations that offer wealth management services.

Data Analysis

KMO and Bartlett's Test

Kaiser-Meyer-Olkin Measure of Sampling Adequacy		.897
Bartlett's Test of Sphericity	Approx. Chi-Square	9654.095
	Df	861
	Sig.	.000

As can be seen from the above table, the KMO sampling adequacy of the data samples is significant at 0.897, and the application of Bartlett's Test of Sphericity is relevant because it is less than 0.05. As a result, the results of this test provide sufficient support for the suitability and adequacy of the data.

After the data was checked for its suitability for factor analysis, Exploratory Factor Analysis (EFA) was conducted. Exploratory

Factor Analysis (EFA) is normally conducted to examine the association between the observed and latent variables which is unknown or uncertain (Byrne, 2010). The analysis extracts the minimum number of factors on the basis of correlation between observed and latent variables (De Coster, 1998). This correlation is represented by factor loadings where, the item that measures the intended factor will load high on that factor (Byrne, 2010). EFA is also used to develop and validate an instrument in case where measures are assessed by the researcher from literature or other sources (Ruscio & Roche, 2012). The factorial validity helps in confirming whether the data collected for a particular group of variables do or do not represent the latent constructs.

In the context of the study, Principle Axis Factoring, an important technique in the Exploratory Factor Analysis process has been used to examine the factors influencing Wealth Management Behavior and their correlations in the data obtained. Usually, the initial factor extraction doesn't give interpretable factors. Rotation makes larger loading even larger and smaller loadings even smaller. Therefore, process of rotation provides factors that can be named and interpreted. Varimax rotation has been used as it provides clearer separation of factors (Dhillon and Goldstein, 1984).

There were 63 items in the study labeled as V1, V2 ... V63. The variable loading value of above 0.50 is considered significant (Hair et. al., 2010). Using Principal Axis factoring and Varimax Rotation, the Exploratory Factor analysis was conducted. We eliminated the variables with factor loadings less than 0.50. (V). The scale was then downsized from 63 items to 61 items. Six components with Eigen values larger than 1.0 that together explain 67.15 percent of the variance

Table 32.1 Summary of rotated component matrix and Cronbach's alpha and variance

Factor No.	Factor	No of Item	(Cumulative) % of Variance Explained	Factor Loadings (Values)	Cronbach Alpha
1	Factor 1. Attitude	V1	30.245 (30.245)	.883	0.976
2	Factor 2. Risk-taking Appetite	V16	12.417 (42.662)	.797	0.946
3	Subjective Norms	V29	8.997 (51.659)	.865	0.969
4	Beliefs of Investors	V39	8.196 (59.855)	.809	0.942
5	Investment Behavior of Investors	V51	3.934 (63.789)	.804	0.912
6	Financial Literacy of Investors	V57	3.368 (67.157)	.758	0.935

Source: Authors

were kept after the extraction process. The factors' extracted items, item loadings, % of variation explained, and Cronbach's alpha are displayed in Table 32.1.

Attitude is the first factor to be extracted. An object's attitude is how you feel about it. This factor is measured by fifteen (15) items (V1, V2,...V15). The measured variables' factor loadings range from 0.742 to 0.883, and this factor accounts for 30.25% of the overall variation. The fifteen items measure the factor based on the investor's attitude toward financial products, perception of the company, duration of investment, behaviour during uncertain times, assessment of stock's future performance, perception of wealth manager's services, and investment. The total variation explained by this factor is 30.25%. The fifteen components assess the factor based on, among other things, the investor's attitude toward financial products, perception of the business, and duration of investment aim.

Risk appetite is the second element that was retrieved. The capacity to take on risk is referred to as risk appetite. This factor is measured by thirteen (13) items with a total variation of 12.42%, and the factor loadings

of the variables range from 0.623 to 0.797. The items assess how investors' mindsets change in response to losses and economic volatility, for example. Additionally, it evaluates how investors perceive investing in particular businesses and equities.

Subjective Norms are the third element that was retrieved. Subjective norms describe how a person views the advice given to him by those who are close to him. This component accounts for a total variance explanation of 8.997%. The factor loadings of the ten (10) items measuring this factor range from 0.777 to 0.865. The items gauge how investors respond to advice on investments from peers, advisors, and friends and relatives' families. The items evaluate investors' responses to publications and adverts for different financial goods. The decisions made by the investors were also evaluated in light of their intuition and prior knowledge.

Beliefs, the fourth item to be extracted, deals with people's presumptions about various things. This factor accounts for 8.196% of the variance in total. This factor is measured by eleven (11) items, with factor loadings ranging from 0.771 to 0.809. The questions assess people's attitudes about their investments, the business in which they invested, a specific stock, the economy, their own investment decision, etc.

Investment Behavior, the fifth factor to be extracted, describes how an investor behaves in relation to the kinds of investments they make or their overall pattern of investing. This factor accounts for 3.934% of the variance in total. This factor was tested by six (6) different items, with factor loadings ranging from 0.620 to 0.804. The questions evaluated the frequency with which investors used services related to wealth management, how they feel about service providers, how they see the future of wealth management, etc.to measure investor behaviour.

Financial literacy, the sixth characteristic identified, reflects the depth of understanding and awareness an investor has regarding financial issues. This factor accounts for 3.37% of the variance in total. This factor was tested by six (6) items, with factor loadings ranging from 0.664 to 0.758. Due to their low factor loadings, the two items were eliminated. The test questions evaluated investors' knowledge of financial topics such as wealth management services, risk involved with them, institutions that offer wealth management services, accessible investment options, investor's rights and duties, and investment plans, among other things.

3. Conclusion

In this paper factors influencing investors' wealth management behaviour were examined. Six factors were found the most influencing factors that influence the wealth management behaviour of investors that includes Attitude, Risk Appetite, subjective norms, beliefs, investment behaviour and financial literacy of investors. The first-

factor Attitude refers to the feelings about a specific object. The total variance explained by this factor is 30.25% and the factor loadings of the measured variables vary between 0.742 - 0.883. Risk is the second extracted factor. The capacity to take on risk is referred to as appetite. This factor is measured by thirteen (13) different things. with a total variance of 12.42% and the factor loadings of the variables vary between 0.623 - 0.797. Beliefs, the fourth item to be extracted, deals with people's presumptions about various things. This factor accounts for 8.196% of the variance in total. This factor is measured by eleven (11) items, with factor loadings ranging from 0.771 to 0.809. The fifth factor extracted is Investment Behavior and it refers to the behaviour of investor towards the type of investments they make or their investment pattern. This factor accounts for 3.934% of the variance in total. A total of six (6) items with factor loadings measured this factor. varying between 0.620 - 0.804. Financial literacy, the sixth characteristic identified, reflects the depth of understanding and awareness an investor has regarding financial issues. This factor accounts for 3.37% of the variance in total. This factor was assessed by six (6) items with factor loadings ranging from 0.664 to 0.758. Factor loading is essentially the association or correlation between the factor and the variable. Factor loading displays the variance that is explained by the individual variable on that factor. As a general rule, a factor loading of 0.7 or above indicates that the factor extracts enough variance from that variable. If the variance is smaller than 0.7, it shouldn't be taken into account. Therefore, it can be considered that belief and attitude are the factors are most important factors that influence the wealth management behaviour of an individual in comparison to the other three factors. However, investor behaviour is not considered a major factor towards wealth management. The research suggests that apart from fundamental and technical analysis used for financial planning there are behavioural factors also that influence the decision of investors. Other behavioural factors like mood, emotions and biases can be considered for further research.

BIBLIOGRAPHY

1. Asia-Pacific Wealth Report 2014, Asia-Pacific Wealth Report 2014 from Capgemini and RBC Wealth Management. Available at: https://www.capgemini.com/thought-leadership/asia-pacific-wealth-report-2014-from-capgemini-and-rbc-wealth-management (Accessed on 2nd Dec 2014).

2. Byrne, B.M., 2010. Structural Equation Modeling with AMOS: Basic Concepts, Applications and Programming. 2nd ed. Ney York: Routledge.

3. Cognizant Report, 2011. Wealth Management in India. Avialable at: http://www.cognizant.com/InsightsWhitepapers/Wealth-Management-in-India-Challenges-and-Strategies.pdf (Accessed on: 27th Nov 2014)

4. DeCoster, Jamie 1998, Overview of Factor Analysis, Available at: http://www.stat-help.com/factor.pdf (Accessed on 23rd November 2014).

5. Evensky, H.R., 1997. Wealth management: the financial advisor's guide to investing and managing Clients Assets. 1st ed. USA: TheMacGraw-Hill Company.

6. Hair, J., Black, W., Babin, B. & Anderson, R., 2010. Multivariate data analysis. 7th ed. Upper Saddle River, NJ, USA: Prentice-Hall, Inc.

7. Nandal. et al., a b-schools service quality measure: scale development and validation, Academy of Strategic Management Journal, Volume 20, Special Issue 6, 2021.

8. Kumar, A., Page, J.K. & Spalt, O.G., 2011. Religious Beliefs, Gambling Attitudes, and Financial Market Outcomes. Journal of Financial Economics, 102(3), pp. 671–708.

9. Nandal. et al. Impact of product innovation on the financial performance of the selected organizations: A study in indian context. Psychol. Educ. J. 2021, 58, 5152–5163.

10. Jora, Neetu and Nandal, Naveen. (2020), Investors Attitude towards Cryptocurrency-based on Gender, Turkish Journal of Computer and Mathematics Education, 11(2), pp. 622–630.

Advancements in Business for Integrating Diversity, and Sustainability – Dimitrios A. Karras et al. (eds)
© 2024 Taylor & Francis Group, London, ISBN 978-1-032-70828-7

33

Human Resource Development as a Component of Long-term HR Management Emphasizing Production Engineers

Alex Khang[1]
University of Science and Technology, Vietnam & USA

Anchal Pathak*
UPES, School of Business, Dehradun, India

Abstract: One of the human resource management (HRM) concepts that should be used consistently along with the others is HR development. To execute the concept of Industry 4.0, it is essential to gain the so-called competences of the future. The purpose of this article is to offer human potential development in the context of other comprehensive sustainable HRM concepts. Industrial engineers in Poland are the professionals tasked with putting the concepts of cleaner production and Industry 4.0 into practise, therefore we will proceed to explore the state of the art in terms of theory and research into the creation of future capabilities. On the basis of the survey technique and representative data from Eurostat and Statistics Poland, the author examined the findings of three research projects. The results of the study suggest that Polish industries have a tendency to see the potential of its engineers with a limited perspective.

Keywords: Human resource management (HRM), Industrial engineers, Industrial companies

1. Introduction

An ongoing controversy has been brewing since the 1980s about what constitutes the "right" method of managing people in the workplace. Several studies have shown that HRM practises, especially those involving the introduction of new strategies and new forms of innovation, directly contribute to an organization's success. Constant reorganisation is a fact

of life in today's business environment (Rezaei, et al., 2021). The Triple Bottom Line framework provides the basis for this idea. Environmental progress is addressed in the first pillar, economic progress in the second, and social progress in the third. It was founded in the 1960s in reaction to the threats posed by a rapidly expanding human population, including but not limited to depletion of natural resources, pollution of the environment, unemployment, hunger,

*Corresponding author: anchal.pathak@ddn.upes.ac.in
[2]alexkhang.ai@gmail.com

DOI: 10.4324/9781032708294-33

and deforestation. The Club of Rome was established in 1968, and its report "The Limits to Growth" e provided a gloomy outlook on the future of Earth (Navaneetha, et al., 2022). Recent years have seen a surge in interest in this idea, although the literature addressing this topic remains sporadic and wide-ranging. At the centre of these shifts is a team of industrial engineers. As long as they continue to bring product and process innovations that are critical to the survival and expansion of organisations, as well as result in the supply of high-quality products to society and produce economic growth, it is appropriate to continue referring to them in this manner. When it comes to environmental responsibility, engineers should prioritise new technologies that promote cleaner production, also known as "preventive environmental management" that "promotes eliminating waste before it is created to systematically reduce overall pollution generation and improve

efficiencies of resource use." One of the many potential outcomes of adopting the Industry 4.0 paradigm is cleaner manufacturing (Alshurideh, et al., 2022). Carbon emissions may be reduced, resource efficiency improved via waste management, and energy usage optimised. Industry 4.0, of which the IoT is a part, has the potential to usher in a wave of novel eco-friendly goods. Against the backdrop of other specific SHRM concepts, this article's theoretical portion aims to describe how human potential in an organisation should be structured. Several studies cited in the article are from peer-reviewed publications that are included in Scopus. The empirical part includes findings from three separate research initiatives that together examine sustainable HR development as it relates to production engineers in Poland. The article also includes a discussion of the practical and theoretical consequences. There are several ways in which this article advances

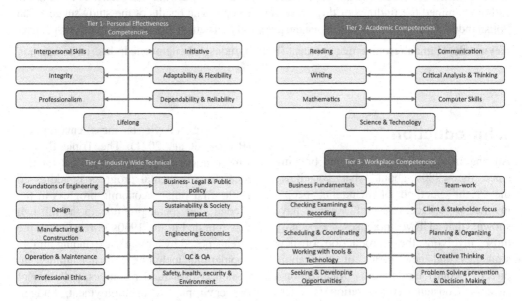

Fig. 33.1 Engineering competency model (ECM)

the state of the idea. The first part of this article describes one SHRM concept and explains the interconnections between it and the other HRM principles. "The Employment and Training Administration (ETA) and the American Association of Engineering Societies (AAES) collaborated in 2017 to create the Engineering Competency Model (ECM) for engineers". Detailed in Fig. 33.1 are the several sub-competency categories that engineers need to demonstrate their mastery of. Competencies are presented by each category (Gupta, et al., 2022).

2. Related Works

A report of an optimum configuration table model of a company's human resources may be formulated with the help of an analysis and processing tool that constructs such a model in the database. According to Liu, et al., 2021 this approach significantly improves the organization's power to optimally allocate human resource management and increases the data combination capacity of the HR department. The purpose of this literature study was to compile all of the available information on how the Industry 4.0 Revolution has affected human capital and customer behaviour so far. 160 publications were found via a search of the Web of Science that were eligible for inclusion (Sima, et al., 2020). Gruzina, et al., 2021 method allows us to compare the growth of human capital across several economic cycles using a common set of calculations. Revunov, et al., 2021 examines how incorporating cutting-edge information and communication technology into the educational process might boost the value of human capital. Alam, A. (2022) to investigate the impact of HR policies on the productivity of college

and university professors via an examination of the mediating role of work satisfaction. Tseng, et al., (2021) contributes to the current literature by conducting a bibliometric evaluation of sustainable industrial and operation engineering at the cutting edge of the subject as it advances toward Industry 4.0 and providing direction for future research and practical accomplishments.

3. Proposed Methodology

The aims of this article were accomplished by combining the findings of three separate studies, as explained in the article's introduction. In 2016, ASTOR Academy launched the first of these initiatives, named "The Development of Engineers' Competencies" (ASTOR, 2017). A total of 114 manufacturing industry engineers participated in the survey. The survey was taken on by the engineering staff of these businesses. Kantar Polska S.A. used a technique called computer-assisted telephone interviews (CATI) to collect data for this research. During these interviews, an interviewer uses specialized software installed on a computer to facilitate conversation with a respondent. In light of this, it may be assumed that the study fairly represents both of these fundamental sectors of the economy. Further, the sample population included engineers with a broad range of professional backgrounds, from those just entering the field (24.5%) to those with over 20 years of relevant experience (15%). Women formed 13% of the responses". Because of this, the researcher was able to assume that the sample was really representative of the population, allowing for more solid conclusions to be drawn from the data.

4. Result and Discussion

According to a 2016 ASTOR survey of industrial engineers' wants and needs, engineers are most driven by the following: the chance to learn and grow in their careers; the prospect of taking on challenging new projects; the chance to work with a wide range of people; the chance to pursue a field they are truly passionate about; the chance to feel like their work matters.

The majority of respondents to the survey conducted for the Smart Industry Poland 2019 initiative recognized that engineers are increasingly taking on the role of change leaders inside their companies, developing innovative approaches to problems like sustainable development. To be successful in engineering, one must be adaptable and open to new ideas, so it's not unexpected that many seasoned professionals, even those in their 50s and 60s, are interested in trying out a novel approach in the hopes of assuming a leadership position in the next wave of transformation. Among the youngest respondents, 84% anticipate changes in the engineering profession, suggesting that people drawn to this field anticipate encountering such a transformation throughout their own professional lives (Fig. 33.2).

Some of the academic skills highlighted in the ECM were the ability to analyze data and use technology effectively. Polish engineers believe that their technical expertise is the most important factor in establishing their credibility. Design thinking in the field of chemical product development has been hampered by engineers' preoccupation with technical details. Considerable personal talents, such as creativity (89% agree) or social skills (81% agree), are seen favorably in this setting. Earlier, we saw how digital skills will play a significant role among the future sets of abilities. It will become more important to have expertise in emerging fields like cyber security, artificial intelligence algorithm development for automation systems, and team programming for industrial robots. Data from Eurostat backs up this outlook. In terms of the criterion "Percentage of persons with basic or above basic overall digital skills," Poland is below the EU average (Table 33.1).

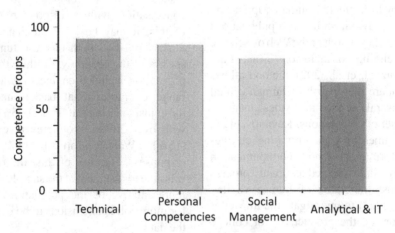

Fig. 33.2 Competencies in future industrial growth scenarios—Smart Industry Poland 2019 survey

Table 33.1   Overall digital skills

Year	EU-28 (2013–2020)	Poland
2015	55	40
2016	56	44
2017	57	46
2019	58	44

It's possible to argue that businesses have reason for optimism with the advent of Generation C workers. The "C" in "always-on" originates from the English term "connected," thus the name of this generation. The term "Generation C" was used to describe those born between 1980 and 2000. To ensure that critical information is not lost, most companies rely on training new staff (83%). However, the majority of training is done informally, with more seasoned workers providing advice and counsel to those less experienced (61%). Despite this, 55.5% of industrial firms were found to lack CVT provision in 2015 according to a Eurostat study of CVT providers. Overall, 85.2% of respondents said that present credentials, abilities, and competences meet the demands of an organization and so there is no need for further training. The course availability rate was found to be 0.316 in industrial enterprises, the lowest of all sectors, according to Statistics Poland (2017). The majority of enterprises (49.6%) who provide training programs report that their workers gain technical, practical, or professional competences via course participation. Most enterprises (76.7% of the total) in the automotive, trailer, and semi-trailer manufacturing, and transportation equipment manufacturing industries used these abilities in their day-to-day operations. The Smart Industry Poland 2019 study found that within the same set of industrial firms, the incidence of internal courses was similarly high (79.5%). Unfortunately, this research ignores the distinction between industrial and non-industrial firms. Creating long-term value for a company requires investing in the next generation's sustainable skillsets. Fifty industrial engineers were polled regarding the procedures used by their respective employers. Table 33.2 displays the breakdown of answers by business category and respondent subset.

Table 33.2   Environmental training outcomes

How frequently do classes on environmental responsibility get offered?	Proportion of a sample that agrees with the statement			
features shared by sampled businesses				
Foreign (n = 40)	35%	50.00%	15%	100%
Polish (n = 10)	65%	35.00%	0%	100%
Small (50 employees)	100%	0.00%	0%	100%
Large (251-5,000 employees)	28.576%	64.27%	7%	100%
Very large (5,000 employees)	25%	15.00%	60%	100%
Medium-sized (51-249 employees)	75%	25%	0%	100%
How much does the lack of such training sessions hinder attitude development?	insignificant/hardly significant	moderately significant	highly significant	Total
Job level: non-supervisory	11.76%	58.82%	29.41%	100%
Job level: managerial/supervisory	0%	62.5%	37.50%	100%

The businesses were classified according to their size and the source of their funding, while the respondents were organized by their level of responsibility within the company. Numerous studies have shown that green training successfully raises levels of green consciousness and pro-environmental actions and attitudes. Therefore, it is essential to educate the workforce of SMEs on environmental issues and cutting-edge technology in order to facilitate sustainable growth. Size is important, but where a corporation gets its money from is as crucial. Polish businesses clearly lag behind their foreign-backed counterparts. Executives have a greater appreciation for the role that training plays in encouraging environmentally friendly actions.

5. Conclusion

Sustainability, Industry 4.0, and SHRM are all explored here. It advances HR development expertise. The essay discusses sustainable HRM concepts and how to accomplish such development. "The competencies of the future" are developed via long-term focus and adaptability. Engineers, who adopt cleaner manufacturing and Industry 4.0, were highlighted in these capabilities. HR practices should also promote teamwork and participation among workers, promote equality, and safeguard people and the planet. Data from Eurostat and Statistics Poland, as well as three other studies, show that Polish industrial firms anticipate increased investment in engineering. Furthermore, environmental sustainability continues to be a poorly trained field of expertise, and there is little collaboration with other educational institutions.

REFERENCES

1. Rezaei, F., Khalilzadeh, M. and Soleimani, P., 2021. Factors affecting knowledge management and its effect on organizational performance: Mediating the role of human capital. Advances in Human-Computer Interaction, 2021.

2. Navaneetha Krishnan Rajagopal, Mankeshva Saini, Rosario Huerta-Soto, Rosa Vílchez-Vásquez, J. N. V. R. Swarup Kumar, Shashi Kant Gupta, Sasikumar Perumal, "Human Resource Demand Prediction and Configuration Model Based on Grey Wolf Optimization and Recurrent Neural Network", Computational Intelligence and Neuroscience, vol. 2022, Article ID 5613407, 11 pages, 2022. https://doi.org/10.1155/2022/5613407

3. Alshurideh, M.T., Al Kurdi, B., Alzoubi, H.M., Ghazal, T.M., Said, R.A., AlHamad, A.Q., Hamadneh, S., Sahawneh, N. and Al-kassem, A.H., 2022. Fuzzy assisted human resource management for supply chain management issues. Annals of Operations Research, pp. 1–19.

4. S. K. Gupta, B. Pattnaik, V. Agrawal, R. S. K. Boddu, A. Srivastava and B. Hazela, "Malware Detection Using Genetic Cascaded Support Vector Machine Classifier in Internet of Things," 2022 Second International Conference on Computer Science, Engineering and Applications (ICCSEA), 2022, pp. 1–6, doi: 10.1109/ICCSEA54677.2022.9936404.

5. Liu, P., Qingqing, W. and Liu, W., 2021. Enterprise human resource management platform based on FPGA and data mining. Microprocessors and Microsystems, 80, p. 103330.

6. Sima, V., Gheorghe, I.G., Subić, J. and Nancu, D., 2020. Influences of the industry 4.0 revolution on the human capital development and consumer behavior: A

systematic review. Sustainability, 12(10), p. 4035.

7. Gruzina, Y., Firsova, I. and Strielkowski, W., 2021. Dynamics of human capital development in economic development cycles. Economies, 9(2), p. 67.

8. Revunov, S.V., Rogova, T.M., Tutaeva, D.R., Murzin, A.D. and Plohotnikova, G.V., 2021. Modern information and communication technologies as a factor of human capital development. In Institute of Scientific Communications Conference (pp. 275–283). Springer, Cham.

9. Alam, A., 2022. Impact of University's Human Resources Practices on Professors' Occupational Performance: Empirical Evidence from India's Higher Education Sector. In Inclusive Businesses in Developing Economies (pp. 107–131). Palgrave Macmillan, Cham.

10. Tseng, M.L., Tran, T.P.T., Ha, H.M., Bui, T.D. and Lim, M.K., 2021. Sustainable industrial and operation engineering trends and challenges Toward Industry 4.0: A data driven analysis. Journal of Industrial and Production Engineering, 38(8), pp. 581–598.

Note: All the figures and tables in this chapter were made by Authors.

Advancements in Business for Integrating Diversity, and Sustainability – Dimitrios A. Karras et al. (eds)
© 2024 Taylor & Francis Group, London, ISBN 978-1-032-70828-7

34

Research on Organizational Behavior and Human Resource Management's Policy Recommendations

Sunil Kumar Vohra[1]

Amity Institute of Travel and Tourism,
Amity University, Noida, UP, India

Anchal Pathak*

UPES, School of Business, Dehradun, India

Abstract: One of the key corporate strategies to withstand and thrive in the quickly changing modern environment is human resource management (HRM) and organizational behavior policy. The globe has recently seen a rise in modernization, where the finances of several nations are linked to encouraging overseas business with organizational behavior and HRM policy. This point of view contends that policy is directly tied to the assessment of the special and particular contribution that each employee has to provide businesses. As a result, we conduct research on organizational behavior and HRM policy recommendations. To improve business achievement in terms of effectiveness and profitability, the policy is an effort to integrate a people-oriented viewpoint into the creation of HRM and organizational behavior standards. According to the study's findings, businesses should adopt policies that will enhance organizational behavior and HRM.

Keywords: Organizational behavior, HRM, Policy, Enterprises

1. Introduction

In the latest days, businesses have made the incorporation of professionally accountable behavior policies a business goal. Over the last thirty years, the field of HRM has changed. An examination of this history demonstrates a shift from a phase when organizational people planning was primarily concerned with behavioral management and assuring optimal human resource performance to a phase where human resources engage a significant position in company development (Barrena, et al., 2019).

The potential to gain a strategic position via the implementation of an effective HRM policy is passed up by a great number of businesses. HRM policies relate to organizational actions designed to manage

*Corresponding author: anchal.pathak@ddn.upes.ac.in
[1]sunilvohra2002@yahoo.co.in

DOI: 10.4324/9781032708294-34

the stock of human assets and guarantee that the assets are used in support of organizational objectives. The goal of managerial HRM is to increase employee performance and dedication in order to provide the company with a long-term financial edge (Anjum, et al., 2022).

The organizational branch of a business that deals with its most precious resource its people has been known as HRM. It is common knowledge that HRM policies and procedures will probably play a large and unique role in day-to-day corporate difficulties. The durability of everything is now being taken into account when discussing HRM in general. In the modern period, human resources have proven to be a crucial kind of asset, making firms' effectiveness and profitability reliant on the conduct and output of their employees. In today's increasingly complicated business world, organizational behavior policy has been acknowledged as a crucial enabler for generating value and achieving durable economic strength in enterprises (Salunke, et al., 2022).

The organizational behavior policy outlines the major firms' foundation, dos and don'ts, and ethical standards of behavior. This policy's guiding principle establishes how workers should behave, choose jobs, take action, and carry out their duties. The degree of respect one party has for the other influences how well the company and its personnel cooperate (Harney, et al., 2021). To involve workers and enable them to follow company rules and procedures, businesses require effective HRM policy. Employment, hiring, career services, the workplace atmosphere, competence, profitability, and contentment concerns are at the centre of HRM's policies and procedures.

International corporations must promote friendly interaction between the company and the workers. The HRM policy concerns that although workers must comply with established laws and standards, the employer must uphold their half of the agreement by providing wages on time, creating a welcoming workplace, and placing a priority on employee learning and advancement (Andjarwati, et al., 2020).

As a consequence of this study substantially conducts research on organizational behavior and HRM's policy recommendations to maintain successful organizational management and increase enhanced profitability.

2. Related Works

The first is that researchers and practitioners in HRM policy need to pay considerably greater attention to the connection between symptoms that employees have experienced at work. They go through the urgent justifications for further research and integrated practice in this field as well as the economic, legal, demographic, and social responsibility considerations. Our second point emphasizes the need of using an integrated economics paradigm in future research and practice to better comprehend the major distinctions with how older women approach transitioning to the workforce. Here, they establish the framework for future study on this important issue by offering reasons that address the global, regional, and microscopic levels of these discrepancies (Atkinson et al. (2021)).

They begin by examining the papers that have been published in the preceding 25 years to analyze the growth of HRM policy in Asia. Then they go into detail on how this special edition got about and highlight the key themes that came out of the reviews in the publication. Global enterprises and their subsidiaries, the affective commitment, the work-life connection, corporate responsibility, consolidation, pure socialism to post-state communism, and integrating the context are among the challenges of global talent management. Additionally, they highlight crucial topics and new concerns for future research, including employee engagement, inclusion and diversity employee resilience, crisis prevention, and sustainability human resource management. They end by providing theoretical insights by highlighting significant recent innovations that are likely to have a bearing on future practice and that scholars should address Cooke, et al., 2020.

To address this issue, the study draws data from a comprehensive review of the literature. The challenges presented by the pursuit of divergent organizational goals are highlighted, and the critical roles played by the HRM in the creation of sustainable businesses are described. The research concludes by highlighting some prospective research directions and providing some sensible advice to professionals on how to manage these opposing agendas to meaningfully affect employees (Podgorodnichenko, et al., 2020).

Chaudhary, et al., 2020 report goal was to comprehend how Green Human Resources Management (GHRM) may improve employees' environmental performance. It especially examines the role of HRM systems on employee green assures optimal effectiveness by using corporate identity as mediation and individual environmental component and gender as moderators (task-related and voluntary). 301 workers

in the Indian auto sector participated in the poll. To use a pass work on the assumption and hierarchical regression analysis, the proposed research model was assessed.

The extensive literature review (Chams, et al., 2019) examines HRM policy's critical role in fostering a found place and supporting management objectives. Based on a compilation of theoretical and empirical works, the study examines the causes and consequences and highlights the barriers to sustainable adoption, not only at the corporate level but also from a broader perspective. They provide four possibilities that might be tested empirically in future studies. There are gaps in the literature that must be addressed, and it is advised that future research be done in the field of sustainable management.

3. Methodology

This research is an explanatory analysis or assessment. The perspectives of businesses and employees about HRM policies, procedures, and productivity management are accurately reflected in policy. The employees were gathered from the enterprises.

Data collection: Customized questions were used to gather the data. 100 employees were selected from 103 enterprises. This decision was made based on many researchers' views, skilled respondents were chosen rather than selected at random. Researchers concluded to have face-to-face discussions with persons who have significant access to the standard of HRM and who are knowledgeable about the HRM procedure in terms of ideas and HRM policies in specific.

Sampling technique: Through the use of sampling techniques, the population quantity was calculated. 100 individuals comprise the number of employees. Equation 1 below indicates the sampling process.

$$n = \frac{S}{1 + S(E)^2} \qquad (1)$$

Where: S is the size of the population, n is the number of needed population size, and E^2 is the maximum allowable error.

Equation 2 is produced when data are entered into the calculation with a 95% confident level and a 5% erroneous level.

$$n = \frac{103}{1 + 103(0.05)^2} \approx 81 \qquad (2)$$

As a consequence, 81 replies would be the bare minimum that could be collected while still maintaining a 95% confident level and a 5% erroneous level.

HRM and organizational behaviour policies:

Employment and Selection (ES): The firm seeks out candidates, encourages them to register, and chooses them intending to match each candidate's beliefs, objectives, aspirations, and skills to the requirements of the job and the business. The most of participants were unsure if the firm actively seeks out candidates, encourages them to apply, and picks them with the intention of matching each applicant's beliefs, objectives, ambitions, and skills to the requirements of the job and the business. On average, participants (26.3%) agreed with this policy.

Interaction (I): The business effectively bonds with its staff members, promoting their happiness at work concerning recognition, relationships, engagement, and interaction. In areas of appreciation, connection, involvement, and interaction,

the most of participants concurred that the company effectively bonds with its workers, enhancing their well-being at the workplace. This policy was highly agreed with by a substantial number (37.0%) of the participants, while only a pitiful 4.7% deeply opposed it.

Coaching, Improvement, and Skills Training: The organization supports structured skill improvement for staff members and promotes lifelong learning and expertise creation. The most of participants (45%) agreed that the organization supports will development of structured skill training among workers and encourages ongoing training and content creation.

Working Circumstances (WC): Regarding advantages, healthcare, security, and innovation, the corporation offers its workers decent working circumstances. Most of the participants agreed that the business offers its workers pleasant working circumstances. Twenty-five percent of the workers supported this policy, while 18% disagreed with this.

Expertise-based quality evaluation: The organization assesses employees' achievement and ability to inform choices regarding advancements, job placement, and growth. The most of respondents weren't sure if the organization assessed employee productivity or growth. 26% of the workers supported this policy.

Salary and Prizes: The Corporation uses incentives and pays to recognize and encourage workers' abilities and achievements. The most of workers said that the corporation should reward employees with compensation and bonuses. A considerable number of participants (28%) completely agreed with this policy.

4. Result and Discussion

Experts and academics in human resources have been creating ideas, policies, protocols, and methods to effectively govern the connection and create solutions for each policy and organization's growth. Both the administration of employees within a company and the achievement of commercial goals are enhanced by HRM and organizational behavior policies. In this research, essential HRM policy was discussed and employee support was analyzed. The HRM policies were evaluated by organizational growth and employee satisfaction.

Organizational growth

A corporation has reached the stage of organizational growth when it can contemplate expanding its operations and may explore other opportunities to increase its income level. Organizational growth is frequently influenced by developments in growing demand, the lifespan of a firm, and the investors' ambition to create enterprise value. All the policies discussed were supported by the employees. It shows that organizational growth is increased by the HRM and organizational behavior policy.

Employee satisfaction

All the HRM policies were helpful to employees. Thus, HRM policies enhance employee satisfaction it leads to increased profitability. The organizational development firm needs the wide word "employee satisfaction" to refer to how comfortable or contented people are with things like their employment, their working environment, and the companies they operate for. A contented employee benefits the business by creating commitment, boosting client satisfaction, and enhancing profitability.

5. Discussion

The fundamental HRM and organizational behavior policies and practices discussed in this research do have a conceptual basis and are mostly consistent with the scientific analyses of each policy and practice. The topic of hiring and choosing policies is pertinent to include both corporate and outside hiring practices, as well as the selection technique and effectiveness. The authenticity of workers' activities and work habits inside firms is helped by policy and its procedures. The workplace has a major role in how people adjust their attitudes and career paths. Professional behavior is taught to workers, and the company cares for their welfare.

6. Conclusion

This paper examines organizational behavior and offers HRM's suggested policy changes. Every organization has to have a strategic human resource management and organizational behavior policy in order to recruit their workers and enable them to commit to their profession efficiently, which is necessary for the development of the business. Employment, hiring, career services, the workplace atmosphere, effectiveness, profitability, and contentment concerns are at the center of HRM's policies and procedures. The employees were on board with and supportive of these policies. It will be beneficial to the growth of the company in terms of both its productivity and income. In organizations, we believe that this paper will serve as a motivator for the formulation and application of policies that are focused on development.

REFERENCES

1. Barrena-Martínez, J., López-Fernández, M. and Romero-Fernández, P.M., 2019. Towards a configuration of socially responsible human resource management policies and practices: Findings from an academic consensus. The International Journal of Human Resource Management, 30(17), pp. 2544–2580.

2. Anjum, A., Ming, X. and Puig, L.C.M., 2022. Analysis of strategic human resource management practices in small and medium enterprises of South Asia. In Research Anthology on Human Resource Practices for the Modern Workforce (pp. 1021–1039). IGI Global.

3. Salunke, D.K., Dadas, A.B. and Bagul, D., 2021. A Study of Effective Implementation of Green HRM Policies and Practices by IT Companies. Int. Interdiscip. Res, 12(1), pp. 478–487.

4. Harney, B. and Alkhalaf, H., 2021. A quarter-century review of HRM in small and medium-sized enterprises: Capturing what we know, exploring where we need to go. Human Resource Management, 60(1), pp. 5–29.

5. Andjarwati, T., Budiarti, E., Audah, A.K., Khouri, S. and Rębilas, R., 2019. The impact of green human resource management to gain enterprise sustainability. Polish journal of management studies, 20.

6. Atkinson, C., Beck, V., Brewis, J., Davies, A. and Duberley, J., 2021. Menopause and the workplace: New directions in HRM research and HR practice. Human Resource Management Journal, 31(1), pp. 49–64.

7. Cooke, F.L., Schuler, R. and Varma, A., 2020. Human resource management research and practice in Asia: Past, present, and future. Human Resource Management Review, 30(4), p. 100778.

8. Podgorodnichenko, N., Edgar, F. and McAndrew, I., 2020. The role of HRM in developing sustainable organizations: Contemporary challenges and contradictions. Human Resource Management Review, 30(3), p. 100685.

9. Chaudhary, R., 2020. Green human resource management and employee green behavior: an empirical analysis. Corporate Social Responsibility and Environmental Management, 27(2), pp. 630–641.

10. Chams, N. and García-Blandón, J., 2019. On the importance of sustainable human resource management for the adoption of sustainable development goals. Resources, Conservation and Recycling, 141, pp. 109–122.

*Advancements in Business for Integrating Diversity, and
Sustainability – Dimitrios A. Karras et al. (eds)*
© 2024 Taylor & Francis Group, London, ISBN 978-1-032-70828-7

35

The Evolution of Human Resource Management through Digitalization

Sunil Kumar Vohra[1]

Amity Institute of Travel and Tourism,
Amity University, Noida, UP, India

Anchal Pathak*

UPES, School of Business, Dehradun, India

Abstract: Digital human resource management (DHRM) is an evolution of HRM that makes use of technological advancements in the realm of computers and the Internet. Mobile devices, electronic media, online social networks, and information technology will all play a role in DHRM's operations. The availability of these technologies will enhance HRM's importance in the contemporary context. It's possible for DHRM to perform human tasks since it's built on software, uses many apps, and is accessible via the internet. HRM will be more effective and relevant in the future if it is digitalized. HRM would fall behind organizational expectations without digital transformation. The purpose of this study is to provide information on the significance of digital HRM in enhancing organisational effectiveness. The findings of this study would be beneficial in assisting organizations to integrate DHRM and boosting their overall efficiency and effectiveness.

Keywords: Digital human resource management (DHRM), Organization, Digital transformation

1. Introduction

As technology has advanced, businesses have been able to improve their digital performance, their social impact, and their operations. The effects of the digital revolution are felt throughout all levels of a business. Additionally, it puts pressure on businesses and employees to adjust to a world that is changing quickly and a growth in digital technologies. The term "digitalization" has recently become popular in the business world, and it is widely acknowledged that this is a trend that organizations must follow to maintain their competitive edge (Rajagopal et al., 2022). All physical labour has been replaced in modern times by computer technology. Artificial

*Corresponding author: anchal.pathak@ddn.upes.ac.in
[1]sunilvohra2002@yahoo.co.in

DOI: 10.4324/9781032708294-35

intelligence (AI)-enabled computer systems have substituted non-repetitive intellectual tasks that might traditionally only be accessed through the use of large amounts of data, or big data. As more digital instruments are connected to the Internet of Things, traceability likewise develops. Everything that can be digitalized has been digitalized. Not only alters the individuals engage and communication with one another as people. Previous studies have focused on the benefits of digitalization in terms of marketing and commercial outcomes. Academic research, especially in the area of human resource management, has focused on the external effects but has given less attention to the internal ripples (Rajagopal et al., 2022). Thus, this research aims to go more deeply into the topic of human resource management in the digital era. More precisely, the purpose of this study is to discover more about the HRM digital research sector and its connection to organisational performance.

2. Related Works

Makarova et al., 2018 provide the created idea of an evaluation system as well as the design of the labour hazards module for project assignments.

The research was based on the notion that businesses are moving toward the ideal of sustainable development as a result of the digitization of work and human resources operations (Kuzior et al., 2022.)

The purpose of this study is to investigate the effect of digitalization variables on the Russian Federation region's human capital. Using ordinary least squares (OLS) estimation, the authors develop a multivariate model to characterise the connection between the Index and digitalization elements (Zaborovskaia et al., 2020).

3. Overview of DHRM and HRM

In the current environment, business is performed to meet global customer wants and desires. Additionally, items are transferred from one nation to another, and services, managerial skills, and technological advancements are shared across nations. Because of globalisation, we now have the ability to communicate with people all over the world. Global economic and financial systems are now more deeply linked. In today's digital era, DHRM has replaced traditional HRM as a key component in meeting organisational needs. Effective and effective DHRM is essential for the success of many businesses today. HR professionals should be open to digital HR transformation and should update HR policy to reflect the necessity of HR digital transformation. To provide the highest quality of work for the organisation on a global scale, digital human resources management must overcome various obstacles. In today's tough business environment, companies that want to succeed need to broaden their trade operations to other parts of the world. Transferring the workflow and its development to a digital platform presents Human Resource Management with several challenges, including dealing with complexity and adapting to new technologies. By generating momentum and developing internal competence, digital HR plays a crucial role in modern organisations and other company operations.

According to (Tayali et al., 2017), modern HR managers' primary goal is to help their companies adjust to the ever-shifting nature of the business market by introducing appropriate changes and boosting employee performance to enable them to develop effective long-term strategies. The success of human resource management may be gauged primarily by examining the hiring process. It would be highly beneficial for the human resource management department to attempt to understand and study the link between information technology and human resources in a society that is highly dependent on the internet. Implementing the analysis in HR is necessary to improve HR performance and use information technology. The use of digital technology will allow every business to achieve a perfect equilibrium between efficiency and innovation. HRM is often in charge of creating the structure under which a company operates, making coordination between it and strategic management crucial.

Conceptual Framework on DHRM

Employees can receive training regardless of their physical location by accessing the necessary materials digitally and participating in the training session via an online platform. According to Margherita, A. (2022) Human Resources (HR) processes benefit greatly from digital human resource management, which also contributes significantly to the growth of the firm. A model was proposed to explain that digital technology contributes significantly by improving the organization's performance. Figure 35.1 depicts the Strategies for Human Resources in the Digital Age.

According to Hagemann et. al., 2022, HRM digital transformation may be divided into three categories, namely Inward, onward, and across. The term "inward" is used to describe a company whose employees primarily use electronic means of communication within the company, such as email, instant messaging, and video conferencing on mobile devices. Digital technologies are used to manage workers' output.

When a company is considered to be "outward," it indicates that its management is encouraging the use of mobile phones and other forms of digital technology in the workplace. An employee who can do their tasks through mobile phones may do so from virtually any location and

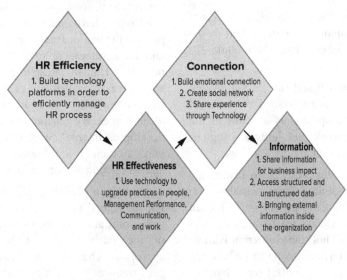

Fig. 35.1 Strategies for HR in digital

at any time. The result will be a rise in employee engagement. HR departments that embrace digitalization have a better chance of fostering creativity, teamwork, and effective strategy inside their respective organisations. Achieving a worldwide presence is facilitated by digitalization, which allows for the sharing and acquisition of information throughout the company's global network of collaborators.

Digital HRM components

Human resource management has evolved in the competitive digital environment (Valipour et. al., 2022). HRM must become digital. HRM transformation requires the following.

Digital tasks and activities

With the use of a digital platform in both work and management, organisational work has undergone a significant revolution. Every firm in the current environment must include digitization in the work process to assist reduce manual work. Additionally, businesses must engage and communicate with employees via digital tools and media. Digital organisation is also required for work and tasks in organisations.

Digital Workforce

The present generation is referred to as the "digital workforce" in the millennial age; they have network-connected devices, and web-based services and apps have always attracted their modern routine. The company must have these workers in order to interact with a digital employee, and it must be digital. As a result, design thinking, video, behavioral economics, and system analytics are all integrated into DHRM.

Management of digital support

HRM entails a wide range of tasks. Digital technologies are increasingly being planned,

implemented, and used to support HRM activities.

Advanced HR

The traditional HR structure is evolving rapidly, with more and more emphasis being placed on digital HR delivered. Traditional office work methods in human resources are being replaced by mobile device-based methods. It is widely agreed that social and mobile features are necessary for the selection and hiring processes.

Advantages of DHRM

Every element of HRM will be impacted by DHR. In the beginning, DHRM assisted the managers and staff of the company with a mentality shift toward using technology and managing the company digitally (Fenech, R., (2022)). All of these factors would eventually cause the biggest change in the company. Table 35.1 shows the old and new digital HR guidelines.

The article emphasizes that changes brought about by digitization have an influence on the way people interact and communicate at work, what they anticipate from their employers and professions, where they work, and when they work. It is necessary to acquire and adopt new information and new working methods since the progress of digitalization impacts businesses on many different levels.

4. Conclusion

HRM software that can be accessed digitally is a fundamental requirement for every modern firm. Every organization still has a way to go before it is fully digitalized. Relationships between employees and management may be maintained on a strong basis with the use of DHRM. Organizational effectiveness may be improved through the

Table 35.1 Old and new digital HR guidelines

Regular guideline	New guidelines
Plans for human resources are created with scalability and uniformity.	HR initiatives focus on certain demographics, personas, and staff segments.
To achieve scale, HR chooses a cloud-based vendor and applies unconventional methods.	Employing the platform for scalability, HR creates creative, company-specific initiatives.
Process quality and design are the emphasis of the HR center of excellence.	HR centers of excellence use chat, APPS, AI, and other advanced technologies.
The HR department focuses on process design and harmonization to establish best practices for HR.	Optimizing employee productivity, teamwork involvement, care, and career progression are the main priorities of the HR department.
HR centers focus on process design and excellence.	HR center focuses on excellent leverage, AI, Chat, APPS, and other advanced technology

development of a DHRM plan. This research aims to provide information on DHRM's value to businesses by demonstrating that developing an app by a market leader may improve the recruiting process. The findings of this work will be important in encouraging more studies on DHRM. Every business should have a digital strategy to boost efficiency. DHRM is not only a crucial issue for every business but also a developing field of study. Organizations may maintain their performance and workers' quality standards with the help of DHR practice and through social networks, the internet, AI, and other technologies.

REFERENCES

1. Rajagopal, N.K., Saini, M., Huerta-Soto, R., Vílchez-Vásquez, R., Kumar, J.N.V.R., Gupta, S.K. and Perumal, S., 2022. Human resource demand prediction and configuration model based on grey wolf optimization and recurrent neural network. Computational Intelligence and Neuroscience, 2022.
2. Rajagopal, N.K., Qureshi, N.I., Durga, S., Ramirez Asis, E.H., Huerta Soto, R.M., Gupta, S.K. and Deepak, S., 2022. Future of business culture: an artificial intelligence-driven digital framework for organization decision-making process. Complexity, 2022.
3. Makarova, I., Shubenkova, K. and Pashkevich, A., 2018, December. Development of an intelligent human resource management system in the era of digitalization and talentism. In 2018 18th international conference on mechatronics-Mechatronika (ME) (pp. 1–6). IEEE.
4. Kuzior, A., Kettler, K. and Rab, Ł., 2022. Digitalization of work and human resources processes as a way to create a sustainable and ethical organization. Energies, 15(1), p. 172.
5. Zaborovskaia, O., Nadezhina, O. and Avduevskaya, E., 2020. The impact of digitalization on the formation of human capital at the regional level. Journal of Open Innovation: Technology, Market, and Complexity, 6(4), p. 184.
6. Tayali, E.M. and Sakyi, K.A., 2020. Reputable Relevant Realistic Reliable and Rigorous Human Resource Management Strategic Approaches and Practices in the 21st Century. Advances in Social Sciences Research Journal, 7(6), pp. 600–621.
7. Margherita, A., 2022. Human resources analytics: A systematization of research topics and directions for future research. Human Resource Management Review, 32(2), p. 100795.

8. Hagemann, V. and Klug, K., 2022. Human resource management in a digital environment.

9. Valipour Damiyeh, S., Hamrahi, M. and Pirzad, A., 2022. Pathology of Strategic Human Resource Management System Based on Digital Transformation Governance. International Journal of Digital Content Management, 3(1), pp. 176–195.

10. Fenech, R., 2022. Human Resource Management in a Digital Era through the Lens of Next Generation Human Resource Managers. Journal of Management Information & Decision Sciences, 25.

Advancements in Business for Integrating Diversity, and
Sustainability – Dimitrios A. Karras et al. (eds)
© 2024 Taylor & Francis Group, London, ISBN 978-1-032-70828-7

Traffic Management and Decision Support System Based on the Internet of Things

36

Alex Khang*

University of Science and Technology, Vietnam & USA

Shashi Kant Gupta[1]

Eudoxia Research University, USA

Abstract: With an ever-increasing population in all over the globe, continuing manufacturing of cars of all different types by manufacturers, and an ever-increasing number of vehicles on the roads, the number of automobiles on the roads will only continue to increase. This inevitably increases traffic congestion, which is particularly problematic in big urban areas and at the busiest times of the day (rush hour). Because of this occurrence, municipal authorities, and urban planners are under continual pressure to find new methods to make traffic control systems that are both safer and more cost-effective. The Decision Support System is a novel approach that was developed to resolve this problem (DSS). The purpose of this article is to investigate and contrast two distinct approaches to the management of traffic, namely Traffic Management Systems (TMS) and Decision Support Systems (DSS), using the Internet of Things (IoT) as our primary research tool.

Keywords: Internet of things, Traffic management system, Decision support system, Traffic light system

1. Introduction

Residents, commuters, municipal authorities, and urban planners in developed and metropolitan centers across the world continue to be plagued by a significant problem that is traffic congestion, particularly during rush hour. Congestion on the roads has a wide range of negative effects and repercussions, including higher rates of environmental pollution and energy consumption as well as slowed rates of economic development. Congestion on the roads, which is caused by a rise in the number of cars on the roadways, will only continue to offer more hurdles and challenges

*Corresponding author: alexkhang.ai@gmail.com
[1]raj2008enator@gmail.com

DOI: 10.4324/9781032708294-36

to economic progress while also having a detrimental influence on the quality of life. As a direct consequence of this, individuals will have a natural tendency to shift to locations that are safer, more efficient, and have less traffic congestion (Avatefipour et al. (2018)). This presents a significant issue for urban planners, who are tasked with developing a system of effective traffic management that is capable of meeting the requirements of a big metropolitan region at the same time being able to readily accommodate the expansion of the population.

The Traffic Management System (TMS) is an attempt to alleviate the problems caused by urban congestion. To begin, more compact devices have been installed in several different locations around the city. As time goes on, new problems, approaches, and technologies are discovered, and more functions are integrated into the system that is already in place to improve the system's overall efficiency (Wang et al. (2022)). To be able to do a comparison between the improvements noticed on the completed system and the original condition (which lacked any kind of traffic management system), we would need access to data that we do not currently possess. The inability to effectively manage traffic is among the most persistent challenges that we face in the world's most populous cities. Congestion on the roads may be caused by a wide variety of factors, including but not limited to: accidents; insufficient road space; traffic infractions; irresponsible driving on the part of drivers; inadequate traffic management systems; etc. The DSS is one of the instruments that has been employed in attaining this significant goal, as it has been one of the few cities in the world that has been successful in reducing the amount of traffic congestion that it

experiences to a tolerable level. The term "Decision Support Systems," or DSS, refers to computer programs that provide support to people engaged in the process of making difficult decisions (Muthukumaran et al. (2022)). Modern decision support systems assist decision-makers in investigating the repercussions of their assessments so that they may make choices depending on their level of comprehension. Because of the inherent diversity of sectors in which people are required to make operational judgments about the management of complex industrial or environmental processes. (Kaushal et al. (2022))

2. Related Works

(Sood et al. 2021)) developed an Edge Cloud-centric IoT-based smart traffic management system for predicting traffic influx and optimizing vehicle routing. The traffic influx forecast modifies the traffic movement phase timing and prevents junction congestion. Smart navigation optimizes traffic allocation and increases junction safety. Baseline classifiers are employed to anticipate traffic influx, and statistical evaluations accept the J48 decision tree's prediction performance. Edge Computing optimizes vehicle navigation and real-time traffic load balancing. Optimal traffic load balance improves junction safety. The findings show how well the proposed system handles smart navigation, traffic load balance, and junction safety. (Khanna et al. 2019)) described an intelligent traffic control system built on Cloud computing, IoT, and Data Analytics. Our method enables traffic management authorities to estimate an optimal route, and reduce the waiting period, traffic congestion, travel costs, and air pollution. The system uses machine learning to forecast optimal routes based on traffic mobilization patterns, vehicle categorization, accident occurrences, and precipitation. Finally, the system creates a green lane where emergency services may pass without traffic. (Kumar et al. 2022)) Analyzed image-processing, deep learning, traffic forecasting, and policy derivation strategies used to handle traffic management problems in recent years. They suggested a hybrid deep learning strategy (CNN and RNN) for detecting and predicting real-time traffic. CNN and RNN can identify real-time traffic and handle it dynamically. (Insaurralde et al. 2022)) provides situational awareness of the decision support system (SAWDAR) technique. SAWDAR uses knowledge representation and semantic reasoning to construct artificial cognition. Ontological SAWDAR includes criteria for the realism of surveillance systems like radars and ADS-B. By employing the ontological SAW, testing findings show improved decision performance in air circumstances, such as when an airliner is ready to take off with potentially harmful drones nearby. The findings show that ontological SAWDAR may help ATCs and pilots determine whether to authorize takeoff. Conclusions and future research areas of aviation analytics ontology for NGATS flight management are also discussed. Ad hoc vehicle networks, cloud services, and the Internet of Things allow novel smart city applications. These applications include smart building automation, healthcare monitoring, and intelligent transportation. The integration of IoT-based vehicle technology will enhance services that will ultimately lead to more sophisticated technological wonders. The paper tackles research concerns such as data acquisition, safety, privacy, quality of data, and network coverage. These difficulties must be solved to implement the VCoT

paradigm and give insights to investors and other parties involved. (Khattak et al. 2019)) Provided real-world application scenarios (smart houses, intelligent traffic lights, and smart cities) employing VCoT for control and automation, along with their problems. It shows early findings on data and energy availability in IoT-based resource-constrained contexts using vehicle clouds. (Rabby et al. 2019)) Examines smart traffic management using IoT. (IoT). It operates as middleware on the IoT and enhances the smart city concept via traffic light management, smart parking, smart emergency assistance, and anti-theft protection. IoT allows web devices to interface with sensing devices, services, controllers, and other networks. IoT analyses traffic flow manages traffic operations and saves the proper choice for future information display. That survey gives a fair overview of IoT in smart traffic management based on previous studies.

3. Methodology

The system contains three vehicle categories—normal, stolen, and emergency—to properly apply Intelligent Transportation System (ITS). These categories may change. System priorities are low, high, and highest. For dynamically updating the database with SMS, we require categories and vehicle priority (SMS). In addition to vehicle types and priority, the database may retain all vehicle information passing through intersections. This method allows traffic tracking in the future. Readers can assist with stolen car direction. They may be placed before traffic signal junctions to identify stolen automobile heading. These readers' primary difficulties are rain or direct sunshine. This distorts reader signals. Software and electrical technologies implement ITS on roads. Controlling traffic starts with detecting and collecting road-bound data. Inductive loop detectors may aid this purpose. IoT technology is increasing data streams, which may be utilized to feed the DSS traffic and weather data. This makes the DSS more dependable, enabling policymakers to make evidence-based decisions and ensure the greatest results.

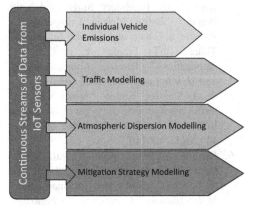

Fig. 36.1 Proposed methodology

Source: Authors

The DSS is going to employ real-time data gathered from IoT devices, and then it is going to use a decision-making process that concentrates on the following four areas shown in Figure 36.1 moreover, these areas are going to build upon each other to form the holistic DSS. Integration of these diverse domains, each of which has its own body of canonical literature as well as a plethora of distinct approaches to modeling them, was one of the principal focuses of this body of study. This procedure requires continual data streams to make and support educated judgments. If the system detected a change in traffic distribution (perhaps due to a community event), it would identify and apply a mitigation approach to modify traffic behavior and emissions. Thus, the system would accommodate these changes. Finally, the DSS may be simulated and

executed by modeling mitigation measures and forecasting how they will affect the traffic network. Traffic accidents, despite precautions, are another concern. The number of cars per traffic policeman and traffic camera is also evaluated. The number of cars per traffic policeman is obtained by dividing the number of vehicles by the number of policemen on duty, whereas the number of vehicles per traffic camera is derived by dividing by the number of cameras. Traffic control and monitoring make these two elements influential factors. Thus, policeman-traffic camera ratios should be low to regulate traffic. These two parameters depend on the number of cars and traffic policemen and cameras at a given time. Traffic jams affect traffic accidents but not traffic decisions, making them the least essential element. The above considerations determine the following decisions:

1. Promote traffic awareness
2. Increase punishment/fine
3. Add traffic cops.
4. Add traffic cameras.

4. Result and Discussion

Traffic management decision support systems (DSS) have the following general discussion: **Real-time data:** System input includes real-time data from network detectors, day of the week, weather conditions, accidents, special events, road works, and refurbishment. **Descriptive statistics:** System input that uses past real-time data to determine scenarios or traffic patterns. **Real-time road network monitoring module:** Traffic and network device status define this condition. Focusing on traffic state, the information can be: Complete or partial on a spatial scale: complete tracking at all levels of the road network or a subgroup of network elements. With various physical and temporal aggregations. **Predictive System:** The system predicts road network status using historical and real-time data. Predicting the network status may offer whole or partial future data on space and traffic factors, depending on the approach. Thus, this module provides indications for each technique to let operators choose the optimal one for the streets. These systems are used to predict traffic congestion and analyze the DSS using IoT.

5. Conclusion

New technology data in network traffic monitoring and forecasting systems presents new problems for traffic management decision support systems. Support systems for mobility management, which increase global mobility in multimodal networks, are another topic of scientific dispute. This paper analyses how various DSS models have solved traffic management issues in major metropolitan areas throughout the world. Based on the models produced, DSS is a highly efficient instrument that solves traffic issues by determining where lanes need to be widened, where traffic people are needed, and where traffic laws need to be tightened.

REFERENCE

1. Avatefipour, Omid, and Froogh Sadry. "Traffic management system using IoT technology-A comparative review." In *2018 IEEE International Conference on Electro/ Information Technology (EIT)*, pp. 1041–1047. IEEE, 2018.

2. Wang, Zhenyan, and Yongjie Ma. "Detection and recognition of stationary vehicles and seat belts in intelligent Internet of Things traffic management system." *Neural Computing and Applications* 34, no. 5 (2022): 3513–3522.

3. Muthukumaran, Venkatesan, Rajesh Natarajan, Amarakundhi Chandrasekaran Kaladevi, Gopu Magesh, and Swapna Babu. "Traffic flow prediction in inland waterways of Assam region using uncertain spatiotemporal correlative features." *Acta Geophysica* 70, no. 6 (2022): 2979–2990.

4. Kaushal, Rajesh Kumar, Rajat Bhardwaj, Naveen Kumar, Abeer A. Aljohani, Shashi Kant Gupta, Prabhdeep Singh, and Nitin Purohit. "Using Mobile Computing to Provide a Smart and Secure Internet of Things (IoT) Framework for Medical Applications." *Wireless Communications and Mobile Computing* 2022 (2022).

5. Sood, Sandeep Kumar. "Smart vehicular traffic management: An edge cloud-centric IoT based framework." *Internet of Things* 14 (2021): 100140.

6. Khanna, Abhirup, Rohit Goyal, Manju Verma, and Deepika Joshi. "Intelligent traffic management system for smart cities." In *International Conference on Futuristic Trends in Network and Communication Technologies*, pp. 152–164. Springer, Singapore, 2019.

7. Kumar, Rahul, and Sandeep Vanjale. "Smart Traffic Management using various Approaches: An Overview." (2022).

8. Insaurralde, Carlos C., and Erik Blasch. "Situation Awareness Decision Support System for Air Traffic Management Using Ontological Reasoning." *Journal of Aerospace Information Systems* 19, no. 3 (2022): 224–245.

9. Khattak, Hasan Ali, Haleem Farman, Bilal Jan, and Ikram Ud Din. "Toward integrating vehicular clouds with IoT for smart city services." *IEEE Network* 33, no. 2 (2019): 65–71.

10. Rabby, Md Khurram Monir, Muhammad Mobaidul Islam, and Salman Monowar Imon. "A review of IoT application in a smart traffic management system." In *2019 5th International Conference on Advances in Electrical Engineering (ICAEE)*, pp. 280–285. IEEE, 2019.

Advancements in Business for Integrating Diversity, and
Sustainability – Dimitrios A. Karras et al. (eds)
© 2024 Taylor & Francis Group, London, ISBN 978-1-032-70828-7

37

Micro, Small, and Medium-sized Businesses' Financial Management Evaluation During the COVID 19 Epidemic

Prabhdeep Singh*

BBD University, Lucknow, UP, India

Abstract: The Indian economy is seeing considerable expansion in "Micro, Small, and Medium-sized Enterprise (MSME)" across a wide range of industries, including manufacturing of machinery and equipment, electrical goods, food and drink, construction and development materials, rubber and plastic products, and robotic technology. All financial sectors have been impacted by the COVID-19 epidemic, but nowhere are they being hit as hard as India's MSMEs. The report examines the examination of financial management during the Covid19 pandemic. MSME's understand that in order to compete, businesses must grow and alter over times after the dust has settled. A more responsive evaluation of "supply chain resilience, an analysis of disaster or emergency management plans, the introduction of protection procedures, sanitation and sanitization methods, an updated sourcing policy, the inclusion of new vendors, the streamlining of their product portfolio", and others are some of the responses to this problem. MSME's may handle COVID-19 this manner.

Keywords: MSMEs, Covid-19, Impact, Financial management

1. Introduction

The COVID-19 pandemic started a worldwide financial and health disaster in March 2020. To quickly adopt preventative and regulatory laws and to relieve the immediate financial strains suffered by people and companies via exceptional expenditure programmes, communities face exceptional finance needs (Gadsden,

et al., 2022). The world economy weakened while also time, dramatically lowering governmental income and spending power. COVID-19 has resulted in more than 2.5 million fatalities as of 1 March 2021. The "Micro, Small and Medium-sized Enterprise (MSME)" market has developed to be a key part of the Indian economy, making a substantial contribution to exports, shared prosperity, output, and creativity. Our

*Corresponding author: prabhdeepcs@gmail.com

DOI: 10.4324/9781032708294-37

nation's development is heavily reliant on MSME. Additionally, it accounts for 40% of all exports, 45% of all industrial production, and a significant portion of GDP. 7.09% of the GDP is generated in the market for MSME development. MSMEs, in contrast, make up 30.5% of the facilities. The MSMED Act of 2006 tackled the issue of under lending to the field by enabling manufacturing expansion and creating a framework for MSMEs, creating a strategy for Micro-enterprises to expand and boost their viability, enabling borrowing to flow through into sector, and laying the foundation for special privileges of MSE products and services in government contracts (Jayesh, et al., 2020). The term "Financial Service Providers (FSPs)" refers to businesses that offer financial services, particularly those related to financing. These businesses may include commercial banks, which give value offer wealth to businesses, as well as online industrial platforms and logistics service providers. FSPs are crucial in addressing capital constraints in MSMEs since they are a substantial external funding provider to businesses. As a result, we investigate how FSPs have thought about helping MSMEs and making the necessary changes in funding MSMEs under the influence of the epidemic (Yang, et al., 2020). The market transaction ranges from 10 to 300 million yen, depending on the sector. At first, public assistance tended to practically treat every MSMEs equally. However, it was anticipated that a particular customised strategy to MSME assistance would be more effective than a one-size-fits-all strategy since MSMEs are seldom uniform. Many authorities started treating MSMEs in various industries differently after seeing how significantly the pandemic's harm varied by industry (Pandey, et al., 2022).

2. Related Works

In the paper (Gondaliya, et al., 2022) six ML algorithms are evaluated on the Indian stock market and a methodology for sentiment analysis and forecasting is proposed. As a consequence, the research emphasises the best algorithm to determine on accuracy outcomes. The natural next step is to construct solid predictive model using the powerful input from these improved algorithms. The goal of the current research (Savitha, et al., 2022) was to clarify the variables influencing consumers' inclination to utilise financial applications during the COVID-19 pandemic outbreak. In order to understand how the flu epidemic affected their businesses, a (Ghosh, et al., 2022) study aims to rank 22 market as per the achievement on 14 chosen financial measures throughout the pre-COVID-19 year, which ended in March 2019, and the comment year, who's ended in March 2021, hoteliers and nine publicly listed travel firms in India were capitalised. The findings of their research (Beloskar, et al., 2022) that was undertaken in response to significant occurrences in India related to the COVID-19 epidemic provide proof that investors might utilise "Environmental, Social and Governance (ESG)" data as an indicator of future share price. In times of crisis, ESG performance most critically offers downside protection. Their findings demonstrate that ESG performance has no negative impact on investment performance under typical circumstances. Additionally, it was discovered that ESG performance decreased volatility of stock returns during the COVID-19 epidemic. Overall, by supporting the excellent management hypothesis, their research aims to provide an investing case for ESG companies in India's developing markets. The author'

(Singh, et al., 2023) goal was to better understand the challenges encountered by the technological changes that preceded COVID-19, MSMEs in the middle of an epidemic, and potential preventative actions that MSMEs might undertake to avert the disaster. They provide a preliminary analysis of how the Covid-19 epidemic affected Indian consumers' attitudes toward the retail sector in the study (Salah, et al., 2023) they address some possible changes in customer responsible decision-making that might result from the pandemic. Data is gathered from a variety of Indian customers who made transactions through organised retail stores in various places. They describe how COVID-19 has affected the retail industry in their discussions of consumer behaviour, as well as how customers' attitudes toward a level higher have changed.

3. Objectives of the Study

1. To investigate how the Corona virus affects MSME's in India
2. To research how the corona virus epidemic has affected Indian MSME's career opportunities
3. To provide recommendations for improving MSME's financial management review amid India's Covid19 pandemic

4. Research Methodology

The current effects of the corona virus on MSME's in India are examined in the article. The research is of a qualitative kind. For the assessment of the MSME's, secondary data is used in the research. The supplementary data came from Indian newspapers, magazines, blogging, and internet. The present situation of India's manufacturing sector and how it

impacts job chances are scrutinised in the research. India is the study's primary country of emphasis. The article initially examines how the corona virus affects MSMEs. The effects of the corona virus epidemic on recruitment in this industry are then researched.

5. Data Analysis and Interpretation

All major industries have been impacted by the Covid 19 epidemic, but nowhere are they being hit as hard as India's MSMEs. All known factual evidence suggests that the Covid-19 lockout was the cause of MSMEs worst fatality, considering the tens of millions of migrant laborers that are trapped across the world. There are 6.34 crore MSMEs in the nation, based on the Department of MSMEs' most recent accessible Annual Report (2018-19). In India's remote regions, they make up around 51% of the total. Together, they employed little over 11 crore people, while urban MSMEs account for 55% of all employment. According to the most recent MSME Ministry Financial Statements (2018–19), there are 6.34 crore MSMEs worldwide. In India's rural areas, around 51% of these are found. They together employ about 11 crore people, although 55% of employment are held by urban MSMEs. Less than two employees per MSME are often reported in these data. based on a foundation that explains why they are so little. The division of all MSME into major, medium, and radical voices is significantly less visible. The data provided showed that 99.5% of MSMEs belonged to the small group. In India, MSME are equally spread across urban and rural areas, although the latter is where they are focused. So, a single person or a housewife who works remotely often counts as a micro-enterprise. This is because it reveals why the efforts being made by the "Bank of India" to improve cash in MSMEs are having such a minimal effect. The majority of the funding still come from unofficial sources. Or to put it another way, this truth is crucial. One of the main reasons why banks shouldn't lend to MSMEs is the high percentage of erroneous loans, which predicts greater slip estimates for relatively bigger enterprises. The business's inability to receive MSME revenues, whether from its clients (such as the government) or other sources like GST refunds, etc., is another major problem.

Impact of Covid-19 on MSME's in India

The globe currently deals with modern atrocities like COVID-19, that has everybody baffled and, in its grasp, as to how one ailment has put the nation to a stop. Because it has touched over 195 nations, the WHO has designated such deadly epidemic as an epidemic. That illness poses a significant risk to the already vulnerable global market. There is no denying that during the last six years, the faltering Indian economy has grown at one of the slowest rates. Currently, a number of sectors are being destroyed by a brand-new set of financial issues caused by the virus. It is a well-known fact that China plays a significant role in the global supply chain for both India and the MSME sector, which is heavily reliant on China for its raw materials. For instance, Chinese manufacturers and $30 billion worth of Chinese goods are the source of over 70% of the chemicals used in Indian medication production. Different worries arise as a result of the complete closure in China and the government shutdown in India, including decreased exports, production halts, job insecurity, unstable market, and sector price volatility. The corona epidemic will also have an impact on MSME digital shopping. Fig. 37.1 depicts COVID-19's impact on MSMEs.

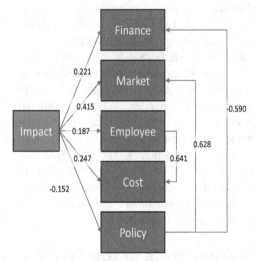

Fig. 37.1 COVID-19's effects

Source: Authors

The economy continues its surveillance system in light of the COVID-19's widespread destruction, and prompt relief actions must be made public in order to rebuild trust in this crucial industry that has been hammered by the govt's flurry of interruptions. Since these companies don't use cash intensively enough to wait for the crisis, the total closure raised a lot of questions. He brought up that due to employment reductions. Based on a recent poll, just 7% of manufacturing "small and medium enterprises" would be able to keep with current cash on hand for roughly 30 days after his organisation is stopped. One of the biggest obstacles to firing up again is the lack of open positions.

According to data from Venture Intelligence's marketplace monitor, they made only $354 in 34 transactions in March 2020, which is less than half of the $714 million they made in 46 agreements in February. As was reported earlier this month, and over a dozen business owners have requested that hazardous debt companies extend the time period during which they must repay their debts. The poll shows that companies in the industry's most adversely hit by the flu epidemic, housing, shipping, and logistics firms—have asked for up to six months longer than initially projected.

6. Conclusion

Throughout COVID-19, a substantial proportion of MSMEs have difficulties getting access to funding and product marketing. They battle to pay their wages, electricity bills, rent, land and local taxes, telephone and internet prices, bank borrowings, as well as other obligations. As a result, it's essential to responsibly solve their main problems, such as enrollment troubles, credit limitations, marketing difficulties, technology adoption issues, inadequate infrastructure, etc. The process of setting up an active evaluation system and proclaim fast remedial measures in light of the widespread COVID-19 disarray in order to boost the trust of the MSMEs industry. Future studies should look at the impact of the change in the definition of MSMEs on their ability to function economically. The updated definition will undoubtedly increase the number of MSME units, which will positively impact production, jobs, market growth, capital, and exports.

REFERENCES

1. Gadsden, T., Ford, B., Angell, B., Sumarac, B., de Oliveira Cruz, V., Wang, H., Tsilaajav, T. and Jan, S., 2022. Health financing policy responses to the COVID-19 pandemic: a review of the first stages in the WHO South-East Asia Region. Health Policy and Planning, 37(10), pp. 1317–1327.
2. Jayesh, G.S., Novaliendry, D., Gupta, S.K., Sharma, A.K. and Hazela, B., 2022. A Comprehensive Analysis of Technologies for Accounting and Finance in Manufacturing Firms. ECS Transactions, 107(1), p. 2715.
3. Song, H., Yang, Y. and Tao, Z., 2020. How different types of financial service providers support small-and medium-enterprises under the impact of COVID-19 pandemic: from the perspective of expectancy theory. Frontiers of Business Research in China, 14(1), pp. 1–27.
4. Pandey, A.K., Singh, R.K., Jayesh, G.S., Khare, N. and Gupta, S.K., 2022. Examining the Role of Enterprise Resource Planning (ERP) in Improving Business Operations in Companies. ECS Transactions, 107(1), p. 2681.
5. Gondaliya, C., Patel, A. and Shah, T., 2021. Sentiment analysis and prediction of Indian stock market amid Covid-19 pandemic. In IOP Conference Series: Materials Science and Engineering (Vol. 1020, No. 1, p. 012023). IOP Publishing.
6. Savitha, B. and Hawaldar, I.T., 2022. What motivates individuals to use FinTech budgeting applications? Evidence from India during the covid-19 pandemic. Cogent Economics & Finance, 10(1), p. 2127482.
5. Ghosh, S. and Bhattacharya, M., 2022. Analyzing the impact of COVID-19 on the financial performance of the hospitality and tourism industries: an ensemble MCDM

approach in the Indian context. International Journal of Contemporary Hospitality Management, (ahead-of-print).

6. Beloskar, V.D. and Rao, S.V.D., 2022. Did ESG Save the Day? Evidence From India During the COVID-19 Crisis. Asia-Pacific Financial Markets, pp.1-35.

7. Singh, S. and Pruthi, N., 2023. SME Survival During the COVID-19 Pandemic: An Outlook of Threats and Digital Transformation. In Strengthening SME Performance Through Social Media Adoption and Usage (pp. 201–212). IGI Global.

8. Salah, A.A., Khaled, A.S., Alomari, K., Tabash, M.I. and Saeed, A.M., 2023. COVID-19 pandemic roles on consumer behaviour towards sustainable transitions: a retail industry survey. International Journal of Innovation and Sustainable Development, 17(1-2), pp. 44–66.

Advancements in Business for Integrating Diversity, and Sustainability – Dimitrios A. Karras et al. (eds)
© 2024 Taylor & Francis Group, London, ISBN 978-1-032-70828-7

38 Green Marketing and its Impact on Supply Chain Management in Industrial Markets

Ashish Kumar Pandey*

Dr. R.M.L. Avadh University, Ayodhya, India

Abstract: Over the last 10 years, interest in sustainable supply chain operations and marketing has increased among researchers and professionals. However, no comprehensive plan for company to make corporate branding and green industrial brands has been devised. It is still not clear whether sustainable green supply chains and green industrial marketing may be integrated in order to develop greener enterprises and industrial brands. Additionally, it is unclear if and how developing green supply chains would aid in the development of new eco friendly industrial products. The special issue aims to highlight the most current advancements in environmentally friendly supply chains, green industrial marketing, and their linkages. Additionally, it searches for new prospective research areas. The invited papers are meant to shed light on how green or sustainable Supply Chains (SC) According to guest editors, effect marketing theory has on commercial and businesstobusiness marketplaces.

Keywords: Industrial marketing, Green supply chains, Sustainability

1. Introduction

Green marketing and sustainable has gotten a lot of attention from researchers and practitioners across a variety of business disciplines, such as marketing, management of supply chains and information management (Jayesh et al., 2022). A fully sustainable and green supply chain also faces additional demands and challenges from a global perspective as a result of globalisation and foreign sourcing (Pandey et al., 2022). For instance, it is not yet completely defined how industrial firms may leverage sustainable supply chains and sustainable industrial marketing to gain an advantage in the market (Gölgeci et al., 2022). For instance, the potential for industrial firms to use green industrial marketing and sustainable supply chains to obtain a competitive edge in the market has not yet been fully realized. Although there has been a lot of focus on

*Corresponding author: ashishkpandey9@gmail.com

DOI: 10.4324/9781032708294-38

green consumers and consumption, is little known about the variables that specifically affect (B2B) advertising and green product buying behaviour (Toorajipour et al., 2021). For green (B2B) marketing, it is important to comprehend how and why businesses select green providers. In order to communicate sustainability potential, green industrial branding may be a crucial component of industrial marketing (Nunes et al., 2020). However, this area still has to be developed further. Additionally, developing green industrial products is necessary for green industrial branding.

Green Marketing Strategy

The adoption of green marketing strategy is also driven by institutional and take holder pressure. Green environmental marketing strategy has drawn a lot of scholarly interest during the past two decades. Environmental issues must now be included into the strategic marketing process in order for businesses to gain institutional legitimacy and a competitive edge (Hofmann et al., 2019). The procedure for developing and putting into practise innovative and environmentally responsible business activities with the goal of generating income by satiating an industry's financial and environmental performance objectives was recommended by them as a means of supporting the marketing strategy's tenets. They assert that environmental marketing is characterised by technological innovation to meet environmental needs, an entrepreneurial attitude, and the convergence of social, ecological, and economic performances. The extent to which businesses have embraced environmentally friendly marketing varies. They suggested that environmental marketing may affect a company's performance and reputation, and that these effects would be more pronounced if the company industry

had a better reputation (Cole et al., 2021). They continued by stating that a company internal policies like those governing tog management and external policies like those governing customer environmental sensibility and regulatory intensity, internal structure (similar to centralised decision making) and external economy would all contribute to the success of the firm environmental marketing (e.g., competitive intensity). Nevertheless, these were only conceptual statements, and there was no data to back them up.

Green SC Management

Sc is a group of companies that collaborate to accomplish the goals (such as customer satisfaction, fulfilment, and other goals) of the entire supply chain.Since SC management and resource allocation are closely related, the literature contains a wide range of optimization strategies to support decisionmaking (Blanchard et al., 2021). This paper's goal is to provide a novel business strategy that might enhance the entire supply chain. Similarly, it could be difficult to distinguish between green marketing and green supply chain management. However, there are several gaps in the interaction of green sc studies and green marketing. If efforts to manage a green supply chain only produce marginal gains, this becomes more obvious. To bolster this, however, the following descriptions of several pertinent study themes are provided:

Corporate performance: The association between environmental supply chain management practices like green supplier management, green purchasing, and environmental marketing activities like green branding doesn't appear to be very strong despite the substantial body of study on the subject (Monczka et al., 2020).

Product development: It has been discovered that green product creation and business performance are related. Innovations in green manufacturing processes and green products are favourably correlated with corporate competitive advantage, according to our research. However, the findings of other investigations are cautious in this regard. For the analysis of green product development options for an electrical device, we proposed a lifecycle technique (Benton et al., 2020). A similar strategy, however, can need excess amounts of time for collecting data, and because the study is difficult to present to clients, it is difficult to link it to green marketing strategies. Additionally, rather than the supply chain level, this strategy is often applied at the product level.

Lean: Lean, sometimes referred to as in just minute, improves the process by getting rid of wastes that frequently occur in such situations. The ability to ensure that resources be used continuously and without interruption is the main premise or prerequisite of lean systems. In other words, owing to the high degree of unpredictability, it will be difficult to apply the lean mentality to both the interface between environmentally conscious supply chains and green marketing initiatives.

Distribution and reverse logistics: The relationship between the supply chain and marketing is significantly influenced by the distribution network. Without a doubt, this is the key area of cost and material flow concerns in supply chain management. A firm might also meet its clients here, especially if it operates in the industrial sector. The lifecycle assessment that was previously addressed is not the only metric for determining how green a product or process is; instead, carbon footprint is

another. Reverse logistics refers to movement in the opposite way from, say, the delivery of goods from a warehouse to clients. Reusing, remanufacturing, and recycling returned goods can all help to lessen a supply chain's negative environmental effects. Unfortunately, regulations are frequently the driving force behind those initiatives, including the aforementioned green product design. However, it is impossible to underestimate the worth of returned goods. Reverse logistics therefore plays a crucial part in industrial marketing and cannot be ignored.

The role that technology and innovation play in making the green SC possible: Two decades ago, governments mostly imposed the green notion. For instance, the U.S. Federal Trade Commission (FTC) began monitoring business branding in Green Marketing in the early 1990s. The Australian Fair-Trading Commission was established at the same period. The Australian Competition and Consumer Commission (ACCC) has taken its position since 1995. Specified several standards for evaluating commercial marketing, but still only two of them pertain to the green (SC). In addition to industry norms and governmental laws, two key enablers help the implementation of an environmentally friendly (SC). Frameworks for performance measurement were developed as one of the enablers (e.g., Godfrey, 1998; Hervani et al., 2005). These tools may be used to organise and assess the effectiveness of sustainable supply chains. They can also be used to ensure benefits like less waste disposal, the creation of byproducts from waste, the systematic tracking of the production of hazardous substances, and less energy use.

Scanning the Issues: His special issue has seven great papers, each of which has been reviewed at least twice by three reviewers. These seven articles cover a variety of topics, covering comparisons between B2B and B2C green SCM, green SCM performance, creating and improving greener products, focusing on sustainability, and integrating green marketing and green SCM. Both the public and private sectors are covered in the papers. They create a framework for new green practises, do qualitative inductive research, or do quantitative research to test a hypothesis. The research explains how the dysfunctional conflict of partnership and opportunistic behaviours might prevent relationship orientation from having a positive impact on the quality of interorganizational strategy. This is in contrast to earlier research, which had a stronger emphasis on the factors that influence the effectiveness of interorganizational strategy.

This study examines how agreements and procurement contracts are affected by a sustainable approach. Public procurement procedures have not previously been covered in company marketing literature. The 6Ps product, marketing, programming, process, people, and project are integrated across a variety of dimensions in the hub and

spoke model outlined in the article. The recommended 6Ps integration approach delivers more accurate data, material, person, and cash mobility across marketing and supply chains as opposed to traditional point to point B2B integration. Industrial managers have participated in an empirical study to evaluate the 6Ps integration model. When trying to adopt a green strategy in their business (Fig. 38.1), managers and logisticians might find some helpful guidance and ideas in this article. The importance of environmental industry analysis and development has been emphasised in the essay in order to boost market edge and financial performance. The majority of resource constrained product innovations are made in tiny numbers for incredibly unique circumstances. Resource constrained product development has drawn more attention during the past five years as large companies have begun to use it. As a result, the process is still the main focus of current study in resource constrained product development. Green supply chain management (GSCM) is typically associated with consumer focused companies and wellknown organisations, although it is sometimes disregarded in the

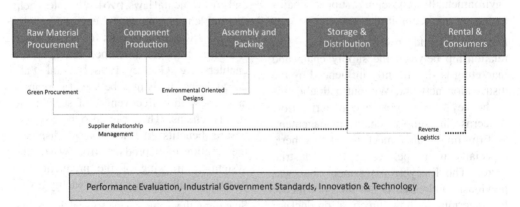

Fig. 38.1 Enablers and activities of green SC

Source: Authors

context of commercial supply chains. The study increases our understanding of how dependant on context GSCM. Additionally, they assess the situations when Supply chain management is most like to be effectively used. This research looks at how GSCM affects respect and support from top management in B2C and B2B supply chains. According to the findings, GSCM is less prevalent in B2B enterprises than it is in B2C firms. These results provide insightful data to B2B supply chain professionals and marketers who are working to meet the growing interest in supply networks' environmental performance. Given that businesses are increasingly using GSCM practises to address the environmental demands of their various key stakeholders and the potential for implementing GSCM to enhance such marketing as good or service and package design, marketing communication, and channel selection, this research is considered timely and significant to add to the existing marketing literature, that has generally paid only limited attention to the strategic implications of GSCM. The expert editors are grateful for everyone's time and work put out during the review process. They surely helped hasten the review process' timely completion and considerably raised the quality of the articles featured in the special edition with their rapid remarks. Finally, we would like to thank all of the writers for their contributions.

REFERENCES

1. Jayesh, G.S., Novaliendry, D., Gupta, S.K., Sharma, A.K. and Hazela, B., 2022. A Comprehensive Analysis of Technologies for Accounting and Finance in Manufacturing Firms. ECS Transactions, 107(1), p. 2715.

2. Pandey, A.K., Singh, R.K., Jayesh, G.S., Khare, N. and Gupta, S.K., 2022. Examining the Role of Enterprise Resource Planning (ERP) in Improving Business Operations in Companies. ECS Transactions, 107(1), p. 2681.

3. Gölgeci, I. and Kuivalainen, O., 2020. Does social capital matter for supply chain resilience? The role of absorptive capacity and marketing-supply chain management alignment. Industrial Marketing Management, 84, pp. 63–74.

4. Toorajipour, R., Sohrabpour, V., Nazarpour, A., Oghazi, P. and Fischl, M., 2021. Artificial intelligence in supply chain management: A systematic literature review. Journal of Business Research, 122, pp. 502–517.

5. Nunes, L.J.R., Causer, T.P. and Ciolkosz, D., 2020. Biomass for energy: A review on supply chain management models. Renewable and Sustainable Energy Reviews, 120, p. 109658.

6. Hofmann, E., Sternberg, H., Chen, H., Pflaum, A. and Prockl, G., 2019. Supply chain management and Industry 4.0: conducting research in the digital age. International Journal of Physical Distribution & Logistics Management.

7. Cole, R., Stevenson, M. and Aitken, J., 2019. Blockchain technology: implications for operations and supply chain management. Supply Chain Management: An International Journal.

8. Blanchard, D., 2021. Supply chain management best practices. John Wiley & Sons.

9. Monczka, R.M., Handfield, R.B., Giunipero, L.C. and Patterson, J.L., 2020. Purchasing and supply chain management. Cengage Learning.

10. Benton Jr, W.C., 2020. Purchasing and supply chain management. Sage Publications.

Advancements in Business for Integrating Diversity, and
Sustainability – Dimitrios A. Karras et al. (eds)
© 2024 Taylor & Francis Group, London, ISBN 978-1-032-70828-7

39 Metaverse Technology in HR and Evaluating its Impact on Balance Scorecard Metric

Smita Singh*, Anjali Saluja[1], Namrata Singh[2]
NIET, Greater Noida, India

Meenakshi Sharma[3]
MIMT, Greater Noida, India

Abstract: This research aims to understand aspect of the impact of Metaverse on Strategic HRM in the context through Metaverse on the drivers of Balance Scorecard. To carry out the present study, a systematic literature review was conducted through previous research papers, journals, and blogs on the key concepts of Metaverse, Strategic HRM-Balance Scorecard. A theoretical framework is being constructed to understand the implications of Metaverse, and Balance Score Card. Through a theoretical framework and systematic literature review, the author(s) have explained the impact of the Metaverse on drivers of Balance Scorecard and also focused on implementing the concept of Metaverse as a long-term strategy.

Keywords: Metaverse, Strategic human resource management balance scorecard

1. Introduction

Whether we are prepared or not the future has already knocked on our doors with the advent of the Pandemic forcing workplaces to think about new workplace landscapes which would be able to deal with uncertainty in times of uncertainty by creating innovations. The five-day working norm has changed from going physical to virtual working and employers need to be more agile to test the platform of Metaverse – the new immersive world. Metaverse concept is not entirely new.

It was created in 1992. Price water house Coopers wrote in his science fiction novel Snow Crash that Metaverse was founded in 1992 and writer Neal Stephenson invented the word "metaverse", roughly 23.5 million occupations will use AR and VR for training, business meetings, or customer service by 2030. Prior to the outbreak, businesses employed a mix of offline and online methods to train their employees. On many platforms, modern technologies are making it possible to demonstrate how technology-enhanced training can increase employee productivity.

---
*Corresponding author: smita29scorpio@gmail.com
[1]anjali.saluja@niet.co.in, [2]namratasingh.mba@niet.co.in, [3]gautam.moni@gmail.com

DOI: 10.4324/9781032708294-39

Many businesses that are making use of virtual platforms, plan to deploy remote working permanently. For Example - The industrial metaverse announcement by Microsoft which shall allow wear augmented reality handsets for managing supply chains virtually. Employees want to work and study whenever and wherever they choose, pushing human resource managers to seek out more interesting work and training environments. According to a recent Accenture survey, 90% of executives believe their present training methods should be more effective and efficient, and 94% of employees claimed that they would have stay longer if company would have invested in their professional development. One such fiction which shall altogether change the experience of Human Resource Function-The Metaverse which is a three-dimensional world wherein individuals using personalized avatars being replica of the user. It is a virtual world where individuals can communicate among each other in an immersive way more realistic and more engaging. HR need to design new hybrid working policies to maintain healthy metaverse working practices in an organization (Robinson, Maria, Moraes, 2022). A wonderful example of Microsoft using Mesh makes the online collaborations fun loving, people engage more in their body language, having water cooler conversations, and having more engaged conversations in team meetings.

2. Literature Review

The Metaverse: A metaverse is a virtual environment in which person can interact with both a computer-generated world and other people. Metaverse term was invented in 1992 and published in Neal Stevenson's book named Snow Crash (Stephenson, N,

2003). This is a shared virtual environment for online communities that is interactive, immersive, and collaborative (Park & Kim, 2022) the current Metaverse is based on the social value of Generation Z that online and offline selves are not different. With the technological development of deep learning-based high-precision recognition models and natural generation models, Metaverse is being strengthened with various factors, from mobile-based always-on access to connectivity with reality using virtual currency. The integration of enhanced social activities and neural-net methods requires a new definition of Metaverse suitable for the present, different from the previous Metaverse. This paper divides the concepts and essential techniques necessary for realizing the Metaverse into three components (*i.e.*, hardware, software, and contents. Metaverse is an interactive network with 3D virtual environments that is continuous and immersive. (Collins, 2008). Metaverse with its infinite capacity of a world which is virtual wherein the interaction of many people can be almost so possible at common platform. it supports a large number of people to boost social significance. Three components: are required to implement metaverse is (i) Advances in hardware; (ii) innovation in expression and recognition drivers; and (iii) Accessibility in subject matter. (Park & Kim, 2022) the current Metaverse is based on the social value of Generation Z that online and offline selves are not different. With the technological development of deep learning-based high-precision recognition models and natural generation models, Metaverse is being strengthened with various factors, from mobile-based always-on access to connectivity with reality using virtual currency. The integration of enhanced social activities and neural-net methods requires a new definition of Metaverse suitable for the present, different from the previous Metaverse. This paper divides the concepts and essential techniques necessary for realizing the Metaverse into three components (i.e., hardware, software, and contents Metaverse is the seamless integration of our physical and digital lives, resulting in a single virtual world where we can learn, play, relax, interact, and connect. The Metaverse is a 3-D imaginary depiction built entirely upon the well-known virtual reality gaming experience. A large influx of our real lives is now hybrid and virtual (Hacker et al., 2020). People working in the physical world may now work fully in the world of Virtual reality as virtual teams. Metaverses can be described as geographically scattered individuals depend upon technology alliance for completing their tasks. (Dubé et al., 2002). A virtual team needs collaboration much more effectively in a virtual world in presence of specific contextual factors and also the influence that leadership might have on these virtual teams. Due to advancements in technological capabilities, Virtual World are now skilled in effective interaction without physically enables (Schroeder et al., 2006). Metaverse is an Internet analogy that combines the powers of social networking, AI, Augmented Reality, and Virtual Reality. (*The Future of the Metaverse – Imagining the Internet*, n.d.). The metaverse has the potential to fill the void between leaders who want to remain connected with their employees and teams who want the flexibility of working remotely. companies related to computer games and social networks like: Facebook is a recent example relating to it are outlined throughout the world, (Egliston & Carter, 2021). The creation of the metaverse has just begun, but avatars with built-in utility will be critical

for digital identification. The metaverse can produce faces to enable real immersive experiences. People communicate both was by verbal communication and as well as by non-verbal communication (Park & Kim, 2022). AI technologies will be required to ensure that all functions is followed by the rules. (Hwang & Chien, 2022).

Metaverse can be categorized into three concepts: Metaverse – "it is a mixture of the transcendence and universe, which refers to a three-dimensional virtual. It is used to refer to computer-generated environment in which both the real and the unreal interaction can be possible" (Metaverse Wiki.) **Avatars** – it is a digital representation of the user's existence created is characterized as an avatar. (Bailenson et al., 2005). A user's identity in the Metaverse will be represented via an avatar. The metaverse will most certainly be used for more advanced tasks as it progresses. **Extended Reality** – it is combination of cybernetic reality, improved reality), and mixed reality. **Balanced Scorecard** – Implementation of Balance Score Card in an organisation increase the Customer satisfaction and the efficient financial performance (Amer, Faten & Hammoud, Sahar & Khatatbeh, Haitham & Lohner, Szimonetta & Boncz, Imre & Endrei, Dora 2022). In organizations, Balance Score Card drivers helps to improve performance of the organizational (Cignitas, C. P., Torrents Arévalo, J. A., & Vilajosana Crusells, J. 2022). It helps to bring efficiency in an organisation (Shalini, S., & Venkatesh, S. 2022 It has a positive relationship with organisational performance (Tibbs, 2016). Each strategy formed under the framework with Balance Score Card increase few areas like: Loyalty, Training, efficiency (Syair et al., 2019). Balance Score Card helps to accomplish the goal of an organisations with high level of success and minimal failure (Setiawan, 2020). It is a complex procedure in which a lot of skills and knowledge and commitment are needed (Scindia Chavan, Meena 2009). the implementation process is required responsible centre, responsible for customer needs, wants, strategy, plan implementations (Nattarinee Kopecka 2015). Balance Score Card focus on quick decision-making process and evaluating production process for sustainable growth in an organization (Deni Ahmad Taufik, Humiras Hardi Purba, Hasbullah 2021). Balanced scorecard helps to improve the profitability of an organisation by improving financial performance (Sahiti, A., Ahmeti, S., Sahiti, A., & Aliu, M. 2016). This strategic helps in converting goal them into action. Balance Score Card method helps to improve internal growth by preparing strong strategies for an organisation.

Objectives of the study

1. To study the implementation of Metaverse on organizations.
2. To examine the role of metaverse in Strategic implementation of Metaverse.

3. To study the impact of application of Metaverse on drivers/ perspectives of Balance Scorecard to measure organizational performance.

3. Research Methodology

This study is based on secondary data from authentic reliable sources and collected from by other researchers for the purpose that are different from this study. For this study, researcher collected information from 80 journal but only 50 journals data is used in this study, rest 30 journal's data were not suitable for this research.

Theoretical Framework

The paper proposes a conceptual model based on our own interpretation of two models for the components of the metaverse (**University of Nebraska at Omaha et al., 2009**) and Balance Scorecard based on the framework suggested by (Kaplan and Norton, 1992). Strategic HRM aims to enhance innovation, flexibility and competitive advantage. The strategic HRM integrates the concept of Metaverse as the new competitive advantage to empower employees, embrace disruption and experiment in innovative ways for

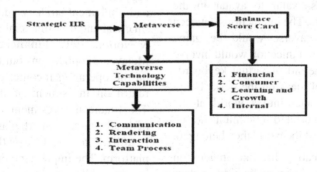

Fig. 39.1 Based on our own interpretation of the models of Components of Metaverse (University of Nebraska at Omaha et al., 2009), and Balance Score Card (Kaplan and Norton, 1992).

enhanced customer experience which could lead to mapping an organization's strategic HRM towards Balance Scorecard drivers.

Discussion on each component of the model

People/Avatars - Avatars are the people who are represented in the universe. Representing themselves as people/avatars they appear and act in interaction with their environment. The metaverse will help in modifying work by encouraging communications with free hand gadgets and avatars rather than laptops and cell phones, making group calls. The virtual representation of oneself through in highly realistic 3D avatars that duplicate our body language as they speak entering the VR and AR environments using those avatars. It would make employees in these avatars more engaged, productive and happier at work. The capabilities of Metaverse as suggested by (University of Nebraska at Omaha et al., 2009) in the model can be summarised as below:

Metaverse Capabilities – The potential features of Metaverse can be developed in the context of interactions in the metaverse.

Communication – The mode of communication is avatar to avatar in the world of metaverse. The interactions between employees in metaverse would be game changer as the communication would involve feedback, with the aid of virtual keyboards to bring out novel ideas on the desk. Using headsets people enter into a world of the virtual environment and communicate no matter which part of the world they belong to.

Rendering – Creating life-like images on the screen to create personalization in their avatars in which people can decide how their avatar would look like would add a real twist to the practices of team management, employee engagement, onboarding, and talent acquisition. In the world of metaverse employees can generate their own avatars with the help of their own choices of clothing, avatar to avatar eye gazing, for more personalized focus and vividness. **Interaction** – The pandemic reduced our mobility to a great extent due to which most of the activities were restricted however the use of metaverse in HR through interactivity and mobility. The metaverse technology would support sharing the content with other employees by increasing files, documents, or other relevant information. The metaverse could help employees by building of texts, figures, three-D models, images, pictures, etc. **Team Process:** (University of Nebraska at Omaha et al., 2009) with an example which is explained in VW helps to understand the capabilities of a metaverse and also provide methods of dealing with activities related with familiar group. These features support in doing interactions in virtual world.

Next component of the model comprises about The Balance Scorecard. **The Balance Scorecard** – The strategic performance of the application of Metaverse can have an impact on the four perspectives as suggested by Norton and Kaplan to manage and implement strategy and to measure the financial and non-financial aspects. (Kaplan & Norton, 1992) **Financial Perspective** – Metaverse application could make an impact on the operating income, profitability, and return on investment of the organization. The financial investment in various types of head glasses, smart glasses, and lenses is utilized to interface with the metaverse platform. The implementation of Metaverse in an agile environment will require immense complexity and collaboration between all stakeholders. **Customer**

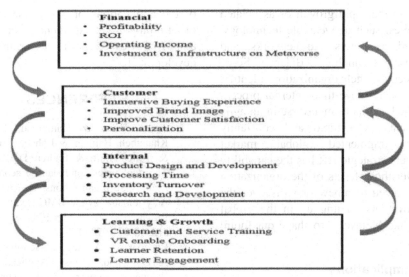

Fig. 39.2 Interpretation of measuring metaverse on perspectives of balance scorecard

Source: Made by Author

Perspective – This perspective in the Balance Scorecard monitors the process of delivering value to its clients and assesses the customer. As a part of the company's strategic success, an organization needs to understand customer needs and satisfaction. The metaverse can create virtual versions of existing products and services in more immersive ways. The future norm is going to be metaverse by putting their customers first to enhance their buying experience uniquely from anywhere. Capitalizing on the new avenues of Metaverse brands like Tanishq, Ceat, M&M and Asian Paints are already end route towards building a virtual world using videos, images, and 3D products. **Internal Process Perspective** – The business operations have the greatest influence on customer satisfaction which could be the source of the internal metrics for the balanced scorecard. High-quality products, operational excellence, and improving the marketing process using avatars, wearables, objects, architecture,

and interiors are possible objectives of internal process perspective. **Learning and Growth Perspective** – According to a latest survey by PWC studied that 51% of companies have already imitated the process of integrating VR into their corporate strategy, or they have already built around one dedicated segment of business into VR. Findings reveals a significant future for the metaverse like Virtual learners were 4 times faster to learn than classroom training, more confident to apply skills learned after training 277 more times, 3.76 more connected to content delivered in training and 4 times more focussed than their e-learning colleagues.

4. Discussion and Conclusions

The volume of research and the number of applications connected to the usage of the metaverse in different sectors is expected to grow significantly over the next ten year due to the rapid growth of associated technologies, such as wearable technology, high-speed computers and networks, and sensor-based technology. Balance Score Card aspects will help organizations identify, measure and improve their internal process to reap the benefits of metaverse in an agile environment. In a rapid and constantly changing fragmented global market environment strategic HR has the capability to discover those facets of the organization where we need to renew or rediscover the new innovations coming up in the global scenario like Metaverse to shape our future workplace.

Future Implications

Developments in VR and AR technology have encouraged the interest in implement in the organisation. This technology will be beneficial in improving the performance of many areas in an organisation like: financial, internal, HRM, etc. this technology will remove the barrier and will be beneficial to the employees living geographically scatter and working together at common platform. **Limitation and directions to future research** - Firstly, the research is based on theoretical literature and based on the authors interpretation of the metaverse on strategic HRM. Secondly, the study concentrates on the impact of Metaverse and how it can be measured on the four perspectives of Balance Scorecard. Thirdly, the application of Metaverse is still in an infancy stage, organizations need to carefully plan the applications of Metaverse owing to the huge costs, issues of data protection and adopting the tools in the metaverse. Fourthly due to the limitations of time the study is limited to the theoretical application of metaverse. Thus, future researches can significantly focus on more exploration

of the applications of Metaverse in terms of Employee engagement, Onboarding employee experiences, Learning and development.

REFERENCES

1. Amer, Faten & Hammoud, Sahar & Khatatbeh, Haitham & Lohner, Szimonetta & Boncz, Imre & Endrei, Dora. (2022). The deployment of balanced scorecard in health care organizations: is it beneficial? A systematic review. BMC Health Services Research. 22. https://doi.org/10.1186/s12913-021-07452-7
2. Banabakova, V. K., & Georgiev, M. P. (2017). Opportunities of Application of the Balanced Scorecard in Management and Control. International Scientific Journal "Internauka," 1(10), 1056–1074. https://doi.org/10.25313/2520-2057-1-10-2780
3. Cignitas, C. P., Torrents Arévalo, J. A., & Vilajosana Crusells, J. (2022). Positive management and the balanced scorecard: a successful strategy for organizations. Journal of Positive School Psychology, 6(3), 2606–2627.
4. Collins, C. (2008). Looking to the Future: Higher Education in the Metaverse. EDUCAUSE Review, 43(5), 50.
5. Dubé, P. L., No, C. D. G., Professor, A., Professor, A., Montréal, H., Montréal, H., Montréal, H., Montréal, H., Dube, L., Dubé, L., Dubé, L., Pare, G., Paré, G., Paré, G., & Paré, G. (2002). The Multi-faceted Nature of Virtual Teams. In D.J. Pauleen (Ed.), Virtual Teams: Projects, Protocols, and Practices, 1–39.
6. Egliston, B., & Carter, M. (2021). Critical questions for Facebook's virtual reality: Data, power and the metaverse. Internet Policy Review, 10(4). https://doi.org/10.14763/2021.4.1610
7. Hacker, J., vom Brocke, J., Handali, J., Otto, M., & Schneider, J. (2020). Virtually in this together – how web-conferencing

systems enabled a new virtual togetherness during the COVID-19 crisis. European Journal of Information Systems, 29(5), 563–584. https://doi.org/10.1080/096008 5X.2020.1814680

8. Hwang, G.-J., & Chien, S.-Y. (2022). Definition, roles, and potential research issues of the metaverse in education: An artificial intelligence perspective. Computers and Education: Artificial Intelligence, 3, 100082. https://doi. org/10.1016/j.caeai.2022.100082

9. Kaplan, R. S., & Norton, D. P. (1992, January 1). The Balanced Scorecard— Measures that Drive Performance. Harvard Business Review. https://hbr.org/1992/01/ the-balanced-scorecard-measures-that-drive-performance-2

10. Park, S.-M., & Kim, Y.-G. (2022). A Metaverse: Taxonomy, Components, Applications, and Open Challenges. IEEE Access, 10, 4209–4251. https://doi. org/10.1109/ACCESS.2021.3140175.

*Advancements in Business for Integrating Diversity, and
Sustainability* – Dimitrios A. Karras et al. (eds)
© 2024 Taylor & Francis Group, London, ISBN 978-1-032-70828-7

40

Enhancing a Commercial Bank's Risk Management Framework as a Prerequisite for Reducing Financial Distress

G. Nirmala*, R. Monisha[1]
St. Joseph's college of Engineering, Chennai, India
Amandeep Nagpal[2]
Lovely Professional University, Phagwara, Punjab, India
Dinesh Chandra Pandey[3]
Graphic Era Deemed to be University,
Dehradun, Uttarakhand, India

Abstract: The goal of this study is to ascertain whether or not the presence of risk management-related corporate governance practices, such as determining whether the Chief Risk Officer (CRO) reports to the Chief Executive Officer (CEO) or the board of directors, is connected to improved bank performance. When evaluating a bank's success, we look at several metrics, such as the CEO's ownership stake, the bank's size and autonomy, the profitability of a buy-and-hold strategy, and the Return on Equity (ROE). We show that when the CRO reported directly to the board of directors rather than the CEO of the bank, stock returns and return on equity were significantly stronger (i.e. less negative) during the financial crisis (or other corporate entities). In some cases, traditional metrics of corporate responsibility have little bearing on the crisis performance of banks, and some have even been shown to have a negative correlation.

Keywords: Chief risk officer (CRO), Chief executive officer (CEO), Return on enquiry (ROE), Corporate governance, Risk governance, Bank performance, Financial crisis

1. Introduction

The purpose and domain of risk management are to guarantee that the investment's risk is handled in a controlled and well-understood fashion (Rajesh, et al., 2022). Internet finance has a major effect on commercial banks because of its resource integration, operational convenience, and customer structure sinking qualities (Jayesh, et al., 2022). The industry has also undergone major changes, particularly in the early

*Corresponding author: nirmala.gopinathan@gmail.com
[1]monisharamaraj89@gmail.com, [2]saranmds@gmail.com, [3]dineshchandra@geu.ac.in

DOI: 10.4324/9781032708294-40

2000s, when there was a significant restructuring as a result of some commercial banks' public declarations of insolvency and eventual liquidation by the Bank of Uganda (Serwadda, I., (2018)). Banking crises in Nigeria have demonstrated that banks frequently take excessive risks and that those risks vary among banks (Olalekan, et al., 2018). An economy's function for financial institutions, particularly commercial banks, is crucial (Aldayel and Fragouli, 2018).

declarations of insolvency and eventual liquidation by the Bank of Uganda (Serwadda, I., (2018)). Banking crises in Nigeria have demonstrated that banks frequently take excessive risks and that those risks vary among banks (Olalekan, et al., 2018). An economy's function for financial institutions, particularly commercial banks, is crucial (Aldayel and Fragouli, 2018).

2. Related works

Permatasari, I., (2020) examined the connection between corporate management and risk mitigation in Indonesian financial institutions. Alhammadi, et al., 2020 highlighted how choosing and continually evaluating a company's business model are $RMRF_t$ is the period t valuation return on average excluding the danger essential components of strategic counsel and how risk management is directly tied to corporate governance (CG). Ayadi, et al. (2021) contrasted how Eurozone banks performed and took risks before and after the 2008 financial crisis, taking into account both internal and external governance financial crisis. The corporate structure, risk management, financial results, and ownership structure of banks are all examined in detail by (kakar, et al., 2021).

3. Methodology

Data samples: Sample selection: In addition, we eliminate any bank years not included in the Centre of Research on Security Prices (CRSP) database. In the end, 573 institutions are still standing, and we are using them as a sample for our attempt to aggregate business and risk governance data from the many sources detailed below. Corporate Governance: The lack of banking-specific Data on management and a dearth of hazard assessment data in commercial governance databases like Risk Metrics led us to rely heavily on the SEC's EDGAR database for key variables for corporate governance. Specifically, we used the Annual survey (10k) and prospectus (Def 14A) types filed by banks. Our initial set of five key corporate governance recommendations covers all 380 banks that had an annual survey done in 2006 and a proxy statement published in 2007. Bank performance metrics: In unreported robustness testing, we replace raw returns with 4-factor model alphas. At the bank level, the precise time regression coefficient is generated as a stand-in for the alphas.

$$R_t = \alpha + \beta_1 RMRF_t + \beta_2 SMB_t + \beta_3 HML_t + \beta_4 MOM_t + \varepsilon_t \qquad (1)$$

percentage, and SMB_t (Small Minus Big), HML_t (High Minus Low) along with the MOM_t. These are the month-to-month returns for factor-mimicking portfolios with no investments that are truly meant to mimic the impacts of dimensions, book-to-market, and momentum. Where R_t is the individual bank's stock's excess return in the corresponding month t financial control variables. At the end of 2006, we started using a wide range of financial institution characteristics in our regressions. This was done so we could better explain how banks did during the financial crash. The COMPUSTAT Banco North America database can be used to produce these variables.

Income diversity =

$$1 - \left| \frac{\text{Net Interest Income} - \text{Other Operating Income}}{\text{Total Operating Income}} \right| \quad (2)$$

Interest revenue less interest expenditure is known as net interest revenue. Net interest earned, net fees revenue, net operating revenue, and net commission income are all included in total operating income.

4. Empirical Analysis

The paper's principal analysis relies on the variables described by their Table 40.1. Descriptive statistics descriptive statistics, from both the small sample (Panel B) and the full sample of 372 banks, which are provided in a Table 40.1 based on information from the Governance Legacy database and personally acquired data on business and risk governance (Panel A). You can see the differences between banks with and without head of risk management on the board of directors in Table 40.2. Table 40.3 displays the variables considered in the multivariate analysis contrasting banks along with or without CRO on the board. Table 40.3: Buy-and-hold returns and measures of sound management practices Examining many factors at once Using Ordinary Least Squares (OLS) regressions, we looked into the connection between buy-and-hold values and several classes of management, business laws, and hazard characteristics. The tabulated outcomes are displayed below. The table below displays the results of ordinary least squares regressions of buy-and-hold returns on multiple sets of risk indicators, corporate governance aspects, and control variables.

Table 40.1 Descriptive statistics

.	Mean	Min	Lower quartile	Median	Upper quartile	Max	Standard	N
Panel B: Small sample								
CRO in the executive board	.4678	0	0	0	1	1	.3742	75
Risk committee	.2456	0	0	0	0	1	.3266	81
CRO reports to the board	.923	0	0	0	0	1	03664	84
CRO reports to the CEO	.0735	0	0	0	0	1	26671	82
ROE	.1066	−.5153	.0473	.1732	.3394	.5235	.243	83
ROE (lagged)	.1293	.0192	.0938	.1246	.1630	.2304	.0581	84
ROA	.106	−.0775	.0057	.0165	.0421	.0346	.0185	84
Panel A: Large sample								
ROE (lagged)	.1074	−0.0561	0.0765	0.116				
ROA	.0066	−.0872	0.0012	0.0120	0.0187	0.0247	.0141	472
ROA (lagged)	.088	−.0031	0.0081	0.0098	0.0135	0.0107	.0042	472
CRO in the executive board	.1263	0	0	0	0	1	.4426	472
Risk committee	.0705	0	0	0	0	1	.2472	369
Board size	11.666	6	9	11	12	23	4.1684	371
Board independence	.7851	.2750	.7000	.8852	.7751	1	.1192	369

Table 40.2 The executive boards of banks with CROs

	CRO in exec. board		Difference	p-value	Number of CROs on the executive board	
	Yes	No			Yes	No
Board independence	0.7514	0.7724	0.0186	0.2823	324	46
CEO is notified by CRO	0.1934	0.0000	0.1934****	0.0005	53	30
CRO updates the board	0.1512	0.0371	0.1234**	0.0452	53	31
Risk committee	0.3530	0.0365	0.3361***	0.0000	325	47
ROA	0.0111	0.0095	0.0011*	0.0713	324	46

Table 40.3 Buy-and-hold return regression with the corporate governance variable

	CRO in exec. board		Difference	p-value	Number of CROs on the executive board	
	Yes	No			Yes	No
CRO reports to the board	0.1512	0.0371	0.1234**	0.0452	53	31
CEO is notified by CRO	0.1934	0.0000	0.1934****	0.0005	53	30
Board size	12.2125	10.5563	16558***	0.0007	324	45
Board independence	0.7514	0.7724	0.0186	0.2823	324	46
ROE	0.1228	0.1065	0.0163**	0.0274	324	46
ROA	0.0111	0.0095	0.0011*	0.0713	324	46
Risk committee	0.3530	0.0365	0.3361***	0.0000	325	47

5. Conclusion

We analyze how the unique aspects of banks' Risk Governance affected the banks' performance throughout the financial crisis. Based on their performance during the financial crisis, our findings suggest that standard governance indicators, which have been used extensively in the literature on governance as well as its effect on valuation with non-financial enterprises, cannot represent the relevant governance model of banks. According to our findings, "risk governance" within financial institutions is crucial. In particular, we found that banks need to better prepare for the next financial crisis by elevating the positions of CEO and CRO to the same level, with both reporting to the board of directors. However, if the market isn't in a state of emergency, that could be detrimental to your success.

REFERENCES

1. Alhammadi, S., Archer, S. and Asutay, M., 2020. Risk management and corporate governance failures in Islamic banks: a case study. Journal of Islamic Accounting and Business Research.

2. Ayadi, M.A., Ayadi, N. and Trabelsi, S., 2019. Corporate governance, European bank performance, and the financial crisis. Managerial Auditing Journal.

3. Zaitul, Z., Melmusi, Z. and Ilona, D., 2019. Corporate Governance and Bank Performance: Global Financial Crisis 2008. Journal of Reviews on Global Economics, 8, pp. 625–636.

4. Serwadda, I., 2018. Impact of credit risk management systems on the financial performance of commercial banks in Uganda. Acta Universitatis Agriculturae et Silviculturae Mendelianae Brunensis.

5. Olalekan, L.I., Olumide, M.L. and Irom, I.M., 2018. Financial risk management and the profitability: empirical evidence from commercial banks in Nigeria. Samuel Analyst Journal of Management Sciences, 16(2), pp. 56–67.

6. Aldayel, M. and Fragouli, E., 2018. Risk management and performance: a case study of credit risk management in commercial banks. The Business & Management Review, 10(1), pp. 169–183.

7. Jayesh, G.S., Novaliendry, D., Gupta, S.K., Sharma, A.K. and Hazela, B., 2022. A Comprehensive Analysis of Technologies for Accounting and Finance in Manufacturing Firms. ECS Transactions, 107(1), p. 2715.

8. Rajesh, N., Irudayasamy, A., Mohideen, M.S.K. and Ranjith, C.P., 2022. Classification of Vital Genetic Syndromes Associated With Diabetes Using ANN-Based CapsNet Approach. International Journal of e-Collaboration (IJeC), 18(3), pp. 1–18.

9. Permatasari, I., 2020. Does corporate governance affect bank risk management? Case study of Indonesian banks. International Trade, Politics and Development, 4(2), pp. 127–139.

Note: All tables in this chapter were made by the Authors.

*Advancements in Business for Integrating Diversity, and
Sustainability – Dimitrios A. Karras et al. (eds)*
© 2024 Taylor & Francis Group, London, ISBN 978-1-032-70828-7

41

Study on the Effects of Credit Risk Management on Commercial Banks' Financial Performance in India

R. Monisha*
St. Joseph's college of Engineering, Chennai, India

Muhammed Shafi M. K.[1]
VIT Business School, Vellore Institute of Technology, Chennai, India

Navdeep Singh[2]
Lovely Professional University, Phagwara, Punjab, India

Shruti Sharma[3]
Graphic Era Deemed to be University, Dehradun, Uttarakhand, India

Abstract: Examining the effects of credit risk (CR) elements on credit risk management's (CRM's) effectiveness and the rise in non-performing resources (NPR) of India's commercial banks is the focus of this article. Sources for the dataset include both original and secondary sources. The main data are gathered by distributing questionnaires to Indian bank risk executives. The ProwessIQ database and annual reports provide another data on the NPRs of Indian banks. The statistical analysis is performed by using ANOVA and multiple linear regression analysis (MLRA) models. The findings imply that the effectiveness of CR is strongly impacted by the detection of CR. The findings are robust because annual loan growth is negatively correlated with CR detection. Evidence exists to support theoretical assumption that private banks will do better in terms of CR versus government banks. This research has consequences for Indian banks that are experiencing significant losses from improper loans.

Keywords: Indian Banks, Credit risk management (CRM), Non-performing resources (NPR), CR detection

1. Introduction

In India, bank lending dominates other sources of funding for businesses. India offers a suitable context in which to study this research subject because it has Asia's largest commercial bank and one of the oldest stock exchanges (Taiwo, et al., 2017). Indian companies' reliance on Indian banks is expected to reduce as they

*Corresponding author: monisharamaraj89@gmail.com
[1]mkshafimba@gmail.com, [2]saranmds@gmail.com, [3]shrutisharma.comm@geu.ac.in

DOI: 10.4324/9781032708294-41

grow and expand abroad (Pandey, et al., 2022). International banks may not lend to these enterprises due to their minimal capital needs. So, these companies choose domestic banks, which should expand and adopt generally acknowledged best practices in order to become more competitive issues, technology issues, inefficient human resources, inattention, and harsh policy approach from sustainable development and resource preservation. With a (Jayesh, et al., 2022). Due to the effective identification of (risk) assets, the major international banks are known for their strong risk management procedures, particularly with regard to CR. To meet the internationally accepted standards, Indian banks are working to enhance their efficiency and risk management procedures (Nabi, et al., 2018). A move in that direction is for international banks to be subject to strict provisioning rules as well as early CR detection. The objective of this research is to discover and assess the key components of the CRM scheme used by Indian banks. Research both corporations' Canadian affiliates approach strategic planning and management (MNEs). It provides a framework for assessing how they would react to the different World Products theoretically and empirically about CRM in banks is rising. This behavior, constructing brand recognition, and trying to recruit best talent in response to the younger generation demands investigations, however, are restricted to the administration, NPRs, and shortcomings in CRM in banks. Comprehending the components of CRM in the setting of emerging economies seems to be lacking (Palamalai, et al., 2017). Additionally, the connection exists between the effectiveness of the CR components and its elements has not been conclusively shown by the existing literature. The objective of the study is to examining the effects of CR elements on CRM's effectiveness in Indian banks.

2. Related Works

Using CRM elements and financial quality measures or measures, Serwadda, I., 2018 sought to examine the effect of CRM on the effectiveness of banks. The effect of CR on firms' profit in the Turkish Banking Sector from 2005 to 2017 was studied by Ekinci, et al., 2019. The study's conclusions showed that commercial banks with well-established internal controls had generally better financial results (Asiligwa, et al., 2017). The impact of internal controls on the financial results of commercial banks is not clear from these studies. Liquidity ratio and net stable financing ratio aspects made up the liquidity risk area (Muriithi, et al., 2017). According to the results, NSFR is both long- and short-term adversely correlated with banks' profitability. The size of the bank, creditworthiness, operational effectiveness, financial services, and debt ratio, according to Nataraja et al. (2018), have a considerable influence considerable influence on the internal achievement, stock performance, and bank revenue, that also demonstrates the economic outcomes of the three selected India's commercial banks.

3. Methodology

Data samples: Raw information is gathered by surveying Indian bank risk executives. Financial statements and the "Centre for Monitoring Indian Economy's ProwessIQ databases" provide secondary data on Indian bank NPRs. The NPR data includes annual records for 40 Indian banks (15 private banks and 25 government banks) having fiscal years that concluded on Mar 2012–2016.

Questionnaires: First question asks about risk executives' opinions of CRM in Indian banks. Concerning CR detection in Indian banks, the next question. The CR valuation in Indian banks is covered in the question 3. Control over CR in Indian banks is covered in the fourth question. The evaluation of investment needs based on Basel (Accord) rules is the subject of the fifth question. The final question concerns CRM's effectiveness in Indian banks.

Hypotheses development:

- Hypothesis-1 (H1): NPR's growth is negatively correlated with CR insight, CR detection, valuation, CR control, and CR investment needs in Indian banks.

- Hypothesis-2 (H2): The effectiveness of CRM procedures and the objectives for CR insight, CR detection, valuation, CR control, and CR investment in Indian banks are positively correlated.

- Hypothesis-3 (H3): The CRM practices of both government banks and private banks in India differ significantly.

Variables: To assess the CRM practices of Indian banks, we use 5 independent factors and 2 analogues for the dependent variable (CR performance).

Dependent variables:

- NPR growth ratio: The NPR growth ratio information were taken from the ProwessIQ directory and verified by bank financial reports. Between 2012 and 2016, we calculated the average annual rate of growth.

- CR performance (CRP): It indicates how well Indian banks are using CRM.

Independent variables (IVs): There are 5 variables as follows, IV-1: CR insight (CRIS); IV-2: CR detection (CRD); IV-3: CR valuation (CRV); IV-4: CR control (CRC); IV-5: CR investment needs (CRIN)

Utilizing MLRA, the two concepts are evaluated. The NPR growth ratio is predicated on 5 explanatory factors in the first concept. The second concept makes an effort to comprehend how CR components affect CRP. To verify the hypotheses, we evaluate the concepts shown in equations (1) and (2).

$$NPR_{gr} = f\{CRIS, CRD, CRV, CRC, CRIN\} \ (1)$$

$$CRP = f\{CRIS, CRD, CRV, CRC, CRIN\} \ (2)$$

4. Results and Discussion

The results of the correlation, MLRA, and ANOVA tests are shown in Table 41.1. The table also contains the summary statistics. The Cronbach's alpha test is used to evaluate the reliability of scales. An appropriate and reliable construct value $\propto \geq 0.70$. The findings show that the majority of the indicators are reliable. The CRIN mean is not very high. For calculating the investment needs for CR, the CRIN is related to Basel rules. The lower mean suggests that Indian banks remain to calculate capital requirements using simple methods. Certain correlation coefficients appear to be strong, according to the table. The greatest VIF score, however, falls within the acceptable range.

CRD's estimated coefficient is both negative and significant, using correlation analysis. This supports H1. MLRA estimates that

Table 41.1 Results of correlation, MLRA, and ANOVA test

Variables	Reliability		Summarized samples		
	Cronbach's A test	Mean	Std. Dev.	Min	Max
CRI	0.68	4.34	0.32	3.70	5
CRD	0.77	4.35	0.37	3.37	5
CRV	0.74	4.37	0.37	3.62	5
CRC	0.66	4.27	0.37	3.56	5
CRIN	0.86	3.79	0.59	1.59	5
CRP	0.66	-	-	-	-
Correlation analysis					
IVs	CRIS	CRD	CRV	CRC	CRIN
CRIS	1				
CRD	0.71	1			
CRV	0.61	0.74	1		
CRC	0.55	0.71	0.72	1	
CRIN	0.22	0.31	0.5	0.42	1

MLRA Variables	Dependent variables	
	NPR growth ratio	CRP
constant	1.62 (1.778)	1.19 (1.21)
CRD	−0.65 (−2.54)**	0.71 (2.55)**
CRIS	0.34 (1.22)	−0.15 (−0.51)
CRIN	0.05 (0.39)	0.091 (0.81)
R^2 value	18%	29%

Note: **(significant at level of 5)

ANOVA results			CRP		
	Significance	F-value	Quantity	Mean	Std. Dev.
CRP	0.02	5.78	-	-	-
Private	-	-	15	4.14	0.43
Government	-	-	25	3.77	0.45
Sum	-	-	40	3.91	0.47

Source: Authors

CRD's coefficient is positive and significant. This supports H2. Government and private banks' CRPs differ significantly, according to the data. Private Banks have a significantly greater CRP than government banks (4.14 vs. 3.77). This supports H3.

Banks and financial organizations initiate risk management by identifying risks. This helps administer risk assessment, administration, minimization, business strategy, performance assessment, and costing. Early risk analysis can enhance stress test cases, risk modelling, risk measurement, and strategy development. Risk assessment enables managers identify the bank's weaknesses. Identifying a bank's credit risk to a specific sector guarantees that industry-specific variables that generate credit losses receive additional risk Outcomes of ANOVA: There is a substantial correlation between absorption and organizational effectiveness.

weights. This improves risk assessment. Identifying risks helps model and quantify complex risks. In circumstances with little evidence, risks are modelled through narrative research. Basel suggests using credit judgement and reasonable estimations to quantify loan losses. An impartial examination of a bank's strategy, rules, processes, and practices linked to credit sanction and asset management should detect credit risk. Prudential restrictions should be imposed to prevent bank risk to a single borrower or associated creditors. Identifying and managing credit risk should include all services and goods. After proper research and official approval, innovative services and goods should fulfill processes for risk management. Complicated credit choices including loans to specialized industries, asset restructuring, and credit risk must be addressed with the best level. Individual company and group credit limitations in banking and trade should be reasonable and relevant. Banks must engage in data and risk management schemes to detect credit riskiness. Branch managers and upper-level leadership should ensure system sufficiency frequently.

5. Conclusion

This report examined CRM's impact on Indian banks' finances. The results supported that RBI's efforts to identify CR

early by requiring banks to reveal potential borrowers' profiles and credit scores. The RBI limits the amount given to a particular firm or group to diversify banks' lending portfolios. It inhibits lending to troubled industries by boosting provisioning requirements. RBI can review banks' books and requires fortnightly compliance reports from banks. Banks can lend to a company or group of companies, subject to regulations. CRD is the primary factor of Indian banks' CR performance. Private Banks have better credit risk performance than government banks. Given private banks' operational flexibility and desire for higher performance, this isn't unexpected. Government agencies interact with government banks.

REFERENCES

1. Taiwo, J.N., Ucheaga, E.G., Achugamonu, B.U., Adetiloye, K. and Okoye, O., 2017. Credit risk management: Implications on bank performance and lending growth. Saudi Journal of Business and Management Studies, 2, pp. 584–590.

2. Pandey, A.K., Singh, R.K., Jayesh, G.S., Khare, N. and Gupta, S.K., 2022. Examining the Role of Enterprise Resource Planning (ERP) in Improving Business Operations in Companies. ECS Transactions, 107(1), p. 2681.

3. Jayesh, G.S., Novaliendry, D., Gupta, S.K., Sharma, A.K. and Hazela, B., 2022. A Comprehensive Analysis of Technologies for Accounting and Finance in Manufacturing Firms. ECS Transactions, 107(1), p. 2715.

4. Nabi, M.N., Gao, Q., Rahman, M.T., Pervez, A.K. and Shah, A.A., 2018. Microfinance institutions of Bangladesh: The effects of credit risk management on credit performance. Journal of Economics and Sustainable Development, 22(8), pp. 104–114.

5. Palamalai, S. and Britto, J., 2017. Analysis of financial performance of selected commercial banks in India. Srinivasan, Palamalai and Britto, John (2017), "Analysis of Financial Performance of Selected Commercial Banks in India", Theoretical Economics Letters, 7(7), pp. 2134–2151.

6. Serwadda, I., 2018. Impact of credit risk management systems on the financial performance of commercial banks in Uganda. Acta Universitatis Agriculturae et Silviculturae Mendelianae Brunensis.

7. Ekinci, R. and Poyraz, G., 2019. The effect of credit risk on financial performance of deposit banks in Turkey. Procedia Computer Science, 158, pp. 979–987.

8. Asiligwa, M. and Rennox, G., 2017. The Effect of internal controls on the financial performance of commercial banks in Kenya. Journal of Economics and Finance, 8(3), pp. 92–105.

9. Muriithi, J.G. and Waweru, K.M., 2017. Liquidity risk and financial performance of commercial banks in Kenya.

*Advancements in Business for Integrating Diversity, and
Sustainability – Dimitrios A. Karras et al. (eds)*
© 2024 Taylor & Francis Group, London, ISBN 978-1-032-70828-7

42

A Study of Consumer Buying Behaviour and Their Shopping Styles for Branded Apparels in NCR

Naveen Nandal*
Assistant Professor, Sushant University, Gurugram

Aarushi Kataria
Assistant Professor, Bharati Vidyapeeth University, New Delhi

Nisha Nandal
Assistant Professor, Sushant University, Gurugram

Anuradha
Assistant Professor, Bharati Vidyapeeth University, New Delhi

Abstract: Branded apparel and promotional apparel will always be a top trending promo product category. The study aims to find out the factor influencing people buy a branded apparel along with the buying decision style and how demography plays a vital role in the buying decisions. Numerous businesses had been producing and promoting branded clothing. Consequently, there were more options available to consumers. A study of consumer behaviour was thought to be necessary in this situation in order to comprehend the purchasing habits and preferences of various consumers. Understanding consumer behaviour will assist businesses in developing strategies to meet customer wants and consequently grow their market share. Consumer preferences and decision-making processes were found to shift quickly, particularly in a dynamic setting. The study will assist marketers in creating marketing strategies for branded garments while keeping in mind the significance of consumer behavior and consumption patterns.

Keywords: Consumer behavior, Brand, Apparel

1. Introduction

In recent years branded products and apparels have captured the consciousness of Indian consumers. The quest to enquire into the consumers is progressively gaining priority among companies and scholars with eagerness among global brands to

*Corresponding author: Naveennandal@sushantuniversity.edu.in

DOI: 10.4324/9781032708294-42

capture the pie of rising Indian middle class market. For this purpose, there is a quest for understanding forces governing consumer behavior, consumer mindset and shopping behavior. The decision making process is essentially cognitive process influenced by diverse forces ranging from culture and socio-psychological to product features. The consumer decision-making process describes the steps a consumer takes before deciding whether or not to buy a certain product. Making rational decisions involves following certain steps: "Identifying the issue, weighing the available options, and selecting the best one given the circumstances at hand". Consumers go through the five steps of "issue detection, information search, alternative appraisal, product choosing, and making a rational buying decision," as described by Engel et al. in 1986. "In the first step, problem recognition (also known as need recognition), a person notices a discrepancy between the current situation and the desired or ideal one.

Effect of Changing Lifestyle on Consumer Behavior Changing way of life are a consequence of changes in statistic attributes and changing estimations of purchasers. These have turned out to be more rival and obvious in 1990's. A few features and their impacts on buyer conduct are as under:

1. Changes in Male Purchasing Roles
   The expansion in number of working ladies especially in urban regions has made a move in part of guys and housewife. Today, the part of male has reached out to shopping, childcare and greater inclusion in cooking and other family unit tasks, which customarily were thought to be female parts. The changing male part is not just a component of socioeconomics. It is additionally critical of progress in male esteems. Guys have begun to search for adornments, healthy skin items, creams and makeup that were thought to be female. The net consequence of the more noteworthy association of men in shopping and housekeeping exercises and their ability to shed a conventional male picture has prompted a merger of male and female acquiring parts.

2. Changes in Female Purchasing Roles:
   Working ladies more noteworthy fortune, autonomy and fearlessness have made a generous change in ladies acquiring parts. As their obtaining power has expanded they utilized more muscle in pretty much every item classification, making no enclave a male save any longer. Because of this many working ladies never again jump at the chance to relate to the promotions that disclose to them how to clean the floors or to satisfy their spouses.

3. Emphasis on Health and Fitness
   Shoppers have turned out to be more mindful of wellbeing and wellness issues and have begun going in for low calorie sustenances, refined oil and low fat nourishment. However, then again because of quick life particularly in urban regions individuals have begun to go in for fast food which is thought to be undesirable by the nutritionist. The sprawling scale increment in wellness related business in India has gradually begun retreating because of quick existence of people.

4. More Isolated Lifestyle Customers
   are investing more energy at home, bringing about more detached way of

life. There are two measurements to this pattern: remaining at home for relaxation and working at home. Today buyers will probably remain at home for relaxation and amusement. The mid 90's saw a considerable measure of TV channels coming into India. The wide decision of cleanser musical drama on these channels has constrained individuals of wide cross segments to adhere to their homes. A moment and more extensive measurement of a more confined shopper is the more prominent open doors for working at home brought forth by the data upset, making it simple for locally established business visionaries to work as though they worked in a corporate office.

5. Greater Time Weights: In the present situation, the regular workers are under gigantic weight with regards to time administration. The regular workers are compelled to put long working hours as the desires of purchasers are ever expanding. Additionally, they are under colossal strain to give identical time to their families too. This wants to purchase merchandise from stores that offer a wide assortment of items. Such a move has expanded the quantity of super stores in huge urban communities. Today, for some buyers shopping is no more a lovely occupation. They don't have room schedule-wise to assess items before acquiring them. They go more towards known brands and master the retail locations to prompt them on item determination. Comfort in buying is getting to be plainly key.

6. Better Means of Information with the appearance of hardware, PCs and web, the awareness level of shoppers

have expanded significantly. Product knowledge has likewise gone up. This is in a route worthwhile to the fabricates as the correspondence procedure ends up plainly rearranged. Then again more item information implies a superior comprehension of item includes. More item information edge prompts sensational lessening in mark unwaveringness. Shoppers wind up plainly hesitant to pay a premium for a brand. This prompts a vast scale increment in value wars and adversary affects the gainfulness of fabricates. This makes a requirement for item separation and for this makes need to persistently redesign their current items and work towards new item advancement.

The consumer decision-making process describes the steps a consumer takes before deciding whether or not to buy a certain product. Making rational decisions involves following certain steps: "Identifying the issue, weighing the available options, and selecting the best one given the circumstances at hand" (Deacon and Firebaugh, 1975). The first five processes in solving a problem are issue recognition, information search, alternative evaluation, product selection, and rational decision-making, according to Engel et al. (1986). "In the first step, problem recognition (also known as need recognition), a person notices a discrepancy between the current situation and the desired or ideal one. It is possible for both internal and external circumstances to cause this urge". A customer may switch out a product that totally meets their wants for another by looking for variety online. Higher purchase frequency may encourage repeat purchases rather than variety-seeking behaviour, according to Van, Hoyer, and Inman (1996).

The study aims to find out the factor influencing people buy a branded apparel along with the buying decision style and how demography plays a vital role in the buying decision. We consume items that we use every day as well as items based on our needs, tastes, and purchasing power. These can be manufacturing materials, durable items, speciality goods, or sensitive goods. What we buy and how much we buy depends on numerous internal and external elements, including our perspective, self-concept, social and informational context, age and family rotation, attitudes, attitude values, motivation, personality, and socioeconomic class. When exchanging, we also think about whether to buy or not to obtain as well as where or from whom to buy.

The marketer makes an effort to understand the needs of various consumers, and having a grasp of Branded apparel is produced and marketed by a number of businesses. Consequently, there were more options available to consumers. A study on consumer behaviour was critical in this situation to comprehend the purchasing patterns and preferences of various consumers. Understanding consumer behaviour will assist businesses in developing strategies to meet customer wants and consequently grow their market share.

Consumer decision-making preferences and patterns have been found to shift quickly, particularly in fast-paced environments. The study will assist marketers in creating marketing strategies for branded clothing while keeping in mind the significance of consumer behavior and consumption patterns.

Levels of Branding

Stage 1: Brand Awareness – When someone thinks of a particular product category,

they immediately think of your product. For instance: SURF for washing powder; DETTOL for antiseptic solution.

Stage 2: After becoming aware, a consumer recognizes the brand name, characteristics, or features of a product based on his or her mental aptitude.

Stage 3: Brand Preference- After learning about a brand, a consumer develops a list of qualities based on his needs and his preference for one brand over another.

Stage 4: Brand Association—At this stage, consumers begin to associate the brand with positive ideas, people, places, etc. For instance: Made in China (Cheap and poor-quality product).

Stage 5: Brand Loyalty: Brand loyalty is the likelihood that a customer will switch to a different brand if the characteristics, cost, or quality of the product change. Customers will react less strongly to competing maneuvers and acts as brand loyalty grows. Customers who are brand loyal stick with the brand, are willing to pay more for it, and constantly advocate it. Customers who are brand loyal to a firm will result in more sales, lower marketing and advertising expenses, and competitive pricing. This is due to the fact that brand loyal customers are less hesitant to switch brands, respond less negatively to price fluctuations, and actively advocate their preferred brand since they believe it offers unique benefits that aren't offered by rival brands.

Through investigation, Sproles and Kendall (1986) identified the following eight characteristics of the fundamental leadership style shown in Figure 42.2:

Product assortment consists of product attributes such as colour, style, size etc. which is a set of parameters used by retailers to

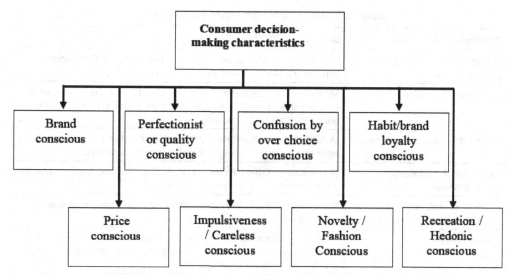

Fig. 42.1   Eight characteristics of consumer decision-making styles

Source: Adapted from Sproles and Kendall, 1986

effectively communicate with their identified target customers. With these parameters in place, planners are able to facilitate the ultimate product assortment in a store. "As consumers consider a product purchase, they are inclined to compare and find distinctions between products which differ from one another in terms of their varying attribute combinations". Product attributes include intrinsic and extrinsic product attributes which are used as cues to communicate various aspects of the product and which consumers use as precursors regarding their perception of quality. Similarly, in the study conducted by Chowdhury and Andaleeb (2007:33), it is postulated that "consumer perceived quality is assembled by various intrinsic and extrinsic cues. The authors argue that product attributes should be emphasized to communicate information to customers regarding the quality of products" (Chowdhury and Andaleeb, 2007:50).

Showing Constructs, Measurement of Variables and Authors

This study identifies research gaps in the extant literature. First, despite its huge population and growth potential, India has only recently gained the attention of consumer behavior scholars (Brokaw and Lakshman, 1995). It's critical for firms to understand Indian consumers' attitudes regarding clothing if they want to enter this profitable industry. Second, despite the presence of international apparel brands in the Indian market and the rising spending power of Indian consumers when it comes to purchasing clothing from foreign brands, there is little clothing research on Indian customers. Only a little amount of consumer research has been done in India, and it was mostly concerned with the branded clothes sector.

Table 42.1 Decision-making style characteristics

Decision-making Traits	Description
Perfectionism or high-quality consciousness	"An attribute that quantifies how thoroughly and methodically a consumer looks for the highest or very best quality in things."
Brand consciousness	Measures a consumer's propensity to purchase expensive, recognisable brands in the mistaken idea that a product's greater price reflects its higher quality.
Novelty-fashion consciousness	"A trait that distinguishes consumers who value novel and cutting-edge goods and find delight in discovering new things."
Recreational, hedonistic consciousness	"An attribute gauging the extent to which a consumer finds shopping a pleasurable activity and shops purely for fun."
Price conscious, and "value-for-money" shopping consciousness	"A defining trait of those consumers who have a strong awareness of discount prices and reduced prices generally."
Impulsiveness	"A trait that characterises those consumers who frequently make impulsive purchases and don't seem to care how much they spend to acquire the greatest deals."
Confused by over choice	"A trait that characterises those consumers who frequently buy on the spur of the moment and seem careless about the amount they spend to get the greatest deals."
Habitual, brand-loyal	"A trait identifying consumers who have favourite products and retailers and have developed habits of repeatedly choosing these."

Source: Authors

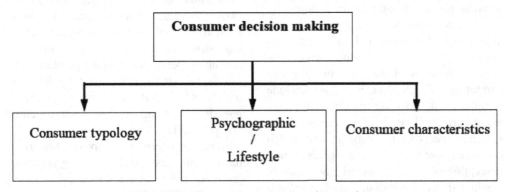

Fig. 42.2 Consumer decision-making styles

Source: Sproles and Kendall, 1986

Problem statement: In a changing lifestyle environment and expanding economic environment, Indian consumers' purchasing behavior has completely changed in a variety of areas, including food consumption and taste, clothing purchases, the use of durable goods, and the purchase of indulgences. Personal income is sharply rising, indicating that Indian consumers have more purchasing power in the luxury market. Additionally, India has the second-largest population in the world after China, and Indians also prefer to buy branded clothing in the market for ready-made garments. Furthermore, Indian and foreign-based branded clothing products influence our customers to wear various designs, prices, and eye-catching colors, so understanding how consumers behave towards branded Apparel is essential in the competitive market.

2. Conclusion

It was found from the study that Product and self-image related Criteria, Quality and easy care, Style and quality criteria and Quality price is a significant determinant of consumer purchasing behavior for branded apparel. This implies that the marketer need to focus on product related attributes which includes quality price style and easy care of the apparels than advertising the country or origin or other attributes of the apparels while targeting the apparels to Indian consumers. Novelty and Impulsive buying style was also prominent in Indian decision making styles. Similarly, Recreational and hedonistic Brand and fashion Perfectionism Habitual and brand loyal Confused by over-choice Price Conscious is significant decision making styles of Indian shoppers. This implies that Indian consumers are very impulsive buyers when it comes to branded apparels. Further Novelty behavior was also a decision making style in Indian consumer which implies that they are aware of new and newest trends driven so marketer can the current trends rather than going for fashion or fads strategy for branded apparels. The marketer can use all the decision making styles into consideration for playing in the

market. Most of the studies have indicated demography playing a very vital role in decision making as well as buying behavior factors.

REFERENCES

1. Ailawadi, K. L., & Keller, K. L. (2004). Understanding retail branding: conceptual insights and research priorities. *Journal of retailing, 80*(4), 331–342.
2. Deacon, R. E., & Firebaugh, F. M. (1975). Home management; context and concepts.
3. Trijp, H. C. V., Hoyer, W. D., & Inman, J. J. (1996). Why switch? product category-level explanations for true variety-seeking behavior. Journal of marketing research, 33(3), 281–292.
4. Nandal, N., Nandal, N., & Malik, R. (2020). "Is loyalty program as a marketing tool effective?". *Journal of Critical Reviews, 7*(6), 1079–1082.
5. Zhou, K. Z., Su, C., & Bao, Y. (2002). A paradox of price–quality and market efficiency: a comparative study of the US and China markets. *International Journal of Research in marketing, 19*(4), 349–365.
6. Sproles, G. B. (1983). Conceptualization and measurement of optimal consumer decision-making. *Journal of Consumer Affairs, 17*(2), 421–438.
7. Nandal, N., Malik, D., & Nandal, D. (2020). Review on India's Baby Care Market. *International Journal of Management, 11*(5).
8. Brokaw, S. C., & Lakshman, C. (1995). Cross-cultural consumer research in India: a review and analysis. *Journal of International Consumer Marketing, 7*(3), 53–80.
9. Engel, J. F., Blackwell, R. D., & Miniard, P. W. (1986). *Consumer behavior*. Dryden Press.

Advancements in Business for Integrating Diversity, and
Sustainability – Dimitrios A. Karras et al. (eds)
© 2024 Taylor & Francis Group, London, ISBN 978-1-032-70828-7

43 Research on the Effect of Talent Management on Employee Attrition and Retention Intentions

Sugandha Agarwal*

Faculty of Management, Canadian University Dubai,
Dubai, United Arab Emirates

Mahesh Singh[1]

Kebri Dehar University, Kebri Dehar, Ethiopia

Sunil Kumar Vohra[2]

Amity Institute of Travel and Tourism,
Amity University, Noida, UP, India

Shashi Kant Gupta[3]

PDF, Eudoxia Research University, USA

Abstract: Surviving and developing commercial contention, a company again has to obtain a competitive edge. The goal of turnover is one of the concerns that organizations or corporations often deal with. The high turnover rate in the company is a result of unfavorable employee attitudes including a lack of commitment and enjoyment at work. PT's case study on staff retention. This research attempts to identify the influence of employee engagement and management of talent's intention to leave the company. Data analysis for this experiment was done with the help of SmartPLS. Employee involvement a significant also negative impact Employee Retention (ER) Has an Impact on Intentional Turnover significant and negative impact on Employee Engagement at a turnover intention and talent management significant and negative impact Employee Engagement has a huge impact on employee retention also negative impact retaining personnel is a topic that may be mediated Employee Engagement on Turnover Intention, according to the study's findings.

Keywords: Employee engagement (EE), Turnover intention, Employee retention (ER), Talent management (TM)

*Corresponding author: drsugandhaagarwaal@gmail.com
[2]mahesh300@gmail.com, [3]sunilvohra2002@yahoo.co.in

DOI: 10.4324/9781032708294-43

1. Introduction

Employee turnover from the firm, also known as staff turnover, is a significant phenomenon in organizational life. When an employee has talent, turnover may be negative for the firm, but it can also be positive since it can draw in superior personnel (Setiawan et al. (2021)). The established talent management (TM) system seeks to develop trustworthy adequate human resources to fulfill certain positions in the organization to ensure the firm's commercial stability (Boonbumroongsuk and Rungruang (2021)). If employees are highly involved in the organization, their performance will be maximized. Here scenario, every business will be able to raise operator productivity through enhancing performance. Therefore, having efficient human resources has a big influence on the organization's conduct, productivity, and workers' quality of life (Kumar (2022)). High staff turnover because of a desire to leave the firm is a result of unfavorable employee attitudes, such as dissatisfaction with and lack of commitment to the organization, which is thought to harm organizational performance in the short and long term (Abdul et al (2019)). The business must spend money on hiring, orientation, training, overtime, and monitoring, a high staff turnover rate may also result in significant cost overruns. Employees must be developed, nurtured, and preserved as corporate assets. The actual reason for turnover frequently results from a combination of issues, including a lack of employee ownership and a lack of managerial trust on the part of the workforce (Dahiya and Rath (2021)). Employee turnover hurts the company in terms of expenses, wasted time, and missed chances to seize advantages.

2. Related Works

The paper is generalizable to other industries, and there is a need for further research on other workforce facets, such as ER being influenced by work-life balance and engagement levels (Hazela et al. (2022)). The processes of talent management (TM) and their relationships to organizational commitment and turnover intentions, among other employee outcomes (Dayeh and Farmanesh (2021)). Information and communication technology ICT personnel are less likely to quit the field. The terms intention to quit and turnover intention have been used interchangeably by prior researchers in the literature (Gupta et al. (2022)). TM has become a strategic concern for firms due to skilled workers' contributions to such organizations in the hypercompetitive and complicated global economy. Although TM has been promoted as a key tactic for keeping outstanding personnel, explore their relationship (Narayanan et al. (2019)). This paper investigates the effects of certain organizational environmental factors on workers' inclinations to leave their jobs (Bindu et al. (2019)).

3. Methodology

This research was gathered through questionnaires that were given to PT employees as part of online surveys conducted using Google Forms. PLS employs two evaluations for the analytical test: the outer model, which is used to assess the measurement's structural model tested against the hypothesis, as well as validity and dependability. The sample was made up of working professionals in the north capital region's IT industries. A standardized questionnaire that was distributed to workers of IT organizations was used to gather the data. There were 400 messages blasted out in all, and 236 surveys that were returned with answers were utilized in the investigation. Additional information was gathered from works on and retention. Analysis of the connection between TM and retention was done using a multiple regression model. Multivariate regression analysis is a technique for investigating the relationship between a dependent variable and more than one independent variable. The influence of TM strategies on ER and turnover intentions will be predicted using a multivariate regression model, which will also quantify the contributions of each independent variable. As a consequence, multiple regression and variation explained by the model fit may be used to estimate the contribution of each TM strategy to ER.

Measures: The view of TM strategies from the staff using a five-point Likert scale, the participants were tasked with assessing their agreement or disagreement with the following TM functions: recruiting and selecting, management support and team spirit, achievement and professional management, and income and reward.

Objectives for Employee Retention and turnover: The desire of employees to remain in the organisation is explained by descriptive scores of ER intentions. It demonstrated the employee's plans to continue working for the organisations. ER is more likely when they respect what they do and the company they work for, which creates a sense of belonging.

Employee turnover and retention objectives and talent management: The development of multiple linear regression to predict employee turnover and retention intentions was based on employee satisfaction with the methods of recruiting and selection, teamwork and management support, performance and career management, and remuneration and pay. The model predicts that employees would have positive intentions to stay if they were happy with the TM procedures. Research Design: Figure 43.1 below includes the design of this study:

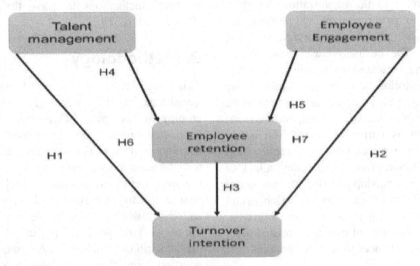

Fig. 43.1 Research design

Hypotheses development:

- H1 = TM has a favorable and substantial influence on turnover intention.
- H2 = Turnover Intention is significantly and favorably affected by employee engagement.
- H3 = Turnover Intention is positively and significantly impacted by ER.
- H4 = ER is positively and significantly impacted by talent management.
- H5 = ER is positively and significantly impacted by employee engagement.
- H6 = ER may act as a buffer management of talent and planned turnover.
- H7 = Turnover Intention and Employee Engagement may be mediated by ER.

4. Results and Discussion

The model predicts that impressed with talent management strategies, employees would have favourable intentions to continue. The dependent variable's connection with the independent variables is estimated by the regression model. Estimates indicate that adding one unit more of independent factors causes the retention intentions to improve.

The findings demonstrated that when employees receive support from managers and supervisors, their intentions to leave the company diminish. The study places a strong emphasis on the impact of remuneration on ER. Organizations must create monetary and nonmonetary compensation schemes that satisfy their workforce and boost their intentions to continue.

R-Square (R^2): The architectural model's performance in predicting the link between latent variables. The proportion of variance described, specifically the R-Square value for endogenous latent components, is used to assess the structural model. The results of table 43.1's R-square test are as follows:

Table 43.1 Results of R-Square

Item	R^2 Adjusted	R-Square
Turnover intention (Y)	.500	.521
ER (Z)	.636	.647

Hypothesis Testing: The research findings may be utilized to address the study's hypothesis in light of the collected research data. The T-Statistics Value and the P-Values value were used to conduct the hypothesis test in this research and shown the table 43.2.

Table 43.2 Results of T-Statistics

Variables	Original sample (O)	Sample Mean (M)	Standard deviation (STDEV)	T statistics (IO/STDEVI)	P values
TM -> ER	.655	.646	.099	6.611	.000
Employee Engagement -> Employee Retention	.242	.259	.098	2.465	.014
-> Turnover Intention	.761	.350	.151	.038	.000
TM -> Turnover Intention	−.429	.429	.157	.729	.007
Employee Engagement -> Turnover Intention	.340	.350	.122	.794	.005

Table 43.3 Specific Indirect Effects

Variables	Original sample (O)	Sample Mean (M)	Standard deviation (STDEV)	T statistics (IO/STDEVI)	P Values
TM -> Employee Retention -> Turnover Intention	.499	.491	.131	3.808	.000
ER -> Employee Retention -> Turnover Intention	.184	.196	.085	2.177	.030

The connection hypothesis is statistically tested in PLS utilizing simulation. Bootstrapping testing seeks to lessen the problem of erroneous research data.

Show table 43.3. Through the mediating variable of ER, which has a P-Value of 0.000 to 0.05, turnover Intention may be indirectly influenced by the TM variable.

5. Discussion

ER as a mediator, this research seeks to understand how talent Employee engagement and management affect intention to leave. The explanation of this study is provided below, based on the SmartPLS result.

TM and Intentional Turnover: It is acceptable to accept the first hypothesis, which claims that TM affects conversion goal.

Employee Engagement and Intentional Turnover: The second theory, according to which there is a connection between intention and employee engagement to leave, do plausible.

Retention of Employees and Intention to Turnover: The Turnover Intention construct benefits from the concept of ER. That the first instance result of 0.761 demonstrates.

TM and ER: The ER Construct is positively impacted by the TM Construct. It is shown by the 0.656 original sample value.

Employee Engagement and Retention: ER is positively impacted by employee engagement structures. It is shown by the 0.242 original sample value.

TM for Intentional Employee Turnover Mediated by Retention: ER mediation benefits from the TM Construct on Turnover Intention. This is shown by the first sample value, which was 0.499.

Mediation of Employee Engagement with Intention to Leave and ER: The Impact of Turnover Intention and Employee Engagement helps ER mediation. This may be seen by the 0.184 initial sample value.

6. Conclusion

Turnover Intention is impacted by talent management, employee engagement, and retention of personnel. Employee engagement and TM have an impact on ER, according to findings from the fourth and fifth hypothesis tests. ER, Employee Engagement, and Intentional Turnover as well as TM to leave the company, may act as a mediator. There are numerous other aspects, such as workplace environment, work-life balance, and employee engagement might influence an employee's desire to stay with the company. These include recruiting, teamwork, performance reviews, and remuneration. Future research may include these factors, and taking into account big samples can provide more reliable findings to decide the procedures for TM and staff retention. The study was conducted with a small sample size and also was based entirely on IT enterprises, comparable studies using the same construct can be undertaken in other industries to obtain conclusions that are more broadly applicable. Using these factors into future studies and taking into account sizable samples can produce more accurate results to establish the rules for talent management and ER.

REFERENCES

1. Setiawan, I. and Prasojo, S., 2021. Effect of TM and Employee Engagement on Turnover Intention with Employee Retention Mediation. Journal of Business, Management, & Accounting, 3(2), pp. 55–63.
2. Boonbumroongsuk, B. and Rungruang, P., 2021. Employee perception of talent management practices and turnover intentions: a multiple mediator models. Employee Relations: The International Journal.
3. Kumar, S., 2022. The impact of talent management practices on employee turnover and retention intentions. Global Business and Organizational Excellence, 41(2), pp. 21–34.
4. Abdul Latif, F.D., Saraih, U.N. and Harada, Y., 2019. Talent management and turnover intention: the moderating effect of employee engagement. Journal of Advanced Research in Business, Marketing and Supply Chain Management, 3(1), pp. 10–17.
5. Dahiya, S. and Rath, R., 2021. Talent Management and Its Impact on Organizational Commitment and Turnover Intention: A Literature Review. IUP Journal of Organizational Behavior, 20(4).
6. Hazela, B., Gupta, S.K., Soni, N. and Saranya, C.N., 2022. Securing the Confidentiality and Integrity of Cloud Computing Data. ECS Transactions, 107(1), p. 2651.
7. Dayeh, K. and Farmanesh, P., 2021. The link between talent management, organizational commitment, and turnover intention: A moderated mediation model. Management Science Letters, 11(7), pp. 2011–2020.
8. Gupta, S.K., Tiwari, S., Abd Jamil, A. and Singh, P., 2022. Faster as Well as Early Measurements from Big Data Predictive Analytics Model. ECS Transactions, 107(1), p. 2927.
9. Narayanan, A., Rajithakumar, S. and Menon, M., 2019. Talent management and employee retention: An integrative research framework. Human Resource Development Review, 18(2), pp. 228–247.
10. Bindu, G.H. and Srikanth, V., 2019. Impact of organizational climate on employee turnover intentions–an empirical study. IPE Journal of Management, 9(1), pp. 1–13.

Note: All tables and figure in this chapter were made by Authors.

*Advancements in Business for Integrating Diversity, and
Sustainability* – *Dimitrios A. Karras et al. (eds)*
© *2024 Taylor & Francis Group, London, ISBN 978-1-032-70828-7*

Implementation of Sustainable Human Resource Management Techniques to Encourage Employees' Pro-environmental Behavior

44

Padma Mahadevan*

Associate Professor,
International School of Business and Research (ISBR),
Bengaluru, India

Juliet Gladies Jayasuria[1]

Assistant Professor, College of Business Management,
University of Doha for Science and Technology, Qatar

Bala V. S. C[2]

Research Scholar, Lovely Professional University, Punjab, India

Mukund P. Singh[3]

Professor, Department of Management Studies,
Graphic Era Deemed to be University, Dehradun, Uttarakhand, India

Abstract: The increasing interest in sustainability and environmental preservation has given rise to an entirely new region of study in the discipline of human resource management (HRM). The phrase "sustainable human resource management" was developed by academics studying that using HRM to achieve sustainable environmental goals could be very beneficial. Despite the increased interest in sustainable HRM research, few studies have looked at it affects employees' positive attitudes and behavior in lowering businesses' environmental footprints and improving corporate sustainability. In order to fill this knowledge gap, the study grown existing sustainable streams of research by examining how sustainable HRM influences pro-environmental behaviors through the mediating sustainable commitment's impact, 342 valid responses were used to validate the theoretical framework using SmartPLS. According to current research findings, sustainable HRM procedures have an impact on employees' sustainable commitment and PEBs. The findings also indicate that sustainable commitment mediates the relationship between sustainable HRM and PEBs.

Keywords: Sustainable human resource management, Environmental behaviors, Sustainable commitment, Employees

*Corresponding author: padma.mahadevan@isbr.in
[1]sundarsms0180@gmail.com, [2]chilukuri.41800662@lpu.in, [3]mpsingh@geu.ac.in

DOI: 10.4324/9781032708294-44

1. Introduction

The study aims to close knowledge gaps by analysing the instant effects of sustainability HRM on PEBs, followed by the indirect mechanisms via which sustainable HRM can affect PEBs. In the context, to investigate the mediating function of sustainable commitment the connection between sustainable HRM and PEBs (Bombiak, et al., 2018). The necessity to establish the idea of sustainable development resulted from the gradual degradation of the environment caused by human use. Within the sustainable HRM concept, the PEBs are seen as key employee behaviours for improving environmental performance. Any quantifiable environmentally responsible business activities that support an ecologically sustainable business model are referred to as PEBs (Chams, et al., 2019). The HRM component of environmental behaviorsis known as sustainable HRM, and it integrates environmental concerns into all HRM operations that identify, value, and promote workplace environmental principles, practice, and initiatives (Ansari, et al., 2021). Employees' voluntary PEB is a new idea that has to be developed in terms of content and proper implementation. There are several terms for equivalent things with different denominations that are described identically. Different conceptualizations lead to the creation of various measures of voluntary PEB at work and the lack of a distinctive theoretical framework, which impedes future study (Feng, et al., 2021). Sustainable human resource techniques motivate employee to participate in environmental preservation and other control actions throughout the operational process (Mousa et al., 2020).

2. Related Works

The Article "Sustainable HRM" refers to the growing body of research that has started looking at how HRM may considerably help achieve long-term environmental goals (Saifulina, et al., 2020). Despite the growing interest in sustainable HRM research, very few studies have examined the effects of the pro-environmental staff attitudes and actions that improve corporate sustainability. Aziz, et al., 2021 mentions that the Planned Behaviour Theory is used to research the way that beliefs of a sustainable workplace climate affect the association between sustainable HRM and PEB. Rubel, et al., 2021 proposed an idea for a sustainable workplace serve as a method for describing how sustainable HRM may encourage sustainable behaviour of employees. Employee PEB, Sustainable HRM has an influence on these activities, which may be equally obligatory and optional, and it can act as a motivator for organization employees to take part, in sustainable behaviours intended to save organisational resources, which may achieve sustainability practices (Nazet, al., 2021). The causes of PEB has received more emphasis in earlier Investigating sustainable HRM could characterised as the use of HRM practises that favourably influence employees' PEBs and, eventually, promote organisations' optimal environmental performance (Rajagopal, et al., 2022). It incorporates environmental management into all HRM procedures, beginning with hiring and screening and continuing through training and development and employee performance management.

3. Hypotheses Development

H1: Employee PEBs are positively impacted by sustainable HRM.

H2: Employee commitment to sustainability is influenced favourable by sustainable HRM.

H3: Employees' PEB is positively influenced by their sustained commitment.

H4: Sustainable commitment acts as a mediator between Sustainable HRM and PEBs.

4. Methodology

Data collection: The researcher contacted and interacted with significant personnel from these chosen sectors, including HR managers, general managers, safety and environmental staff, to discuss the presence and acceptability of sustainable HRM practises. Employees received questionnaire from the researcher, and reducing the chances of bias in social desire. To start, names of dimensions and variables were left out in order to lessen the chance that participants would know what was being examined. Second, the participants received a very explicit explanation on how their privacy would be guaranteed. Finally, participants were given their own envelopes in which to place their completed surveys.

Measures: Three important variables such as sustainable HRM, sustainable commitment, and PEBs were examined in the study and each were graded on a five-point Likert scale, to measure sustainable HRM a six-item scale was used. Sample items: "Employee

interactions at the workplace". The eight-item scale was used to evaluate the sustainable commitment. Sample items: "I want to help my organization's environmental initiatives". The PEB were evaluated using a seven-item scale. Sample items: "I turn off my lights while not being used".

Analysis: The first method to evaluate connections between the indicators and the relevant latent variables. Second, eminent academics recommended PLS-SEM as a useful tool for complex research frameworks. Third, in contrast to a variety of alternative route modeling systems. Four, this strategy is a strong component-based strategy. PLS-SEM is a two-stage analytical method used to assess the measurement model's accuracy and reliability.

Evaluation of measurement models

The evaluation's findings are shown in Table 44.1. As can be observed, the outer loading levels are far above the 0.70 threshold. The composite dependability values were also significantly higher than the 0.70 cutoff. The attainment of consistent validity was shown by the general retrieved variance values, which were over 0.50. Then assessed using HTMT criteria in accordance with the discriminant validity of the measuring model. Table 44.2 depict the legality of the discrimination. The HTMT ratios were below the cutoff point of 0.85.

Table 44.1 Measuring model's reliability and validity

First order	Items	Loadings	CR	AVE
PEB			0.569	0.902
	PEB-1	0.748		
	PEB-2	0.713		
	PEB-3	0.738		
	PEB-4	0.686		
	PEB-5	0.757		
	PEB-6	0.762		
	PEB-7	0.865		

First order	Items	Loadings	CR	AVE
SHRM			0.712	0.936
	SH1	0.722		
	SH2	0.765		
	SH3	0.815		
	SH4	0.878		
	SH5	0.928		
	SH6	0.928		
sustainable commitment			.641	.934
	SC-1	0.887		
	SC-2	0.866		
	SC-3	0.816		
	SC-4	0.815		
	SC-5	0.812		
	SC-6	0.741		
	SC-7	0.735		
	SC-8	0.715		

Table 44.2 Discrimination's legality

	SHRM	Sustainable commitment PEBs
SHRM		
Sustainable commitment	0.247	
PEBs	0.321	0.487

Structural path assessment

The assessment of the structural model is the following phase in PLS-SEM. The study utilized 5,000 iterations and 300 cases of bootstrap resampling were used in order to assess the importance of the direction coefficients. The amount of the dependent factors' variance that the model's study variables can explain, is represented by R^2. This determines the model's forecast accuracy. Sustainable HRM and sustainable commitment, two independent factors in the study, accounted for 25.9% of the variation in the PEB. Table 44.3 demonstrates that sustainable HRM significantly improves PEB, which supports the initial idea. Similar to this, sustainable HRM has a supportive and significant effect on sustainable commitment, and sustainable commitment has a relationship with PEB; Hence, both of the third and fourth hypotheses are confirmed.

Table 44.3 Process of bootstrapping to generate a hypothesis

	Path coefficients	T statistics	p-values
SHRM-> PEBs	0.232	4.597	.000
SHRM->sustainable commitment	0.271	5.679	.000
sustainable commitment -> pro-environmental	0.394	8.713	.000

Table 44.4 Evaluation of the mediation

	Direct effect	Range of confidence for the immediate impact at 95%	T value for the immediate impact	Significance?	Indirect impact	95% confidence interval of the direct impact	T coefficient for the indirect impact	Significance?	Mediation style
HPWS ->IB	0.232	[0.327–0.131]	4.597	True	0.107	[0.115–0.064]	4.559	True	Additional mediation

Mediation analysis

The bootstrapping feature of Smart PLS was used to analyse the significance of the indirect impact in order to assess the mediation influence of sustainable commitment in the relationship between sustainable HRM and PEBs. According to Table 44.4, the indirect impact of sustainable HRM on PEBs via sustainable commitment was appreciable (Beta is 107 and T is 4.559).

5. Conclusion

As a result, the present work fills a significant gap in the literature by examining the mediating mechanism between sustainable HRM and employee behavioural outcomes via sustainable commitment. The studies still need to address a few issues, despite the fact that research provided useful implications for both theory and practise. It's important to note that the present study is restricted to the chemical and fertiliser industries, raising concerns about the external validity of its findings. Second, Pakistan is the only rising economy that this study examines for its impact on sustainable HRM practises. The study has useful implications for both theory and practise, but more work is required to confirm its findings in various contexts.

REFERENCES

1. Bombiak, E. and Marciniuk-Kluska, A., 2018. Green human resource management as a tool for the sustainable development of enterprises: Polish young company experience. Sustainability, 10(6), p. 1739.
2. Chams, N. and García-Blandón, J., 2019. On the importance of sustainable human resource management for the adoption of sustainable development goals. Resources, Conservation and Recycling, 141, pp. 109–122.
3. Ansari, N. Y., Farrukh, M. and Raza, A., 2021. Green human resource management and employees pro-environmental behaviours: Examining the underlying mechanism. Corporate Social Responsibility and Environmental Management, 28(1), pp. 229–238.
4. Mi, S., Feng, Y., Zheng, H., Wang, Y., Gao, Y. and Tan, J., 2021. Prediction maintenance integrated decision-making approach supported by digital twin-driven cooperative awareness and interconnection framework. Journal of Manufacturing Systems, 58, pp. 329–345.
5. Mousa, S. K. and Othman, M., 2020. The impact of green human resource management practices on sustainable performance in healthcare organisations: A conceptual framework. Journal of Cleaner Production, 243, p. 118595.

6. Saifulina, N., Carballo-Penela, A. and Ruzo-Sanmartín, E., 2020. Sustainable HRM and green HRM: The role of green HRM in influencing employee pro-environmental behavior at work. Journal of Sustainability Research, 2(3).

7. Rubel, M.R.B., Kee, D.M.H. and Rimi, N.N., 2021. Green human resource management and supervisor pro-environmental behavior: The role of green work climate perceptions. Journal of Cleaner Production, 313, p. 127669.

8. Naz, S., Jamshed, S., Nisar, Q.A. and Nasir, N., 2022. Green HRM, psychological green climate and pro-environmental behaviors: An efficacious drive towards environmental performance in China. In Key Topics in Health, Nature, and Behavior (pp. 95–110). Cham: Springer Nature Switzerland.

9. Aziz, F., Md Rami, A.A., Zaremohzzabieh, Z. and Ahrari, S., 2021. Effects of emotions and ethics on pro-environmental behavior of university employees: A model based on the theory of planned behavior. Sustainability, 13(13), p. 7062.

10. Rajagopal, N.K., Qureshi, N.I., Durga, S., Ramirez Asis, E.H., Huerta Soto, R.M., Gupta, S.K. and Deepak, S., 2022. Future of business culture: an artificial intelligence-driven digital framework for organization decision-making process. Complexity, 2022.

Note: All the tables in this chapter were made by the Authors.

Advancements in Business for Integrating Diversity, and
Sustainability – Dimitrios A. Karras et al. (eds)
© 2024 Taylor & Francis Group, London, ISBN 978-1-032-70828-7

Sustainability in Organisations and the Role of Eco-friendly Human Resource Management Practices

45

Shubhendu Shekher Shukla*
Department of Business Administration,
SRM Business School, Lucknow, India

Kolachina Srinivas[1]
K L Business School, KL University KLEF,
Vaddeswaram, Andhra Pradesh, India

Lavanya L[2]
Principal-Jeppiaar College of Arts and Science,
Chennai, India

Praveen Singh[3]
Department of Management Studies,
Graphic Era Deemed to be University, Dehradun, Uttarakhand, India

Abstract: Human resource management (HRM) techniques that are good for the environment could help businesses work environmental concerns into their business plans. This research, which is based on a company's resources, uses cross-sectional data from 113 big manufacturing companies in Malaysia to find out how eco-friendly HRM practices affect sustainability. The results show that hiring and training employees to be eco-friendly is good for sustainability. But it was found that none of the eco-friendly factors eco-friendly selection, eco-friendly performance evaluation, and eco-friendly rewards had any noticeable effect on sustainability. This paper's model shows how eco-friendly HRM can help manufacturing firms be more sustainable. Few studies have looked at the relationship between HRM and sustainability using real-world data from Malaysian manufacturing firms, so this study is very important for both academics and practitioners. Future research may also take into account each feature of eco-friendly HRM, in connection to the many facets of sustainability.

Keywords: eco-friendly HRM, Malaysia, Manufacturing firms, Sustainable human resource

*Corresponding author: shubhendusshukla@gmail.com
[1]srikolachina81@gmail.com, [2]lavanya.official18@gmail.com, [3]praveensingh@geu.ac.in

DOI: 10.4324/9781032708294-45

1. Introduction

There are a variety of factors that might inspire businesses to embrace sustainable Practices Human resource (HR) demand forecast is the process of determining the quantity and caliber of workers which will be needed. If the forecast is to be a trustworthy predictor, the annual budget and long-term company plan must be converted into levels of activity for each function and department. To plan supply and demand for human resources effectively, anticipating HR demand is necessary. The creation of a precise HR demand forecasting model that denotes connected company's growth may help with the implementation of an enterprise development plan (Rajagopal, et al., 2022). Supervisors and decision-makers across a range of business professions have prioritised the resources of the natural ecosystem. Businesses today confront sharper competition, which forces managers to continually devise innovative ways to maximise their essential organisational resources, specifically their human resources (HR), where HR is seen as a major success factor for implementing measures, practises, and also improving resource efficiency (Mousa, S.K., 2020).

2. Related Works

Chams, et al., 2019 highlighted that HRM systems can have huge effects on workers' health and lives, both directly and indirectly. These effects can be caused by things like how jobs are made or by stress caused by long hours at work. So, organisations care regarding the social effects of their own HRM activities and take effects into account as a part of their plan for long-term success,

along with remuneration and economic stability. But it hasn't been proven yet that eco-friendly analysis and job descriptions might result in sustainability (Shah, M., (2019)). Recruiting people with an eco-friendly attitude may help businesses more easily find workers who comprehend how to do things sustainably and give the company a chance to stand out from its competitors (Saeed, et al., 2019). According to Gilal, et al., 2019, Eco-friendly training is a good investment, and organisations should offer it to their employees all the time. Eco-friendly training is a big part of getting people to work towards goals for environmental sustainability. From an eco-friendly viewpoint, "eco-friendly selection" refers to the process of choosing individuals who are devoted to protecting the environment, sensitive to its needs, and capable of helping firms manage their environmental impact. So, a company that focuses on environmental management should choose employees who are devoted to and aware of environmental concerns. Nevertheless, there is little information available on how to choose people who are environmentally conscious or who have the necessary technical expertise in environmental management (Yusoff, et al., 2020). Performance evaluations are often used for salary administration, determining a worker's superiors and shortcomings, and providing performance feedback to boost transformational processes and performance in addition to improving operational competence and company development (Amrutha, et al., 2020). Rewards encourage the growth of new information, behaviors, and talents to meet corporate objectives while also working to recruit, retain, and motivate the best personnel (Macke, et al., 2019).

The following hypotheses were put out to collect empirical data supporting the conclusion predicted.

H1. Sustainability has a favorable relationship with eco-friendly analyses and job descriptions.

H2. Sustainable development has a good connection with eco-friendly hiring.

H3. Sustainability has a favorable relationship with the eco-friendly selection

H4. Sustainability and eco-friendly training are favorably correlated.

H5. Sustainability and the evaluation of eco-friendly performance are favorably associated.

H6. Sustainability and eco-friendly incentives are favorably correlated.

3. Proposed Methodology

Survey and data collection:

The current research uses a correlational methodology to assess the effect of eco-friendly HRM on sustainability. Using cross-sectional empirical analysis, the research's focus is narrowed to the organisational level. A survey instrument and measurement scales were created to evaluate conceptual model. The scale's content validity was evaluated using a pretest, and it was then refined with input from four academics and four business professionals. The questionnaire was finally developed and utilised to test the suggested hypotheses. The questionnaire's measuring scales included elements that represented eco-friendly HRM practices and sustainability. Fig. 45.1 represents the suggested conceptual model.

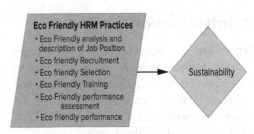

Fig. 45.1 Conceptual model

Measurements

Sustainability was measured using a 15-item scale and for each item, responses ranged from 1 (not at all) to 7 (to a very considerable degree) on a 7-point Likert-type scale. Six factors, including eco-friendly analysis and job descriptions (3 items), eco-friendly recruitment (2 items), eco-friendly selection (2 items), eco-friendly training (3 items), eco-friendly performance assessment (3 items), and eco-friendly rewards, were used to measure eco-friendly HRM practices (2 items). Each item was graded on a 7-point Likert-type scale, with 1 being the least, 7 being the most. Data accuracy decreases significantly when assessed by scale points with values less than 5 or more than 7, according to earlier investigations. While the 5-point Likert scale denoted often utilized in research, a 7-point Likert-type scale was used in the current study. This is such that even while a short scale would be easy cognitively; it might not distinguish between respondents' perspectives. A 7-point response scale may help humans comprehend information more efficiently.

4. Results

The Federation of Malaysian Manufacturers (FMM) Directory 2015 lists 661 big manufacturing companies as the study's complete sample. The population of the study, however, was 649 after the eight businesses utilised for the surveys as well as the four businesses used for the questionnaire's pretesting were taken into account. Thus, 649 questionnaires in all were sent to responders. After a telephonic reminder, With 113 completed questionnaires received; the response percentage was 18.3%. Considering that the required sample size was meant to be 97, they often showed lower postal survey response rates, and typically this kind of correlational research in Malaysia has a low response rate, this response rate may be considered as good (Sekaran and Bougie, 2016).

Data analysis

Measurement model

Partial least squares (PLS) analysis was performed on the research model created for this study using SmartPLS 3.2.8 software. A second-generation statistical program called SmartPLS is capable of analyzing smaller non-normally distributed data sets. As survey research data is often nonnormal, this method is best suited to our study.

Structural model

HTMT criteria were used to evaluate discriminant validity (see Table 45.1), and it passed the .95 cutoff point, suggesting that discriminant validity was established.

Table 45.1 Discriminant validity (HTMT criterion)

Construct	I	II	II	IV	V	VI	VII
Eco-friendly analysis and job description							
Eco-friendly recruitment	.722						
Eco-friendly reward	.523	.667					
Eco-friendly performance assessment	.601	.752	.881				
Eco-friendly selection	.626	.821	.771	.828			
Eco-friendly training	.609	.602	.647	.680	.648		
Sustainability	.255	.408	.357	.361	.364	.409	

Table 45.2 Hypothesis testing

Hypothesis		Std beta	Std error	n value	Z value	BCI LL	BCI UL	P2	VID
H1	Analysis sustainability	−.104	.114	.911	.175	.067	.065	.002	2.001
H2	Recruitment sustainability	.241	.142	1.670	.047	.491	.492	.024	3.821
H3	Selection sustainability	−.104	.071	.072	.471	.374	.371	0	4.421
H4	Training sustainability	.260	2.052	2.052	.018	.462	.465	.041	1.945
H5	Assessment sustainability	.008	.038	.038	.481	.36	.36	0	4.312
H6	Reward sustainability	.071	.451	.451	.321	.345	.335	.002	3.002

We used a bootstrapping approach to generate n values, p values, and bootstrapped confidence intervals to test hypotheses. Table 45.2 presents the outcomes.

The six hypotheses that we analyzed were as follows, Just two were determined to be important. Especially, ecofriendly recruitment (β = .234, n = 1.772, Z < .02) with P^2 of .035 and ecofriendly training (β = .254, n = 2.046, Z < .02) with P^2 of .044 were significant, meanwhile ecofriendly analysis and job description, ecofriendly selection, ecofriendly performance assessment, and ecofriendly reward were inconsequential.

5. Discussion

The study into the connection between sustainable HRM practices and innovation is what makes this study unique. This study evaluates the theoretical paradigm using Malaysian empirical data, which advances our perception of sustainability in major manufacturing enterprises. Finally, future developments might be investigated by concentrating on the importance of environmental performance, given the time constraints of this research and the importance of taking environmental factors into account in the administration of the business. We expect that this study will provide a different perspective for those researching consequences of sustainable practices and eco-friendly HRM.

6. Conclusion

The industrial sector in Malaysia contributes significantly to environmental problems while also being one of the major economic drivers of the nation. As a result, it is becoming more important to pursue the adoption of environmentally friendly practices that is eco-friendly HRM, to reduce environmental issues. The present study fills a significant research vacuum in the literature by examining the results of eco-friendly HRM practices (*i.e.*, eco-friendly analysis and job descriptions, eco-friendly recruiting, eco-friendly selection, eco-friendly training, and eco-friendly performance assessment and rewards) on sustainability. The results demonstrated that the industrial industry in Malaysia can only become sustainable via eco-friendly training and eco-friendly recruiting. We consequently recommend future scholars look into these connections in various businesses, utilizing the information presented here as a guide for their work in Malaysia.

REFERENCES

1. Rajagopal, N.K., Saini, M., Huerta-Soto, R., Vílchez-Vásquez, R., Kumar, J.N.V.R., Gupta, S.K. and Perumal, S., 2022. Human resource demand prediction and configuration model based on grey wolf optimization and recurrent neural network. Computational Intelligence and Neuroscience, 2022.

2. Mousa, S.K. and Othman, M., 2020. The impact of green human resource management practices on sustainable performance in healthcare organisations: A conceptual framework. Journal of Cleaner Production, 243, p. 118595.

3. Chams, N. and García-Blandón, J., 2019. On the importance of sustainable human resource management for the adoption of sustainable development goals. Resources, Conservation, and Recycling, 141, pp. 109–122.

4. Saeed, B.B., Afsar, B., Hafeez, S., Khan, I., Tahir, M. and Afridi, M.A., 2019. Promoting employee pro-environmental behavior through green human resource management practices. Corporate Social Responsibility and Environmental Management, 26(2), pp. 424–438.

5. Gilal, F.G., Ashraf, Z., Gilal, N.G., Gilal, R.G. and Channa, N.A., 2019. Promoting environmental performance through green human resource management practices in higher education institutions: A moderated mediation model. Corporate Social Responsibility and Environmental Management, 26(6), pp. 1579–1590.

6. Yusoff, Y.M., Nejati, M., Kee, D.M.H. and Amran, A., 2020. Linking green human resource management practices to environmental performance in the hotel industry. Global Business Review, 21(3), pp.663-680.Gompers, P. A. and Metrick, A. (2001). Institutional investors and equity prices. Q. J. Econ. 116(1):229 259.

7. Amrutha, V.N. and Geetha, S.N., 2020. A systematic review on green human resource management: Implications for social sustainability. Journal of Cleaner Production, 247, p. 119131.

8. Macke, J. and Genari, D., 2019. Systematic literature review on sustainable human resource management. Journal of cleaner production, 208, pp. 806–815.

9. Sekaran, U. and Bougie, R., 2016. Research methods for business: A skill building approach. john wiley and sons.

10. Shah, M., 2019. Green human resource management: Development of a valid measurement scale. Business Strategy and the Environment, 28(5), pp. 771–785.

Note: All the tables and the figure in this chapter were made by the Authors.

Advancements in Business for Integrating Diversity, and Sustainability – Dimitrios A. Karras et al. (eds)
© 2024 Taylor & Francis Group, London, ISBN 978-1-032-70828-7

46

Investigation on Influence of Sustainable Social and Environmental Practices on Financial Behavior of Banking Sector

K. Bhavana Raj*

Department of Management Studies,
Institute of Public Enterprise, Hyderabad, India

J. P. Senthil Kumar[1]

Department of Finance, GITAM School of Business- GITAM
(Deemed to be University), Bengaluru, India

D. Saravanan[2]

Department of CSE, Sathyabama Institute of Science and Technology,
Chennai

Priti Sharma[3]

Assistant Professor, Department of Commerce,
Graphic Era Deemed to be University, Dehradun, Uttarakhand, India

Abstract: Financial institutions, as intermediaries between economies and investment sectors, help economies expand and maintain. In order to support the Socially Responsible Investing (SRI) concept which promotes both financial gain and benefit to society in order to bring about societal change, Sustainability Management processes have recently been adopted. This research investigates the connection with both green banking practises, banks' perceptions of being green, and bank employees' behaviour. According to the study's results, there is a substantial positive association among both green banking practises and banks' assessments of their own environmental friendliness. This conclusion suggests that the more green banking activities a bank participates in, the better its reputation becomes. The link amongst green banking practises and banks' green reputation is unaffected by an employer's green banking practises, though. Because it is depicted in some studies as optional activities rather than required ones, it may change how seriously workers take compliance.

Keywords: Financial institutions, Socially responsible investing (SRI), Green banking practises, Banks' green image

*Corresponding author: bhavana_raj_83@yahoo.com
[1]sjayapra@gitam.edu, [2]saranmds@gmail.com, [3]pritisharma@geu.ac.in

DOI: 10.4324/9781032708294-46

1. Introduction

The financial transaction between a bank and a customer occurs inside the financial system have organised and regulated environment. Alshebami, A. (2021). It provides the essential resources in terms of money for the creation of products and services. It has become challenging for financial firms to provide the level of services required to keep customers due to the homogeneity of the banking sector (Siueia, et al., 2019). Thus, it has been difficult for the banking business globally these days to discover strategies to foster customer satisfaction, particularly green trust. The findings support SRI claim that it increases customer loyalty, and they also suggest that co-creation may partly mitigate this link. Developments in green banking likewise reinforce this connection by (Jan, et al., 2019). Whether they are investors in a particular business, social responsible investors must bear social costs. SRI includes both ethical and financial concepts (Rajagopal, et al., 2022). A major gap between the topics and a preoccupation on the financial paradigm are shown by this systematic literature evaluation. Here examines three important study themes within the SRI literature Widyawati, L. (2020). A crucial part in setting the standard must be played by banks. Before introducing this mindset to their customers, they may start by making improvements to their own sustainability. They may put money into green businesses that sell sustainable goods. The banking sector makes a substantial contribution to sustainable development. At the moment, sustainability is one of the largest trends on the market. Investors preference for sustainable and ethical investment (SRI). Illustrations must include the focus placed on social responsibility by a company management or the respect paid to sustainability and environmental impact issues by investors (Navaneetha, et al., 2022).

2. Related Works

The research recommends continued assistance for green banking procedures to ensure greater employee commitment to green banking and to improve banks perceptions of the environment (Falcone, et al., 2017). The literature began to focus on combining a social-environmental perspective with a comprehensive sustainability approach to business performance. The issue with this combined strategy is that it downplays the environmental sustainability while ignoring the economic sustainability (Yuan, et al., 2018). The many financial measurements used to evaluate performance are another element that contributes to the diversity in outcomes. The results showing a link between corporate sustainability practises and financial success also rely on the size of the organisation, the industry, and the stewardship that were examined (Alshehhi, et al., 2018). Its programmes attempt to strike a balance between the requirements of the economy, society, and environment. As for achieving shareholder expectations both public and private companies are concerned about their level of performance, which may be expressed either formally using organisational evaluations or objectively using financial data (Oncioiuet, et al., 2020). It is an anticipated that there would be a stronger correlation between sustainability practises and company performance in established countries than in emerging nations.

Hypotheses development

H1: The adoption of sustainable banking processes and the green conduct of bank workers are strongly correlated.

H2: Green banking practices and banks' reputations for being environmentally friendly are strongly correlated.

H3: The green behavior and attitude connects the institutions green reputation to its green financial practices.

3. Methods & Material

Conceptual framework

The assumption is that the control variable is the banking service practices, which are defined by environmental policies and goals, green loans, green processes, and green methodology. It was believed that the employee's environmental behavior would act as a mediator between the independent and dependent variables.

4. Analysis and Hypotheses Testing

Confirmatory Factor Analysis (CFA)

CFA has the validity and reliability of the constructs, researchers frequently utilize and accept the confirmatory factor analysis as an instrument. The variation between the real and observed scores is determined by several factors taken into account by the CFA model. For the purposes of observing the variables validity and reliability, three methods-Cronbach Alpha, Composite Reliability, and Average Variance Collected often utilized.

Cronbach's alpha is a reliability indicator that, as its name suggests, analyses the internal consistency of the variables. When Cronbach Alpha and composite reliability are higher than 0.70, the concept of dependability is attained. Variables that are discovered as being lower than 0.6 indicate a weak internal consistency among the variables. Table 46.1 depicts the Cronbach's alpha results.

The square root of the AVE for each construct in Table 46.2 must be higher than its evidence-based practice with any other construct in the research in order to meet the Fornell-Larcker criteria. An indicators outer loading on a build, like cross-loading, should be greater than all of its cross-loadings with other structures. The relationships between the various buildings are shown in Table 46.3.

Table 46.1 Constructs Reliability and Validity

Constructs	Cronbach Alpha	Composite Reliability	Average Variance Extracted
Green Lending	0.880	0.916	0.678
Operations & Procedures	0.870	0.906	0.659
Environmental Policies & Goals	0.980	0.960	0.750
Green Products & Services	0.762	0.855	0.650
Employee's Green Behavior	0.920	0.940	0.760
Bank's Green Image	0.930	0.956	0.790

Source: Made by Author

Table 46.2 Discriminant Validity

Form	Environmental Policies & Goals	Green Products & Services	Operations & Procedures	Green Lending	Employees Green Behavior	Banks Green Image
Environmental Policies & Goals	0.860	0.580	0.743	0.810	0.742	0.532
Green Products & Services		0.803	0.650	0.695	0.540	0.554
Operations & Procedures			0.808	0.750	0.695	0.777
Green Lending				0.822	0.750	0.530
Employees' Green Behavior					0,867	0.493
Banks Green Image						0.883

Source: Made by Author

Table 46.3 Correlation Matrix

	Green Policies	Green Lending	Products & Services	Operations & Procedures	Employee's Green Behaviour	Bank's Green Image
Green Policies	1.000					
Green Lending	0.770**	1.000				
Products & Services	.550**	.525**	1.000			
Operations & Procedures	.706**	.686**	.620**	1.000		
Employee' Green Behavior	.729**	.730**	.490**	.681**	1.000	
Bank's Green Behavior	.510**	.510**	.535**	.668**	.485**	1.000

Source: Made by Author

5. Conclusion

Banks should make sure that their internal activities don't harm the environment or produce an environmental footprint. It is claimed that banks indirectly cause environmental destruction but have no direct effects on the environment. According to popular belief when a financial institution engages in green banking practices, this will enhance public perception of the institution and highlight its contribution to the preservation and sustainability of society, demonstrating that it is an ethical organization and earning more money as a result. The received sample was still small, which would make it difficult to generalize to larger banks. Future work might target this problem.

REFERENCES

1. Jan, A., Marimuthu, M., bin Mohd, M.P. and Isa, M., 2019. The nexus of sustainability practices and financial performance: From the perspective of Islamic banking. Journal of Cleaner Production, 228, pp. 703–717.

2. Widyawati, L., 2020. A systematic literature review of socially responsible investment and environmental social governance metrics. Business Strategy and the Environment, 29(2), pp. 619–637.

3. Alshebami, A.S., 2021. Evaluating the relevance of green banking practices on Saudi Banks' green image: The mediating effect of employees' green behaviour. Journal of Banking Regulation, 22(4), pp. 275–286.

4. Rajagopal, N.K., Saini, M., Huerta-Soto, R., Vílchez-Vásquez, R., Kumar, J.N.V.R., Gupta, S.K. and Perumal, S., 2022. Human resource demand prediction and configuration model based on grey wolf optimization and recurrent neural network. Computational Intelligence and Neuroscience, 2022.

5. Navaneetha Krishnan Rajagopal, Naila Iqbal Qureshi, S. Durga, Edwin Hernan Ramirez Asis, Rosario Mercedes Huerta Soto, Shashi Kant Gupta, S. Deepak, "Future of Business Culture: An Artificial Intelligence-Driven Digital Framework for Organization Decision-Making Process", Complexity, vol. 2022, Article ID 7796507, 14 pages, 2022.https://doi.org/10.1155/2022/779650.

6. Falcone, P.M., P. Morone, and E. Sica. 2018. Greening of thefinancial system and fuelling a sustainability transition: A discursive approach to assess landscape pressures on the Italian financial system. Technological Forecasting and Social Change 127:23–37. https://doi.org/10.1016/j.techfore.2017.05.020.

7. Siueia, T.T., Wang, J. and Deladem, T.G., 2019. Corporate Social Responsibility and financial performance: A comparative study in the Sub-Saharan Africa banking sector. Journal of Cleaner Production, 226, pp. 658–668.

8. Yuan, F., and K.P. Gallagher. 2018. Greening development lending in the Americas: Trends and determinants. Ecological Economics 154 (April): 189–200. https://doi.org/10.1016/j.ecolecon.2018.07.009.

9. Alshehhi, A., Nobanee, H. and Khare, N., 2018. The impact of sustainability practices on corporate financial performance: Literature trends and future research potential. Sustainability, 10(2), p. 494.

10. Oncioiu, I., Petrescu, A.G., Bilcan, F.R., Petrescu, M., Fülöp, M.T. and Topor, D.I., 2020. The influence of corporate governance systems on a company's market value. Sustainability, 12(8), p. 3114.

Advancements in Business for Integrating Diversity, and
Sustainability – Dimitrios A. Karras et al. (eds)
© 2024 Taylor & Francis Group, London, ISBN 978-1-032-70828-7

Influence of Globalization of SMEs on Digitalization: The Moderating Effect of Marketing and Entrepreneurial Behavior

Niyati Joshi*
Department of Management, Assistant Professor,
Rajeev Gandhi College of Management Studies, Navi Mumbai

Padma Mahadevan[1]
Associate Professor, International School of
Business and Research (ISBR), Bengaluru, India

M. V. Rama Prasad[2]
Professor and UGC Research Awardee GITAM School of Business-Bengaluru (GSBB),
GITAM (Deemed to be University), Bangalore Campus, Bengaluru, India

Dinesh Chandra Pandey[3]
Associate Professor, Department of Management Studies,
Graphic Era Deemed to be University, Dehradun, Uttarakhand, India

Abstract: Digitalization is not a new phenomenon, but it is evolving and altering in ways that affect businesses worldwide and open doors for Small and medium-sized enterprises (SMEs) to participate in the global economy. Although digitalization, globalization and SMEs are major concerns for global and European corporations alike, Digitalization and SMEs' international strategic choices, which have not been thoroughly explored, are critical to investigate. Both globalization and the increase of SMEs with an international presence are significant developments on a global scale. The multidimensional behavior of an entrepreneur who is imaginative, proactive, independent, proactive, and willing to compete aggressively to capitalize on market possibilities is known as entrepreneurial behavior. This research investigates at marketing and entrepreneurial behavior have a role in the effects of digitalization and globalization on SMEs.To help SME managers, this research offers hypotheses data and conclusions on the crucial roles of moderating the effect of entrepreneurial behavior and marketing.

Keywords: Small and medium-sized enterprises, Digitalization, Marketing, Entrepreneurial performance, Globalization

---

*Corresponding author: niyatihjoshi.15@gmail.com
[1]padma.mahadevan@isbr.in, [2]rmusunur@gitam.edu, [4]dineshchandra@geu.ac.in

DOI: 10.4324/9781032708294-47

1. Introduction

SMEs are crucial to the growth and development of both established and developing economies, particularly when it comes to creating jobs, raising gross domestic product (GDP), redistributing wealth, and other factors (Mpi, D.L. (2019)). Yet, survival and improved SME performance rely on supportive government policies, superior organizational cultures, and entrepreneurial behavior that may advance and build a nation's SME sector (Park, et al., 2020).

The entrepreneurial orientation is a reflection of the entrepreneurial behaviors of creativity, initiative, and risk-taking. Entrepreneurial orientation (EO) enables small organizations to find new business prospects, and the finding of new chances strengthens their distinction from other companies (Rajagopal, et al., 2022).

In this sense, marketing leadership entails the development of original marketing plans, the utilization of professional sales associates, and the vigilant administration of channels of distribution. Since it often sits at the center of a company's overall strategic plan, a strong marketing strategy may be the most crucial element to success for most businesses (Irudayasamy, et al., 2022).

The term "globalization reaction" is used to characterize how seriously businesses take the benefits and risks brought about by globalization. Changes in corporate strategy, advertising methods, and other quick fixes are all the result of management's initiative (Naradda Gamage, et al., 2020). In this Study, the impact of digitalization and globalization on SMEs is studied, along with the role played by marketing and entrepreneurial behavior.

2. Literature Survey

Nuseir, et al., 2020 collects empirical evidence linking digital marketing strategies to increased revenue generation among UAE's SMEs. Agyapong, et al., 2020 investigates how a global perspective might shape the connection between entrepreneurial behaviour and financial success. Al-Hakimi, et al., 2022 aims to examine the moderating role of marketing ethics and competitive intensity on the correlation between cost and profit. Arzubiaga, et al., 2018 explored the moderate impacts of two primary sources of board diversity in family enterprises, family engagement level and gender diversity, as possible strategies for boosting family firms' performance when utilizing entrepreneurial ideas. Genc, et al., 2019 investigates whether or not there are mitigating elements in the connection between EO and the success of SMEs.

3. Hypothesized Relationships

According to Webster's (1992) theory, an entrepreneurial perspective predates Marketing plans, which come before results. Figure 47.1 suggests the hypothesized links.

H1: Marketing leadership strategy, quality leadership strategy, and product specialization strategy are all more likely to be pursued by a company with a higher entrepreneurial orientation than they are otherwise.

H2: The more aggressively a company pursues a marketing leadership approach, the more likely it is to acquire new technologies, adapt to the effects of globalization, and make preparations to enter overseas markets.

Fig. 47.1 Predicted Correlations Among
Research Hypotheses

Source: Authors

H3: There is a positive correlation between a company's pursuit of a quality leadership strategy and its interest in acquiring new technologies.

H4: The greater the company's emphasis on product segmentation, the more likely it is to actively seek out and acquire cutting-edge technological capabilities.

H5: The performance of the firm improves as it adds more technology.

H6: The firm performs better the more it adapts to globalization, in general.

H7: The performance of the company improves as it makes more preparations in advance to access international markets.

4. Methods

The data was collected in three different stages: (1) semi-structured interviews with business leaders, policymakers, and industry advocates to refine research topics and develop survey instruments; (2) a pilot test of the questionnaire with 100 companies; and (3) mailing the finalized questionnaire to 800 randomly selected manufacturers in industries that reflect electronic systems. The selection of these sectors is based on the fact that many companies operating inside them have been impacted by globalization. Key criteria such as the number of workers, yearly sales activity, minor vs dominating market standing, in contrast to the later entrance to the market, and company performance were compared across these several industry classifications.

As there were no significant differences discovered (p>.05), we do not anticipate that contextual variables in the industry had any substantial impact on the findings. The survey was sent out in three separate waves, with each wave separated by about two weeks, and respondents were incentivized to fill it out. A total of 273 completed questions were reverted after this process, with 268 of them being considered valid. This represents a response rate of 32%. Nonresponse bias was evaluated by comparing the workers, sales, founding year, and four-digit Standard Industrial Classification (SIC) code of the businesses who responded with those of a random sample of 50 businesses that did not answer. Nonresponse bias is unlikely to impact outcomes since there were no statistically significant differences detected (p >.05).

5. Measures

To get the most granular answers possible, we presented each question on a 7-point scale. We utilized exploratory factor analysis on the entire marketing strategy construct scale to derive the aforementioned dimensions. Principal component analysis followed by varimax rotation yielded the factors, and the number of factors was established by using an eigenvalue threshold of 1.00 to separate composite eigenvalues.

Items that have weak or strong cross-factor loadings were taken out of the running. Leadership in marketing, quality, and product specialization were the resulting factors. Finally, to get a full picture of each company's health, we used a variety of performance metrics. Measures were validated by factor analysis in linear structural relations (LISREL) 8 structural equations computational modeling to determine if they accurately captured the construct validity of the measures used in the study. A high level of fit was achieved across all models (all indices less than or equal to 0.93). Finally, Cronbach's alpha tests showed that all multi-item measures were either highly reliable or sufficiently reliable.

6. Result and Discussion

The hypotheses were tested using three different types of model testing procedures. Initially, t-tests were used to compare the primary study construct scores of highly globalized and less globalized enterprises. Second, we used multivariate regression and correlation analysis to test our hypotheses.

Finally, the hypotheses testing outcomes for the two sets of companies were compared and contrasted. A subsample of SMEs with an international presence (n = 216) was initially chosen to establish the analysis. These companies average 143 people (ranging from 5 to 500), generated $100 million in yearly sales, exported to three countries, and saw 25% of their revenue come from exports. This subsample was then divided in half (n = 108 each) based on the median of globalization; that is, one group scored highly on globalization, and the other group scored poorly. All statistical tests employed these classifications. Also, SMEs that are having trouble adapting to globalization may benefit greatly from adopting an entrepreneurial mindset. Businesses with an entrepreneurial spirit are more likely to use marketing tactics to break into untapped markets and navigate challenging settings. Particularly for SMEs, implementing creative advertising strategies, placing an emphasis on quality, and setting themselves apart through product specialization is likely to yield positive results. The results of the subsequent set of studies, which evaluate the study's hypotheses, are described in Table 47.1. To evaluate H1–H4, which are all bivariate relations, we used correlation analysis (Pearson's correlation coefficient). As the dependent variable is the same for hypotheses H5–H7, we only needed to test one regression equation. Both hypotheses (H1a and H1b; $p < .01$) about the connection between an entrepreneurial mindset and success in marketing and quality management were supported. The hypothesis (H1c; $p < .05$) that an entrepreneurial mindset is positively associated with product specialization receives moderate support, globalization responses and market preparation in advance ($p < .01$). According to managers, these are crucial strategies for contending with globalization's forces.

Table 47.1 Discussion of the differences between the groups and the study hypotheses

Implied Relationship	Hypothesis	High-Globalization Group	Low-Globalization Group	Assessment
Entrepreneurial Behaviors				
Marketing leadership	H1a	.41**	.38	Supported
Quality leadership	H1b	.26**	.03	Supported
Product specialization	H1c	.21*	.39**	Supported
Marketing leadership				
Technology Acquisition	H2a	.36**	.31**	Supported
Globalization response	H2b	.37**	.22*	Supported
Internationalization preparation	H2c	.17	.11	Not significant
Quality leadership				
Technology Acquisition	H3	.15	.26**	Supported
Product specialization				
Technology acquisition	H4	.26**	.25**	Supported
Technology acquisition Performance	H5	-0.7	0.1	Not significant
Globalization response⇒Performance	H6	.34**	.13	Supported
Internationalization preparation⇒Performance	H7	.25**	.08	Supported

Source: Authors

7. Conclusion

The study is a cross sectional picture of business conditions, a method that frequently ignores causality in construct interactions and is unable to capture all the ramifications of a dynamic system across time. The research was also restricted to a few key globalization-affected industries. Future research should take into account businesses in different industries to test the generalizability of findings. Future longitudinal research that compares changes in business strategy with specific globalization events occurring at particular times may be helpful. This strategy would also clarify the relationship between marketing and performance over an extended period. In-depth discussions with leading companies provide the most useful information for constructing case histories that can be used to track changes in strategy and methods and to fully account for their reasons.

REFERENCES

1. Mpi, D.L., 2019. Encouraging Micro, Small and Medium Enterprises (MSMES) for economic growth and development in Nigeria and other developing economies: The role of 'the Igbo apprenticeship system'. The Strategic Journal of Business & Change Management, 6(1), pp. 535–543.

2. Park, S., Lee, I.H. and Kim, J.E., 2020. Government support and small-and medium-sized enterprise (SME) performance: the moderating effects of diagnostic and support services. Asian Business & Management, 19, pp. 213–238.

4. Rajagopal, N.K., Qureshi, N.I., Durga, S., Ramirez Asis, E.H., Huerta Soto, R.M., Gupta, S.K. and Deepak, S., 2022. Future of business culture: an artificial intelligence-driven digital framework for organization decision-making process. Complexity, 2022.

5. Irudayasamy, A., Christotodoss, P.R. and Natarajan, R., 2022. Multilingual Novel Summarizer for Visually Challenged Peoples. In Handbook of Research on Technologies and Systems for E-Collaboration During Global Crises (pp. 27–46). IGI Global.

6. Naradda Gamage, S.K., Ekanayake, E.M.S., Abeyrathne, G.A.K.N.J., Prasanna, R.P.I.R., Jayasundara, J.M.S.B. and Rajapakshe, P.S.K., 2020. A review of global challenges and survival strategies of small and medium enterprises (SMEs). Economies, 8(4), p. 79. implementation. Industrial Marketing Management, 69, pp. 62–73.

7. Nuseir, M.T. and Aljumah, A., 2020. The role of digital marketing in business performance with the moderating effect of environment factors among SMEs of UAE. International Journal of Innovation, Creativity and Change, 11(3), pp. 310–324.

8. Agyapong, A., Maaledidong, P.D. and Mensah, H.K., 2021. Performance outcome of entrepreneurial behavior of SMEs in a developing economy: the role of international mindset. Journal of Strategy and Management, 14(2), pp. 227–245.

9. Al-Hakimi, M.A., Saleh, M.H., Borade, D.B., Hasan, M.B. and Sharma, D., 2022. Competitor orientation and SME performance in competitive environments: the moderating effect of marketing ethics. Journal of Entrepreneurship in Emerging Economies, (ahead-of-print).

10. Arzubiaga, U., Iturralde, T., Maseda, A. and Kotlar, J., 2018. Entrepreneurial orientation and firm performance in family SMEs: the moderating effects of family, women, and strategic involvement in the board of directors. International Entrepreneurship and Management Journal, 14, pp. 217–244.

11. Genc, E., Dayan, M. and Genc, O.F., 2019. The impact of SME internationalization on innovation: The mediating role of market and entrepreneurial orientation. Industrial Marketing Management, 82, pp. 253–264.

Advancements in Business for Integrating Diversity, and
Sustainability – Dimitrios A. Karras et al. (eds)
© 2024 Taylor & Francis Group, London, ISBN 978-1-032-70828-7

48

Sales Promotion, Advertising and Product Appeal: Effects on Customer Impulsive Buying Behavior

Alden O. Obuyes, Rayan C. Soriano
Polytechnic University of the Philippines 1016
Anonas Sta. Mesa Manila, Metro Manila

Mark Justine P. Vicera*
Palawan State University Coron Bgy. Poblacion 6 Coron,
Palawan Polytechnic University of the Philippines 1016
Anonas Sta. Mesa Manila, Metro Manila

Rock Bryan B. Matias, Cresilda M. Bragas
Polytechnic University of the Philippines 1016
Anonas Sta. Mesa Manila, Metro Manila

Abstract: Customer impulse buying habits have led to various consumer-based research. The consumer behavior towards acquiring a certain product or service is intriguing since it can be affected by external, market-related inputs and several internal psychological factors. This article's analysis was compiled using data from 385 samples of working millennials in Metro Manila, Philippines, whose impulsive buying behavior was affected by sales promotion, advertising, and product appeal. According to the findings of the study, working millennials in the country are often influenced by three external factors in addition to their gender when it comes to their tendency in making impulsive purchases. Lastly, it was discovered that women are more prone than males to engage in such purchasing activities.

Keywords: Consumer behavior, Impulse buying behavior, Working millennials impulse buying, Partial least square approach

1. Introduction

The initial definition of an 'impulse buy,' according to the DuPont Consumer Purchasing Habits Research, which took place between 1948 and 1 The concept of impulsive buying behaviors was further extended to relate to a consumer's overwhelming desire to purchase a product straight away, which typically causes ambivalence in the purchasers. Zhang and Shrum (2009) discovered that impulse

*Corresponding author: markjustinevicera@gmail.com

DOI: 10.4324/9781032708294-48

buying happens when a person's desire to satisfy their demands clashes with their own logical and inner outlook. It's no wonder that individuals all across nations have developed a habit of making rash buying to counter against their inability to control themselves. 965, was an unanticipated transaction made by the client. There are various aspects that affect the impulsive buying behavior of consumers which could be classified as the enterprise's sales promotion, advertising, and product appeal.

Many researchers developed the work of Stern's (1962) study, in which he presented the structure of impulse buying classified as planned, unplanned, or impulse. Planned buying include information-gathering and logical decision-making, while unplanned shopping doesn't require initial purchasing decisions. Quick decision-making distinguishes impulsive purchases from unexpected purchasing. In addition to being unplanned, an impulsive purchase is characterized by a sudden, intense, and overpowering need to purchase. According to the theorist of the Theory of Impulsive Buying, there are four impulsive buying behaviors, and these are *planned, reminder, suggestive and pure*. Planned impulse purchases are largely organized, but the customer does not have the option of selecting specific products or categories. Consumers are also influenced by the store's numerous promotional offers. Reminder impulsive purchases occur when a buyer is notified of the product's requirement while shopping. A pure impulse purchase is a novelty or escapes purchase made by a purchaser who detracts from his or her usual buying habits. Reminded impulse buying is a type of impulsive buying behavior in which the buyer has knowledge or familiarity with the item yet lacks any plans to buy it - and then purchases it. The researchers used this theory to understand how the identified factors encourage impulse buying among working millennials in Metro Manila and will explain which category of impulse buyers the consumers will fall into. This study will attempt to determine the influences of sales promotion, advertising, and product appeal on impulse buying behavior among working millennials in Metro Manila. Ultimately, the aim of this study is to investigate how sales promotion, advertising, and product appeal of certain products and services influence impulsive buying behavior using a Partial Least Square (PLS) approach.

2. Review of Related Literature

Product Appeal and Impulse Buying Behavior

Marketing communications and consumer characteristics influence reminder impulse buying behavior, (Shu-Ling Liao, et al., 2019). The study applied antecedent, process, and consequence approaches to examine the important differences between pure and reminder impulse buying. The study revealed that reminder impulse buying is significantly dissimilar from pure impulse buying in motivation, buying goal, and decision evaluation. According to Kacen et al 2012, product characteristics and retailing factors affect the consumer's impulse purchase. The study was conducted in three major grocery shopping stores in Houston Texas, and the results found that product characteristics have a 50% greater influence on impulse buying than retailing factors. Among the characteristics studied, hedonic nature has the greatest influence on unplanned buying and the immediate usability of an impulse item was not a significant factor in shoppers' impulse purchase decisions. Brand-related cues like brand awareness and brand variety on the other hand are infrequently studied in the literature about online impulse buying. Brand knowledge may improve the likelihood of online impulse buying since consumers are likely to pay more attention to known brands than to new ones. Another important factor is brand diversity which appears to be more likely than not that greater brand variety causes online impulse purchases.

Sales Promotion and Impulse Buying Behavior

Zulfiqar, Ambreen, and Bushra presented research on the effect of sales promotion on impulsive purchasing (2018). Vouchers, special offers, rebates, freebies, various schemes, bonus packs, loyalty programs, contests, price packs, and promotional signs all influence customers' impulse purchasing habits. Nagadeepa, Selvi, and Pushpa (2015) stated the definition of sales promotion as an action that operates as a direct enticement by delivering added value or incentive to resellers, salespeople, or customers for a product. In addition, it defined sales promotion as special offers designed to boost product demand. However, in this study, sales promotion is described as products offered in deals and discounts. In the marketing domain, promotion in any shape or form is seen as a strategic and vital tool to facilitate the marketer in supporting the business to achieve its goals (Alvarez and Casielles, 2005). Modern retailers nowadays conduct campaigns for sales such as discounts, displays, and in-store promotions. Efforts to promote sales inspire a keen interest in buying. According to the study of Lovelock and Wirtz (2004: 138), one of the motives why buyers are compelled to acquire is their feelings and emotions. Furthermore, Cummins and Mullin (2004: 41) discovered

that pricing desire and distraction are drivers of customer eagerness to purchase.

Social Media Advertising and Impulse Buying Behavior

Online impulse purchases are a crucial component that might yield favorable results for online businesses and advertisers. Personalization is employed in social media marketing practices. However, the relationship between personalization and social media impulse purchasing has not been properly investigated. The study by Dodoo and Linwan of 2019 provides insights into the importance of personalization on social media as an antecedent of customers' online impulse tendency, which is an important topic for online retailers these days. Likewise, the findings indicate the influence of perceived personalization on perceptions of value, relevance, and novelty of social media ads (Dodoo, Linwan Wu 2019). According to the study of Nuseir in 2020, buying behavior tends to adopt a certain pattern: need identification, search between alternatives, buying, and post-buy evaluation. This sequence has been reviewed based on certain principles. Any buying habits that do not conform to the said pattern are unplanned or impulse buying. Facebook users, on the other hand, tend to adapt to social media reactions and indicators like comments, tags and likes which lead to impulsive buying behavior. Former studies on impulse buying have determined Facebook as a catalyst or driving force of impulsive buying. However, little evidence has proven Facebook's role in motivating impulse buys.

Gender and Impulse Buying Behavior

Gender is the social division between women and men, their employment, and the growth of society. It is found to be a key determinant in driving purchasing practices. For a very long time, the market has been segmented by gender (Schmitt et al., 2008), mostly due to the fact that in some cultures, women and men have different social roles and personality trajectories that affect the act of consumption (Dholakia, 2000). According to studies, women spend more time shopping than men do (Fischer and Arnold, 1990). In addition, women analyze information from product publicity with greater detail (Kempf et al., 2006). It was determined that advertising, product displays, surroundings, innovations, sales promotions, and the perspective of the salesperson had a significant impact on the purchase behavior of female consumers. Generally, women receive items that are expressive and indicative of their passionate perspectives and appearance. Thus, young women have a stronger propensity to buy indiscreetly, whereas the indiscreet shopping propensity of young men is of a more utilitarian kind. In general, people will find what they require quickly and with a minimal level of commitment. Thus, for them, impulsive shopping is a faster decision and the quickest possible usage of the purchased goods. In addition, for men, indiscreet shopping propensities are increasingly associated with aspects of financial perspectives (Akram, Hui, Khan, Hashim, & Rasheed, 2016).

3. Results and Discussions

The study was able to analyze the demographic profile of the working millennials in Metro Manila. It can be noted that one-third of the respondents are working in Manila City accounting for 32.5% followed by Quezon City with 26%. The National Capital Region (NCR)

is the country's political, economic, and educational center making it a more viable option to study. According to the 2020 census of PSA, the most populous city in Metro Manila is Quezon City with more than 2.8 million people followed by the City of Manila with 1.8 million residents. Considering that the respondents of this study are all millennials, it was revealed that out of 385 samples, 182 respondents have an age range from 31-40 years old followed by 21-30 years old with 163 responses. Researchers have done a great job focusing the study on millennials who were born between 1981 and 1996 (Rauch, 2018). They are described as the first global generation that grew up in the internet age (Pendleton et al., 2021) and are sometimes referred to as "digital natives" because of their significantly increased use of and familiarity with the internet, mobile devices, and social media. (Prensky & Mark, 2013). The study found that 70.9% or 273 responses were females. Contrary to what the Philippines Statistics Authority (PSA) stated that there is more male than female in the country (2020 PSA census), the study explicitly shows that females are more than males. It can be dissected that females are more inclined to shop and buy stuff than males making them more susceptible to buying habits offline or online (Dholakia, 2000).

Furthermore, the profiles of the respondents such as marital status, business sector belonging, and monthly income were dissected. It can be gleaned that the majority of the respondents are single accounting to 79.7%. According to Invespcro.com, single shoppers make 45% more impulse buys than married shoppers. Hence, there is really a high tendency for single individuals to purchase impulsively since they don't have families to feed. Meanwhile, the top two business sectors where most working millennials are connected are the service and banking and finance industries with 18.7% and 16.9% respectively. The services sector is made up of a wide variety of services, including, among others, business and retail services, educational services, and health services.

Within the context of validity and reliability analysis of the structures used in the research, reliability, convergent validity, and discriminant validity of the data were examined. Cronbach's Alpha and Composite

Reliability (CR) ratings were computed for reliability. For the investigation of convergent validity, the average variance values explained by factor loadings (AVE = Average Variance Extracted) were employed. While the Average Variance Extracted (AVE) value is used to determine the measure of the convergence between specific items reflecting the latent structure, and Composite Reliability (CR) and Cronbach's Alpha values were used to determine the consistency of items in the scale; all values were above 0.80, which is regarded as a very good level (Hair et. al, 2014). Table 48.1

Table 48.1 Descriptive, validity, and reliability tests

Constructs	Mean	Std. Deviation	Std. Loading	AVE	CA	CR
Impulsive Buying Behavior						
BB2	2.7195	1.22443	0.869			
BB5	2.5377	1.24552	0.854			
BB4	2.4779	1.22906	0.843	0.699	0.921	0.892
BB3	3.1065	1.24649	0.810			
BB1	3.1870	1.26505	0.803			
Sales Promotion						
S5	3.8935	1.09525	0.823			
S2	3.9351	1.09137	0.817			
S6	4.1169	.98126	0.795			
S1	3.9896	1.11799	0.785	0.614	0.918	0.895
S4	3.7532	1.13371	0.774			
S7	3.8623	1.13618	0.767			
S3	3.5481	1.14264	0.720			
Advertisement						
A3	2.5922	1.16924	0.888			
A4	2.6675	1.22202	0.874			
A6	2.1584	1.15621	0.866			
A5	2.1766	1.19023	0.848	0.683	0.927	0.904
A2	2.9221	1.15206	0.836			
A1	3.5273	1.15014	0.617			
A7	3.9117	.96690	Deleted			
Product Appeal						
P1	3.6312	1.11293	0.748			
P6	3.4104	1.16722	0.744			
P8	3.8831	1.05542	0.737			
P9	3.8909	1.04010	0.716			
P2	3.8156	1.01795	0.714	0.529	0.871	0.822
P4	3.6312	1.07241	0.704			
P3	4.4701	.72512	Deleted			
P5	4.4338	.75788	Deleted			
P7	4.1714	.84884	Deleted			

Average variance extracted (AVE) must be 0.5 or higher based on Fornell-Larcker criterion. CR and CA must be 0.70 and greater

Table 48.2 Square root of average variance extracted

	Impulsive Buying Behavior	Product Appeal	Sales Promotion	Advertisement
Impulsive Buying Behavior	**0.836**			
Product Appeal	0.458	**0.727**		
Sales Promotion	0.439	0.602	**0.784**	
Advertisement	0.588	0.565	0.461	**0.827**

The diagonal values must be higher than the off-diagonal values (Kock, 2012)

Table 48.3 HTMT ratio

	Impulsive Buying Behavior	Product Appeal	Sales Promotion	Advertisement
Impulsive Buying Behavior				
Product Appeal	0.533			
Sales Promotion	0.493	0.703		
Advertisement	0.663	0.667	0.527	

(good if < 0.90, best if < 0.85)

presents statistics for both measurement items and constructs. Almost all factor loadings were higher than the cutoff of 0.70. Only one item (A1) received a loading that was somewhat lower than this, but it was nevertheless kept because all of the item-to-total correlation coefficients had residual variances that were below the recommended cutoff range of 0.35.

Table 48.2 presents the square roots of the average extracted variance (on the diagonal) and the inter-construct correlations (below the diagonal) for the first-order constructs. The table demonstrates that the average variance extracted for all first-order factors had a square root that was greater than their combined variances. The HTMT criterion, according to Henseler et al. (2015), expresses the ratio mean of the correlations between the items of all the study variables to the geometric means of the correlations between the same variable's items. According to him, the HTMT value should be less than 0.85, although it is possible for structures with equal content to have HTMT

values as high as 0.90. This reaffirms the model constructs' discriminant validity as shown on the next table.

Table 48.3 shows the results of HTMT. All constructs such as product appeal, sales promotion, and advertisement have had less than 0.85 which means all of them are not highly correlated with one another. As a result, it was determined that the study's structures were appropriate for structural equation analysis.

Table 48.4 indicated that the five hypotheses of five direct effects and two hypotheses of indirect effects were supported. As theorized, product appeal directly affects sales promotion, impulse buying behavior, and advertising. Sales promotion alongside advertising directly and significantly affects impulse buying behavior. Indirect effect constructs meanwhile: the sales promotion significantly and indirectly affects the relationship between product appeal and impulsive behavior, and advertising significantly and indirectly affects the relationship between product appeal and

Table 48.4 Direct and indirect effects of the PLS model

Hypothesis	Path Coefficient	p-value	Standard Error	Effect Size	Decision
Direct Effects					
H1a. PA -> SP	0.615	<0.001	0.047	0.379	Supported
H1b. PA -> IBB	0.094	0.031	0.050	0.043	Supported
H1c. PA -> AD	0.579	<0.001	0.047	0.335	Supported
H2. SP -> IBB	0.174	<0.001	0.050	0.076	Supported
H3. AD -> IBB	0.456	<0.001	0.048	0.269	Supported
Indirect Effects					
H4. PA -> SP -> IBB	0.107	0.001	0.036	0.049	Supported
H5. PA -> AD -> IBB	0.264	<0.001	0.035	0.121	Supported

Effect sizes were measured using the following criteria: 0.02 – small effect; 0.15 – medium effect; 0.35 – large effect (Cohen, 1988).

Table 48.5 Measurement invariances for moderating analysis of gender

Items	ALGC for Loadings	p-value
Male vs. Female		
BB1	0.045	0.190
BB2	0.016	0.381
BB3	0.034	0.256
BB4	0.029	0.289
BB5	0.002	0.483
P1	0.001	0.494
P2	0.012	0.408
P4	0.035	0.246
P6	0.025	0.314
P8	0.028	0.292
P9	0.051	0.161
S1	0.044	0.194
S2	0.047	0.180
S3	0.021	0.340
S4	0.025	0.315
S5	0.057	0.133
S6	0.067	0.095
S7	0.039	0.224
A1	0.018	0.361
A2	0.041	0.211
A3	0.032	0.265
A4	0.006	0.454
A5	0.029	0.288
A6	0.026	0.308

* ALGC is the Absolute latent growth coefficient for loadings (ALGCs)

impulsive behavior. As recommended by Cohen, 1988, the effect size values of H1b, H2, H4, and H5 correspond to the value of small effect with values 0.043, 0.076, 0.049, and 0.121 respectively. H1c, 0.335, and H3, 0.269 on the other hand have a medium effect and H1a has the largest effect with an effect size of 0.379. Therefore, all hypotheses are supported.

Table 48.6 shows the moderating effect of gender on sales promotion and impulse buying and gender on product appeal and impulse buying. There is a very low effect of gender on sales promotion and impulse buying with a p-value of 0.306. Therefore, it failed to reject the null hypothesis and it is not significant in nature. This result is supported by Ndubisi (2005). Meanwhile, the moderating effect of gender on product appeal and impulse buying showed significance in context and had a p-value of 0.030 which is less than the alpha 0.05 and therefore rejects the null hypothesis. In a study on cross-gender brand extensions published in 2006 by Kwon Jung, he looked at product categories, brands, perceived risks related to those categories, and the companies' perceived gender images. The success of cross-gender extensions that result in purchases is seen to be strongly conditioned by the gender of the brand, the gender of consumers, and the type of product (Jung, 2006).

Table 48.6 Hypothesis testing – moderating effect of gender

Hypothesis	Path Coefficient		ALGC	p-value	t-ratio	Decision
Gender	**Male**	**Female**				
H6a. Gender* SP-> IBB	0.173	0.184	0.052	0.306	1.025	Not Supported
H6b. Gender* PA->IBB	0.242	0.032	0.110	0.030	2.171	Supported

Table 48.7 Common method bias test, coefficients of determination, and predictive relevance

Construct	FCVIF	R^2	Q^2
Product Appeal	1.894		
Impulsive Buying Behavior	1.632	0.389	0.389
Sales Promotion	1.670	0.379	0.379
Advertisement	1.857	0.335	0.334

The threshold for FCVIF is 3.30 or lower; R^2 is evaluated using the following: 0.67 – substantial; 0.33 – moderate; 0.19 – weak (Chin, 1998). Q squared must be greater than 0.

4. Conclusion

Based on the study's findings, over 50% of the respondents work in Manila City and Quezon City. The Philippine Statistics Authority states that these two cities are the ones with the highest population densities in NCR. Since millennials made up the majority of the respondents in this study, 70.9 percent of the replies came from those under the age of 40 who are female. Women are anticipated to make more purchases than males because they are more detailed in their analysis of information from product promotions during the buying process (Kempf et al., 2006). Additionally, it was discovered that millennials in the workforce were 79.7% single and make between P10,000 and P20,000 monthly salary as evidenced by the minimum wage in the NCR. Finally, with 18.7% percent and 16.9% respectively, the top two industries where the majority of respondents work are services and banking and finance.

Table 48.1 of this research provides evidence that the study also had a legitimate setting for validity and reliability analysis. In addition to Composite Reliability (CR) and Cronbach's Alpha values, the average variance retrieved was utilized to calculate the degree of convergence between particular items indicating the latent structure. It should be emphasized that all values are over 0.80, indicating that the constructs used in the study are excellent. The factor loadings, on the other hand, are all higher than 0.70, with the exception of one item (A1). The validity and reliability tests of the study's constructs were thus passed. Meanwhile, the HTMT model showed that the variables such as impulse buying behavior, product appeal, sales promotion, and advertisement had values less than 0.85 which tells that the four aforementioned constructs are not correlated with one another. On the hypotheses testing, it was summarized that all constructs are supported. Product appeal such as brand awareness, product aesthetics, packaging, and among others directly influences sales promotion, impulse buying behavior, and advertising. Sales promotions such as price discounts and coupons alongside advertising have a significant influence on the impulse buying behavior of working millennials. Quoted from Cohen, 1988, the effect size values of H1b, H2, H4, and

H5 correspond to the value of small effect with values 0.043, 0.076, 0.049, and 0.121 respectively. H1c, 0.335, and H3, 0.269 on the other hand have a medium effect and H1a has the largest effect with an effect size of 0.379. Therefore, all hypotheses are supported. Table 48.6 demonstrated that gender had a significant p-value of 0.030 on the moderating influence of product appeal on impulse purchases. This demonstrates the widespread use of gender sensitivity by brands around the world, which affects both men's and women's purchasing behaviors, especially impulse purchases. Since some goods and services are appropriate for particular gender identities, Kwon (2006) published that images, product categories, and perceived risks on brands were among the factors influencing this. On the other side, the impact of gender on sales promotion was minimal, indicating that gender has no bearing on how sales promotion materials like coupons, reductions on prices, samples, etc. are presented.

In summary, the study revealed that the impulse buying behavior of working millennials in Metro Manila was influenced by product appeal, sales promotion, and advertising. It was also noted that gender particularly females have a high tendency of getting impacted by such sudden bursts of emotions when buying. And lastly, the researchers hope that this paper will shed new opportunities, especially for companies and brands in their pursuit of a better understanding of impulse buying.

REFERENCES

1. Bansal, M., & Kumar, S. (2018, July). Impact of Social Media Marketing on Online Impulse Buying Behaviour. Research Gate.
2. Hilmi, L. D., & Pratika, Y. (2021). Paylater feature: impulsive buying driver for e-commerce in indonesia. International Journal of Economics, Business and Accounting Research, Volume 5 (Issue 2), 63–74.
3. Huang, L.-T. (2016). Exploring utilitarian and hedonic antecedents for adopting information from a recommendation agent and unplanned purchase behaviour. New Review of Hypermedia and Multimedia, Volume 22 (Issue 1-2), 139–165.
4. Hussain, S., & Siddiqui, D. A. (2019, March 16). The Influence of Impulsive Personality Traits and Store Environment on Impulse Buying of Consumer in Karachi. International Journal of Business Administration, Vol. 10(No. 3), 50–73.
5. Kazi, A. G., Khokhar, A. A., Qureshi, P. A. B., & Murtaza, F. (2019). The Impact of Social Media on Impulse Buying Behaviour in Hyderabad Sindh Pakistan. International Journal of Entrepreneurial Research, Volume 2(Issue 2), 8–12.
6. Rodrigues RI, Lopes P, Varela M. Factors Affecting Impulse Buying Behavior of Consumers. Front Psychol. 2021 Jun 2;12:697080.
7. Fassnacht, M., Wriedt, S. (2011). Online grocery shopping: Determinants of online impulse buying behavior. In: Wagner, U., Wiedmann, KP., von der Oelsnitz, D. (eds) Das Internet der Zukunft. Gabler.
8. Sigal Tifferet, Ram Herstein, (2012),"Gender differences in brand commitment, impulse buying, and hedonic consumption", Journal of Product & Brand Management, Vol. 21 Iss: 3 pp. 176–182.
9. Covell, K. (1992). The Appeal of Image Advertisements: Age, Gender, and Product Differences. The Journal of Early Adolescence, 12(1), 46–60.
10. Tifferet, S. and Herstein, R. (2012), "Gender differences in brand commitment, impulse buying, and hedonic consumption", Journal of Product & Brand Management, Vol. 21 No. 3, pp. 176–182.

Note: All the tables in this chapter were made by the Authors.

Advancements in Business for Integrating Diversity, and
Sustainability – Dimitrios A. Karras et al. (eds)
© 2024 Taylor & Francis Group, London, ISBN 978-1-032-70828-7

The Effect Between ServQual, Trust, and Leadership Toward Inpatient's Satisfaction at Lawang Municipal's CMC

49

Bambang Sugiyono Agus Purwono*
School of Business and Management,
Universitas Ciputra Surabaya, Indonesia

Mochammad Jasin
Universitas Islam Negeri Syarif Hidayatullah,
Jakarta, Indonesia

Imanuel Teguh Harisantoso
Universitas Kristen Satya Wacana, Salatiga, Indonesia

M. Fahim Tharaba, Ali Nasith
Fakultas Ilmu Tarbiyah dan Keguruan,
Universitas Islam Negeri Maliki Malang, Indonesia

Abstract: The purpose of this study is to analysis how trust, leadership, and service quality affect inpatient satisfaction at Community Medical Center, Lawang Municipal, South Sumatra. Inpatient satisfaction is one of the dependent variables, while service quality, trust, and leadership are the independent variables. There were 40 patients who responded to the survey. This research is the quantitative method using multiple regression analysis. Trust, leadership, and service quality had found to have a positive impact toward inpatient's satisfaction at the Pendopo Inpatient Community Medical Center, while service quality had a negative impact. The trust variable makes the most contribution to inpatient satisfaction, followed by the leadership variable and the service quality variable (negative contribution).

Keywords: Inpatient's Satisfaction, Leadership, Service quality, Trust

1. Introduction

World Health Organization (WHO) defined health is a condition of complete physical, mental and social prosperity and not simply the shortfall of illness or ailment. If someone becomes sick, the patient will try to look for the health facility near their place. Indonesia

*Corresponding author: bambang.sugiyono@ciputra.ac.id

DOI: 10.4324/9781032708294-49

had two health facilities, there are private and state health facilities. Two state facilities are hospital (Class A, B, and C) and Community Medical Center (CMC/"Puskesmas").

2. Research Background

CMC is a health care facility or health administration office that provides individual and local medical services at the highest level while also providing health promotion and preventive services in their operating area. The social class clinical consideration runs a piece of specific useful of the prosperity impact in the common or city, to additionally foster prosperity and getting, status and to deal with the expense of strong life for every individual so every one can have an optimal sound life. In all civil and urban areas throughout Indonesia, the CMC is the primary stage and exact office. Since each CMC receives a functional endowment from the public authority to provide the best health care to the general public, it is essential for a large number of Indonesians because it is small and affordable. The primary level and precise office, which can be observed in all civil and urban areas of Indonesia. Because each CMC receives a functional endowment from the public authority to provide the best health care to the general public—the highest level and exact office that can be seen in all civil and urban areas throughout Indonesia—the local wellness center is essential for a large number of Indonesians. Since each CMC receives a functional endowment from the public authority to provide the best health care to the general public, it is essential for a large number of Indonesians because it is small and affordable.

Despite the fact that the health service CMC actually needs to provide the best quality, prompt, and expert assistance.

CMC must provide medical and health services, but they must constantly strive to improve service quality, patient trust, and patient and community satisfaction. In order for a patient to truly be satisfied with the service, a CMC must be accurate in knowing the patient's need and hopes.

When people need CMC services, there are issues with the system, regulations, and complicated bureaucracy. For instance: Because of their unsatisfactory service, the medical director and the paramedics are not pleasant to the patient. Additionally, the paramedics are not punctual due to their lack of discipline.

One of the CMCs in Indonesia is the CMC in Pendopo, Lawang Municipal, South Sumatra. It is also one of the CMCs that can provide the best service to the surrounding community with high perfectionism and high responsibility in order to achieve a high patient satisfaction score that can be recorded as data for the CMC's inpatients (Table 49.1).

In 2017, there were 215 inpatients at the CMC Pendopo. Of those, 40 were dissatisfied, while 175 were satisfied. In 2019, there were 301 inpatients, 290 of whom were satisfied and eleven who were not.

Table 49.1 Data Inpatient's Satisfaction in Lawang Puskesmas year 2017 till 2019

Inpatient	2017	2018	2019
Satisfied	175	215	290
Dissatisfied	40	5	11
Total	215	220	301

Source: Anwar (2020).

Table 49.2 shows the functioning ethic that can be utilized by supervisor as a method for speaking with the sub-ordinates, so they will

Table 49.2 Previous research

Researcher	Year	Description
Rivai, V and Ella Sagala.	2015	Discipline. There are, for instance, holes: Workers frequently arrive late to care for patients. Senior laborers were occasionally unreliable. Authorization for infractions is not granted consistently and reasonably.
Wibowo	2016	Competence. It's about the expert's ability to complete the task given their knowledge, experience, and perspectives supported by work.
Rusmiati, Abdullah, and Tamsah	2018	Quality of service. There are gaps between what people think is real and what they expect to be real, for instance: Poor bureaucracy delays attending to the impatient desire for the initial medical action; and they lack sufficient tangibles or specific facilities.
Dian Fitry Anwar	2020	Patient's satisfactory. In 2017, 215 inpatients were discharged, of which 175 were satisfied and 40 were dissatisfied. There were 220 inpatients in total in 2018, of which 215 were satisfied and 5 were dissatisfied. The total number of inpatients in 2019 was 301, of which 290 were completed and 11 were not.

Source: Authors

actually want to change their lead. It can also be used to increase employees' awareness of the need to adhere to all workplace social and systemic norms.

Competence defines as the willingness to perform a job or task based on one's knowledge, skills, and attitude.

Other issues include factors like service quality, trust, and leadership that can make patients happy.

The Research Objective

The research objective is to analyze the effect between service quality, trust, and leadership to the inpatient's satisfaction at CMC, Lawang Municipal, South Sumatra.

3. Literature Study

This paper discussed about the operational variables of Trust, Leadership, Service quality, and Inpatient's Satisfaction.

Service Quality

The five dimensions of the, accessability, reliability, tangibles, empatyy, and responsiveness. Service quality is a multi-dimensional research instrument or variable that aims to capture consumer expectations and perceptions of service quality. Table 49.3 shows the variables of the service quality, which can be summarized as the degree to which customers' actual perceptions of the service experience confirm or disprove their pre-consumption expectations of quality.

Trust

Robbins, S. P. (2018) stated that: "…. five aspects that make up the idea of trust. Trust is characterized as a faith in the honesty, character, and capacity of a leader."

Table 49.4 shows that five attributes of trust are Competence, Consistency, Integrity, Loyalty, and Openness.

Table 49.3   The definition of the five dimensions of service quality

No.	ServQual Variables	Description
1	Tangibles	The facilities, equipment, personnel, and communication materials is the physical aspects of what is provided to inpatients' satisfaction.
2	Reliability	The ability to play out the surefire organization continually and unequivocally or ability to fulfill what was ensured exactly.
3	Tangibles	The facilities, equipment, personnel, and communication materials is the physical aspects of what is provided to inpatients' satisfaction.
4	Empathy	The provision of care and individualized attention to customers or inpatients (access, comprehension, and communication with patients).
5	Responsiveness	The capacity to extend to ongoing issues and provide assistance quickly or the eagerness to assist in the long run. recognizing the concept of adaptability and adaptability to the client's requirements.

Source: Nastih (2019) and Parasuraman (2022)

Table 49.4   Five dimensions of trust

No.	Trust Dimensions	Definition
1	Competence	Attitudes, skills, and knowledge in both interpersonal and technical areas
2	Consistency	Good judgment, predictability, and dependability in handling situations
3	Integrity	Honesty and truthfulness
4	Loyalty	Willingness to physically and emotionally defend oneself, one's organization, and others
5	Openness	Willingness to freely share with stakeholders information and ideas

Source: Robbins S.P (2008).

4. Leadership

Robbins, S. P. (2008) stated that: "The act of persuading a group of people to achieve a goal is called leadership. Leader is defined as someone who has managerial authority and can influence others." Influence, authority, and followership are all characteristics of leadership. The most common method of influencing a group to achieve its goals is through leadership. Pioneer is defined as someone with administrative authority and the ability to influence others. Pioneers, influence, authority, and supporters are all attributes of an initiative.

Satisfaction is a person's feeling of pleasure or disappointment resulting from comparing the perceived performance (or result) of a product with their expectations is called satisfaction." Perceived performance and expectations influence satisfaction The customer is not satisfied as mentioned performance is not as expected. Perceived performance and expectations play a role satisfaction. The customer is satisfied if the perceived performance meets his expectations.

5. Research Method

This research method discussed about Likert Scale, Mathematical model, and conceptual framework.

Likert Scale

Likert Scale is the basic and most widely used psychometric assessment impact of respondents on educational and social science research.

The Likert scale category using five scale, like: Disagree Strongly (1), Disagree (2), Neutral (3), Agree (4), and Agree Strongly (5) and makes the impression to measure each person's view point [4]. The Quantitative approach of multiple linear regression analysis.

6. Mathematical Model

Mathematical model of this research is:

$$b_0 + b_1x_1 + b_2x_2 + b_3x_3 + e_{ij} = y_{ij} \qquad (1)$$

Where:

y_{ij} = Inpatient satisfaction variable

x_1 = Service Quality

x_2 = Trust

x_3 = Leadership

b_0 = intercept or constant.

b_1, b_2, b_3 = coefficients of regression.

e_{ij} = Error.

Null Hypothesis

The null hypothesis is rejected, it means that is a relationship between Service quality, Trust, Leadership toward Inpatient's Satisfaction.

The Research Conceptual Framework

Figure 49.1 shows the flow chart of the research conceptual framework.

Place and When the Research was Carried Out

The research was conducted at Jalan Nurdin Panji - Puskesmas Pendopo, Kabupaten Empat Lawang, Sumatera. The data were collected from May until July 2020.

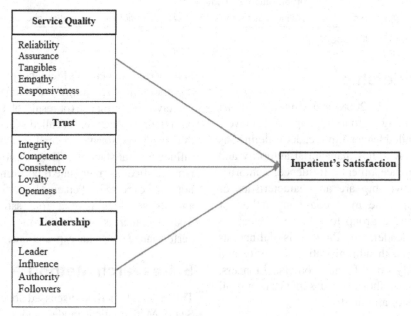

Fig. 49.1 The research conceptual framework

Source: Anwar (2020), Nasith (2019), Oshan (2016), Parsuraman (2002), Zeithaml (1990)

7. Results and Discussion

This sub-chapter discussed about results and discussion.

Description of the Research Results

The result was obtained from the primary and simulated data computation obtained from data distributions of questionnaires to the subjects of the research who are the inpatient respondents numbering to 40.

Multiple Regression Analysis

Table 49.5 shows that the regression coefficient of the research variables outputs. The value here counted the Service quality, Trust, and Leadership, as an independent variables respectively is −0.049, 0.093, and 0.061, and the intercept is 4.196. Inpatient's satisfaction as dependent variable

Table 49.5 Coefficients of regression[a]

Variables	Coefficients B	t test	Significance
(Constant)	4.196	7.783	0.000
Servqual	−0.049	−0.595	0.555
Trust	0.093	0.855	0.393
Leadership	0.061	1.029	0.310

[a]Dependent variable: Satisfaction
Source: Authors

The mathematical representation are:

$$y = 4.196 - 0.049x_1 + 0.093x_2 + 0.061x_3 \quad (2)$$

or

Inpatient's satisfaction = 4.196 − 0.049 Service quality + 0.093 Trust + 0.061 Leadership $\quad (3)$

Equation 2 and 3 shows that the biggest contribution to inpatient satisfaction is trust variable (regression coefficient is 0.093), the second is Leadership variable (regression coefficient is 0.061), and the third is Service quality variable (regression coefficient is -0.049) and negative contribution.

8. Conclusion

At Community Medical Center, Lawang Municipal, South Sumatra, the mean values of the variables for service quality, trust, leadership, and inpatient satisfaction scores are above 3.0 (neutral or close to better).

The trust variable makes the largest contribution to inpatient satisfaction, followed by the leadership variable and the service quality variable (negative contribution).

Acknowledgment

The authors are thankful to all those who have assisted in this research. Especially to the Rector of Universitas Ciputra Surabaya, Indonesia, Indonesia for his support.

REFERENCES

1. Anwar, D. F. (2020). The effect of Service Quality, Competency, Discipline, and Facility towards Patient's Satisfaction at Puskesmas Hospitalization Pendopo Kabupaten Empat Lawang Sumatera Selatan. Thesis. Faculty of Economics, Master Degree in Management Study Program, Universitas Bina Insan Lubuklinggau.

2. Jasin, M., Vincent, S. S., Masroni. & Purwono, B. S. A. (2021). Dominant Factors for Enhancing Product Quality, Service Quality, Promotion Efforts, and Decision Making Toward The XBCA Bank Customer's Satisfactions. Journal of Tianjin University Science and Technology. ISSN (Online): 0493-2137 E-Publication: Online Open Access. 54(6): 185–192.

3. Kotler, P. E. (2000). Marketing Management. International Edition. Prentice Hall International, Inc.

4. Nasith, A., & Purwono, B. S. A. (2019). Service Quality Implementation to Increase the Youngsters' Parishes Satisfaction at ABC Church. Journal of Advance Research in Dynamical & Control Systems. 11(11): 157–162.

5. Oshan. M. K. (2016). Providing Good Service Quality and Customer Satisfaction for Airline Ground Services. Master of Science Thesis, Management of Technology. Delft University of Technology.

6. Permenker No 43 (2019) about the Community Medical Center (Pusat Kesehatan Masyarakat). Accessed 10 November 2021.

7. Parasuraman, A. (2002). Service Quality and productivity: a synergistic perspective. Journal Managing Quality. 12(1): 6 9.

8. Robbins, S. P., Bergman, R., Stagg, I., and Coulter, M. (2008). Foundations of Management. Third Edition. Pearson Education.

9. Rusmiati, R. A., & Hasmin, T. (2018). The Effect of Service Quality, Facility, and Image toward Patient's Satisfaction at Puskesmas Solo Kabupaten Wajo. Journal of Management. 1(3): 1 12.

10. Zeithaml, V. A., Parasuraman, A., & Berry, L. L. (1990). Delivering Quality Service. The Free Press.

Advancements in Business for Integrating Diversity, and
Sustainability – Dimitrios A. Karras et al. (eds)
© 2024 Taylor & Francis Group, London, ISBN 978-1-032-70828-7

Stock Accuracy Analysis in Warehouse: A Daily Cycle Calculation Based on ABC Method

50

Resista Vikaliana*

Universitas Pertamina, Indonesia

Eric Hermawan, Rifan Indra Setiawan

Institut Ilmu Sosial dan Manajemen Stiami, Indonesia

Irwansyah

STIES Gasantara, Indonesia

Abstract: The purpose of this study was to analyze the implementation of cycle counting with the ABC method in measuring stock accuracy in the warehouse. The type of the study was descriptive quantitative, with case study at PT Bintang Dagang Internasional (Haistar). The methodology used was the ABC method based on the category of fast moving goods (sales). Based on the results of the cycle counting analysis using the ABC method, it was found that the results of the calculation of inventory analysis using the ABC method for food and beverage (F&B) product at PT Bintang Dagang Internasional (Haistar) on the Sarinah Client had the total absorption value of Rp. 155,195,800 from 185 SKUs with 3596 pcs. This results showed that the sales with the largest value were in category A, which had a absorption value of 75% with a sales value of Rp. 116,396,850 and the products sold of 2703 pcs from 41 SKUs. Category B had an absorption value of 20% with a sales value of Rp. 31,039,160 and the products sold of 676 pcs from 61 SKUs. Category C had an absorption value of 5% with a sales value of Rp. 7,759,790 and the products sold of 217 pcs from 83 SKUs.

Keywords: Cycle counting, ABC method, Inventory control

1. Introduction

In Indonesia, electronic commerce has increased in recent years. Especially after the emergence of various marketplace websites such as Tokopedia, Lazada, Shopee, Bukalapak, Akulaku, Blibli, JD.ID, and many others. E-commerce is electronic commerce for the process of buying or selling products. Along with the growth of the e-commerce business, companies need fullfilment services as a fulfillment of the

*Corresponding author: resista.vikaliana@universitaspertamina.ac.id

DOI: 10.4324/9781032708294-50

sales process so that they can get mutual satisfaction. As a company grows, it requires inventory management to control the amount of targeted profit. Companies must minimize technical problems that interfere with company activities so that the process runs smoothly.

The e-commerce business in Indonesia is increasingly promising. During the pandemic, this digital-based trading business is even projected to grow 33.2% from 2020 which reached Rp. 253 trillion in 2021. From Bank Indonesia's records, not only the e-commerce business has increased. The use of electronic money increased by 32.3% or equivalent to Rp. 266 trillion in 2020, the central bank estimate states that the use of electronic money reaches Rp. 201 Trillion" (source website kominfo.go.id).

In achieving business goals, a company has business processes that must be implemented and integrated properly. If there is an inhibiting process, it will affect other main processes. One process that has an important role in supporting the business of a retail company is the inventory management process, a common problem is the comparison between the stock of goods recorded and the amount of stock in the warehouse (Handoko, 2010). With the physical inventory process, it can be seen the level of accuracy of the stock of objects between the number of stock items recorded and those in the industrial warehouse.

There has been a lot of research done related to inventory management, both in the method of grouping objects or developing information systems. However, because each industry has unique characteristics, whether in the field of business, customers or transaction patterns, research in this field is still being carried out (Wardana & Sukmono, 2019).

Therefore, it is necessary to have a correct calculation in controlling the correct inventory (Siagian, 2005), one of which is by using the Cycle Counting method using the ABC method, to minimize the possibility of lost items or damage, and the following is a list of clients from haistar is a client of PT Sarinah. John Mark McDaugal (2013) defined of cycle counting is a process designed to replace a comprehensive annual inventory with smaller amounts that are carried out continuously throughout the year. This can be done when business activities are carried out on a daily basis and eliminates the need for annual overtime.

This principle states that "Critical View and Trial Many" this principle teaches to focus inventory control on types of high value or critical inventory rather than low value or trival According to Heizer and Render ABC Classification as follows:

(a) Class A are products that provide high value. although group A is only represented by 20% of the total inventory in the warehouse, it has a value of 80%

(b) Class B are products that provide moderate value. this class B inventory group is represented by 30% of the total inventory and the resulting value is 15%

(c) Class C are products that provide low value. Class C inventory group is represented by 50% of the total inventory and the resulting value is 5%. (Kasuma Dewi Nila, 2012).

During the period from July 2021 to January 2022, it was recorded for lost items (Quarantine 4) and damaged items at the location (Quarantine 2) of the total lost items and location damage there were 18 pcs of which the total loss was for replacement.

the goods are worth Rp. 884,200. In this study will analyze how the cycle counting carried out by the warehouse on the accuracy of stock in the warehouse. The research aim is knowing the application of cycle counting with the ABC method carried out by inventory at PT Bintang Dagang Internasional in measuring stock accuracy in its warehouses.

Research on daily cycle counting with the ABC method has been carried out by previous researchers. Research on inventory control of pharmaceutical products using the ABC method shows a better inventory cycle calculation policy (Fathoni, 2018). In line with these studies, other studies have produced more accurate inventory control using the ABC method (Cu, Ching Wu et al, 2008). This study uses the ABC method of inventory control applied in the warehouse. This is different from previous research. In addition, the products observed in this study are food and beverage (F&B) products.

2. Method

In this research, the researcher uses a quantitative approach with descriptive method, which aims to present data on the sample individually or singly on each research variable, then perform calculations to clarify the characteristics or situations of the relevant data. Descriptive analysis using Likert Scale to analyze Daily Cycle Counting (x1), ABC Method (x2), and Stock Accuracy in warehouse (y).

The collection technique is to observe by direct observation and systematic recording of the object to be studied and documentation by using historical data from the Daily Cycle Counting at Sarinah, along with the collective supporting documents for research, both hardcopy and softcopy.

The population in this study is the inventory data of PT Bintang Dagang Internasional (Haistar) for clients from Sarinah. Sampling was carried out with the consideration that the existing population was very large in number, so it was not possible to examine the entire existing population, so that a representative population was formed. Researchers will take a sample of F&B product inventory data for Sarinah's clients from October 2021 - March 2022 at PT Bintang Dagang Internasional (haistar). In this study, researchers used purposive sampling by using inventory data and history cycle counting data on f&b products at the Sarinah Official store.

The analysis in this study follows the analysis in the inventory section using a cycle counting system with the ABC method based on Pareto's law, ABC analysis will be carried out by classifying goods based on the highest price value to the lowest and then dividing them into major priority classes marked by groups A, B, C where the counting cycle is calculated. continuously, in this case the effectiveness will be known. on the accuracy of stock in the warehouse. large priority classes marked by groups. A, B, C where the counting cycle is calculated continuously, in this case it will be known how effective it is on stock accuracy in the warehouse. The theory used in this research is Heizer and Render (1991) theory.

3. Results and Discussion

Results

The process is carried out by the Distribution Center carried out by PT Bintang Dagang Internasional (Haistar) on the Sarinah client using the by Grid (Location) and SKU (Stock Keeping Unit) system, the results of the daily cycle counting on Sarinah consist of 292 SKUs consisting of 199 f&b products and and 103 craft and fashion products, from the dcc results there were 18 pcs of 7 F&B product SKUs that were included in the quarantine 4 (lost item) location which caused a loss of 405,956.

Based on the summary daily cycle counting carried out by the inventory division of PT Bintang Dagang Internasional (Haistar) on the Sarinah client for F&B products, there are 18 pcs consisting of 7 SKUs (Stock Keeping Units) declared Shortage. Collection of inventory data for f&b products sold July 2021 – April 2022, inventory data at PT Bintang Dagang Internasional on the Sarinah Official Store client, steps in making a Pareto diagram.

1. Number of items managed
2. Total usage of each type of goods (in one year)
3. Unit price of goods

4. Discussion

Based on the results of the study, it was found that the results of the calculation of inventory analysis using the ABC method for product f&b at PT Bintang Dagang Internasional (haistar) at the Sarinah Client, namely from the total absorption value of Rp. 155,195,800 of 185 SKUs of 3596 pcs. from this it can be seen that the sales with the largest value are in category A, which has a absorption value of 75% witsalesvalue of Rp. 116,396,850 with products sold as many as 2703 pcs from 41 SKUs. Category B has an absorption value of 20% with a sales value of Rp. 31,039,160 with products sold as many as 676 pcs from 61 SKUs. Category C has an absorption value of 5% with a sales value of Rp. 7,759,790 with products sold as many as 217 pcs from 83 SKUs.

Table 50.1 Summary of daily cycle counting

Item Name	Q'ty_system Before Reconcile	Count_1	Count_2	Count_3	Diff	Status
BEEMA RAMBUTAN BLOSSOM 300 GR	1	0	0		-1	Shortage
BEEMA DARK ACACIA 300 GR	2	0	0		-2	Shortage
WOH KERIPIK TEMPE RASA KUNYIT CURCUMIN - 50GR	6	0	0		-6	Shortage
WOH - KERIPIK TEMPE RASA ORIGINAL - 50GR	47	48	46	46	−1	Shortage
WOH - KERIPIK UBI UNGU ORIGINAL - 50GR	6	0	0		−6	Shortage
PROSPERO CHOBAYOO BISKUIT BALL KOPI SALUT COKELAT - 100GR	8	7	7		−1	Shortage
UNI TUTIE - RENDANG JENGKOL 250GR	3	2	2		−1	Shortage

Source: Research, 2022

This is in line with previous research on inventory control conducted by (Cut Fiarni, Arief Samuel Gunawan & William, 2018). The results of the study found that this physical inventory recommendation system can make it easier for companies to carry out regular checks, especially in sorting goods to be checked according to the level of demand for goods based on classification results, so as to reduce and prevent differences in stock of goods between what is written and what is on the list. warehouse system. This recommendation is based on the opinion of Heizer and Render (1991) on ABC analysis. ABC analysis is carried out by classifying goods based on the highest price value to the lowest and then divided into major priority classes marked by groups A, B, C where the counting cycle is calculated continuously, in this case the effectiveness will be known. on the accuracy of stock in the warehouse.

Based on the results of research on Daily Cycle Counting Analysis using the ABC Method Against Stock Accuracy in PT Bintang Dagang Internasional (Haistar) Case Study Warehouse, it is recommended to do cycle counting with the category of fast moving goods or for products with sales with the highest value, for products with categories A or category is important to be controlled more intensively so the attention must be more and for checking which must also be more careful and continuously. Inventory efficiency can be done with tight control on supply control and scheduling, especially in category A and followed by categories B and C, by applying rescheduling to products with fast moving categories or with sales with the highest value. For products with category C, which are slow moving, to create an economical package from every consumer purchase by combining it with several fast moving products to form an economical

package at a price that can be adjusted to profits (Vikaliana, 2020).

5. Conclusion

Based on the results of the daily cycle counting analysis using the abc method on stock accuracy in the case study warehouse at PT Bintang Dagang Internasional (Haistar) on the Sarinah client, it can be concluded that the f&b product classification in Sarinah consists of 185 sku using the ABC method, namely for Category A consisting of 41 SKUs with a percentage of 75% absorption value with a value of Rp. 116,396,850 with a usage quantity of 2703 pcs. Category B consists of 61 SKUs with a percentage of the absorption value of funds of 20% with a value of Rp. 31,039,160 with a usage quantity of 676 pcs. Category C consists of 83 SKUs with a percentage of the absorption value of funds of 5% with a value of Rp. 7,759,790 with a usage quantity of 217 pcs. The application of cycle counting with the ABC method carried out by inventory at PT Bintang Dagang Internasional in measuring the accuracy of stock in the warehouse has been properly carried out. Inventory efficiency can be done with tight control on supply control and scheduling, especially in category A and followed by categories B and C, by applying rescheduling to products with fast moving categories or with sales with the highest value.

REFERENCES

1. Fiarni, Cut et al. 2018. Implementasi Metode ABC-Cycle Counting pada Sistem Rekomendasi Physical Inventory Perusahaan Retail. (Prosiding SISFOTEK, Nomor 1, II, Hlm. 206-212). Jakarta: Organisasi Profesi Ikatan Ahli Informatika Indonesia (IAII).

2. Handoko, T. Hani. 2010. Dasar-dasar Manajemen Produksi dan Operasi. Yogyakarta: BPFE.

3. Heizer, Jay dan Barry Render. 1991. Production and Operations Management: Strategies and Tactics. Boston: Allyn and Bacon.

4. McDougal, John Mark. 2013. Cycle Counting Exposes Inventory Ills. Nashville: Material Handling & Logistics.

5. Siagian, Yolanda M. 2005. Aplikasi Supply Chain Management dalam Dunia Bisnis. Jakarta: Gramedia Widiasarana Indonesia.

6. Vikaliana, Resista et al. 2020. Manajemen Persediaan. Bandung: Media Sains Indonesia.

7. Wardana, M. Rafi dan Yudi Sukmono. 2019. Perancangan Cycle Inventory Policy Menggunakan Metode Cycle Counting pada Gudang PT. Badak NGL. (Prosiding Seminar Nasional Teknologi, Inovasi dan Aplikasi di Lingkungan Tropis, Nomor 2, I, Hlm. 78–87). Samarinda: Universitas Mulawarman.

8. Fathoni, Fadhilah Amin, Ari Yanuar Ridwan, Budi Santosa. 2018. Development of Inventory Control Application for Pharmaceutical Product Using ABC-VED Cycle Counting Method to Increase Inventory Record Accuracy. Atlantis Highlights in Engineering (AHE) Volume 2. International Conference on Industrial Enterprise and System Engineering (IcoIESE).

Advancements in Business for Integrating Diversity, and
Sustainability – Dimitrios A. Karras et al. (eds)
© 2024 Taylor & Francis Group, London, ISBN 978-1-032-70828-7

51

365 Days of Business 2 Business (B2B) Marketing Turnaround: A Fact Driven, Bullet Proof Showcase Guide

Radhika Bajaj

Dr. Ambedkar Institute of
Management Studies & Research, Nagpur

Pankaj Pethe

G H Raisoni College of Commerce Science and
Technology, Nagpur

Shweta Pethe, Amit Sahu

G H Raisoni College of Engineering, Nagpur

Abstract: We try to explain the historical background of the current major developments in industrial goods marketing in this chapter. I have to overhaul entire economic sectors because it takes the larger picture into account. Globalization and digitalization are just two of the many factors at work here. What changed to make Germany's economy, which used to be the third largest in the world, less powerful? Or why is the once-ubiquitous "Made in Germany" logo now seen as a warning sign of a collapsing heavy and automotive industry? In light of these recent standard changes, this part explores Business to Business (BUSINESS 2 BUSINESS (B2B)) marketing in the future.

The goals of a Business to Business (BUSINESS 2 BUSINESS (B2B)) marketing strategy essential to successfully position industrial firms in western side in worldwide markets that are characterised by developing financial authorities and their nimble businesses with constantly changing products. Engineers form Western side and their old, inflexible conducts of thinking and operating are not extended sufficient for the companies to survive. The different areas of expertise within the companies must intersect at eye level in order to deliver customer-centered innovations in the appropriate marketplaces over the long period using recent Business to Business (BUSINESS 2 BUSINESS) (B2B)).

Keywords: Business to business, Markeging, Manufacturing, Branding

DOI: 10.4324/9781032708294-51

1. Introduction

The worldwide economy was purportedly going through a tough time. I gave the following description of the situation at the time. The international economy is in an unheard-of situation for the past 40 years; instead of aiming to focus higher, all three of the main economies are drained and on a road of slowing development. What is so unique about the current situation? Remember the most recent financial turmoil and consider about the 3 largest markets: Europe, Asia, and the USA.

The two other economies could gain from the strength of the one strong economy to understand the move from a economic slowdown or a negative marketplace scenario to a rising and more steady one. The "bandwagon effect" is the name of this causation. At the time, no one could have imagined How the worldwide budget would change or grow?

This also suggests that conventional engineering, which supported the worldwide economy after the 2 global conflicts, will slowly need to take on a new role. Future engineers won't describe and require fresh goods and scientific advancements on their own; rather, they'll work with customers to help them make decisions about what will become a company's future cash cows. In Europe, region, debate started about whether need to issue common debts in Euro bonds for helping Italy and Spain, which have been rigorously harmed by the present epidemic. This should avoid a "Italexit" if Brexit is less or more effective. The purpose of this joint debt is to assistance the tightly integrated sales marketplaces of the European internal market soon regain its dominance. Nonetheless, the return of border controls as

a result of COVID-19 raises concerns about how the EU will grow as a collection of states. Will there ever be a free exchange of products within the internal market of the European Union? Or will the reintroduced border controls eventually have an impact on how goods move within the EU? Every now and then, economists and futurologists speculate about the emergence of a completely new culture following the corona. Optimists hope or anticipate that the changes in travel patterns brought on by the COVID Crisis and the accompanying tourism limitations will cause a significant reevaluation even after the restrictions are repealed. It conveys the sense that our world is utopian and populist. The few realists today have serious doubts about the European Union's ability to withstand this test.

Without a doubt, a country may seek to safeguard and develop its own commercial region. Nonetheless, these plans must always be able to stand up to examination from the perspective of global economic policy. But, the questionable principles that permeate the geopolitical landscape of the world also have an impact on financial activity.

2. Looking Back and Forward

Without a doubt, a medal always has two sides. Digitalization and globalisation have both shown to have a large optimistic result on the world economy. Globally, the relationship between supply and demand is opening up. Resources can be used effectively globally through planning, controlling, and optimising supply and value chains. Businesses can always order products through online marketplaces with an eye towards a streamlined, effective delivery approach, lowering CO_2 emissions and transportation costs. All of these have an equal capacity to association of financial and business communal accountability. Yet, the rewards and abilities of a worldwide economy made stronger by digitalization and globalisation are wasted when leaders start to reject any CSR notion in order to reward for their own country's declining competitiveness.

The truly unfortunate aspect of such political behaviour is that it ultimately hurts their voters and constituency, which amounts to a betrayal of the trust placed in them by their own country.

Another feature of present financial strategy growth is the reappearance and implementation of disciplinary charges on imported goods under the excuse of long-term employment security for one's own business site. The difference is that the latter group is oblivious of it in the long run, even though all of this is hurting their own people. The creation of new technologies is delayed by a lack of exertible pressure as pathetic financial segments, outdated industries, and their firms are kept preciously alive throughout time.

Commercial law practices the expression or the evidences of deliberate postponement in filing for liquidation for such an action. The burden will be borne by taxpayers or future generations. Hence, by taking all necessary steps, governments should try to avoid economic policy returning to the older one. Our worldwide financial organization and all associated with it are too important to be jeopardised by outdated practises, including, amongst other belongings, the return of corrective rates or the restart of entirely antiquated, resource-wasting making techniques.

The World Is Crazy: What Now?

It is reasonable to wonder how the aforementioned relates to manufacturing merchandises marketing in the modern day. The standard Business to business (BUSINESS 2 BUSINESS (B2B)) marketing manager joins manufacturing organisation after finishing his marketing trainings or training. There, he or she gains immediate knowledge of and hands-on experience with the main responsibilities of a marketing department, including the management of relevant trade exhibitions and the fabrication of brochures. Most of the time, after that, one might remain working at this company in marketing till their own retirement. The unfortunate pleasure of learning everything from big advertising director with a comparable background—viz. UG completion, entry, and superannuation—is usually also enjoyed by the ambitious young professional. In conclusion, this suggests that the blind are instructed by the one-eyed. The excited young professional quickly realises that engineering, the "Gods in Grey," are the heroes and that marketing is just the company's extended workbench. Therefore, marketing offers little value and only generates expenses. This is further corroborated by the following statement made by a highly recognised German marketing colleague in a letter to me: Short-term work was adopted in our division. R & D must be condensed by 50%, merchandise administration by 40%, calculations by 30%, sales by 50%, and advertising by 90% over the following 3 months. according to a management team-wide email that was sent. As a result, the promotion section will only be open for four hours each week. To express the valuation or obligation of the company's marketing department, it is not essential to read between the lines At this point, it should be noted that the anxious marketing manager performs admirably. As engineers' works are always immaculate and sell themselves, it should not be surprising that they are more learned and skilled than experts in other fields. They are not aware of the need for marketing, thus. The specialists that produced this image had backgrounds in technology and, ideally, had at least once encountered clients, markets, and sales during their academic careers. As a result, as crazy significantly suppresses self-reflection and self-criticism, it not only has an impact on the entire world but also on enterprises. Because they are already benefiting from the longer, adapted training techniques, the present-day, rising, youthful, and highly trained engineers deserve commendation. Together with comprehensive technical training materials, these include modules on sales, market analysis, and customer orientation. As a result, as crazy significantly suppresses self-reflection and self-criticism, it not only has an impact on the entire world but also on enterprises. Because they are already helping from the longer, adapted training techniques, the present-day, rising, youthful, and highly trained engineers deserve commendation. Together with complete technical training materials, these include units on sales, market analysis, and customer orientation. Business to Business (BUSINESS 2 BUSINESS (B2B)) marketing, however, can and must make an important input to the long-term stabilisation and defence of the manufacturing enterprises they support and work for. The development of technology in this area has made this possible. This makes the following essential specialties for "next-generation" BUSINESS 2 BUSINESS (B2B) marketing, which are addressed in more detail below, emerge:

• Expertise in procedures and techniques knowledge of data and IT

Proficiency with Procedures and methods

The 1892–1938 Russian physicist Nikolai Dmitrievich Kondratieff is credited with creating the concept of long waves. He observed that lengthier time periods which cab business series waves—with a span of 45 to 60 years in addition to short time periods last up to three years and medium period cycles last up to 11 years during his business cycle investigations in 1919 and 1921. In 1926, Kondratieff.

In the end of eighteenth century, he observed, the financial development of the industrial nations in the western area had been defined by 3 key improvements and depressions. Joseph Schumpeter was the first researcher to emphasise the significance of fundamental inventions.

The term "Kondratieff cycle," which he later connected with the long wave phenomenon, was also coined by Schumpeter. Kondratieff predicted that as the economy became more automated and technical; people would become the weakest link in the chain in his work on Next-Generation BUSINESS 2 BUSINESS (B2B) Marketing. The greatest challenge of the twenty-first century, in his opinion, is that in order for people to completely realise the probable of mechanization and technology in the first place, it is crucial to first maintain the overall health of the human being. Then, it is important to provide people with the necessary procedural and mechanical competence.

The recent high-pitched increase in the prevalence of mental diseases in humans provides strong evidence in favour of Kondratieff's hypothesis. A significant financial sector for business wellbeing organization has recently evolved under the heading of "business mental wellbeing" (Güpner et al. 2010). The cost to nationwide markets of treating intellectual infection now represents high double-digit percentages of all healthcare spending. The economic damage caused by businesses without technique and process proficiency is far worse.

Process proficiency as a Basic Requirement

What causes this harm? Lack of procedural and mechanical competence is evidenced by ineffective procedures, repetition, interface difficulties, insufficient use of data technologies, and even the disappointment to attain specified areas within the allotted time and within the allotted budget.

A good illustration would be the premature release of a product as a result of poor project management by the project manager for the R & D department. Another common problem that can result in significant delays in fulfilling delivery dates is a lack of coordination between project management and manufacturing. Absence of comprehensive process specifications for marketing and communication operations, current job explanations, precise purposes, and unmistakable performance pointers of the procedures taken are all indications of structural and methodological competency in BUSINESS 2 BUSINESS (B2B) marketing. These essential structural elements are absent from marketing organisations; hence this department will continuously function in "firefighting mode." Marketing will always be on the defensive, working as swiftly and accurately as possible to execute duties given to it or required by other departments. As a result, marketing is frequently driven by

and played with by the other departments. With the right mechanical and procedural knowledge, the aforementioned well-known exercise can be recognized and made available to the public. If someone fails to submit a effort direction in agreement with the set procedures and timeframes, the section of marketing may make reference to it. It progressively acquires control over its own period and scheduling in this way. xiv BUSINESS 2 BUSINESS (B2B)

Marketing That Is Future-Proof

If these mechanical basics are not developed, an in-house department of marketing will never have the inflexible and consistent construction it requires to act and debate with the internal consumer groups with the essential power. At this point, we want to emphasise once more that the marketing department is where change always begins. If you have the necessary structural competency, you can design a clear organisational diagram for your own department of marketing in relation to other organisational units, both strictly speaking and generally speaking. As a result of the well-defined interfaces, cross-team and cross-departmental processes become more effective.

Everything Must Come Together

Additional significant feature that decreases under the purview of procedural capability is the presentation and analysis of all conditions in light of economic efficiency difficulties. Every small movement up to the procurement of new MarTech equipment falls under this. 2 Next-generation BUSINESS 2 BUSINESS (B2B) marketing does away with the awkward alternative up and asking for new properties and money, but it does start to modestly hint at how things can function. This establishes confrontational foundation for itself in order to show the resistant of idea within the situation of the attainment of additional means and assets and to produce the primary business case based on it. Next-generation BUSINESS 2 BUSINESS (B2B) advertising declares to always be one step ahead, breaking out from the murky realm of marketing. The simple remedy is to be empathetic. Think of yourself as your opposite. Imagine that your CEO is sat across from you. What query would he put to you? The reply is the same 90% of the time: "What does it cost me and what does it gain us?" Always shining and not putting yourself out there must be your goal. In other words, you must constantly plan the crucial step forward. Find the aspects in your idea that need improvement. Find the structure's inconsistencies and weak spots. Start thinking structurally. Many structures come in the following varieties: •Models of management (BCG matrix, SWOT analysis) Business practises (production, buying, and customer experience).

3. Data Competence

In 21st century, analysing and comprehending information of all types is a second essential element for effective BUSINESS 2 BUSINESS (B2B) marketing. This has long been a vital part of current instruction and practise in traditional management education. The 2 disciplines of HRM and promotion have effectively avoided discussing performance management and measurement for years.

It wasn't till the latter half of the 20th era that the first accurate pointers for the field of HRM were made available. At that time, the marketing sector has also gone through a process of reconsidering crystal clear dimension and assessment of promotion return on investment (MRoI) in relation to the marketing resource management (MRM) plan (Seebacher and Güpner 2021). Despite this, recent years have seen a major advancement in the research of data literacy. According to business intelligence (BI) systems that are getting more complex, ever-increasing measurements of facts can now be administered, comprehended, and assessed more effortlessly and rapidly. Famous saying "knowledge is power" is not new, but in light of recent events, it has had a considerable resurgence. Next-generation BUSINESS 2 BUSINESS (B2B) marketing requires the capacity to continuously stay abreast of markets, clients, initiatives, and items. Maintaining the content power of all facts and data, especially that pertaining to customer relationship management, must entirely falls under the purview of marketing (CRM). In many firms, the CRM system is under the supervision of the deals section or even the IT department. most marketing executives. The operational IT department is the optimum location for pure IT power in the sense of system-technical sovereignty, but not for content responsibility, according to the structural analysis of the situation that was described above. This should logically fall within the purview of the marketing department, which is responsible for defining the types of data that are collected, entered, measured, and used in the perspective of the additional marketing value chain, as well as their location and timing.

IT knowledge

This may be difficult for some readers to accept, but the fact remains. In the 21st century, BUSINESS 2 BUSINESS (B2B) marketing is becoming more dependent on modern data tools. As a part of the community of next-generation BUSINESS 2

BUSINESS (B2B) marketing managers, you must have the knowledge required to speak intelligently about the most recent MarTech solutions. As a result, you don't have to learn how to code. But you must be able to perform a transparent collection procedure for a new marketing clarification using the essential procedural abilities. You'll also need to be able to connect with co-workers in other sections, particularly IT, via edges and information grounds to confirm that you always have the precise facts obtainable in the essential setup. You must be able to work with your co-workers to coordinate talks about system-related problems from a content perspective. Strategically speaking, your area of competence in IT also requires you to develop a plan for the MarTech architecture of the company. Which software, platforms, and marketing-related technologies should the company use moving ahead and over the long term, and through what interfaces should they be connected?

4. Summary

This indicates that other people will choose the most effective way to market. In light of the pervasive business insanity over the comprehension of marketing, it might be expected that the appropriate choices will only seldom be complete. In conclusion, any transformation starts with itself. The number of employees in a marketing department is a question you hear quite regularly. It is frequently said that minor and medium-sized initiatives deficiency the marketing resources necessary to implement all of these methods.

You always hear complaints that everything is too expensive and that there would be no budget anyhow. In all honesty, if you have read this book and comprehend its ideology and philosophy, you shouldn't be asking these questions. The only thing needed for next-generation BUSINESS 2 BUSINESS (B2B) marketing to be successfully applied in a business is a marketing manager who actively jumps performing his own homework for Next-Generation BUSINESS 2 BUSINESS (B2B) Marketing.

How many people are employed in marketing it does not matter really but it is always a process of deliberate and progressive internal development. With the help of this technique, it is likely to display and record one's own movements in the form of assessable outcomes.

As a result, trust and transparency are encouraged. On this basis, and with the resulting confidence boost, new initiatives and projects can be launched. Always know what is practical on a small scale and then and only then, approach your superior for additional resources or financial aid.

REFERENCES

1. Güpner, A. Hillert, and U. G. Seebacher (2010).
2. Occupational mental health. Munich: USP Publishing. Schumpeter, JA (2008).
3. Business cycles. Göttingen: Vandenhoeck & Ruprecht. A. Güpner and U. G. Seebacher (2021).
4. Marketing resource management. Munich, Germany: AQPS Inc. It was written by U. G. (2003).

Advancements in Business for Integrating Diversity, and
Sustainability – Dimitrios A. Karras et al. (eds)

52 Study of Determinants of Follow-on Round in SaaS Subsectors: Venture Capitalist's Outlook

Kavita Ingale

Assistant Professor, School of Economics,
MIT World Peace University, Pune, India

Babasaheb Jadhav*

Associate Professor, Global Business School & Research Centre,
Dr. D. Y. Patil Vidyapeeth, Pune, India

Paridhi Singhania

Research Scholar, School of Economics,
MIT World Peace University, Pune, India

Manisha Paliwal

Professor, Balaji Institue of International Business,
Sri Balaji University, Pune, India

Abstract: Venture capital firms have been the key to funding young startups when no one else in the market trusted them. Venture Capital firms have been a major source of funding for the majority of startups in India and abroad. Enterprise SaaS being evolutionary in nature has been an attractive area for investors to invest in. To ensure the safety of Funds Venture capitalists tend to look for parameters that help them make a viable investment decision and this is where the study finds out whether general parameters at different stages affect the valuation of the company or not.

The study considers four sectors under enterprise SaaS: marketing tech, sales force automation, enterprise collaboration, and in-store retail tech. The factors taken into account shows the consideration for all stages companies in stores retail tech while in other sectors the valuation is impacted only in case of early stage.

This study allows Venture Capitalists to look backward in terms of performance and make better investment decisions rather than vague decisions though these decisions are affected by various other factors while Venture capitalists look to invest further in specific companies in a particular sector.

Keywords: Venture capital, Enterprise SaaS, Marketing tech, In-stores retail tech, Enterprise Collaboration, Sales force automation, etc.

---

*Corresponding author: babasaheb.jadhav@dpu.edu.in

DOI: 10.4324/9781032708294-52

1. Introduction

Indian Venture capital markets have seen a rise in terms of broadening investments by 3.8x times in 2021 over 2020. The investments grew up in India more than that in china (1.3x). There has been increasing in deal transactions from 609 to 1500+ which is a drastic increase. Venture Capital funding in India accounted for more than 50% of overall private equity and VC investments in the country. (Sheth et al., 2022)

Growth drivers for Indian SaaS:

- Indian companies are building innovative solutions in India for global clients
- Rapid pace of innovation through the creation of new categories
- Distinct competitive advantage over global peers

2. Literature Review

(Sheth et al., 2022) talks about how India's start-up landscape is growing in terms of investments and potential growth drivers the country possesses. India tends to replace the UK in terms of the number of unicorns growing to 73 in 2021. The investment base grew by 3.5x over 2020 reaching $38.5B amount. The SaaS segment tends to grow in terms of deal size and has grown 3x times from 2020 to 2021. SaaS is mostly focused on bringing out CRM-focused solutions and conversational AI. Exits have seen momentum and 40% of exits were through IPO.

(Pai and Vats, (2022)) studies growth in Indus Valley which is used as a catch for Indian start-up ecosystems through various evolutions seen through the backward and forward-looking lens.

(Chaudhary, (2022)) the research report discusses the definitive comparison between Horizontal SaaS and Vertical SaaS solutions and brings out the advantages that the company will be gaining while providing vertical SaaS solutions.

(Sharma and Ahmad, 2022) The researcher tries to understand the major transformations caused by covid 19 pandemic within the Indian Venture capital industry.

3. Research Gap

The article aims to focus on the factors that are still considered by venture capital firms when they invest in their portfolio company's next funding round. The study aims to understand whether they impact the valuation for the next funding round the wholesome venture capitalists and entrepreneurs rely on. This study is bridging the gap as none of the previous research focused on identifying the importance of next-stage funding.

4. Research Methods

Problem Statement

The research study is done in VC-backed startups. This research is important to understand whether investments should be made in startups and to study the approach for funding in subsequent rounds or not. In venture capital also there are different sectors and the sector in which the intern worked is Enterprise SaaS Sector.

Enterprise SaaS is a broad domain and research has been carried out to understand Horizontal SaaS: Marketing Tech, Retail Tech, HR tech, IT Operations, Sales Force Automation, Supply Chain Automation, etc.

Research in this domain in a broad sense revolves around digging deep to understand the activities of the portfolio companies and their performance analysis and whether the venture capital firm should proceed with providing funding for them or should go for returns through the exit as per foreseeing future trends in the respective SaaS sub-sectors.

Objectives

(a) To study the trends in each sub-sector: Marketing tech, In-stores retail tech, enterprise collaboration space, and Salesforce automation space.

(b) To study the impact of factors - team size, social networking, and annual revenue on the valuation of the companies in sectors- Marketing tech, Enterprise Collaboration, Sales Force Automation, and in-store retail in different stages whether early stage or in growth stage & late stage.

(c) To analyze the impact of annual revenue, Twitter followers and employees count on the valuation of the company

Hypothesis

H0: Factors-Team Size, annual revenue, and social network do impact the valuation for next-stage funding in the respective sector in all stages whether it be early or growth and late stage.

H1: Factors-Team Size, annual revenue, and social network do not impact the valuation for next-stage funding in the respective sector in the growth and late stage but it does impact in the early stage.

Source of Data

Secondary data (for quantitative analysis)- The data has been taken from Tracxn, Rocket reach, your story, and Owler regarding Twitter followers (which is a proxy for social media reach), Employee count (a proxy for employee size), and post-money

valuation (proxy for next funding round from founder's perspective and investment from Venture capitalist perspective). The latest figures available on the site have been taken. Qualitative analysis has been done through discussion in person and represented as part of trend analysis. To understand that since Venture capital firms lend to Entrepreneurs, they also need some assurance in terms of safety whether their funds are safe or not. But unlike a listed company start-ups do not have annual reports or documents in the public domain, so there are factors that they consider to study the impact on valuation, and based on valuation they decide the amount to invest in for the percent of equity taken up.

For the early stage, some typical metrics that become difficult to track are customer NPS score, Customer LTV, Gross profit margins, EV/ EBITDA multiple, MRR& ARR as the early stage companies have just entered the market and have not reached the entire targeted population yet. So for the early stage what factors do VCs consider including the idea of a Founder in that space and has it generated any revenue and if then how much market it has addressed, they consider the social media reach and do the company has a capable team which is the mixture of potential talent?

Methods of Data Analysis

In this process, researchers interacted with people from venture capital firms that invest in Enterprise SaaS space and certain founders to understand how and what parameters they have been using to measure the growth of their company in terms of revenue, spending, customer relations and how that varies across different stages of funding and different sub-sectors. The factors that were used by entrepreneurs and founders to measure growth in the early stage and growth stages were social media reach, employee count, and annual revenue. The main aim was to understand whether these factors affect the decision of funding by impacting valuation only when they are in the early stage or growth stage or if it applies to the companies in both Stages in different Sectors. If they are likely to impact by what percentage they impact valuation is the main focus of the study. To test the hypothesis least Squares Method is used along with a dummy variable (for the early stage).

The dummy variable is being used in combination with two factors revenue and employee count.

The least squares method is used as it provides the best fit among the data points being studied.

The regression equation used in different sub-sectors looks like this:

$$Y = \beta 1 X1 + \beta 2 D11 + \beta 3 D10 + \beta 4 D21 + \beta 5 D22 + Ui$$

Y is the dependent variable that represents a post-money valuation.

$\beta 1$, $\beta 2$, $\beta 3$, $\beta 4$, and $\beta 5$ are the coefficients where $\beta 1$ shows that holding the difference between the early stage and growth stage companies in terms of annual revenue and employees count (a proxy for team size) constant, how does the post-money valuation of a startup is being impacted when there is an increase in Twitter followers by 1 unit.

Equation with symbols used in E views:

$$Lv = \beta 1 (T\_F) + \beta 2 (AR01 \ (Early \ stage = 1)) + \beta 3 (AR01 \ (Early \ Stage = 0, \ Growth \ stage = 1)) + \beta 4 (EC \ (Early \ stage = 1)) + \beta 5 (EC \ (Early \ Stage = 0, \ Growth \ Stage = 1))$$

No constant variable is used as one additional variable for defining the impact of non-early

stage companies in terms of revenue on valuation for the next follow on a round in each sub-sectors.

To check the stability of data in terms of variance between the residual terms that might arise and to avoid correlation between any two explanatory variables, the heteroscedasticity test (BP test) and Variance Inflation factor were conducted in E-views.

To understand the trend in the industry and selective sub-sectors personal interaction was done with the people in the market and their opinion was taken as the part of trend analysis that is likely to be seen four to five years down the line.

The least square method is used to study the impact of the variables social media reach, employee count, and annual revenue on valuation considering the respective stages where most of the companies are in the sector. Heteroscedasticity tests have also been conducted to minimize the influence of residuals on the dependent variable and get significant results.

The data points being considered to evaluate the impact of early-stage and growth and late-stage company which is going for the next level of funding is uneven due to the unavailability of data across sectors in the public domain.

The factors and data that are affecting the valuation in the sector in the respective stage have been gathered using secondary sources. For insights on trends in different sub-sectors, many founders reached out to the sub-sectors with a standard set of questions that forms part of primary data.

The research is associated with bringing the typical Venture Capitalist mindset and testing the same in economics. Due to the lack of data, these small companies or the ones who are entering the market, the Venture Capital firms are highly dependent on some or the other metrics. Usually, these metrics are ARR, MRR, churn rate, customer retention rate, sales cycle, total addressable market, and customer lifetime value.

The choice of metrics varies from sector to sector but certain metrics are considered as part of all sectors in all stages of investment moving from one funding round to another. Working in a Venture Capital firm, the researcher gives importance to trends as well as other qualitative factors while going for the next funding round apart from establishing one. The study follows a bottom-up approach to evaluate the worth of follow-on rounds from a micro to macro lens.

Factors that are considered for evaluating growth at every level and are considered to be part of a study to:

a) Annual Revenue: This variable is used as a proxy for sales the start-ups are making. The higher the revenue the higher is level of motivation of the sales team to make efforts.

b) Employee Count: This is the representation of the team. In the venture capital world, the investors look at how strong a team the company has and what expertise they possess, whether they are diversified in their talents or not.

c) Twitter Followers: This variable is used as a proxy for understanding how many potential leads can a company get in a particular sector. On a sectoral basis, it analyses whether the leads impact the valuation of the sector that investors are looking to invest in.

d) Annual Recurring Revenue (ARR): It is the forecasted revenue figures that companies tend to forecast at the beginning of the financial year based on the MRR they get for the year.

e) Monthly Recurring Revenue (MRR): It is the actual incurred revenue for the first month based on which revenue for the next months is calculated.

f) Customer Retention rate: this rate tells how much percentage of the customers were retained from the previous sales. The higher the rate better it is.

g) Total Addressable Market: Every company in a particular sector has a targeted market and venture capital wants this market to be defined in terms of customers and geographic areas.

h) Customer Lifetime Value: This is the value company is likely to generate for a customer over certain years and it should be more than customer acquisition costs.

Data Analysis, Hypothesis Testing, and Results

Enterprise SaaS has a maturing landscape in the

1) Regression Analysis

The method used is the least squares method along with the dummy variable. This method is to study the impact on the dependent variable as the least square regression line is the line that minimizes the sum of the residuals squared. This model was chosen to reduce the impact of outliers that might arise in terms of widening variances between residuals.

The method was able to capture the non-impact of the factors on valuation for the next funding round except in the early stage in sub-sectors-marketing tech, in-store retail tech, enterprise collaboration, and sales force automation.

A) Marketing Tech

Table 52.1 Regression results of the marketing tech sector

Dependent Variable: Valuation (post-money)			
Method - Least Squares			
Variables	Coefficients	t-statistics	p-value
Twitter Followers (T_F)	5397.37	4.242785	0.0002
AR01(early stage=1)	1.559725	5.582040	0.0000
AR01(growth stage=1)	0.984436	3.652630	0.0011
EC(Early stage=1)	−17225.65	−1.699463	0.1003
EC(Growth stage=1)	−21756.01	−2.150759	0.0403
R^2	0.744966		
Adjusted R^2	0.699425		

In the above model, the dependent variable is the valuation of a company. The dummy variables are annual revenue (AR01) & employee count (EC) and the independent variable is Twitter followers (T_F).

The adjusted R^2 value is the goodness of fit statistic. The value is 0.699425 Or 69.94%. It implies that over 69% of the variation of values of the dependent variable is explained by independent variables.

The probability values are less than 0.1 which is considered to be very good, therefore any estimates done in the future, their result will be more likely to be significant.

Hypothesis Testing

H0: B1=B2=B3=B4=B5=0 at all stages

H1: B1=B2=B3=B4=B5≠0 at all stages except early stage

The null hypothesis which describes the coefficients of Twitter followers, media reach, and employee count as Zero is successfully rejected at a 0.01% significance level in favor of the alternative hypothesis.

B) In-store retail tech

Table 52.2 Regression results of In-stores retail tech

Dependent Variable: Valuation (post-money)			
Method - Least Squares			
Variables	Coefficients	t-statistics	p-value
Twitter followers (T_F)	15035.61	1.169967	0.3070
AR01(early stage=1)	2.698465	1.683050	0.1677
AR01(growth stage=1)	13.17546	1.412810	0.2306
EC(Early stage=1)	406359.6	2.726857	0.0526
EC(Growth stage=1)	−318149.0	−0.746282	0.4970
R^2	0.963083		
Adjusted R^2	0.926166		

The adjusted R^2 value which is the goodness of fit statistic has the value of 0.963083 or 96.30% which implies that over 96% of the variation of values of the dependent variable. These results have been obtained after overcoming the issue of heteroscedasticity by assigning inverse variance of the Latest Valuation and use of Huber White as a co-variance method.

The probability values are more than 0.1 which indicates insignificant results.

Hypothesis results:

The null hypothesis which describes the coefficients of Twitter followers, media reach, and employee count as Zero is successfully accepted at a 0.01% significance level.

The factors do affect the valuation of the company in subsequent rounds irrespective of the stage the company is in In-stores retail tech.

a) Salesforce Automation

Table 52.3 Regression results of sales force automation

Dependent Variable: Valuation (post-money)			
Method - Least Squares			
Variables	Coefficients	t-statistics	p-value
Twitter followers (T_F)	395740.5	5.441796	0.0122
AR01(early stage=1)	45.93027	3.168947	0.0505
AR01(growth stage=1)	−364.0916	−7.039390	0.0059
EC(Early stage=1)	−3529266	−4.932593	0.0036
EC(Growth stage=1)	12626813	8.368987	0.0160
R^2	0.915327		
Adjusted R^2	0.802429		

The adjusted R^2 squared value which is the goodness of fit statistic has a value of 0.915327 or 91.53% which implies that over 91% of the variation of values of the dependent variable are explained by independent variables. These results have been obtained after overcoming the issue of heteroscedasticity by assigning inverse variance of Twitter Followers and use of Huber White as a co-variance method.

Hypothesis Test results:

The null hypothesis which describes the coefficients of Twitter followers, media reach, and employee count as zero is successfully rejected at a 0.01% significance level in favor of the alternative hypothesis.

b) Enterprise Collaboration

Table 52.4 Regression results of enterprise collaboration

Dependent Variable: Valuation (post-money)			
Method - Least Squares			
Variables	Coefficients	t-statistics	p-value
Twitter followers (T_F)	−1080.054	−2.815493	0.0183
AR01(early stage=1)	2.062422	6.180243	0.0001
EC(Early stage=1)	−46436.12	−4.443467	0.0012
R^2	0.752917		
Adjusted R^2	0.703500		

The above result does not show the impact of the growth stage companies on the post-money valuation of the company due to lack of data and not many companies are in the growth and late stage in the Indian SaaS domain in the Enterprise Collaboration space.

The adjusted R^2 value which is the goodness of fit statistic has a value of 0.752917 or 75.29% which implies that over 75% of the variation of values of the dependent variable is explained by independent variables. The null hypothesis which describes the coefficients of Twitter followers, media reach, and employee count as zero is successfully rejected at a 0.01% significance level in favor of the alternative hypothesis.

2) Trend Analysis in SaaS-based on Interaction with Founders

a) Marketing Tech

- Marketing tech is being been likely to contribute the maximum to

Enterprise SaaS as it is the backbone of Globalisation and it is currently growing at a CAGR of 23.67%. There has also been the emergence of Vertical SaaS and optionality in the adoption of format whether it could be AI/ML or blockchain code.

- Indian SaaS market has certain limiting factors to get rid of like brain drain, delivering quality products and making better products, and then focusing on growing in terms of revenue & expansion to compete globally.

- The trends that have been seen in marketing tech are automation of content creation and graphics automation which is likely to contribute maximum to the Enterprise SaaS markets in coming years.

b) In stores Retail tech

- SaaS in this area has worked out through a literacy bridge from when the founder of Zobaze started his startup to where he sees they are aware but relativity sets it. He sees relativity boosting SaaS-based in-store retail in near future to compete in the challenging market.

- The factors that have contributed to boosting demand for In-stores retail are the arrival of Covid and the switch from offline to online presence merging with small players in the market. This is where the sub-sector grows at 5-10% from 3% year on year.

- The underlying challenge in this segment is to release all of the stuck revenue in delivery charges which arise out of reluctance to pay systems in Tier 2 & Tier 3 cities for shorter distances & boosting literacy.

c) Sales Force Automation

- The trends that are foreseen on a Global level including the USA the adoption of DevOps and sales force automation

- For Indian SaaS solutions to reach abroad there is a challenge that is of raising capital as more capital better talents and better quality products.

- CRM and cyber security are such sectors in the opinion of VCs which have the power to incentivize sales teams and motivate them for pre and post-sales as solutions have become complex and they are the areas that need to play out.

d) Enterprise Collaboration

- With the increase in digitization of business and high reliability on employee demand, there is huge potential of currently 9 million rooms to 35 million rooms target in video conferencing space which remains untapped we see other risks being faced by employees like the security of data, standardization of experience and integration of data sets in.

- This is where we see other risks being faced by employees like the security of data, standardization of experience, and integration of data sets.

- The Key SaaS category which has been in the market for the last 4 years is Hyper Intelligent automation (HIA) which according to me is likely to grow in correlation with Collaboration further excelling in the consolidation of different sectors not keeping it to legacy by the SaaS players in the SaaS markets. Currently, HIA is growing at an 18% YoY basis which has been seen at the same pace with which it will be growing in coming years.

5. Conclusion

The results prove that factors such as Twitter followers, annual revenue, and employee count are only acceptable to be considered when investing in-store retail tech at any stage company going for the next round of funding whereas in other sectors such as marketing tech, enterprise collaboration, and sales force automation it is only applicable for early stage companies.

Enterprise SaaS has been evolving for decades and currently is in the 4.0 industry which is more focused on product-led growth and user-based pricing. Investments in Indian SaaS markets have grown by 3X in the 2021 financial year which shows SaaS has long tailwinds to many other sectors which have not yet been replaced by SaaS. Since investments have been flowing into SaaS the major sub-sectors which have seen immense growth or are likely to see growth shortly includes marketing tech, In-stores retail tech, Sales force automation, and enterprise collaboration.

While looking forward to investing in companies in follow-on rounds Venture capital firms have been evaluating performance using certain general parameters on valuation (post-money) and certain sector-specific and stage-specific parameters are also being considered by them. The research proves that there has been no impact of these general factors on valuation except in the early stage in marketing tech, sales force automation, and enterprise collaboration space whereas these factors do impact the valuation of companies in In-stores retail tech.

The investment decision is not only decided based on sectoral performance but influenced by forward and backward-looking trends as SaaS is such a model which can monetize from delivered services as software.

Marketing tech and In-stores retail tech are likely to see growth as both are associated with catering and developing solutions for SMBs. Sales force automation is seeing adoptive trends and huge demand potential to cater to customers' spontaneous needs and tickets raised whereas collaboration space is likely to see rising demand because of Hybrid work culture and the need for standardization in terms of experience.

In the end, the ball is in VCs' court which will decide based on how earlier funds were used, competitor's scenario, less explored sector trends and market scenario, and standard parameters and were the companies able to keep up to the expectations or not and the relations with co-investors.

REFERENCES

1. Arpan Sheth, Aditya Shukla, Prabhav Kashyap, and Gustaf Ericson. (2021). Indian SaaS Report 2021. Mumbai: Bain & Company.
2. Chaudhary, L. a. ((2022)). Vertical SaaS. Mumbai: Blume Ventures.
3. Jadhav, B. (2022). Study of Perception and Use of Generic Medicine with Special Reference to Pradhan Mantri Bharatiya Janaushadhi Pariyojana. Journal of Pharmaceutical Negative Results, 13(9).
4. Pai and Vats. ((2022)). Indus Valley Annual Report. Mumbai: Blume Ventures.
5. Panda and Dash. ((2016)). Exploring the venture capitalist-entrepreneur relationship: evidence from India. Journal of Small business & Enterprise Development.
6. Sharma and Ahmad. (2022). Venture Capital Financing in India during Covid-19. EPRA International Journal of Multidisciplinary Research, 31–36.

7. Sheth et al. (2022). Indian Venture Capital Report 2022.

8. Swathi. ((2018)). Venture Capital Funding-Recent trends and challenges in India. Emperor International Journal of Finance and Management Research, 6.

9. Venkatesh Peddi, Tarang Mittal, Praveen Bhadada, Vaibhav Gupta, Vikram Godbole, Mathew Makkah. (2022). India SaaS-Punching through the Global pecking order. Banglore: Chiratae Ventures & Zinnov.

10. Yang and Cui. ((2021)). Modeling Investment Choice Preference of Government Venture Capital Guiding Funds. Hindawi Publications.

Note: All the tables in this chapter were made by the Authors.

*Advancements in Business for Integrating Diversity, and
Sustainability – Dimitrios A. Karras et al. (eds)*
© 2024 Taylor & Francis Group, London, ISBN 978-1-032-70828-7

Sustainable and Technology-Driven Solutions for Overcoming the Impact of Energy Consumption and Pollution on Consumer's Health

Renuka Deshmukh
Assistant Professor, Faculty of Management,
MIT World Peace University, Pune, India

Babasaheb Jadhav*
Associate Professor, Global Business School & Research Centre,
Dr. D. Y. Patil Vidyapeeth, Pune, India

Pragati Hiwarkar
Mentor, NKC Inurture, Mumbai, India

Sangjukta Halder
Assistant Professor, Shree L. R. Tiwari Degree College of Arts,
Commerce and Science, Mumbai, India

Abstract: The objective of the study is to evaluate the relationship between the use of renewable energy, socioeconomic factors, and health using data from 18 Asian countries between 1990 and 2021 using the generalized method of moments estimation strategy. Asia has been found to have a higher prevalence of lung and respiratory diseases as a result of CO_2 emissions.

The results also demonstrate the magnitude of the impact that fossil fuel use and CO_2 emissions have on the rate of malnutrition and mortality. Furthermore, we discover that healthcare spending and GDP per capita may help to lower the ratio of mortality to undernourishment. The conclusion suggests launching swift energy transition initiatives, increasing energy efficiency, and reducing energy intensity to improve the national health security of developing Asian nations.

In this study, the effects of air pollution, as measured by particles with an aerodynamic diameter of less than 10 mm (PM10), on the variables affecting mental health and well-being are further investigated. A representative sample of N=3020 Indian adults was employed, with 54% of the sample being female and 46% of the sample being male. The participants' ages ranged from 18 to 92 (M=49.04, SD 17.27). According to multivariate linear regression models, less air pollution is linked to higher levels of life satisfaction, self-esteem, and stress tolerance (PM10). The individual's income, age, and gender were all taken into account in each regression model. PM10 and self-esteem were only significantly associated with women, gender-specific and

---

*Corresponding author: babasaheb.jadhav@dpu.edu.in

DOI: 10.4324/9781032708294-53

sub-analyses revealed similar results for PM10 and stress resistance. Relationships between mental health characteristics were examined in the representative Indian sample.

Keywords: Energy Consumption, Pollution, Consumers Health, Mental Health, Stress Resilience, Self-Esteem, etc.

1. Introduction

Energy use and national health security have been connected. The use of fossil fuels increases risks to human well-being, changing climate in the future, & other types of environmental harm.

India's production of coal and oil continued to fall, while its imports of oil increased. In all cities, the average level of environmental air quality was 78.8%. India's brisk economic expansion has been accompanied by significant environmental and energy issues. To promote sustainable growth, the Indian government has been developing policies to limit energy use.

At the 2020 Climate Ambition Summit, India likewise promised a reduction in the carbon intensity of more than 65% from 2005 to 2030. To assist in achieving these goals, India has put in place several emission reduction policies, but there is still significant pressure to cut carbon emissions.

2. Research Methods & Model Specifications

Research Objectives

1. To evaluate the association between energy consumption & health problems from the database of 20 developing countries.
2. To examine the correlation between air pollution and mental health.
3. To explore emerging technologies and sustainable solutions for curbing air contamination in India.

For Attaining Objective 1 - The study has used secondary data. The principal component analysis (PCA) technique was used to break down the four selected dependent health variables into two constituents: lung and respiratory illnesses, and under and malnutrition and death ratio. Further based on the two constituents LRD & UDR, the author finalized two prototypes, which are put forth below.

Table 53.1 Principle component analysis method outcome

Constituent	Original Eigenvalues			Sums of Squared Loadings		
	Total	% of Deviation	Accumulative %	Total	% of Deviation	Accumulative %
1	2.640	46.671	54.871	1.741	44.650	46.850
2	1.221	31.349	74.879	1.320	31.349	76.887
3	.638	14.322	86.337			
4	.520	10.681	99.000			

Source: Made by Author

Table 53.2 Principle Component Analysis

	Constituent	
	I	II
Variable 1	–.538	–.689
Variable 2	–.370	.747
Variable 3	.947	–.069
Variable 4	834	–.087

Source: Made by Author

In addition to setting up the dependent variables, the study also selects explanatory variables namely, Variable 5-CO_2 releases, Variable 6-fossil fuel consumption, Variable 7-GDP, Variable 8-health care spending per capita, and Variable 9-Metropolitan inhabitant's evolution. The above data was collected from secondary sources from databases across 20 developing nations.

Table 53.3 Descriptive data of the selected Attributes

Attributes	Component	Observation	Mean	SD	Maximum	Minimum
Tracheal Lung Cancer	%	550	1.146	2.65	1.645	0.0023
Respiratory Diseases	Demises	550	189,435	5.8	352,912	8,093
Undernourishment	%	550	22.4	46.58	18.18	22.04
Death Ratio	%	550	20.19	44.03	38.57	11.03
CO_2 releases	Metric tons per capita	550	9.19	14.15	23.83	6.12
Fossil petroleum usage	%	580	94.27	131.27	100	24.55
Gross Domestic Product	Present US Dollar	580	6,848.68	2,201.82	22,126.56	52.35
Metropolitan inhabitants	%	580	32.30	52.25	25.65	2.64
Well-being outlay	Current US$	580	526.85	2,723.44	2,824.81	43.80

Source: Made by Author

For Attaining Objective 2: The research model is developed and the hypothesis framed is put forth. A demonstrative sample of 300 Indian adults was used to get at outcomes, multivariate linear regression analysis was employed.

Statistical Procedure: To determine how air pollution PM10 will affect factors that contribute to subjective mental well-being, multivariate linear regressions were computed. Regression analysis and t-statistics were determined.

3. Results and Discussions

For objective 1: Empirical Outcomes for the Energy Consumption, Air Contamination & Well-being Connection: A Panel Data Analysis - Variance Inflation Factor and Hausman tests were conducted.

Table 53.4 Variance inflation factor and Hausman assessment outcome (Prototype I)

Samples	Independent attributes						
20 Developing countries	Lung & respiratory disorders	0.20	2.21	2.54	2.14	2.20	2.45
	CO_2 releases	1.14	--	2.22	2.30	2.25	2.65
	Fossil petroleum firewood usage	2.25	2.42	--	2.45	2.40	2.60
	Gross Domestic Product	2.30	2.42	2.55	–	2.38	2.42
	Metropolitan inhabitants growth	2.02	2.21	2.54	2.14	2.20	2.45
	Well-being related outlay	2.22	--	2.22	2.30	2.25	2.65
	Mean VIF	2.25	2.53	2.45	2.52	2.42	2.46
	Chi2(5)	42.32					

Source: Made by Author

Table 53.5 VIF and Hausman assessment outcome (Prototype II)

Samples	Independent Variables						
20 Developing countries	Lung & respiratory disorders	–	2.54	1.62	1.28	1.45	3.35
	CO2 releases	2.28	–	2.36	2.44	3.65	2.48
	Fossil petroleum firewood usage	2.52	2.54	–	2.38	3.26	2.38
	Gross Domestic Product	2.48	4.52	3.46	–	3.49	2.58
	Metropolitan inhabitants growth	2.25	2.35	2.45	2.34	–	2.25
	Well-being related outlay	2.35	2.25	2.36	2.38	3.52	--
	Mean VIF	2.38	2.39	2.48	2.35	2.38	2.39
	Chi2(5)	25.25					

Source: Made by Author

Table 53.6 Cross-segment reliance assessment outcomes

Samples	Attributes	CSD Assessment	Correlation	Abstract Correlation	Substantial at 1%
20 Developing countries	Lung & respiratory diseases	8.25	0.452	0.456	Yes
	Demises to malnutrition	9.28	0.514	0.521	Yes
	CO2 releases	12.02	0.481	0.481	Yes
	Fossil fuel consumption	7.32	0.587	0.577	Yes
	Gross domestic product	9.17	0.428	0.449	Yes
	Urban inhabitants growth	9.45	0.568	0.469	Yes
	Healthcare spending per person	9.27	0.586	0.560	Yes

Source: Made by Author

Table 53.7 Pesaran (2007) panel unit root assessment outcomes

Samples	Attributes	Exclusive inclination tendency	Inclusive inclination tendency
20 Developing Countries	Tracheal Lung Cancer	1.622	2.520
	Respiratory Diseases	1.594	2.530
	CO2 releases	1.536	−1.920
	Fossil Fuel Consumption	1.480	−1.820
	Gross Domestic Product	1.450	−1.840
	Urban Population Growth	1.560	−1.790
	Health Expenditure	1.650	1.590

Source: Made by Author

Table 53.8 Prediction outcome for prototype I (Dependent variable: Lung and respiratory disorders)

Descriptive Attributes	Constants	Substantial at 1%
Constant	0.20	Rejected
Carbon releases	1.85	Accepted
Fossil Fuel Petroleum and Firewood usage	1.48	Accepted
Gross Domestic Product	−0.21	Accepted
Metropolitan Inhabitants growth	0.65	Accepted
Well-being related to outlay	−0.52	Accepted
Total number of comments	580	
Category	1992–2020	
Total segments covered	30	
Chi2	725.40	Accepted

Source: Made by Author

Table 53.9 Prediction outcome for prototype I (Dependent variable: URD)

Descriptive Attributes	Constants	Substantial at 1%
Constant	1.40	Rejected
Carbon releases	2.35	Accepted
Fossil Fuel Petroleum and Firewood usage	2.25	Accepted
Gross Domestic Product	1.45	Accepted
Metropolitan Inhabitants growth	1.60	Accepted
Well −being related to outlay	1.40	Accepted
Total number of comments	580	
Category	1921–2021	
Total segments covered	40	
Chi2	825.40	Accepted

Source: Made by Author

For objective 2: Empirical results of the survey

Table 53.10 Regression analysis forecasting psychological well-being and welfare factors

Prototype/Attributes	Un-Uniform coefficient	Uniform regression coefficient	t-statistics	p-value	Adjusted R-square
Nervousness					0.018
Age	1.114 (0.00)	1.138	3.45	0.018*	
Revenue	0.072 (0.02)	1.258	−8.46	<0.005***	
PM_{10}	1.112 (0.00)	1.149	2.45	0.170	
Unhappiness					0.038
Age	1.014 (0.00)	1.25	2.45	<0.002	
Revenue	1.345 (0.02)	1.29	−7.25	<0.051*	
PM_{10}	1.118 (0.00)	1.68	2.18	0.372	
Stress resilience					**0.074**
Age	−1.65 (0.01)	1.69	−25.14	<0.021***	
Revenue	3.25 (0.20)	1.28	20.12	<0.003***	
PM_{10}	−1.68 (0.03)	−1.45	−2.44	<0.006***	
Life fulfillment					0.068
Age	−1.35 (0.04)	−1.25	−5.74	<0.002***	
Revenue	6.86 (0.72)	1.48	13.48	<0.001***	
PM_{10}	−1.56 (0.13)	−1.36	−3.80	0.011*	
Self-worth					0.034
Age	−1.24 (0.01)	−1.56	−2.48	0.254	
Revenue	2.45 (0.17)	1.78	8.50	<0.002***	
PM_{10}	−1.78 (0.03)	−1.98	−3.78	0.012*	

Source: Made by Author

Table 53.11 Regression analysis forecasting emotional well-being & welfare factors for men

Prototype/Attributes	Un-Uniform coefficient	Uniform regression coefficient	t-statistics	p-value	Adjusted R-square
Nervousness					0.009
Age	0.00 (0.00)	0.03	1.30	0.19	
Revenue	−0.11 (0.03)	−0.10	−3.68	<0.001***	
PM_{10}	−0.00 (0.00)	−0.00	−0.13	0.893	
Unhappiness					**0.028**
Age	0.00 (0.00)	0.01	0.44	0.658	
Revenue	−0.21 (0.03)	−0.17	−6.34	<0.001***	
PM_{10}	0.00 (0.00)	0.00	0.33	0.737	

Prototype/Attributes	Un-Uniform coefficient	Uniform regression coefficient	t-statistics	p-value	Adjusted R-square
Stress resilience					**0.085**
Age	−0.01 (0.01)	−0.18	−6.72	<0.001***	
Revenue	2.50 (0.28)	0.23	8.70	<0.001***	
PM$_{10}$	−0.15 (0.05)	−0.07	−2.87	0.004**	
Life fulfillment					**0.124**
Age	−0.15 (0.05)	−0.07	−2.81	0.005**	
Revenue	2.01 (0.24)	0.22	8.34	<0.001***	
PM$_{10}$	−0.04 (0.04)	−0.02	−1.03	0.299	
Self-worth					**0.050**
Age	−0.00 (0.01)	−0.00	−0.22	0.826	
Revenue	2.01 (0.24)	0.22	8.34	<0.001***	
PM$_{10}$	−0.04 (0.04)	−0.02	−1.03	0.299	

Source: Made by Author

Table 53.12 Regression analysis predicting mental health & well-being factor for females

Model/variables	Un-Uniform coefficient	Uniform regression coefficient	t-statistics	p-value	Adjusted R-square
Nervousness					0.022
Age	0.02(0.01)	1.22	2.65	0.054	
Revenue	1.25 (0.04)	1.25	3.39	<0.002***	
PM$_{10}$	1.05 (0.01)	−1.04	2.78	0.050	
Unhappiness					**0.044**
Age	0.006 (0.01)	1.24	3.23	<0.002***	
Revenue	−0.25 (0.05)	1.28	2.22	<0.003***	
PM$_{10}$	0.02 (0.01)	1.05	2.00	0.258	
Stress resilience					0.092
Age	0.24 (0.02)	2.15	8.24	<0.002***	
Revenue	2.89 (0.40)	1.24	6.86	<0.001***	
PM$_{10}$	1.24 (0.04)	1.08	3.68	0.001*	
Life fulfillment					
Age	0.36 (0.04)	2.48	3.45	<0.011***	
Revenue	3.86 (2.20)	1.25	3.45	0.12*	
PM$_{10}$	1.22 (0.22)	2.56	1.12	0.17	
Self-worth					0.008
Age	1.42 (0.02)	−1.05	−0.25	0.082	
Revenue	1.62 (0.28)	1.24	3.97	0.003**	
PM$_{10}$	1.02 (0.03)	−1.08	−1.15	0.033*	

Source: Made by Author

Dependent variables include stress resilience, sadness, anxiety, life satisfaction, and self-worth. 10 g/m^3 of PM10 particulate matter

4. Conclusion and Implications

Based on the findings, we have concluded that rising lung and respiratory disorders are a result of rising CO_2 emissions in Asian countries. Furthermore, the estimation has shown that the use of fossil fuels promotes lung & respiratory conditions. In Asian countries, we discovered a substantial correlation between the growth of the urban population and the rise in lung and respiratory disorders. The findings have shown how rising levels of undernourishment and mortality are a result of CO_2 emissions and fuel consumption.

Therefore, advise developing nations to implement various policies to enhance the energy transition, which calls for a switch from fossil fuel to renewable energy sources. The use of fossil fuel energy results in the destruction of human habitats and the growth of deadly diseases like cancer. It is strongly advised that urban lifestyles be improved, which may result in better human health in cities.

The present study's data collection, which included subjective psychological characteristics and was linked with accurate pollution data, is a key strength (PM10).

The study reveals correlations between mental health indicators and air pollution. Poor air quality affects a significant portion of Indians because the country has not yet attained WHO air quality guidelines.

REFERENCES

1. Alper A, (2016) Environmental Kuznets curve hypothesis for sub-elements of the carbon emissions in India. Nature Hazards 82(2).
2. Binti H (2012) FDI, growth and the environment: impact on quality of life in Malaysia. Procedia Soc Behav Sci 50.
3. Pinar M, Stengos T (2020) Renewable energy consumption and economic growth nexus: evidence from a threshold model. Energy Policy.
4. Huang Z (2021), Regional low carbon development pathways for the Yangtze River Delta region in China. Energy Policy.
4. Ming Z (2021) Provincial comparison and factor decomposition of energy carbon emissions in eastern China. Contemporary economic management.
5. Makridakis S (2017) The forthcoming artificial intelligence revolution: Its impact on society and firms. Futures 90:46–60.
6. Jadhav, B. (2022). Psychological Resilience- A Conceptual Framework. Nova Science Publisher, USA
7. Chen C, Pinar M, Stengos T (2020) Renewable energy consumption and economic growth nexus: evidence from a threshold model.
8. Elmorsy SS (2015) Determinants of trade intensity of Egypt with COMESA countries. Journal of Global South.
9. Yuan S, Musibau HO, Genç SY, Shaheen R, Ameen A, Tan Z (2021) Digitalization of the economy is the key factor behind the fourth industrial revolution: how G7 countries overcoming the financing issues?
10. Zambrono-Monserrate MA, Fernandez MA (2017) An environmental Kuznets curve for N2O emissions in Germany: an ARDL approach.

Advancements in Business for Integrating Diversity, and
Sustainability – Dimitrios A. Karras et al. (eds)
© 2024 Taylor & Francis Group, London, ISBN 978-1-032-70828-7

54 Study of Prospects of Pre- and Post-Pandemic Transnational Mergers and Acquisitions in India

Babasaheb Jadhav*

Associate Professor, Global Business School & Research Centre,
Dr. D. Y. Patil Vidyapeeth, Pune, India

Nilesh Limbore

Assistant Professor, Sharadchandra Pawar Institute of
Management & Research, Pune, India

Dhanashri Havale

Associate Professor, Global Business School & Research Centre,
Dr. D. Y. Patil Vidyapeeth, Pune, India

Ashish Kulkarni

Associate Professor,
Dr. D. Y. Patil B-School, Pune, India

Abstract: Purpose: Covid-19 has caused business disruption across the globe. The significant aim of this research was to examine the impact assessment of pre and post-Covid-19 pandemics on mergers & acquisitions concerning Indian Corporates.

Methodology: The measurement and evaluation of the impact assessment of the pre- and post-Covid-19 pandemic on mergers & acquisitions concerning Indian corporates have been studied from the year 2012 onwards. Statistical techniques such as Levene's t-test, factor analysis, correlation, KMO, etc. were used for testing the hypothesis.

Findings: As per the factor analysis, FDI outflows from India are significantly loaded on factor 3 while the total number of transnational mergers & acquisitions in India by sellers and the value of transnational mergers & acquisitions in India by sellers are significantly loaded on Factor 2.

Keywords: Covid-19 disruptions, Covid-19 pandemic, Pre- and Post-Covid-19 Impact Assessment, Mergers & Acquisitions, Indian businesses, Corporates, Markets, Indian Economy, etc.

*Corresponding author: babasaheb.jadhav@dpu.edu.in

DOI: 10.4324/9781032708294-54

1. Introduction

Global transnational mergers & acquisitions deals hit a new high in the year 2021 and broke the prior records with a huge difference. The No. of announced mergers & acquisitions deals exceeded 62,000 globally in the year 2021. It was observed that a 24% rise in mergers & acquisitions deals as compared with the last year 2020.

It is seen that mergers & acquisitions activities are always high in India. The pandemic has created a global impact on corporate mergers & acquisitions. On a larger scale and in a very short period, hundreds of businesses have closed down or stopped their significant operations, lakhs of workers have been terminated or laid off, consumers spending has drastically declined, logistics and supply chains networks have been disturbed, demand for health care products, oil, and energy resources has dramatically increased.

Meaning of Mergers: It refers to a combination of two or more companies into one company. In legal jargon, mergers are also referred to as Amalgamation.

The recent examples of mergers in India are Vodaphone and Idea, Housing.com and Proptiger.com, Tata Steel and ThyssenKrupp, Flipkart and E-Bay India, etc.

Meaning of Acquisitions: The acquisition is the purchase by one company over another company by governing its interest in the share capital, assets, and liabilities.

The recent examples of acquisitions in India are Zomato and Uber Eat, LIC and IDBI Bank, Tata Steel and Bhushan Steel, Walmart, and Flipkart, ONGC, and HPCL, etc.

2. Review of Literature

Kooli, C. stated the influence of the Pandemic on Corporates. The study further investigated the impact of global mergers and acquisitions and restructurings.

Natika Poddar evaluated the impact assessment of companies by comparing the pre and post-merger by using ratios and paired t-tests.

Harpreet Singh Bedi explored the new trends of M&A in India and explored the growth factors of the growth of M&A in India.

Upendrabhai Pandya tried to measure the M&A in India. The study categorized the trends of M&A and the prospective future of India.

Rabi Narayan Kar and Amit Soni highlighted M&A as a strategic plan to boost business value. They analyzed the impact of M&A on the economy.

Agnihotri investigated and analyzed the determinants of M&A in India and their significant impact on M&A.

3. Methodology

Purpose of Research: The study aimed to find, compare and analyze M&A in India pre and post-pandemic.

Objectives of Research: The significant objectives are enlisted below:

   a) To study and analyze the M&A of Indian Corporates.

   b) To study the post-pandemic prospectus for M&A of Indian Corporates.

   c) To evaluate and analyze the trend of M&A of Indian Corporates pre and post-pandemic.

Scope of Research: The scope of the research was M&A of Indian Corporates from 2012 to 2021.

Research Design

Types of Data: The study was based upon secondary data of mergers and acquisitions of Indian Corporates pre and post Pandemic.

Sources of Data: Authenticate data were gathered from journals, the internet, and government websites.

Data Presentation Tools: Tables and graphical representations were used for data presentation and analysis.

Hypothesis Testing: Statistical tools such as standard deviation, t-test, factor analysis, correlation, KMO, variances, etc. were used for hypothesis testing.

Statistical Software and techniques used for Analysis: SPSS was used for the analysis and testing of the hypothesis.

Data Analysis, Results & Testing of Hypothesis

Table 54.1 Factor Analysis

Descriptive Statistics[a]			
	Mean	S	N
No. of M&A in India by Purchasers	58.9000	13.62555	10
GDP	5.4900	4.50196	10
No. of M&A in India by Sellers	133.1000	12.55610	10
Value M&A in India by Purchasers	3227.1900	2760.00978	10
Value M&A in India by Sellers	13076.3200	11023.00541	10
FDI Inflows	41694.7600	11275.73228	10
FDI Outflows	9695.5700	4068.46223	10

Results: From the table of descriptive statistics, the average number of transnational M&A in India by purchasers is 58.9 and the standard deviation is 13.62. Similarly, the average GDP is 5.49 and the standard deviation is 4.50.

Table 54.2 Correlation Matrix[a,b]

		No. of M&A in by Purchasers	GDP	No. of M&A in India by Sellers	Value of M&A by Purchasers	Value of M&A by Sellers	FDI Inflows	FDI Outflows
Correlation	No. of M&A in India by Purchasers	1.000	.601	−.163	.377	−.168	−.380	−.220
	GDP	.601	1.000	.455	−.123	−.492	−.635	−.130
	No. of M&A in India by Sellers	−.163	.455	1.000	.043	−.405	−.277	−.039
	Value of M&A by Purchasers	.377	−.123	.043	1.000	−.185	.000	−.228
	Value of M&A by Sellers	−.168	−.492	−.405	−.185	1.000	.534	.407
	FDI Inflows	−.380	−.635	−.277	.000	.534	1.000	.423
	FDI Outflows	−.220	−.130	−.039	−.228	.407	.423	1.000

Results: The analysis of the correlation coefficient showed that the principal diagonal is the same for factors.

Table 54.3 KMO and bartlett's test[a]

Kaiser-Meyer-Olkin Sampling Adeq.		0.421
Bartlett's Test of Sphericity	Chi-Square	23.332
	df	21
	Sig.	0.027

Results: The researcher saw that the Test of Sphericity is significant i.e. 0.027. Sig. Value or significance value is less than 0.05 then the researcher may reject the null hypothesis.

Table 54.4 Commonalities[a]

	Initial	Extraction
No. of M&A in India by Purchasers	1.000	.942
GDP	1.000	.938
No. of M&A in India by Sellers	1.000	.715
Value of M&A in India by Purchasers	1.000	.708
Value of M&A in India by Sellers	1.000	.726
FDI Inflows	1.000	.700
FDI Outflows	1.000	.582

Results: From the analysis, commonalities, and variance have been accounted for extracted factors. 94.2 % of the variance in

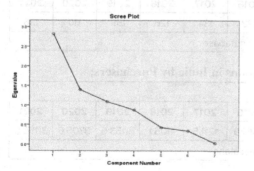

Fig. 54.1 Plot chart

"the number of transnational M&A in India by Purchasers" is accounted for, while 71.5 % of the variance in the "no. of transnational M&A in India by Sellers" is accounted for.

Results: In the Fig. 54.1, the researcher observed that the curve is flattening from factors 3 and 4. Also here researcher observed that the eigenvalue from factor 4 is less than 1 that's why only 3 factors were retained.

Table 54.5 Component Matrix[a,b]

	Component		
	1	2	3
No. of M&A in India by Purchasers	−.582	.580	.517
GDP	−.824		
No. of M&A in India by Sellers		−.616	
Value of M&A in India by Purchasers		.692	
Value of M&A in India by Sellers	.762		
FDI Inflows	.825		
FDI Outflows	.528		

Results: The table represents loadings that are less than 0.5, this makes the reading of the table easier.

Table 54.6 Rotated Component Matrix[a,b]

	Component		
	1	2	3
No. of M&A in India by Purchasers	.870		
GDP	.852		
No. of M&A in India by Sellers		−.841	
Value of M&A in India by Purchasers			−.832
Value of M&A in India by Sellers		.704	
FDI Inflows	−.658		
FDI Outflows			.687

Results: The value of transnational M&A by Purchasers and FDI Outflows is significantly loaded on Factor 3 while the number of transnational M&A by Sellers and the Value of transnational M&A by Sellers is significantly loaded on Factor 2.

4. Conclusion

Owing to the Amid Covid-19 pandemic challenges, corporate mergers and acquisitions have undergone a phenomenal change, which has created ample growth opportunities for M&A deals not only in India but also at the global level.

Now a day's, M&A are reflected as significant change agents, growth opportunities, and important components of business restructuring and strategies. As per the factor analysis the value of transnational M&A in India by Purchasers.

FDI from India is significantly loaded on Factor 3 while the number of M&A by Sellers and the Value of M&A purchasers are significantly loaded on Factor 2.

DATA TABLES:

1. GDP Growth in India

Annual Percentage Growth										
Economy	2012	2013	2014	2015	2016	2017	2018	2019	2020	2021
India	5.5	6.4	7.4	8.0	8.3	6.8	6.5	3.7	−6.6	8.9
Source: World Bank database										

2. No. of Transnational Mergers & Acquisitions in India by Purchasers:

No. of deals										
Economy	2012	2013	2014	2015	2016	2017	2018	2019	2020	2021
India	67	49	60	54	87	67	63	43	40	59
Source: UNCTAD transnational mergers & acquisitions database										

3. No. of Transnational Mergers & Acquisitions in India by Sellers:

No. of deals										
Economy	2012	2013	2014	2015	2016	2017	2018	2019	2020	2021
India	133	142	125	139	128	134	126	158	110	136
Source: UNCTAD transnational mergers & acquisitions database										

4. Value of Transnational Mergers & Acquisitions in India by Purchasers:

Million US Dollar										
Economy	2012	2013	2014	2015	2016	2017	2018	2019	2020	2021
India	6281.7	2988.4	1021.2	−612.5	8461.9	1211.5	1105.1	5053.5	3705.6	3055.5
Source: UNCTAD transnational mergers & acquisitions database										

5. Value of Transnational Mergers & Acquisitions in India by Sellers:

Million US Dollar										
Economy	2012	2013	2014	2015	2016	2017	2018	2019	2020	2021
India	2805.2	4644.3	7857.5	1323.4	7958.0	22762.6	33178.3	14887	27211.3	8135.6
Source: UNCTAD transnational mergers & acquisitions database										

6. FDI Inflows in India:

Million US Dollar										
Economy	2012	2013	2014	2015	2016	2017	2018	2019	2020	2021
India	24195.8	28199.4	34582.1	44064.1	44480.6	39903.8	42156.2	50558.3	64072.2	44735.1
Source: UNCTAD FDI database										

7. FDI Outflows from India:

Million US Dollar										
Economy	2012	2013	2014	2015	2016	2017	2018	2019	2020	2021
India	8485.7	1678.7	11783.5	7572.4	5072.4	11140.5	11446.9	13144.1	11109.2	15522.3
Source: UNCTAD FDI database										

REFERENCES

1. Kooli, C., (2021). Impact of COVID-19 on M&A and Corporate Restructurings.
2. Macmillan, I.; Purowitz, M., (2021). M&A, and Covid-19: Charting New Horizons. Deloitte.
3. Jadhav, B. (2014). FDI: A Growth Perspective from India. Research Journal of Social Science & Management.
4. Seetharaman, P. Business models shift: Impact of Covid-19. International Journal of Information Management. 2020.
5. Poddar, N. (2019). A Study on M&A in India and Its Impact on the Operating Efficiency of Indian Acquiring Company.
6. Ekaterina A. Degtereva, and Alexander M. Zobov. (2021). The Impact of the COVID-19 Pandemic on Cross-Border M&A Determinants.
7. Jadhav, B. (2020). The Study of Direction of India's BOP and BOT Position. The Journal of Indian Management, 10(2).

Note: All the numbered figures and tables in the chapter were made by the Authors.

Advancements in Business for Integrating Diversity, and
Sustainability – Dimitrios A. Karras et al. (eds)
© 2024 Taylor & Francis Group, London, ISBN 978-1-032-70828-7

55 Transitions and Developments in Indian Aviation Industry (2022)

Ravi Phadke

Assistant Professor, Bharati Vidyapeeth,
Centre for Distance and Online Education, Pune, India

Babasaheb Jadhav*

Associate Professor, Global Business School & Research Centre,
Dr. D. Y. Patil Vidyapeeth, Pune, India

Sonali Dharmadhikari

Asociate Professor, Bharati Vidyapeeth,
Institute of Management & Entrepreneurship Development, Pune, India

Ameya Lonkar

Research Scholar, Bharati Vidyapeeth,
Institute of Management and Entrepreneurship Development, Pune, India

Abstract: The aviation sector is considered to be one of the most dynamic sectors in the Indian economy. The speed at which the industry is changing is unprecedented. In the last 2 decades, the industry has seen the expansion of the aviation sector like never in the history of independent India. The industry experienced changes in the capacities, technology, number of passengers, business models, the role of government, strategic alliances, etc. The industry has responded to every single environmental change happening in the economy and has seen its effects, both positive and negative, immediately after the implantation of strategies. It was therefore required to conduct a comprehensive study that will encompass all the changes in the aviation environment in India and will lead to brainstorming and a better understanding of the same.

This case presents the transitions and developments in the Indian aviation sector to initiate the discussion on the topic of the Business Environment.

Keywords: Civil aviation, Low cost, Full service, Environment, Sustainability, etc.

*Corresponding author: babasaheb.jadhav@dpu.edu.in

DOI: 10.4324/9781032708294-55

1. Introduction

Indian aviation sector changed dramatically post-1991. As soon as the sector was opened for the private sector, the companies started implementing diverse and innovative strategies. Post liberalization, the aviation space went through testing different business models, different offerings, and different customer expectations. The sector experienced all the methods of strategic alliances including partnerships, acquisitions, joint ventures, and liquidation. Despite all these factors, the Indian market is considered to be the most lucrative for the aviation industry and the most attractive destination for investment (See Table 55.1 for Performance of India's Service Sector).

2. Recent Developments in Indian Aviation

Regulatory Changes: In the last few years, the growth in the aviation sector in India has resulted in making the Indian domestic aviation market the third largest in the world. It is expected that India overtakes the UK to become the world's third-largest in air passenger space (IBEF, 2022). The government of India lifted the FDI Cap for Domestic Scheduled Passenger Airlines to 100% out of which, up to 49% was through the automatic route while above 49% it will be through the clearances from the government of India (See Table 55.2).

New Airlines in India: Foreign airlines have entered the Indian aviation space with joint ownership with an Indian partner. Malaysian budget airline AirAsia entered India with a Joint venture with Tata Sons. The company established itself as AirAsia India headquartered in Bengaluru and commenced its operations in the year 2014.

Similarly, Singapore Airlines also entered the Indian aviation market by entering into a joint venture with Tata Group.

Operating Challenges: These are not the only challenges before the airlines today in India. Companies today are fighting on all fronts for meeting the challenges.

Cost of Operations: The operating cost of an airline has risen considering the rise in fuel prices, tax rates, landing charges, and increased cost of MRO activities. The government is adding to the challenges faced by air service providers. Though efforts taken to improve the infrastructure base to support the aviation sector, the privatization of two major Airports, Mumbai and Delhi, has brought new challenges to operating Airline companies in these cities. Companies have to pay the maximum charges to operate at these busy Airports. The cost of maintaining the ground staff, the parking space, and the space required to perform all the pre-travel activities including the check-in procedure, baggage, security checks, sales and marketing, ticketing, etc. has shot up (See Table 55.3 for Profit/Loss made by major airlines in India).

Challenges on the Procurement side: Some other challenges for the aviation industry today include some from the procurement side. Procuring resources like fuel, equipment including aircraft, and human resources have also become costly (See Fig. 55.3 for changes in Fuel prices). The rupee has depreciated to almost 20% in a very short period. All the procurements have to be done in Dollar terms. This has made all the procurements costly. Not only aircraft but hiring people, including on-board and ground staff, engineering contracts, the space occupied by the companies in the airports, and most important, Aviation Fuel, have become the focus of reducing costs. In an interview

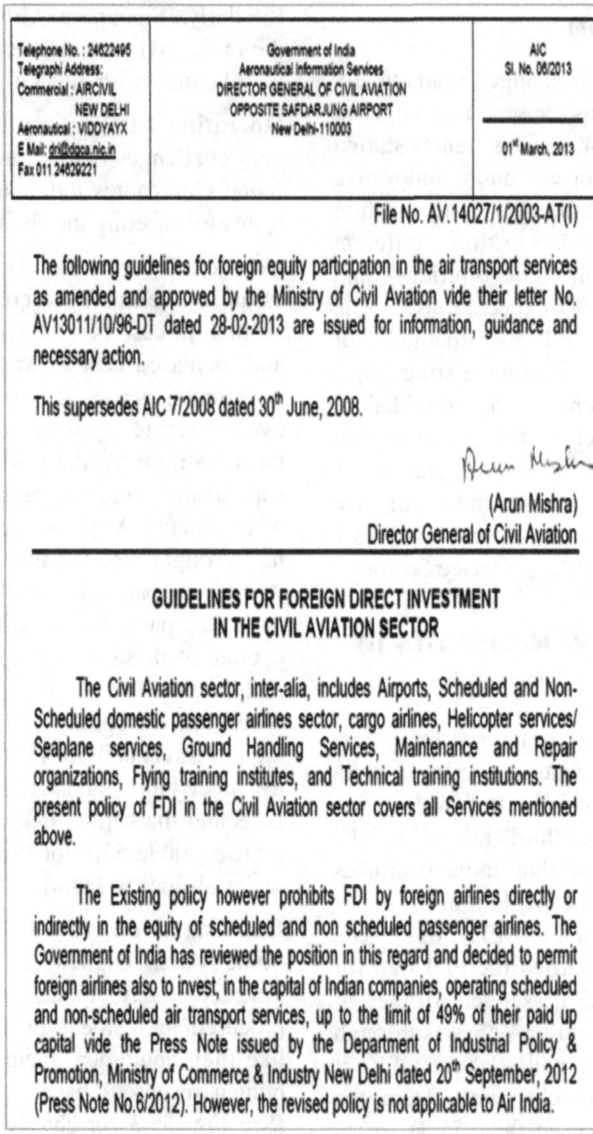

| Telephone No. : 24822495
Telegraphi Address:
Commercial : AIRCIVIL
NEW DELHI
Aeronautical : VIDDYAYX
E Mail: dri@dgca.nic.in
Fax 011 24629221 | Government of India
Aeronautical Information Services
DIRECTOR GENERAL OF CIVIL AVIATION
OPPOSITE SAFDARJUNG AIRPORT
New Delhi-110003 | AIC
Sl. No. 06/2013

01ˢᵗ March, 2013 |

File No. AV.14027/1/2003-AT(I)

The following guidelines for foreign equity participation in the air transport services as amended and approved by the Ministry of Civil Aviation vide their letter No. AV13011/10/96-DT dated 28-02-2013 are issued for information, guidance and necessary action.

This supersedes AIC 7/2008 dated 30ᵗʰ June, 2008.

(Arun Mishra)
Director General of Civil Aviation

**GUIDELINES FOR FOREIGN DIRECT INVESTMENT
IN THE CIVIL AVIATION SECTOR**

The Civil Aviation sector, inter-alia, includes Airports, Scheduled and Non-Scheduled domestic passenger airlines sector, cargo airlines, Helicopter services/ Seaplane services, Ground Handling Services, Maintenance and Repair organizations, Flying training institutes, and Technical training institutions. The present policy of FDI in the Civil Aviation sector covers all Services mentioned above.

The Existing policy however prohibits FDI by foreign airlines directly or indirectly in the equity of scheduled and non scheduled passenger airlines. The Government of India has reviewed the position in this regard and decided to permit foreign airlines also to invest, in the capital of Indian companies, operating scheduled and non-scheduled air transport services, up to the limit of 49% of their paid up capital vide the Press Note issued by the Department of Industrial Policy & Promotion, Ministry of Commerce & Industry New Delhi dated 20ᵗʰ September, 2012 (Press Note No.6/2012). However, the revised policy is not applicable to Air India.

Fig. 55.1   Changes in the FDI norms in the civil aviation sector (2014)

Source: DGCA, dgca.nic.in

given by JET Airways CEO Nikos Kardassis to INSEAD (Kardassis, 2012), he discussed the cost control measures adopted by Jet Airways to fight the competitive environment today. He said that Jet has stopped hiring since Aug 2011. The companies have started adopted taking various cost control measures to manage the cost of operating. Some of these cost measures include negotiation with the existing engineering and maintenance contracts, reduction in the space occupied by Airports, no fresh recruitments, etc.

Table 55.1 Performance of India's Service Sector

Sector	Indicators	Unit	Period														
			2008-09	2009-10	2010-11	2011-12	2012-13	2014-15	2015-16	2016-17	2017-18	2018-19	2019-20	2020-21	2021-22
Aviation	Airline Passengers	Million	49.5	54.5	64.5	70.2	67.5	115.8	135.0	158.4	183.9	344.7	340.9	115.7	106.5
Telecom	Telecom connections	Millions	4297.25**	4297.25**	8436.2**	9513.4**	8955.1**	1,252.80**	1,356.30	1,571.10	1,656.10	1,744.60	1,878.60	1,980.30	1,990.90*
Tourism	Foreign Tourists Arrivals	Million	5.28	5.17	5.78	6.31	6.65	7.8	8.2	9.1	10.0	10.6	10.9	2.74#	
	Tourist Foreign Exchange	US$ Million	11832	11136	14193	16564	17737	20.4	21.4	23.8	27.3	28.6	30.1	6.96#	-
Shipping	Gross Shipping	Million GT	9.28	9.69	10.45	11.06	10.45	10.5	10.9	11.6	12.6	12.8	12.7	13	12.96##
	No. of ships	Numbers	925	1003	1071	1122	1158	1210.0	1273	1316	1382	1405	1431	1463	1488##

*Forecasted figures, **Wireless and Wired Telephones (in Lakhs), #As of June 2021, ##As on Aug 2021

Sources: DGCA

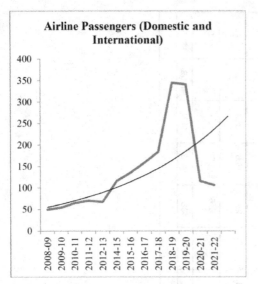

Fig. 55.2 Trend of airline passengers in India

Source: DGCA

Table 55.2 Change in FDI limit for scheduled air transport service as per FDI policy (2017)

Sector/Activity	% of Equity/ FDI Cap	Entry Route
(1) (a) Scheduled Air Transport Service/ Domestic Scheduled Passenger Airline (b) Regional Air Transport Service	100%	Automatic up to 49% (Automatic up to 100% for NRIs) Government route beyond 49%
(2)Non-Scheduled Air Transport Services	100%	Automatic

Source: DIPP

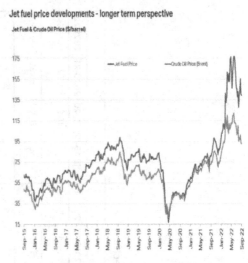

Fig. 55.3 Trend of jet fuel prices

Source: S&P Global

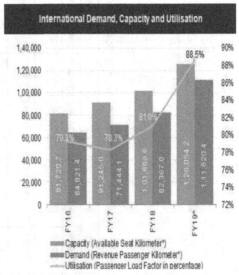

Fig. 55.4 Snapshot of Indian aviation - international demand, capacity, and utilization

Source: dgca.nic.in

Table 55.3 Comparison of profit after Tax (Rs. Millions)

Particulars	Mar-11	Mar-12	Mar-13	Mar-14	Mar-15	Mar-16	Mar-17	Mar-18	Mar-19	Mar-20	Mar-21	Mar-22
Jet Airways	10	-1,236	-486	-3,668	-1,814	1,174	1,483	-768	-5,536	-2,841	-152	-773
SpiceJet	101	-606	-191	-1,003	-687	450	431	567	-316	-935	-998	-1,725
Go Air	-	-	-	-	-	-	205.25	294.88	123.34	-1278.6	-	-
Indigo	1,203	-1,062	496	-871	-2,844	-1,195	-620	-1,147	-3,174	-1,436	130	-1,682
Air Asia	-	-	-	-	-	-	-	-	-	-	-3.3757566	-
Air India				-	-	-	-	-	-8556.36	-7982.82	-7083.91	-

Source: Compiled from CMIE

3. Conclusion

Indian aviation space is changing rapidly. Exposure to International environmental factors has brought a paradigm change in the sector. On one hand, new trends are being set, new business models are being developed, new strategic alliances are taking place and new challenges are emerging, whereas, on the other hand, the Indian middle class is increasing, leading to an increased number of passenger traffic. The entire industry is undergoing fundamental changes and hence it becomes very important to critically understand how businesses will sustain themselves in such a dynamic external environment.

REFERENCES

1. Airport Authority of India. (2011). AAI's tryst with Aviation.
2. Chakravarty, M. (2011). 100 Years of Civil Aviation in India - Milestones
3. Director General of Civil Aviation. (2013). Guidelines for Foreign Direct Investment in the Aviation sector
4. Kardassis, C. N. (2012). Indian Airline Industry. (I. K. Grace Segran, Interviewer)
5. Mehta, G. C. (2011). 100 Years of Aviation in India - Airport Authority of India
6. The Economic Times. (2022). Latest Infra News: Aviation.

Advancements in Business for Integrating Diversity, and
Sustainability – Dimitrios A. Karras et al. (eds)
© 2024 Taylor & Francis Group, London, ISBN 978-1-032-70828-7

56

Agro Tourism: An Opportunity to Doubling Farmer's Income

Dhanashri Havale*, Babasaheb Jadhav

Assistant Professor, Global Business School & Research Centre,
Dr. D. Y. Patil Vidyapeeth, Pune, India

Sphurti Birajdar

Assistant Professor, Department of Commerce,
College of Arts, Science and Commerce, Mumbai, India

Hrishikesh Kokate

Research Scholar, M.Sc. (Agri) Dept. of Agronomy,
G. H. Raisoni University, Nagpur, India

Abstract: **Purpose:** Agro-Tourism is well acknowledged as a locomotive of development in many economic sectors around the globe. It has emerged as one of the world's largest economies. Most countries have shifted their economies by mounting the agro-tourism industry. Agro-Tourism has countless potentials to create extensive employment, providing a supplementary source of income for the skilled and unskilled workforce.

This paper mainly focuses on the relationship between agro-tourism and the increasing income of the farmer.

Methodology: This research paper consists descriptive in nature and is based on primary data collected by interviewing Agro tourism owners in Maharashtra. Secondary data from various literature sources, websites of ATCs, various research papers, newspaper articles, and papers. The data is gathered from the website of the Government of India, Maharashtra, and the Ministry of Agriculture.

Findings: The study stated that there is a direct relationship between agro-tourism and doubling farmers' income. Various activities in agro-tourism make additional revenue for farmers and the revenue goes on increasing since 2017. Agro-tourism sector strengthens the farmers economically.

Originality Value: According to estimates by the WTTC, agro-tourism generates over US$5 trillion in output for his, which is about 8% of the global GDP. India's share in global tourism was just 4% in its Tourism Vision 2020. WTTO predicts that by 2023 there will be approximately 1.6 billion international tourists visiting every country in the world. According

*Corresponding author: dhanashri.havale@dpu.edu.in

DOI: 10.4324/9781032708294-56

to the same assessment, India is scheduled to refuel. India welcomes an escape from the hectic pace of daily life in the peaceful rural heart of, with great potential and potential for agritourism development.

Keywords: Agro-tourism, Farmer's income, Doubling income, Potentials opportunities, Indian economy, etc.

1. Introduction

The government's efforts to double the incomes of farmers have got very positive results. In this connection, the Government has announced in its April 2016 Inter-Ministerial Committee to consider issues related to "Double Farmer Income (DPI)" and to recommend strategies to achieve the same was installed. The commission submitted its final 14-volume report to the government in September 2018, outlining strategies to double the farmers' incomes through various policies, reforms, and programs. Agri-tourism brings agriculture closer to the working sector and gains more consideration for the improvement of local transport networks. India has previously established itself as one of the topmost travel destinations in the world. The added importance of the introduction of new products such as agritourism only strengthens the spirit of India. The advancement of tourism brings direct and indirect profits to people. 4,444 farmers have significant potential to generate 4,444 additional income streams and employment opportunities. Agritourism uses local culture as a tourist repulsion. It is the same as ecotourism, but its main attraction is the cultural landscape rather than the natural landscape. Agrotourism can promote local development if the provision of tourism contributes to increased income

for residents. For it to also contribute to the conservation of biodiversity, agricultural biodiversity must be documented by rural residents themselves as important and worthy of conservation. Agrotourism is known as "travel that binds agricultural or rural environments with agricultural products in a tourism and experience". It offers tourists the chance to experience genuine contact with the truly fascinating rural life, taste local and authentic cuisine and become acquainted with various agricultural practices during their visit.

2. Literature Review

Pawar, (2018) in his research paper stated that Agritourism is the well relevant key to promoting rural areas, and most people are busy with agricultural activities. This new concept of agritourism has come over the past years to establish the agricultural sector. Agri-tourism has great potential to generate extra income and employment opportunities for farmers.

ATDC studies conducted in 2014, 2015, and 2016 show that 400,000, 530,000, and 700,000 tourists visited agritourism centers, generating INR 35.79 million for farmers. increase. Jobs are also being created for females and the young in rural areas. Agri-tourism can create a wonderful environment for both farmers and tourists.

Ayala (1995) stated tourism enables the enjoyment and appreciation of the environment and culture. At the same time, it achieves a satisfying visitor experience and improves the living standards in the public (Lim & McAleer, 2005).

M. Sunitha's (2021) role of agrotourism in rural development in her research paper stated that Agritourism plays a major role in revitalizing rural areas. Its position and market power influence many external components and mechanisms. While positive impacts on economic and social development in rural areas are felt, many associated obstacles are also revealed. An important aspect is to raise community awareness of the benefits of developing this non-agricultural income source.

United Nation World Tourism Organization stated that Rural tourism is a key player in regional development due to its complementarity with other economic activities, its role in GDP and employment creation, its diversification of demand over time, and its ability to transcend social change. It has a high potential to stimulate economic growth.

Kharaishvili, Eter; Lazariashvili, Tamar; Natsvlishvili, Ia (2019) explained that the triumph of developing countries in strengthening agricultural production has a worldwide impact on strengthening food market resilience, bettering food security, improving well-being, and promoting sustainability. In addition to agriculture, the tourism sector generally has a good impact on production and production capacity, especially in poorer economies. Tourism has one of the most important levers for development and development-related forms in developing countries. However, such countries have many more political, institutional, and economic problems that should be resolved to break the catchy cycle of bareness and promote national prosperity.

3. Research Methods

This research paper consists of descriptive in nature. Based on primary data which is collected through interviewing Agro tourism owners in Maharashtra. Secondary data from various literature sources, websites of ATCs, various research papers, newspaper articles, and papers. The data was gathered from the website of the Government of India, Maharashtra, and the Ministry of Agriculture.

- Geographical scope: All districts and Talukas of the Maharashtra region
- Sample Size: 100
- Sample Unit: Agro-tourism owners
- Sampling Method: Random sampling method was used for interviewing agro-tourism owners
- Source of data: By interviewing agro-tourism owners in Maharashtra

Objectives

1) To examine the role of agro-tourism in the economic development of farmers.
2) To evaluate the need and significance of agro-tourism in doubling farmers' income.
3) To identify the potential opportunities and the limitations of agro-tourism.

Data Collection

Table 56.1   Agro- tourism Centers

Sr. No.	Name of ATCs	Location	Establishment Year	Operating Experience in Years
1	Jay Malhar Agri tourism Centre (JMAT)	Pune	2005	14
2	Silver Oak Agri tourism center (SOAT)	Nashik	2014	5
3	Tarapa agri tourism center (TAT)	Thane	2009	10
4	Rajput Agri tourism center (RAT)	Aurangabad	2011	8
5	Vednandini Agri tourism center (VAT)	Akola	2015	4
6	Mahajan vavar agri tourism center (MVAT)	Nagpur	2015	4

Source: https://savefarm.in

Table 56.2   Income of ATCs

(Figures in Rs)

Sr. No.	Particulars		JMAT	SOAT	TAT	RAT	VAT	MVAT	Average
1	No. of tourists arrived in a day	M	874	1708	318	134	1223	222	747
		F	833	1681	310	128	1170	226	725
		C/S	723	1632	182	112	914	228	631
	Total		2428 (50.00)	5024 (50.00)	812 (50.00)	371 (50.00)	3307 (50.00)	671 (61.66)	2504 (50.52)
	Total Income (Rs)	M	699100	1281100	254300	93700	1467500	144200	656718
		F	666400	1260650	248100	89500	1404100	146800	635941
		C/S	288700	571800	73100	38750	640400	80250	282232
	Total		1654400 (34.52)	3113650 (37.35)	575600 (34.60)	222250 (35.30)	3512100 (42.54)	371350 (45.18)	1574892 (38.57)
2	No. of tourists stayed at Night	M	874	1708	318	134	1223	149	734
		F	833	1681	310	128	1170	151	712
		C/S	722	1634	183	111	915	121	614
	Total		2429 (50.00)	5023 (50.00)	811 (50.00)	373 (50.00)	3308 (50.00)	421 (38.34)	2061 (49.48)
	Total Income (Night tourists stay)	M	1311100	2220300	477100	174100	1956700	193600	1055516
		F	1249400	2185200	465100	166300	1872100	196200	1022427
		C/S	577500	817100	146300	66500	915100	60400	430527
	Total		3138100 (65.48)	5222700 (62.65)	1088400 (65.40)	407200 (64.70)	4743800 (57.46)	450500 (54.82)	2508450 (61.43)
	Total of tourists (M+F+C/S)		4858 (100.00)	10046 (100.00)	1622 (100.00)	746 (100.00)	6616 (100.00)	1098 (100.00)	4164 (100.00)
	Total income (Rs) (M+F+C/S)		4792500 (100.00)	8336350 (100.00)	1664000 (100.00)	629450 (100.00)	8255900 (100.00)	821850 (100.00)	4083342 (100.00)

Source: https://www.agritourism.in

Table 56.3 Gross income of ATC

(Figures in Rs)

Sr. No.	Name of ATCs	Sources of Income			Total Income
		ATCs	Crop production	Livestock	
1	JMAT	4792500 (85.70)	800000 (14.30)	-- (0.00)	5592500 (100)
2	SOAT	8336350 (85.24)	1403000 (14.36)	40000 (0.40)	9779350 (100)
3	TAT	1664000 (83.53)	328200 (16.47)	-- (0.00)	1992200 (100)
4	RAT	629450 (67.87)	263000 (28.35)	35000 (3.78)	927450 (100)
5	VAT	8255900 (92.62)	658000 (7.38)	-- (0.00)	8913900 (100)
6	MVAT	821850 (87.72)	115000 (12.28)	-- (0.00)	936850 (100)
	Total	24500051 (87.04)	3567201 (12.67)	75100 (0.28)	28142250 (100)
	Average	4083341 (87.03)	594532 (12.65)	12400 (0.28)	4690375 (100)

Source: https://tourdefarm.in

Table 56.4 Number of Visitors

(Figures in Rs)

Sr. No	Name of ATCs	2017	2018	2019	2020	2021	2022
1	JMAT	1586	1687	1784	1987	2257	2489
2	SOAT	1423	1582	1655	2029	2173	2367
3	TAT	1655	1728	1985	2175	2219	2289
4	RAT	1247	1359	1685	1893	2029	2284
5	VAT	1365	1497	1671	1987	2157	2387
6	MVAT	1458	1567	1787	2027	2258	2478
	Total	8734	9420	10567	12098	13093	14294
	Average	1456	1570	1762	2016	2182	2383

Source: STAD and Official websites of ATC

Table 56.5 Income Earned

(Figures in Rs)

Sr. No.	Name of ATCs	2017	2018	2019	2020	2021	2022
1	JMAT	845600	1058400	1273900	1429400	1687500	1975100
2	SOAT	985600	1172300	1371200	1542900	1823400	2014700
3	TAT	724500	974120	1087600	1219700	1425900	1702900
4	RAT	942300	1126900	1317900	1539700	1639700	1945300
5	VAT	658400	715200	914700	1142300	1345800	1647800
6	MVAT	542300	725600	958700	1178500	1459700	1789200

Source: TAT and Official website of ATC

4. Results and Discussions

Income of ATC

The total outturn of ATC proprietors from various things such as ATC, crop and yield production, and animal husbandry has been calculated. The data shown in Table 5, stated that the total gross income of ATC was projected to be around Rs. 2,81,42,251 of which, a foremost share came from agritourism companies. 87.05% and 12.95% from these ATC crop production and ranching operations. The mean income of ATC from such agricultural activities is estimated at Rs. 46,90,370.

The data then analyzed showed that agritourism was the main source of outturn in 2018 for all these surveyed ATCs. Agriculture and animal husbandry are considered side businesses that make up a very large percentage of total income.

The prime purpose of establishing ATC farmers is to supplement or increase the income of farmers. The surveyed ATCs have been analyzed for their yearly income from various sources, including income/revenue.

The data presented in Table 56.2 demonstrate that ATC's income was calculated for his two categories of tourists. H. Income from daytime visitors to ATC and their overnight guests in 2018. 48,83,342, of which 38.57% is revenue from tourists who visit ATC during the day and 61.43% is from a guest who visits ATC at night. ATC, SOAT income from these two types of tourists in 2021 was Rs. 83,36,340 surveyed by ATC BGEM revenue of Rs. 82,55,800. In total, the number of day guests and tourists staying at ATC is 4164 per year, of which about 50.52% are day visitors and 49% are night visitors.

Economic Perspectives

Agro-tourism is the economic movement that happens when people combine travel with agricultural aftermath, duties, or experiences. Agro-tourism prospects rely on agriculture and related sectors. Agro-tourism turns out to be a foremost source of revenue for farmers and farm workers by generating improved employment opportunities and quality production. Other economic benefits are also brought to local transportation companies and others associated with their tourism activities.

Agro-tourism offers rural residents the opportunity to reward their products and services promptly and appropriately. It controls the immigration of village people to cities to find employment chances by creating job and agribusiness opportunities. It gives residents and farmers a substantial amount of revenue for their work and culture. Agro-tourism will have a good bearing on the understanding of wildlife, natural resources, ecology, wild plants, and the importance of their conservation concepts to domestic and international tourists as well as locals. Economic exploitation through a combination of traditional and advanced agricultural techniques. It is also expected that agro-tourism centers and tourist attractions will serve as potential sources of information for adapting and expanding new technological developments among residents and domestic and international tourists.

Potential Opportunities

India's tourism industry growing at 10.2%: Indian tourism industry growing at 10.2%. World Tourism Organization says the tourism industry is growing at 4% per annum, 10% in 2020. It is estimated that there will be greater than 100 million tourists. Visit his different regions of the globe. However, India's tourism industry is emerging at a rate of 10.2%, which is 2.5 times quicker than the global growth rate. The introduction of the agritourism concept will not only maintain the existing growth rate but also contribute to further growth through this added value.

India Makes Top 10 Travel Destinations List Worldwide: The added value from the introduction of new products such as agritourism will only increase the race of India's tourism industry in the world market.

India is home to diverse cultures and geographies: India has vast and limitless possibilities for the development of business because of agro-climatic conditions, a variety of crops, peoples, cultures, deserts, coastal systems, islands, and mountains.

Increase in unwilling tourists: Increase in tourists preferring non-urban tourist attractions Therefore, the inland villages have room to promote non-urban tourist attractions through the establishment of agritourism centers. I have. However, proper amenities and outreach are essential to facilitate such ATCs.

Government Initiatives: The five-year plan allocation increased from 526 million to 290 billion. The budget increase confirms the government's commitment. The six-fold increase in funding will be available for service provider capacity building, infrastructure creation, and outreach.

Constraints of the Agro Tourism

A survey of existing units reveals important aspects when considering agro-tourism, such as unclear definitions, as the agrotourism product consists of various components. Definitions must be approved at the national level. Agro-tourism destinations are not always good and may take place in remote localities. In such situations, lack of transportation and escort facilities, a lack of consciousness of potential benefits for farmers and tourists, a lack of basic information on how to finance such projects/entrepreneurs, and a market Such as a survey's lack of integration with the overall tourism economy is the main obstacle. Another bottleneck is the lack of coordination between mainstream tourism and agrotourism regarding the different elements that make up the local agro ecotourism industry.

Issues to be considered when promoting agro-tourism are Publicity, Transport, Accommodation, Farmer Capacity Building, Tourist Safety, etc.

Findings

1) Study stated that there is a direct relationship between agro-tourism and doubling farmers' income. Various activities in agro-tourism produce extra revenue for farmers.

2) The income goes on increasing since 2017. Agro-tourism strengthens the farmers economically.

3) Agro-tourism boosts the farmer's income and become a trend in India for many years.

4) Income of the farmers goes on increasing after starting agro-tourism as a side business. And now agro-tourism becomes their core income source.

5) Number of operating ATCs is increasing, and the Number of tourists or visitors visiting ATCs is increasing & through that profit of farmers is increasing.

6) Agro-tourism is a way to double farmers' income and helps in the socioeconomic development of farmers.

5. Conclusion

Indian agribusiness is facing declining profitability due to declining yields from agricultural production. The survival and stability of many farms are dependent on the ability of farmers to generate supplementary revenue from their existing agricultural activities. Agritourism is a scheme to encourage agricultural advances in India.

It is intended to educate policymakers and farmers about the nature of agritourist activities and how much they increase agricultural profitability. Over the years, farmers have taken over a lot of agritourism activities. To maximize farm-based agritourist appeal and produce more cash, they continue to adjust current activities in response to shifting market prospects. They also anticipate establishing new activities. Agritourist frequently maintains the health of farm youngsters. The growth of agritourists in India is compatible with previous and current government policies that support agriculture and is a logical step in the development of many agribusinesses.

Equally important, agritourism is a cultural complement to agricultural production. There is a great opportunity to promote the development of agritourism in the country through pre-emptive strategies and speculation of resources. This can reassure farmers interested in providing recreational and educational farming activities to the public. As such, agritourism is a surplus source of revenue for farmers and supports rural development to help the Indian economy.

REFERENCES

1. Singh, P. (2016). Identifying the potential of Agri-Tourism in India: Overriding challenges and recommend strategies, Volume 3, Issue 3, International Journal of Core Engineering & Management
2. Shores John N, (2008). Challenges of Agro Ecotourism, K. Suresh (Ed), Travel and Tourism Challenges and Opportunities, ICFAI University Press
3. Jadhav, B. (2022). Analytical Study of CSR Spending in Indian Banking. ECS Transactions, 107(1).
4. Singh, L., Gantait. M., Puri, G., and Swamy, A. (2018). Rural Tourism: Need, Scope and Challenges in Indian Context. Research Gate.
5. Singh, G. (2019). Potential and Growth Opportunities through Agri-Tourism: A study of Maharashtra and Punjab State, Vol 68, Issue 5, Our Heritage
6. Kumbhar, S. M. (2018). Agro Tourism: A Cash Crop for Farmers in Maharashtra, APRA Paper No. 25587.
7. Adriana, M. (2019). Environmental supply chain management in tourism: The case of large tour operators. Journal of Cleaner Production,
8. L. Makhana, (2018). Sustainable agro eco-tourism, Volume 4, Issue 1, Paripex - Indian Journal of Research.
9. P. Anujkumar, (2019). Farmer's development tourism, A Journal of Asia for Democracy and Development. Volume - IX. No-4.

Advancements in Business for Integrating Diversity, and Sustainability – Dimitrios A. Karras et al. (eds)
© 2024 Taylor & Francis Group, London, ISBN 978-1-032-70828-7

57

Study of Impact of Employer Branding on Employee Attraction and Retention in the Education Sector

Sphurti Birajdar, Dhanashri Havale*,
Babasaheb Jadhav, Komal Singh
Global Business School & Research Centre,
Dr. D. Y. Patil Vidyapeeth, Pune, India

Abstract: Purpose: This study aims to investigate how corporate branding affects recruiting and retaining talent, notably in the educational sector.

Methodology: A questionnaire is used for collecting data from employees currently working in educational institutions. A Questionnaire constitutes of demographic questions, questions on employer branding, influential factors with employers to attract new employees, retention and attraction policy, etc. To determine whether or not the hypothesized relationship between the variables holds a true picture a quantitative research design was used. Data was collected through a questionnaire consisting of 128 responses. Academic professionals including lecturers and administrative staff served as a unit of analysis. To measure the impact ANOVA was undertaken using SPSS version 26.

Findings: The result of this research highlights an employer branding development value and a factor of balanced work-life balance which has a favorable impact on retaining and attracting a critical talent pool.

Keywords: Employee retention, Employee attraction, Employer branding, Education sector, Employee engagement, etc.

1. Introduction

The pace of today's economic world & job market is unprecedented. Those aged 20–29 will decrease by 20% during the next decade; while workers aged 50–60 will increase by 25%. However, India is making rapid progress toward establishing itself as a major player in the international human capital market. According to a report by the Indian organization for technical education, about 25% of the global workforce will be Indian by 2025. This trend is likely to continue at least through the year 2040. In today's globalized

*Corresponding author: dhanashri.havale@dpu.edu.in

DOI: 10.4324/9781032708294-57

world, corporations are increasingly enlisting the help of governments in other nations to recruit & keep domestic workers.

Modern businesses increasingly employ branding as a strategic strategy to help them compete in today's complex marketplace. Branding is an integral aspect of HRM, serving both to recruit new employees & to encourage current workers to stay with the organization. Brands include the company's name, products, services, and unique log type. In other words, branding is all about making an effort to bring in new customers and keep the ones you already have. Human resource management's incorporation of the "employer brand" is a recent development. However, the phrase is commonly used to describe how businesses advertise their products and services to employees, interact with them, and keep them loyal. Many human resource managers in today's labour market use the umbrella of employer branding to coordinate their many employee recruiting & retention efforts.

In addition to attracting & retaining top talent, a company's ability to stand out as an employer thanks to its unique culture is a key competitive advantage that can be communicated through an Employer Branding plan.

Value of Branding

These businesses may benefit from a larger pool of applicants, which could result in better hires, and from enhanced employee loyalty, which has been related to higher levels of output. The diagram below illustrates a representation The diagram below illustrates a representation of what possible way employer branding affects the success of a firm.

Fig. 57.1 Model of employer branding
Source: Gaddam 2008, p. 47

Figure 57.1 shows how employer branding affects customer satisfaction & loyalty, which in turn leads to higher output through satisfied & loyal customers. Moreover, the brand image helps enhance an organization's internal atmosphere. The central idea is that if employees are happy, they will become advocates for the company and tell their friends and family about it. Mosley (2007) agrees, noting the correlations between employer brand, culture, loyalty, & productivity, all of which lead to happier customers because of more dedicated staff members.

Employer Branding

Ambler & Berrow (1996) originally developed the notion of "Employer Branding" whose definition is considered as " the package of operational, financial, and emotional support provided by occupation and acknowledged by the organization's employees." The following elements make up a well-rounded employer brand:

Interest Value: It evaluates the allure of a prospective employer in light of their responsibility to provide a workplace that encourages and supports innovation & creativity.

Economic Value: It predicts how much employees would be interested in working for a company that offered competitive salaries & profit sharing.

Application Value: It's a key factor in determining how appealing a place is that offers the chance to put knowledge into practice.

Social Value: An organization's or business's attractiveness is measured if they provide its employees with a pleasant place to work that fosters a sense of belonging and a reasonable level of civility amongst coworkers.

Dabirian et al. in the year 2017 extended the concept with additional two parameters, which are:

Work-Life Balance: It's a quality that indicates the staff has achieved a healthy equilibrium between their professional & personal lives, which in turn helps them to express their full potential in their jobs. The term "employee" undersells the value of employees. Remember that they are people outside of the workplace as well. Employees are more productive when they can maintain a healthy work-life balance.

Management Value: It claims that a firm's capacity to retain its employees depends on the quality of its management. Employees tend to stay or quit a firm less because of the company itself and more because of the attitude & behavior of their managers. Both good and bad managers have significant effects on their staff. Both a good & bad working connection with the employer can have an impact on an employee's personal life.

Rationale of study

Opportunity for businesses & workers alike in the realm of employer branding is expanding rapidly. Because of this, employer branding has rapidly become an established HRM technique of the present day. In addition, prior research on the topic of employee retention has shed light on several interconnected aspects, most of which pertain to overarching management techniques. Few studies have examined how effective employer branding is in the academic sector for attracting & retaining top talent. Therefore, inadequate research has been conducted thus far. Because there is so little written of a connection between employee retention and employer branding, more investigation into the topic is warranted. It is expected that by adopting this model, people can gain a deeper understanding of what makes an effective brand that represents an employer. It explains how employer branding can help or hurt keeping staff. It also gives us a clue as to how to win the devotion of our staff. The study's results are anticipated to also offer organizations a template for creating and maintaining a favorable perception of their business as an employer. Furthermore, it will help point future researchers in the right direction by identifying the central and important features of brand loyalty. Considering of the foregoing, this research offers researchers a solid justification for their investigations.

3. Literature Review

Styvén, M. E., et al. (2022) studied current workers' opinions of their employers' support for innovation & creativity in the hospitality

& tourism industries. The research uses the Employer Attractiveness scale, zeroing in on the section measuring innovative & creative traits. Workers in the Swedish hospitality & tourism industry were polled via an online survey and in-depth interviews. It appears from the data that many workers value their jobs as creative and that the opportunity to be innovative & original on the job tends to be a considerable inspiration to those who wish to continue with their present employment.

The mediating effect of motivation for public service, individual fit, and user fit on people's intent to apply for a position are examined by **Sievert, M., et al. (2022)** examined the impact of institutionalization & regulatory encumbrance in government employment adverts. The findings show that mathematical formalism reduces program intents. Costs associated with compliance and other administrative difficulties are insignificant. The results demonstrate the unfavorable signals of institutionalization in job postings for the public sector, which tends to deter people from applying for these positions.

Mark B. and Hugo M. (2019) studied the impact of employee branding on expectations for compensation and staff retention. This survey included five South African insurers. To investigate different hypotheses methods used were correlation tests and variance. Said study discovered a favorable correlation between participants' perceptions of their employer's brand and both retention and wage expectations. Interestingly, despite observable trends in potential age disparities and the total number of years spent at the same job, demographic variables were not found to be significant in the analysis. The report offers a detailed roadmap for putting

a successful corporate marketing strategy into practice. This proposed model takes into account the strategy's design, execution, & monitoring stages.

Christopher N. and Aishwarya K., (2019) studied the correlation between staff retention and firm cooperation as an employer branding feature in a New Zealand government agency. 134 research participants were surveyed through the Internet for this cross-sectional study. In New Zealand, research subjects were recruited through a local municipality. To analyze and interpret the available data, the Process Macro Regression technique was considered. First, this study demonstrates the fact that determined organizational support as a tool for company branding influences employee retention. Second, POS had a substantial impact on organizational engagement in the purview of the diviner or as a medium for retaining employees. In this study, OC mediated the association between organizational support & employee retention.

Hadi, Noor Ul, & Shahjehan Ahmed (2018) investigated the question of what values organizations prioritize when trying to keep their employees. This research made use of the theoretical frameworks of social learning theory and reciprocity theory, and its methodology included the systematic collection of data from 204 participants at educational institutions in Pakistan. According to the results, development value has a significant impact on whether or not employees stick with an organization. As a result of gaining expertise in new areas, one can become more effective in their current position. The study's potential ramifications & limitations are also discussed.

4. Research Methodology

Objectives

1. To study the impact of employer branding on employee retention in the Indian education sector in the Pune region.
2. To find out the impact of Application Value, Interest Value, Development Value, & Work-Life Balance on employee attraction and retention.

Hypothesis

H1: Application Value, Interest Value, Development Value, & Work-Life Balance has a major impact on employee attraction and retention.

5. Research Design

Type of Sources of Data

Primary data collected from Education professionals, including lecturers & administrators, who served as the units of analysis.

Research Instruments

For data collection questionnaires were used as a research instrument.

Sampling Method

In this paper, the convenience sampling method is considered for data collection.

Sample Size

Sample sizes for the collection of data were 105 educational institutes.

Analysis Tool

SPSS version 26 was used for the data analysis.

Hypothesis Testing

Statistical techniques such as percentage, reliability statistics, and ANOVA were used for hypothesis testing.

6. Data Analysis & Hypothesis Testing

Table 57.1 Descriptive statistics based on demographic profile

Demography	Frequency	%
Gender		
Male	89	69.53
Female	39	30.46
Total	128	100
Profession		
Teacher	81	63.28
Administrative Staff	47	36.71
Total	128	100
Age		
21-30	40	31.25
31-40	50	39.06
41-50	26	20.31
51 & Above	11	8.59
Total	128	100
Qualification		
Graduate	38	29.68
Post Graduate	57	44.53
Doctorate	33	25.78
Total	128	100
Experience		
1-5 years	47	36.71
6-10 years	36	28.12
11-15 years	26	20.31
16-20 years	19	14.84
Total	**128**	**100**

Results: Descriptive statistics (table 57.1) reveal that there were 69.53 % males & 30.46 % females. Respondents included 63.28 % of teachers & 36.71 % of office managers. The ages of the respondents ranged from 21 to 50+, with 30.06% being in the 31-40 range. Out of the total respondents, 25.68% held a doctoral degree, 44.53% held a master's, and 29.68% held a bachelor's.

The reliability statistics have provided the actual value for Cronbach's alpha, which is highlighted in the below table:

Table 57.2 Reliability analysis for attractiveness and retention dimensions

Sr. No.	Attraction and Retention Dimensions	Cronbach's Alpha
1	Application	0.836
2	Interest	0.812
3	Development	0.876
4	Work-Life Balance	0.805

Results: All four dimensions' Cronbach's alpha coefficient values were discovered to be more than 0.7.

Table 57.3 ANOVA

Hypothesis	Path	Beta	Std. Error	t-statistics	P-value	Decision
H1	AV-EAR	0.08	0.073	1.194	0.32	Rejected
H2	IV-EAR	0.016	0.082	2.15	0.01	Accepted
H3	DV-EAR	0.057	0.056	0.763	0.13	Rejected
H4	WLB-EAR	0.059	0.046	0.732	0.03	Accepted
	R^2			0.607		
	Adjusted R^2			0.273		
	F-value			11.35		
	Sig			0.000		

Results: The development value and work-life balance are related to the aspects of the corporate brand image along with the recruitment & retention of employees, as shown by the results of the aforementioned test, less than 0.05 p-value. Although, the significance of other aspects is not established in this situation.

According to Table 57.2 description of the multiple regression model, which has an R square value of 0.607.

7. Conclusion

Any organization's stability and success largely depend on its ability to recruit and retain outstanding employees, which is where employer branding comes in. Therefore, this study concludes that development value is an important one for employees because it helps keep employers around, while the other variables have no observable effect on luring in new employees or keeping existing ones.

Employees are more inclined to look for work elsewhere if they are not appreciated for their contributions or if management complains excessively and pointlessly. This research will provide educational sector employers with important insights into what areas to prioritize in their efforts to attract & retain their workforce. The growth of employees is an area that should receive more focus from employers. An employer should never undervalue the relevance of complementing his staff to show performance progress, as appreciation is the cornerstone of development value. Giving employees the essential knowledge and training they require to perform their jobs well will also improve employee performance. By doing this, everyone benefits.

Furthermore, since most of the study's data came from the education sector, it stands to reason that this sector's emphasis on employee growth would have a significant impact on retention rates. Though additional research is needed to establish a causal link between the remaining three dimensions & employee attraction and retention. However, similar research conducted in the education sector may find different factors to be the primary motivators of employee attraction and retention. Therefore, it will be impossible to extrapolate the findings to the public and private sectors.

REFERENCES

1. Adibah N., and Daud S. (2016). Engaging People with Employer Branding. Procedia Economics and Finance 35: 690–98.
2. Das S., Lahkar B., and Baruah M. (2013). Employee Retention: A Review of Literature. Journal of Business and Management 14: 8–16.
3. Jadhav, B. (2022). Psychological Resilience-A Conceptual Framework. Nova Science Publisher, USA (pp 223-240). DOI: https://doi.org/10.52305/KRLL5890
4. Mita, K, Mehta S., Kurbetti A., and Dhankhar R., (2014). Study on Employee Retention and Commitment. International Journal of Advance Research in Computer Science and Management Studies 2: 154–64.
5. Mark B., and Hugo M. (2019). Effectiveness of employer branding on staff retention and compensation expectations. South African Journal of Economic and Management Sciences, 22(1), 1–8.
6. Sivertzen L., & Olafsen O. (2013). Employer branding: Employer attractiveness and the use of social media. Journal of Product and Brand Management. 22. 10.1108/JPBM-09-2013-0393.
7. Steven, M. E., Napa, A., Mariana, M., & Natarajan, R. (2022). Employee perceptions of employers' creativity and innovation: Implications for employer attractiveness and branding in tourism and hospitality. Journal of Business Research, 141, 290–298.

Note: All the tables in this chapter were made by the Authors.

Advancements in Business for Integrating Diversity, and Sustainability – Dimitrios A. Karras et al. (eds)
© 2024 Taylor & Francis Group, London, ISBN 978-1-032-70828-7

58

Market Growth and the Impact of IoT: The Moderating Effect of an Entrepreneurial Performance

V. J. Chakravarthy*
Principal, Arulmigu Kapaleeswarar Arts and Science College,
Kolathur, Chennai Tamilnadu, India

Anitha Christy Angelin P.[1]
Assistant Professor, Department of Computer Science and Engineering,
PSNA College of Engineering and Technology, Dindigul, India

Rajalakshmi R.[2]
Assistant Professor, Department of Computer Science and Engineering,
Sathyabama Institute of Science and Technology, Chennai, India

K. Vimala[3]
Assistant Professor, Department of MBA,
Karpagam College of Engineering, Coimbatore, India

Abstract: The Internet of Things (IoT) has its own distinct set of concerns about data privacy. New marketing methods created by IoT advances are slowing its expansion. Security problems can restrict imaginative marketing techniques. This research examines the ways the IoT influences the efficiency of marketing as well taking into account the potential mediating role of an entrepreneurial orientation. The respondents were from the small-to-medium firms market. With the use of Smart Partial Least Squares (PLS) software programs, the acquired data were examined using structural equation modelling and employing both inferential and descriptive statistical approaches. The results show that IoT significantly improves marketing performance as well as entrepreneurial orientation. The entrepreneurial approach enhances marketing effectiveness. The research also investigated the mediating effects of entrepreneurial attitude and IoT on marketing effectiveness. The study findings provide corporate management and strategy specialists with a clearer understanding of the relationship between IoT and marketing success.

Keywords: Internet of things (IoT), Entrepreneurship orientation, Marketing performance, Partial least squares (PLS), Business model, Entrepreneurial strategy

*Corresponding author: principalakasc@gmail.com
[1]anithaangelin1@psnacet.edu.in, [2]rajalakshmi.cse@sathyabama.ac.in, [3]vimalark56@gmail.com

DOI: 10.4324/9781032708294-58

1. Introduction

Technological advances and facilities management methods are now being done concurrently. The IoT relies on internet technologies to connect practical objects to networks. The IoT connects important components and collects operational data to enhance activities or related components, such as machines and gadgets, and regulate them (Buntak, et al., 2019). As a consequence of all these technical advances, which have been together referred to as the IoT, inventive alterations are occurring throughout all industries. Since the rate at which these advancements are developing quickens, various economic sub-networks are seeing the emergence of unique combinations of markets and technology (Yun, et al., 2019). IoT's distinctive qualities create new attack surfaces and vulnerabilities that cause severe security and privacy issues. The IoT's extraordinary developments inspire the development of new business models, even through its growth. And the widespread adoption of new marketing strategies is hampered by the absence of practical security solutions (Viriyasitavat, et al., 2019). Industries may be thought of an assessment processes that need to be structured to achieve corporate objectives. An effective methodology, such as including specialists in decision-making or merging participant evaluations, may have a significant impact on the success of a business marketing plan (Rajagopal, et al., 2022). The goal of technological advancement is to minimize the quantity of data that has to be communicated and the level of network performance that needs to be managed. The IoT has enabled several innovations that make it feasible to link devices constantly, everywhere. IoT communication protocols have a variety of problems as a consequence of instability-restricted communication lines and few resources that frequently fall short of the standard service quality requirements (Refaee, et al., 2022).

2. Related Works

Ziyae, et al., 2021 presented new insights on how Iranian IoT-based companies may enhance their Strategic Entrepreneurship (SE) to recognize marketing opportunities and take advantage of them. Yerpude, et al., 2021 developed an approach to customer engagement for a rising market employing real-time data analytics from the IoT for the traditional retail company to customer domain. Mehralian, et al., 2022 examined the impact of the IoT on marketing performance while taking into consideration the possible mediating influence of entrepreneurial attitude. Nistor, et al., 2022 determine the effect of the IoT via theories and the expansion of market growth in order to better understand how the IoT may influence global growth. Ding, et al., 2019 Integrate IoT technology with Gray market management and examine the impact on the gray market and company revenues taken into account in the current research. The producer can trace the circulation of gray market goods and maintain surveillance on gray market activities due to IoT technology.

Hypothesis Development

H1 - the IoT significantly improves the effectiveness of marketing.

H2 - the IoT significantly improves entrepreneurial orientation.

H3 - The effectiveness of marketing is significantly enhanced by entrepreneurial focus.

3. Methodology

The approach's goal was to examine how IoT affects marketing success and the role that entrepreneurial attitude provides as a mediating factor in this relationship; consequently, it could be classified as practical research. The research was carried out in the form of a field experiment, and thus the data were acquired by means of a descriptive method. Smart-PLS was utilized to assess the measurement model and the modelling of structural equations was utilized to analyze the gathered data. According to the model shown in Fig. 58.1, the link between the collected data was assessed. Tehran, Iran-based businesses of all sizes made up the statistical population. These firms' marketing and IT managers served as the responders. The analysis of data utilized 229 of the 350 questionnaires submitted for data collection and retrieved with full replies.

It is necessary to show composite reliability, discriminate reliability, and convergent validity when using the measurement model

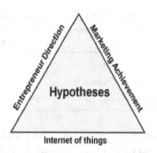

Fig. 58.1 Hypothesis structure

to assess the hypotheses. Also, it implies that the outcomes of the PLS analysis may only be used to evaluate the research hypothesis if the PLS model measures meet the measurement model, divergent validity, and reliability requirements. Convergent validity evaluation entails measuring the loading factor of each variable instead of the concept (Fig. 58.2). All indicators obtained factor loadings over 0.4 in the estimate findings of the model, demonstrating that the model satisfies the criterion for convergent validity. The Average Variance Extracted (AVE) of each concept was also examined for convergent validity evaluation in addition to factor loadings. It was determined that the

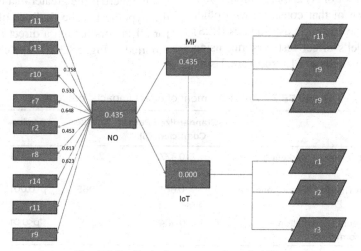

Fig. 58.2 Tests for composite reliability

Table 58.1 Component durability, mean variation, and Cronbach's alpha

	Cronbach's Alpha	Composite Reliability	(AVE)
IoT	0.796	0.883	0.714
Entrepreneurial Orientation	0.828	0.840	0.507
Marketingperformance	0.741	0.854	0.660

study model complies with the standards for convergent validity because all AVE obtained values for each concept were greater than 0.5. Table 58.1 includes the calculated factor loadings, Cronbach's alphas, reliability coefficient values, and AVE value system for each construct.

All constructions were determined to fulfil the composite reliability criteria and had a Cronbach's alpha of better than 0.7, as shown by the reliability test results in Table 58.1. As a result, it was determined that all constructions had enough dependability. To make sure each notion of each latent construct is sufficiently distinct from other latent variables, discriminant validity evaluation is used. A model is said to have good discriminant validity when every aspect of an ecosystem (values on the main diagonal) has a square root of AVE that is higher than the association of that construct with other constructs. The Partial Least Squares (PLS) analysis model's effect test was run using the t-statistic and Smart PLS software. Using the bootstrapping method, the R-squared and the significant statistic were produced. Table 58.2 displays the outcomes of this process.

Table 58.2 R-Squared calculating outcomes

	R-Squared
Entrepreneurial Orientation	0.433
Marketing performance	0.480

In PLS, testing for hypotheses is often referred to as internal model testing and includes determining if there are any significant indirect or direct effects as well as determining how exogenous factors affect endogenous variables. The t-value calculates that the difference varies from the variability in the sample data. The t-value is, that computed difference expressed in terms of standard deviation. The more t-value there is the greater that data supports the hypothesis. The findings of hypotheses for all factors having a direct influence are reported in Fig. 58.3 and Table 58.3.

Table 58.3 An assessment of direct impacts' outcomes

Hypothesis	Standardized Path Coefficient (β)	t-value	p-value	Test Result
H1: Internet of Things → Marketing performance	0.377	2.590	**p<0.01	supported
H2: Internet of Things → Entrepreneurial Orientation	0.661	10.965	p<0.001	supported
H3: Entrepreneurial Orientation → Marketing performance	0.384	2.872	**p<0.01	supported

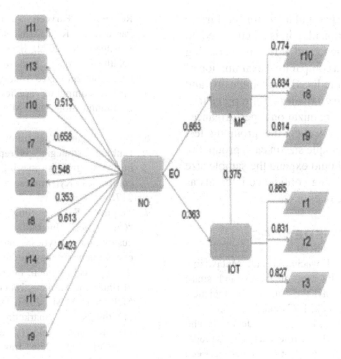

Fig. 58.3 Hypotheses testing

4. Discussion and Conclusion

This research explored the influence of IoT on marketing and the possible mediating function of market intention in this impact. The results of the research may allow corporate management and strategy experts to better grasp the link between IoT and marketing success. On the link between IoT and marketing performance, this research found a mediator. Our results also imply that the relationshipbetween IoT capabilities and market, performance is somewhat mediated by entrepreneurial attitude, even if IoT capability favorably influences marketing performance.

This indicates that, in addition to having a direct impact on marketing success,

IoTcapacity also influences marketing performance indirectly via a focus on entrepreneurship. These two impacts work together to increase marketing performance via IoT capabilities.The findings imply that IoT has the potential to transform into a powerful source of competitive advantage for businesses, provide them with entrepreneurial chances, and potentially alter future markets. Also, businesses need to design and carry out their business plans while focusing on IoT advancements.Given the assumption that IoT may assist with strategic decisions, businesses may use it to identify new entrepreneurial opportunities, identify potential threats, and improve their marketing efficacy. The methodology of the research was tested on a large sample of medium- and small-sized businesses. So, it could be worthwhile to evaluate the approach to a particular sector in further research. Additionally, it is encouraged to study the influence of IoT on marketing performance in a comparative examination of businesses with reduced, high-intensity, and hyper-competitive rivalry. Entrepreneurial orientation and organizational performances are not linear, however, the grouping test may lower the sample size in each group. So, future studies should expand the sample size and categorize using confidence intervals as well as negative ones.

REFERENCES

1. Buntak, K., Kovačić, M. and Mutavdžija, M., 2019. Internet of things and smart warehouses as the future of logistics. Tehnički glasnik, 13(3), pp. 248–253.

2. Yun, J.J., Won, D., Park, K., Jeong, E. and Zhao, X., 2019. The role of a business model in market growth: The difference between the converted industry and the emerging industry. Technological Forecasting and Social Change, 146, pp. 534–562.

3. Viriyasitavat, W., Anuphaptrirong, T. and Hoonsopon, D., 2019. When blockchain meets the Internet of Things: Characteristics, challenges, and business opportunities. Journal of industrial information integration, 15, pp. 21–28.

4. Rajagopal, N.K., Qureshi, N.I., Durga, S., Ramirez Asis, E.H., Huerta Soto, R.M., Gupta, S.K. and Deepak, S., 2022. Future of business culture: an artificial intelligence-driven digital framework for the organization decision-making process. Complexity, 2022.

5. Refaee, E., Parveen, S., Begum, K.M.J., Parveen, F., Raja, M.C., Gupta, S.K. and Krishnan, S., 2022. Secure and scalable healthcare data transmission in IoT based on optimized routing protocols for mobile computing applications. Wireless Communications and Mobile Computing, 2022.

6. Ziyae, B. and Vagharmousavi, M., 2021. Linking strategic entrepreneurship to business growth in Iranian IoT-based companies. Kybernetes, 50(7), pp. 2155–2178.

7. Yerpude, S. and Singhal, T.K., 2021. "Custolytics" Internet of Things based customer analytics aiding customer engagement strategy in emerging markets–an empirical research. International Journal of Emerging Markets, 16(1), pp. 92–112.

8. Mehralian, M.M., 2022. Effect of internet of things on marketing performance: the mediating role of entrepreneurship orientation. In 25th Iranian Conference on Business Development and Digital Transformation.

9. Nistor, A. and Zadobrischi, E., 2022, March. Analysis and estimation of economic influence of IoT and telecommunication in regional media based on evolution and electronic markets in Romania. In Telecom (Vol. 3, No. 1, pp. 195–217). MDPI.

10. Ding, L., Hu, B., Ke, C., Wang, T. and Chang, S., 2019. Effects of IoT technology on gray market: An analysis based on traceability system design. Computers & Industrial Engineering, 136, pp. 80–94.

Note: All the figures and tables in this chapter were made by the Authors.

Printed in the United States
by Baker & Taylor Publisher Services

Printed in the United States
by Baker & Taylor Publisher Services